By Design or by Chance?

Also by Denyse O'Leary:

Faith@Science: Why Science Needs Faith in the Twenty-First Century (Winnipeg: J. Gordon Shillingford Publishing, 2001) $19.95 ISBN 1-896239-83-8.

Intelligent Design: Beyond Creation and Evolution? (Toronto: Dare Connexions, 2002).

By
Design
or by
Chance?

Denyse O'Leary

Augsburg Books
MINNEAPOLIS

BY DESIGN OR BY CHANCE?

Large-quantity purchases or custom editions of this book are available at a discount
from the publisher. For more information, contact the sales department at
Augsburg Fortress, Publishers, 1-800-328-4648, or write to: Sales Director,
Augsburg Fortress, Publishers, P.O. Box 1209, Minneapolis, MN 55440-1209.

Cover design by John Cowie, *eyetodeye, design*

ISBN 0-8066-5177-6

The paper used in this publication meets the minimum requirements of American
National Standard for Information Sciences—Permanence of Paper for Printed
Library Materials, ANSI Z329.48-1984. ♾ ™

Manufactured in the U.S.A.

08   07   06   05   04   1   2   3   4   5   6   7   8   9   10

For Johnny
(1948–1957)

Contents

Part Four / Design... the Picture Is Coming In

The most important question for any society to ask is the one that is forbidden.

—*Richard Halvorson*, Harvard Crimson *(2003)*

Preface

As a freelance journalist based in Toronto, Canada, I have frequently been asked to write on science topics. One such topic was Darwinian evolution and the new, competing theory of intelligent design. When I first started looking into this subject, I had no clear convictions about it, nor any desire to enter a controversy. I am a Christian, but my church does not require any position on evolution. The idea that God is somehow behind the universe accommodates all positions except, obviously, atheism.

It was a tough but rewarding slog for an arts major. Through reading, study, arguments, and interviews, I began to see clearly that Darwinism is a theory of evolution that explicitly denies design in biology in order to leave God out of the picture—at a point in history when, from the science evidence available, it appears that the whole universe is screaming DESIGN!

The design may not be real. The designer may not be God. The reader must judge. But the implications of this state of affairs seemed worth a book. So here is a book. Its topic is huge: the slow, sure—and strongly opposed—reorganization of sciences around the theme of design, as opposed to no-design. The book is written in what I hope is an accessible, journalistic style. Timelines, tables, focus boxes, and definitions are offered. Readers are urged, as much as possible, to read the notes and go to the resources found there, and to other resources as well, to find additional, alternative, or correcting views. Wherever possible, Internet resources as well as print resources are referenced, for the reader's convenience. Above all, sit back, and enjoy the journey.

Most writers ascribe all improvements to their editors and all faults to themselves. So do I, and I *mean* it. Without a patient and visionary publisher like Larry Willard, a gifted and perceptive editor like Don Bastian, and a talented designer like John Cowie, this book would have ended up as nothing more than a mass of overstuffed file folders, a pile of overdue library books, thousands of links and e-mail messages, and a zip disk.

I especially want to take this opportunity to thank Stephen Jones for his help in pointing out errors and providing additional material. Stephen, an Australian, is an old earth creationist who is in the final stages of a biology degree. He is also in the early stages of writing a book of his own, *Problems of Evolution*. A summary of Stephen's book is on his Web site: http://members.iinet.net.au/~sejones/. As sections of his book are written, they are posted to his Internet discussion Yahoo group, CreationEvolution Design, for vigorous debate.

Thanks to Mike Coren, Ted Davis, Bill Dembski, Elizabeth Dunning, Bob Giza (and Paul, and other great teachers at Chaminade!), Phil Johnson, Steve Jones, Forrest Mims III, Dan Osmond, Phil Skell, Tim Standish, CPS Taylor, and Jonathan Wells for reading the manuscript and offering comments. I listened to everything, and made the changes I could. And thanks to Elizabeth Dunning and Steve Jones for proofreading the manuscript along with me, a chore everyone needs and no one wants.

Thanks to Renée VanderWindt and artist Willow Hales for the layout and the necessary but ever-tiresome corrections.

Thanks to kind members of my professional associations and groups, who supported me, *whether or not* they clearly understood what I was trying to do,—and tolerated my long absences from the confabs I have always loved so much.

Thanks also to my mom Blanche O'Leary, who cooked when I couldn't (or wouldn't), my favorite computer guy Sandy McMurray, and the prayer team at Little Trinity Church in Toronto, who heard me out when I was convinced that my health would not hold up under the deadlines. I particularly want to thank the biology instructor on the prayer team who simply prayed, "Lord, we know that you did it, but we don't know how. Please support Denyse's health." Hey, pal, my health's okay now. And the book is in print. Cheers!

Lastly, I want to thank my daughter Cindy and my friends Elizabeth and Theresa, who never doubted that the year I disappeared into the files to write this book was well spent. Or if they did, they never said so.

Denyse O'Leary, Toronto, 2004

Introduction

Nature has been kinder to us than we had any right to expect.[1]

—Freeman J. Dyson, cosmologist

The origin of life in the universe has unexpectedly become *the* question of our time.

We peer into space, fire off spacecraft in every direction, land on the moon and on Mars, always looking for signs of life. We peer through electron microscopes, below the wavelength of visible light, trying to understand life. Life ... what is it? How does it come about? What does it mean? Where did the universe come from?

The controversy over the origin of life was supposed to have been settled in the 1950s by the tidy doctrine of Darwinian evolution. Now, Darwin seems to be going the way of Marx and Freud, and we once again confront the age-old questions.

Did the universe have no beginning? No end? Was it designed? Did it arise by chance? A roll of supercosmic dice? Though many people think so, the most recent evidence does not support their view.

That is the great, unnoticed revolution of the 20th century. Just a few decades ago, the overwhelming evidence from science was thought to support a self-perpetuating universe that did not need God as designer. But there was one serious problem. Most of the evidence was not in.

Now that we know much more about the universe and about life on earth, a surprising thing has happened. Far from supporting an atheistic, meaningless universe, <u>the evidence supports</u> a universe that is <u>bursting with design.</u> Was it orchestrated by an omnipotent God?

This evidence does not prove the Christian doctrine of God. But <u>it makes belief in God a reasonable idea.</u>

What is this evidence? And if it is so evident, why is our culture taking so long to accept it? This book attempts to answer these questions. Not with 10,000 pages of scientific or philosophical jargon, but with brief, simply expressed concepts and examples.

The Beginning: Why, the Very Idea of a *Beginning* Is Radical!

Before the 18th century, most people believed that the universe and time began when God created it. But from the 18th century until the mid-20th century, many scientists doubted that the universe even had a beginning. The idea of a beginning to the universe was considered a religious belief.[2] Typically, scientists accepted an eternal universe, of never-ending binding and unbinding atoms over an infinity of space and time. Listen carefully to the scripts of some old science fiction movies, and you will still hear the echoes from the eternal void.

The earth having a "beginning" is a new idea for scientists...

Then, in 1927, an obscure Belgian priest and cosmologist, <u>Georges Lemaître (1894–1966),</u> an early follower of Einstein, proposed that the universe popped into existence between 10 and 20 billion years ago, beginning with a single point.

Lemaître's theory was revolutionary. It overturned a century and a half of science. Initially, many scientists did not like the theory much, and some, like Arthur Eddington (1882–1944), said so. His comment was: "Philosophically, the notion of a beginning to the present order is repugnant to me. I should like to find a genuine loophole."[3] To most scientists of the day, it sounded too much like religion. Thus, Lemaître, a priest, was in the unusual position of trying to focus attention on the science that supported his idea, while many

> **Definition**
>
> **Big Bang**   the origin of the universe in an explosion about 14 billion years ago.

> **Definition**
>
> **cosmology**   the study of the origin and structure of the universe. It includes such questions as laws, chance, space, time, causes of things, and freedom. The cosmologist relies heavily on astronomy.

atheists were more concerned with the religious implications. This odd turnabout continues to the present day, as we will see.

The Difference a Beginning Makes

If the universe has existed forever—or waxes and wanes in cycles—absolutely anything can happen, given the infinite amount of time available.

Now, just for a moment, let's picture the universe as a Universal Lottery. Perhaps neither you nor I are in the habit of buying lottery tickets, but for our illustration we must use

> ### Timeline for the Big Bang
> 10^{-43} seconds Gravity separates from other forces. (This is called Planck time.)
> 10^{-36} seconds Force that holds atoms together emerges.
> 10^{-35} seconds The universe expands by a great deal.
> 10^{-33} to 10^{-4} seconds Universe is very hot but cools down to 10 million degrees Kelvin. 3 minutes later, the elements hydrogen, helium, and lithium have formed. Heavier elements are cooked in stars, much later.[4]
>
> Note: 10^{-43} is a decimal point followed by 42 zeroes, followed by a 1. The other numbers are interpreted in the same way.
>
> Amazingly, it takes more time to microwave frozen food than it did to cook up a universe.

the assumptions of scientists who view the universe that way. Well then, suppose we have pooled our money and bought a book of 10 consecutive lottery tickets.

There is nothing unusual about our winning a lottery in which we have bought tickets. Indeed, suppose the universe is eternal. Over time, if tickets continue to be drawn indefinitely, our numbers will eventually come up. In fact, they will come up an infinite number of times, long after we are no longer around to claim our reward.

An eternal universe would work that way. All physically possible events would happen at some point. Its Universal Lottery is not guided by anyone because no guidance is needed. It just goes on drawing tickets forever. So the universe goes on and on, eternally evolving new and surprising situations—eventually it evolves the very situation we are now experiencing.

However … if the universe has a beginning—even if that beginning was a very long time ago—what happens to our Universal Lottery? Think about it.

Here are some ways in which the Universal Lottery must change:

1. The number of tickets that can win shrinks dramatically. That is because only a certain number of draws can be made *in the allowable time*. Perhaps none of our tickets will be drawn.

If the earth doesn't have a beginning then the possibilities are limitless.
"   "   "   does have a   "   "   "   "   limited.

3

2. Lots of unlikely things can still happen. For example, one of our tickets might win the lottery anyway.

The "created Universe" would be limited by time.

3. However, every unlikely thing cannot happen because there is not enough *time*.

Suppose that in our Universal Lottery, there are 50 billion tickets. The odds that a ticket in our book will be a winner are very small but possible. Yet, what if, suddenly, every one of our 10 tickets is called in perfect order, in a row, as a prizewinner. We know that is highly unlikely, even impossible. The lottery, which is now time limited, could not possibly randomly draw every ticket in our book, and no others, in the exact order in which the tickets are numbered. The lottery must have been "fixed"—designed so that we would win. As this book will show, that is indeed the universe we are living in. It appears fixed so that we would win.

Now, science is turning away from the concept of an eternal universe. The universe is thought by most cosmologists to have begun no more than 14 billion years ago. Its future life is estimated at about 100 trillion years. That sounds like a lot of time, and it is. The important thing to see, however, is that any finite amount of time, even if it is very large, enables us to calculate the odds of a given event.

And as we will see in the next few chapters, from the science evidence available today, our tickets have come up an amazing number of times. The coincidences that enable us humans to exist—which is what the Universal Lottery represents—now seem statistically impossible. Unless, that is, there is some sort of design at work.

The next question is: Does this mean that there would be an impact on "modern" culture? The answer is yes. Let's look at the ways.

Why "Modern" Culture Is On the Way Out

It may not be apparent at first glance, but the concept of the universe as an endless lottery of meaningless events actually shaped the "modern" culture of our society, from about the 1850s on. Modern culture, better known as "modernism," was the culture created by the theories of Darwin, Marx, and Freud. We humans were believed to be just an accident, living on a mediocre planet, circling a suburban star, in an irrelevantly repetitious universe. For culture, that means, among other things, "no God," "no meaning," "no purpose," and "no rules!" Not surprisingly, we have all heard these themes

Modernism said our existance was meaningless.

sounded every day from every source. They have driven the key questions that dominate modern society, such as:

- ■ "Can we find meaning in a world without God?" (God's absence is taken for granted because there is no need for a creator in an eternal universe.)

- ■ "How can a human life be important?" (If we just happen to exist, then we aren't important.)

- ■ "What kind of morality should we have, if any, if God does not exist?" (A random universe can offer no moral guidance, and it is presumptuous to assume that we can really decide between right and wrong, or determine truth.)

Henri Frédéric Amiel expressed this modern view clearly when he wrote, in 1868:

> The universe is but a kaleidoscope which turns within the mind of the so-called thinking being, who is himself a curiosity without a cause, an accident conscious of the great accident around him, and who amuses himself with it so long as the phenomenon of his vision lasts.[5]

And, continuing the theme well over a century later, in 1986, zoologist Richard Dawkins wrote:

> Natural selection, the blind, unconscious, automatic process which Darwin discovered, and which we now know is the explanation for the existence and apparently purposeful form of all life, has no purpose in mind. It has no mind and no mind's eye. It does not plan for the future. It has no vision, no foresight, no sight at all. If it can be said to play the role of the watchmaker in nature, it is the blind watchmaker.[6]

Yet, even as art, literature, and science were churning out endless riffs based on these propositions, a critical change was taking hold in science. A key moment was Lemaître's idea. Once science accepted the idea that the universe might have a beginning—and perhaps an end—it confronted a radically different picture of the universe from the "meaningless universe" of modernism. In some ways, it is a scarier one. But because it comes from the findings of contemporary science, it will have as much of an impact on our culture as the meaningless universe of modernism did. Key new findings in science usually do change culture and society.

What Does This Mean for Religion?

Many people, sensing a change in the wind, assume that the basic assumptions of modernism are false.[7] Increasing numbers are looking elsewhere for answers. Ironically, one outcome is a worldwide resurgence of traditional religion. In North America, for example, liberal religious denominations that have aligned themselves with modernist philosophy are stagnant and graying, while non-modernist ones are growing rapidly.

Some commentators argue that this situation simply reflects the "political muscle" of orthodox religious believers. In other words, it is merely a political event. They are mistaken. The change is a fundamental shift in how people look at questions about God, life, and the universe. It is a result of a change in the picture of the universe provided by science.

Shortly before he died, in 1966, Lemaître, who in his life had never sought or received much publicity, learned a critical piece of news. Two American physicists had discovered what is called the "signature" of the Big Bang: the microwaves that have been spreading throughout the universe ever since it took place.[8]

The idea that the universe has a beginning is now overwhelmingly accepted by cosmologists.[9] But that did not happen without conflict, as we will see in Chapter 1. And what is even more interesting, the conflict had far more to do with defending the modernist religion of a meaningless, God-free universe than with science evidence.

Where This Book Is Going

Fortunately, the controversies that this book will deal with are exciting as well as instructive. In Part One, we will look at changes in recent cosmology and the difference they make to how people see themselves and their world. These changes include the Big Bang, anthropic coincidences (the odd

---

How big is the universe we are talking about, anyway?

Scientists today work with a scale that goes from "way too large to grasp" to "way too small to grasp." To see this, fire up your browser and go to

http://www.micro.magnet.fsu.edu/primer/java/scienceopticsu/powersof10/

You can see the Milky Way at a distance of 10 million light years and then work your way down through successively smaller sizes of things, until you find yourself inside the parts of an atom.

By the way, can you guess where we humans fit? The universe has a radius of 10^{27} metres and the tiniest part of an atom has a radius of 10^{-26} of a metre. Human beings, at roughly a metre or two in size, are right in the middle.

coincidences that make our existence possible), and the Rare Earth principle. These changes have made the ideas that God designed the universe and that human beings are important seem reasonable again. We will also begin to appreciate the impact of the new cosmology on biology, which is the focus of the remainder of the book. Part Two considers modern culture's view of how life started and developed, and why it is approaching a crisis. Part Three examines creation science, which developed in opposition to modern culture. And Part Four looks at the new intelligent design movement and asks whether it promises a way out of the confusion.

The main effect of the new cosmology on biology is this: Some scientists now view life forms as designed rather than accidental—that is the *intelligent design* hypothesis. Intelligent design is most controversial among Darwinian evolutionists, of course. Darwinism, the only type of evolution taught in most of our schools, is based explicitly on the idea that life has no purpose and no design. But if a respectable argument can be made for design or purpose in the rest of the universe, why not for design or purpose in life?

Here are some brief facts and definitions that will help us enjoy the story that follows:

A Brief Summary

Until the 19th century, scientists assumed that the universe was held together by three principles: law, chance, and design:

Law—is what must happen (laws of gravity, for example).

Chance—is all the things that might happen randomly within the life of the universe.

Design—means the operation of an intelligence that organizes the effects of law and chance, creating information. (Christians and other theists assume that the "intelligence" is God, who created the design. However, to some people, the fact that we can see a design would not necessarily mean our God was its creator.)

So Evolution Means What?

Evolution is the theory that all life forms are descended from one or several common ancestors that were present on the early earth, three to four billion years ago. It includes the process by which one species is transformed into another, for example a dinosaur species into a bird species. There have been a number of models of how evolution works, including models that assume divine guidance or perhaps divine intervention at various points along the way.

So Darwinism Means Exactly What?

The fundamental principle of Darwinian evolution is _common descent_ by _fully naturalistic_ means. Common descent is the belief that all life forms, including ourselves, are descendants of a common ancestor (or possibly several common ancestors) billions of years ago. Scientists differ, often sharply, about the details. "Naturalistic means" is a way of saying that natural law acting on chance events explains everything that happens. Life came into existence by chance and developed by chance, without design, guidance, or intervention by God or an intelligent designer. Or, if there were any divine design, guidance, or intervention, it could never be scientifically detectable.

In his epoch-making _On the Origin of Species,_ published in 1859, Englishman Charles Darwin argued that there was no actual design to nature; the laws of nature acted by chance and created all the life forms that we see from a common ancestor. The fittest ones survived by developing endless adaptations (changes). In other words, Darwin provided a theory for how life forms develop from a common ancestor _without_ design or outside intelligent influence.

He called the process _natural selection._ Scientists liked Darwin's simplification. It especially suited the materialistic world of 19th-century England. It provided a powerful support for a belief that was already rapidly growing among intellectuals that the universe was Godless and meaningless, and that human beings were a random outcome of its processes. Thus, Darwin became the popular central figure in biology in the same way that Freud had in psychology, and Marx in politics. The fact that these men were elevated as dominant figures did not, of course, mean that everyone agreed with them. It did mean that everyone had to take their claims seriously, and if they disagreed, they had to construct a viable alternative view.

From the beginning, scientists identified problems with Darwin's assumptions. These problems did not attract much attention, because scientists assumed that they would just be sorted out one day. For example, Darwin thought that the world under the microscope consisted of simple jellies and crystals that could easily form randomly. He could not have been more wrong. It was only with the dawn of biochemistry in the 1950s—when scientists were able to look into cells deeply and in detail—that they

Problems of Darwinism

8

realized how wrong he was. The world at a microscopic level is almost as complex as the world above it.

It was difficult to understand how complex cells can be created simply by law acting on chance. We do not know of an "early, simple version" of cells or organs. Even the "simple" version had to be complex in order to exist. Respected scientists, such as Fred Hoyle checked out of believing in a simple Darwinist explanation for the origin of life in the early 1970s, for precisely this reason. So why is Darwinism still entrenched?

Darwinism continues partly because it is the historical model of biology and partly because it underwrites the modernist religion, as we will see later. But more and more of the evidence supporting Darwinism just does not withstand close scrutiny. We will look at that issue in detail in this book.

The growing political uproar around the teaching of evolution is fuelled by the fact that Darwinism is the only model of evolution that is permitted in most school systems. Indeed, some teachers have been forbidden even to bring up known problems with the theory. This is because modernism is the unacknowledged religion of tax-supported public school systems, and Darwinism is one of modernism's most important teachings. Just as you would not be permitted to argue against Christianity in the pulpit of a traditional church, so teachers are not permitted to argue against Darwinism in the lectern of a modernist school or university. In this book, we will look at the fate of dissenters.

> **Definition**
>
> **evolution** the theory that all life forms are descended from one or several common ancestors that were present on the early earth, three to four billion years ago.

> **Definition**
>
> **Darwinism** each life form has certain random mutations that make it either more or less fit to survive in a given environment. Over time, these random mutations create the vast array of life forms that we see, from sponges to elephants to people. There is no need for design. This was Charles Darwin's explanation of evolution.

So What's Young Earth Creationism?

During the 20th century, when Darwinism was the biology of modernists, some evangelical Christians, who have historically opposed modernism, came up with their own model of the history of life, based on the assumption that the earth is not more than 10,000 years old. They rely on a literal interpretation of Genesis 1 through 7.[10] Their model applies principles from this assumption. As we will see in Part Three, young earth creationism has become an important force in evangelical Christian church life in North America, and has also spread to many other parts of the world.

What's Intelligent Design (ID) Theory?

ID theory started to take shape in the late 1970s, as an outcome of information theory. Faced with the enormous complexity of living things—for example, the fact that complete instructions for creating DNA would be as long as the DNA code itself—ID theorists argue that it makes more sense to assume that the information is a language. In other words, it is a product of design. This is the complete opposite of Darwinism.

Reintroducing design would, of course, change the way many problems in science are perceived. The ID scientist does not try to figure out how things happened by chance, but rather looks for intentional patterns that suggest general laws of development. The laws that prevail in one situation may shed light on another.

Darwinists view ID as heresy because they are committed to a "no-design model" and would prefer to continue looking for solutions to the mystery of life via law and chance.

Isn't This Just 'Religion' Versus 'No Religion' All Over Again?

No. All parties to the debates have a religious stance of some type. Many atheists who are Darwinists actively promote a "no-God religion," which they think is better suited to the times we live in than traditional religions.[11] Many other Darwinists are religious people, sometimes devout Christians. One example is the American biochemist Ken Miller, a practicing Roman Catholic who is the author of *Finding Darwin's God*. During my research, I also ran across a number of atheists or agnostics who are non-Darwinists or post-Darwinists.

In the end, the conflict that this book describes is between those who think that Darwinism can survive the collapse of modernism—a collapse that has already taken out Marx and Freud—and those who think that, on the contrary, design belongs as much in biology as in cosmology.

History Check: "Hey, Man, It Just Happens." Then and Now

Many people believe that the idea of an eternal, random universe was discovered by modern science. For example, here is a description of the modernist universe:

> An ongoing cosmic event—a never-ending binding and unbinding of atoms resulting in the gradual emergence of entire new worlds and the gradual disintegration of old ones. Our world, our bodies, our minds are but atoms in motion. They did not occur because of some purpose or final cause. Nor were they created by some god for our special use and benefit. They simply happened, more or less randomly and entirely naturally, through the effective operation of immutable and eternal physical laws.[12]

Does this sound familiar? Scientific and modern? Something your high school teacher told you, years ago?

Well, it's familiar, yes.

Scientific? That's debatable.

Modern? No.

These are the ideas of the ancient philosophers Epicurus and Lucretius. The Greek Epicurus lived from about 341 to 271 BC, a generation after Plato and Aristotle. The Roman Lucretius, who popularized his ideas, lived from about 99 to 55 BC. That makes him a contemporary of Julius Caesar.

Epicurus's and Lucretius's ideas did not arise from scientific discoveries. In their days, almost no one was doing what we now call science. There simply were no relevant discoveries. These philosophers were describing life as they knew it.[13]

This "casino" universe (chance governed by laws) sounds familiar to us because the scientific assumptions of the 18th and 19th centuries provided support for it. However, the ideas themselves are very old.

Twentieth-century science described a universe more like the one you read about in the Bible, a masterwork of complex design. Nobel Prize–winning physicist Arno Penzias, who helped uncover evidence of the Big Bang, told the New York Times: "The best data we have (concerning the big bang) are exactly what I would have predicted, had I nothing to go on but the five books of Moses, the Psalms, the Bible as a whole."[14]

Was the Universe Created or Was It Always Here?

PART ONE

By Design or by Chance?

CHAPTER 1

On both scientific and philosophical grounds, the concept of an eternal Universe seems more acceptable than the concept of a transient Universe that springs into being suddenly, and then fades slowly into darkness.

—Robert Jastrow, astronomer[1]

As we look out into the universe and identify the many accidents of physics and astronomy that have worked to our benefit, it almost seems as if the universe must in some sense have known that we were coming.

—Freeman J. Dyson, cosmologist[2]

Can an eternal universe die? Well, maybe the *idea* of an eternal universe can die. During the 20th century, the idea did die. However intellectually preferable scientists found the concept of an eternal universe, as opposed to the Big Bang theory, evidence forced them to abandon it. The cause of death? American astronomer Edwin Hubble (1889–1953) had discovered in 1929 that the galaxies are moving away from each other.[3] His discovery raised a key question: If the universe is really eternal, why have the galaxies that we see on a clear night not disappeared from view ages ago?[4] Any rival theory to Lemaître's Big Bang had to answer that key question. And none did. So even before the Big Bang theory was widely known, the eternal universe was dead—dead and buried.

The Godfather

The godfather of the Big Bang was the famous British astronomer Sir Fred Hoyle (1915–2001). He gave the theory its name in one of his papers.[5] He hated the theory. As an atheist, he recognized its theological implications, and he didn't like them at all.

So Hoyle set out to disprove the Big Bang. Transferring eternity away from God and back to the universe again would require a sophisticated strategy, but, as one of the world's best-known scientists, he stood a better chance than most of coming up with it.

Little by Little . . . One Atom at a Time?

The story goes that Hoyle and two other physicists, Hermann Bondi and Thomas Gold, went out one night in Cambridge in 1946 to see a horror movie. It was one of those movies with a circular plot so the final scene is the same as the opening scene. Later that night, over glasses of brandy in Bondi's apartment, the physicists were inspired to wonder if the universe is really like that movie. The end is just replaced by the beginning, over and over again.[6]

In 1948, in a bold move, they proposed a new theory, the Steady State universe.[7] They began by noting that the best evidence for the Big Bang is the fact that the universe is expanding. Most scientists assume that the universe is expanding from its own origin in a single point, as Lemaître had said.[8]

Why Is the sky dark at night?

In 1823, German astronomer Heinrich Olbers asked a simple but important question: Why is the sky dark at night? If the universe is unchanging, eternal, and infinite, shouldn't the night sky be ablaze with the light from all the stars that have ever shone? Edwin Hubble helped resolve the paradox by showing that the universe is not unchanging, as Olbers had supposed. The galaxies, including our own, are moving away from each other. Thus we should expect dark spaces in the sky. Later, the Big Bang theory showed that the universe is not eternal and infinite, so we should not expect to see an infinite number of stars.

Sometimes the simple questions are the most important.

However, Hoyle's team argued, suppose the universe is expanding a little bit at a time, from everywhere at once? Perhaps hydrogen atoms, the simplest ones, can come into existence all by themselves by spontaneous generation. Just a few here and there, maybe one particle per cubic kilometer per year.[9] It would add up, they said. The galaxies move apart because the new atoms shove other matter aside, and create an expanding—but still eternal—universe.

Definition

Steady State Universe the universe does not have a beginning. Its expansion is explained by the continuous, spontaneous creation of hydrogen atoms.

So . . . not with a Bang, but with a *whimper*, the universe leaks into existence. Such a small whimper of creation eludes strict bookkeeping.

To sticklers who demanded to know where all the individual newborn hydrogen atoms were coming from, the Steady State physicists replied with a question of their own: Is spontaneous creation of single atoms a bigger mystery than a Big Bang, according to which the *whole universe* comes into existence suddenly from nothing?

So on either side there is a mystery. But which mystery is the real one? And which is just a good plot device for a science fiction movie? *That* was the question they were posing.

A Pin in the Big Bang Balloon?

The stakes were high: the history of the universe. In 1964, Hoyle, the strongest promoter of the Steady State theory, had the courage to participate in studies that subjected his own theory to a test.[10] The specific question was: Did the Steady State theory or the Big Bang theory better explain the fact that about one quarter of the universe consists of helium gas?[11]

Many scientists were anxious for the results. The Big Bang was an embarrassment to many of them. Like Hoyle, they did not like it, primarily for religious reasons: It inevitably gets scientists talking about God even when they do not mean to.[12] Astronomer Robert Jastrow, author of *God and the Astronomers*, puts it like this:

> For the scientist who has lived by his faith in the power of reason, the story ends like a bad dream. He has scaled the mountains of ignorance; he is about to conquer the highest peak; as he pulls himself over the final rock, he is greeted by a band of theologians who have been sitting there for centuries.[13]

Similarly, Stephen Hawking says:

> Many people do not like the idea that time has a beginning, probably because it smacks of divine intervention. …There were therefore a number of attempts to avoid the conclusion that there had been a big bang.[14]

Of course they hoped that Hoyle would show that the Big Bang never happened and that in some way the universe really was eternal after all. Remember, as we saw in the Universal Lottery discussed in the Introduction, in an eternal universe anything can happen, given enough time. A Steady State universe, which has always existed, provides plenty of time for everything to happen, without any divine intervention at all.

The Envelope, Please . . .

In the study that tested the two theories, the Big Bang predicted the correct amount of helium—about 25 percent—but the Steady State was way off.[15] In Hoyle's own words:

> Our results, together with further developments by William Fowler, Robert Wagoner and myself, became what even to this day is pretty well the strongest evidence for the big bang, particularly as the arguments were produced by members of what was seen as the steady state camp.[16]

That did not stop Hoyle, who stubbornly continued to search for a No Bang theory to the end of his life. Most scientists respected him for his stubbornness, as was evident in the many eulogies written at the time of his death in 2001.[17] Because he needed to find a source for atoms other than the Big Bang, he ended up doing important research on the way in which heavier elements are produced inside stars.[18]

Great Scientists *Are* Stubborn

Contrary to popular belief, great scientists do not simply abandon their theories just because the evidence of an experiment does not confirm them. Usually, a theory has taken many years to work out, and, for all the scientist knows, a later experiment may confirm it after all. As philosopher of science Thomas Kuhn notes: "All historically significant theories have agreed with the facts, but only more or less."[19] In other words, the question is whether one theory fits the facts better than another overall. No theory agrees precisely with all observations. But the Big Bang agreed with more facts than the Steady State.

Snapshots from a Baby Universe

There were other reasons, besides helium, for thinking that Hoyle's Steady State universe could not be true. No mechanism was found to account for the continuous creation of hydrogen atoms. Granted, no mechanism was found to account for the Big Bang, either. But most scientists found the idea of one original, inexplicable event like the Big Bang easier to take than constant inexplicable events like the spontaneous creation of each individual hydrogen atom.

Another problem is that all the galaxies near us are middle-aged, like our own. If the Steady State model is correct, there should be newborn galaxies around us.

When astronomers look out to the edges of the universe, they do see galaxies in an earlier stage of formation than ours. There is a good reason for that. The light from these galaxies takes billions of years to reach their telescopes, so the astronomers are really looking backwards in time. This picture fits the Big Bang model of an early cosmic explosion very well. The younger-looking stars do not prove that the Big Bang happened, but they are the sort of thing that a scientist would expect to see if the Big Bang model is correct.[20]

Then in 1965 came an unexpected discovery. Two physicists at AT&T Bell Laboratories in New Jersey, Arno Penzias and Robert Wilson, accidentally discovered the cosmic microwave background (CMB). This is the background radiation that is assumed to be left over from the Big Bang. It spreads out as space expands in all directions, at a temperature just a little below three degrees above absolute zero.[21]

Pictures delayed in the cosmic mail?

If the concept of "looking backwards in time" sounds a little tricky, picture it like this: Suppose it takes 10 years for you to receive photos of your infant nephew in the mail. By the time you get the baby picture, he is 10 years old. By the time you get the picture of him when he is 10, he is a college senior. It's the same with galaxies. Astronomers using the Hubble Space Telescope are getting the galaxies' baby pictures billions of years later because the light takes that long to get here. So the astronomers know what the galaxies look like as babies. However, the galaxies may be long dead by now. We have no way of knowing for sure what happened to them later.

Definition

cosmic microwave background (CMB) electromagnetic radiation from all points in the universe, considered a remnant of the Big Bang.

Big Bang Theory vs. Steady State Theory Timeline

Hubble shows that universe is expanding.	1929	
	1933	Lemaître proposes Big Bang theory.
Alternative Steady State theory proposed.	1948	
	1964	The two theories are tested; Big Bang wins.
Radiation from Big Bang discovered.	1965	
	1992	Satellite studies confirm Big Bang observations.

Note: Some scientists continue to work on Steady State assumptions.[22]

In 1990, NASA's Cosmic Background Explorer (COBE) satellite made more accurate measurements. The atmosphere was tense as scientists gathered at the Goddard Space Flight Center near Washington, D.C., to hear the numbers read out. The numbers vindicated the Big Bang beautifully, which caused the head of the team, George Smoot, to say: "I felt like I was looking God in the face."[23]

These discoveries were taken by most scientists as showing that the Big Bang theory best fits the facts of our universe. The theory still has its detractors, mainly for philosophical (in other words, mainly for theological) reasons. In 1989, the prestigious British science journal *Nature* published an editorial by its physics editor John Maddox titled "Down with the Big Bang."[24] "Apart from being philosophically unacceptable, the Big-Bang is an over-simple view of how the Universe began, and it is unlikely to survive the decade ahead," he wrote.

Maddox's obituary for the cosmic bang was premature. From the early 1990s on, most cosmologists have simply taken the Big Bang for granted and have turned their attention to working out the details, such as the age of the universe and when various types of stars and elements formed.

Key Big Bang Scientists and What They Did

Scientists	Key Year	Key Idea/Action	Significance
Georges Lemaître (1894–1966)	1927	Universe expanded from single "cosmic egg."	Universe is located in finite time and measurable space.
Edwin Hubble (1889–1953)	1929	Galaxies are moving away from each other.	Universe is expanding.
George Gamow (1904–1968)	1948	There should still be radiation from the Big Bang.	Colleagues calculated likely temperature of radiation.
Arno Penzias (1933–) and Robert Wilson (1936–)	1965	Detected the radiation.	Radiation was correct temperature for Big Bang.
George Smoot, and Cosmic Background Explorer team	1992	Satellite showed how galaxies formed from post-Bang clumps.	Big Bang model confirmed.

Our Dreary Little Suburb?

In the meantime, another related change was taking place in the way scientists viewed the universe. In the 20th century, it was fashionable to view it as blind, pitiless, and indifferent, and to describe earth as a mediocre planet in a suburban galaxy, far from the center of things. This was one of the most popular themes in the art and literature of the period. As cosmologist Stephen Hawking has said:

We are such insignificant creatures on a minor planet of a very average star in the outer suburbs of one of a hundred billion galaxies. So it is difficult to believe in a God that would care about us or even notice our existence.[26]

This was also a key theme of *Pale Blue Dot: A Vision of the Human Future in Space*, by astronomer Carl Sagan (1934–1996). In this book, Sagan muses on the idea that the universe is favorable to us, saying:

> You might imagine an uncharitable extraterrestrial observer looking down on our species over all that time—with us excitedly chattering, "The Universe is created for us! We're at the center! Everything pays homage to us!"—and concluding that our pretensions are amusing, our aspirations pathetic, that this must be the planet of the idiots.[27]

Sagan's alien is, of course, really Sagan himself, an atheist giving his own view. In the next paragraph, he says that his judgment is too harsh. Indeed, it is. But not just because the judgment isn't polite. Sagan is in fact simply wrong. There is good reason to think that the cosmos is fine-tuned to allow for our existence. Ironically, Fred Hoyle, also an atheist, was one of the first people to say that Sagan's mediocrity theme is just coffee-house nonsense (see Chapter 3). Later in this chapter, we will look at some of the many reasons why, in reality, we inhabit a favored universe—and a rare earth.

> ### Space and Time Are Created in the Big Bang
>
> In the present understanding of the universe (Big Bang cosmology), the universe is not expanding within space and time. Space and time did not exist before the universe; they came into existence with the universe. Space itself has been expanding, starting at the creation of time, about 14 billion years ago.[25] In other words, contrary to the voiceovers of old sci-fi films, there is no "Eternal Void" out there. In fact, there is no "out there" out there at all. Space creates itself by expanding from the Big Bang explosion, and time is traveling with it.

Enter, God

The Big Bang caused a significant philosophical shift during Fred Hoyle's lifetime, one he found most unwelcome: Based on scientific evidence alone, the assumption that there is a God who designed the universe is reasonable. It is *not* an act of faith, undertaken against the evidence. Arno Penzias, co-discoverer of the cosmic microwave background of the Big Bang in 1964, explains the situation like this:

Astronomy leads us to a unique event, a universe that was created out of nothing and delicately balanced to provide exactly the conditions required to support life. In the absence of an absurdly-improbable accident, the observations of modern science seem to suggest an underlying, one might say, supernatural plan.[28]

Our culture has yet to catch up with Penzias. On the contrary, what we commonly hear about the universe and our place in it dates from scientific beliefs that prevailed from the mid-1850s to the mid-1950s.

The Curious Accident in the Backwater

In an eternal or Steady State universe, there can be an infinite number of accidental earths. So there would be nothing special about our planet or about us. This notion is called the *Copernican Principle*, or, sometimes, the Principle of Mediocrity.

During the 20th century, any evidence that appeared to support the Copernican Principle was played up. For example, British intellectual Bertrand Russell declared in his book *Religion and Science*, published in 1935, that humanity is a "curious accident in a backwater."[29] He meant that we must be unimportant because we are on a spiral arm of the Milky Way galaxy, rather than in the center of the galaxy.

The real situation has turned out to be somewhat different. In Russell's day, people did not know about the black holes[30] in the centers of galaxies. A black hole relentlessly sucks up and destroys all "information," that is to say, everything that means anything or has characteristics. Our galaxy has a supermassive black hole, so we definitely would not want to be near it.[31] It would suck up our lives, our history, and our earth. The fact that we are not mid galaxy is hardly proof of our insignificance.

Platitudes like Russell's continue to be advanced relentlessly, even though science has been going in a different direction for decades. Science has in fact discovered the *Rare Earth Principle*, which claims that the earth is very special. Let's contrast the Copernican Principle with the Anthropic Principle and the Rare Earth Principle.

Copernicus's Real Principles (Not the Copernican Principle)

In the spring of 1543, Polish monk and astronomer Nicolas Copernicus suffered a stroke and died. For many years, he had been working on a theory, completed in 1530, that the earth revolved around the sun (heliocentric), not the other way around. He had made bits of his theory available here and there and had even presented it to the Pope (Paul III). But Copernicus knew that his idea would be controversial among astronomers. Actually, it sounded ridiculous to most astronomers of his day.

Myths and Facts About Copernicus and His Times

Myth: In Copernicus's time, most people believed that the earth was flat.
Fact: No educated person believed that the earth was flat. All schools in Copernicus's day taught the ancient Greek view that the earth is a sphere. Nineteenth-century American writer Washington Irving gave legs to the story that medieval Europeans believed that the earth was flat.[34]

Myth: Medieval philosophers thought that the earth was in the center of the universe because it was special.
Fact: Medieval philosophers thought that the earth was in the center of the universe because it was heavier than other planets, and was not really a "heavenly" body.[35]

Myth: Copernicus's sun-centered (heliocentric) theory was obviously simpler and more accurate than the old Ptolemaic (earth-centered) theory.
Fact: Copernicus's theory, as he formulated it, was neither simpler nor more accurate than Ptolemy's system. For one thing, he insisted that the planets' orbits were circular. About a century after Copernicus's death, Johannes Kepler (1571–1630) correctly identified the orbits as elliptical and straightened out other problems, which paved the way for the theory's general acceptance.[36]

Myth: Copernicus was persecuted by the Catholic Church, and therefore was reluctant to publish his theory.
Fact: Copernicus received a lot of support from the Catholic Church. For one thing, Pope Paul III hoped that the Polish astronomer could help with the vexing problem of calendar reform, by making more accurate observations. It was Protestant leaders such as Martin Luther who originally opposed the Copernican theory.[37] When he was old and in failing health, Copernicus finally yielded to the wishes of high-ranking Catholic clergy and published his theory as a book. Partly because of the many myths that grew up around his theory, Copernicus's name became attached to an idea that developed much later, that human beings were insignificant in the scheme of things.

But he felt that there was just a chance that astronomers would give his theory some consideration. They were definitely looking for new answers. The Ptolemaic system that had been used for over 1200 years assumed that the sun revolved around the earth (geocentric). The system worked, but it was awkward and time-consuming, because it required constant correction. Alfonso the Wise of Castile (1221–1284) had said, hundreds of years earlier: "Had I been present at the Creation, I would have given some useful hints for the better ordering of the universe."[32] And nothing had changed.

In 1543, at the urging of local clergy, Copernicus permitted a friend to publish his book, *On the Revolutions of the Heavenly Spheres*. A copy is said to have been handed to him on his deathbed.[33]

Copernicus had good reason to think that his theory would be controversial. Medieval cosmology, following the ancient Greek philosophers, placed earth at the center of the universe because earth was considered dull, debased, and heavy. Heavy things fell toward earth. Many people pictured hell as the hot interior of the planet, the lowest and least desirable place in the universe.[38] Under these circumstances, working out a brand new way of understanding earth as a planet that was not inferior to the others was quite a challenge.[39] Still, Copernicus would have been amazed by the 20th-century take on his theory. As astronomers Guillermo Gonzalez and Hugh Ross explain:

> Over the last four centuries the CP [Copernican Principle] has evolved from a simple claim that the Earth is not located at the center of the solar system to an expansive philosophical doctrine that the Earth, and particularly its inhabitants, are not special in any significant way.[40]

Despite the fact that Copernicus would be unlikely to agree with it, the principle that "observers must assume (as far as is possible) that they occupy an unexceptional location in the Universe"[41] was named after him.

Anthropic Principle: So Why Are We Even Here, Wondering About This?

New information about our universe, our sun, and our earth has challenged the easy, conventional assumptions about our mediocrity.

It slowly began to be recognized, especially in the late 20th century, that the universe has a sort of "cosmic DNA." A number of factors work together in great detail to enable our existence. These *anthropic coincidences*, as they are called, are the genes of the universe, coding for the formation of life.

Remarkable coincidences can be found among the gravitational constant,[43] Planck's constant, the unusual properties of water, and many other natural facts.[44] Even a slight deviation from these balances would effectively prevent our existence. As physicist Stephen Hawking admits: "The remarkable fact is that the values of these numbers seem to have been very finely adjusted to make possible the development of life."[45]

> ### Why We Would Not Exist If the Universe Were Not Fine-Tuned:
>
> "If protons were 0.2 percent heavier, they could decay into neutrons, destabilizing atoms. If the electromagnetic force were 4 percent weaker, there would be no hydrogen and no normal stars. If the weak interaction were much weaker, hydrogen would not exist; if it were much stronger, supernovae would fail to seed interstellar space with heavy elements. If the cosmological constant were much larger, the universe would have blown itself apart before galaxies could form."
>
> —Max Tegmark[42]

The upshot is, as physicist Paul Davies puts it, that "we can't avoid some anthropic component in our science, which is interesting, because after three hundred years we finally realize that we do matter."[46]

Many cosmologists are profoundly uncomfortable with anthropic coincidences and try to find ways around them. There are three ways to dump on our cosmic good luck:

Weak Anthropic Principle

This argument simply says that if conditions did not all work together to enable our existence, we would not be here to think about it. Therefore, even talking about it is a tautology, and that's all we need to know. However, this Weak Anthropic Principle is a "weak" form of reasoning. It begs the very question at issue. Suppose, for example, you win five door prizes in a row

> ### Just one "anthropic coincidence" that makes our existence possible:
>
> When two helium nuclei collide in the interior of a star they cannot fuse permanently, but they do remain stuck together momentarily—for about a hundredth of a millionth of a billionth of a second. In that tiny sliver of time a third helium nucleus comes along and hits the other two in a three-way collision. Three heliums, as it happens, do have enough sticking power to fuse together permanently. When they do so they form a nucleus called "carbon-12." This highly unusual triple collision process is called the "three-alpha process," and it is the way that almost all of the carbon in the universe is made. Without it, the only elements around would be hydrogen and helium, leading to an almost certainly lifeless universe.
>
> —Stephen Barr, particle physicist[47]

while shopping at the local plaza. You wonder out loud how you got to be so lucky. Someone responds, "Well, the answer is simple. If you didn't shop at those stores, you wouldn't have won." Would you be satisfied with this explanation? Probably not. The fact that you qualify to win any prizes at all does not explain why you should win an astounding number of them.

Scientific Legalism

Another argument says that there is no way of determining what sort of a universe we should expect; therefore, it isn't "scientific" to notice all the anthropic coincidences. Thus, Heinz R. Pagels, executive director of the New York Academy of Sciences, suggests throwing out the Anthropic Principle, as "needless clutter in the conceptual repertoire of science."[48] As political scientist Patrick Glynn notes: "Whether the Anthropic Principle meets the technical qualifications of a formal scientific theory is irrelevant to what it suggests about the fundamental nature of the universe." He also notes an essential hypocrisy underlying Pagels' comments:

> The double standard of work here is breathtaking: a host of scientists, from Russell to Richard Dawkins to Carl Sagan, are free to use loose surmises based on Darwin's theory to buttress the public case for atheism; but the moment scientists begin marshalling rather considerable and persuasive evidence for the opposite case, their speculation risks being branded by colleagues as "unscientific."[49]

Multiple Universes

Cosmologist Max Tegmark argues that the anthropic coincidences are best explained by assuming there are many universes. Not only are we not alone, our universe is not alone either. "Although the degree of fine-tuning is still debated, these examples suggest the existence of parallel universes with other values of the physical constants."[50] Are there really infinite numbers of parallel universes ballooning out there? This is a big topic, and we will discuss it in Chapter 2.

Rare Earth Principle

Not only does the universe appear to be fine-tuned for our existence, our earth is not the backwater that some philosophers have claimed. It may even be unique. Here are just three reasons:

■ *We live in a nice neighborhood.* People used to wonder why our sun and earth, if they are significant, are not at the center of the galaxy. One reason is that, in addition to the supermassive black hole, there are plenty of supernovas (exploding stars) and magnetars (deadly radiation sources) at the center. Not a good place to raise kids. Our location is just right, far from all that, but not so far from the center that we lack heavy elements such as iron.[51]

■ *We have nice neighbors.* Our giant planet neighbor Jupiter stays far away and sucks up the asteroids that would otherwise kill us all. That's not something a rocky planet like earth can take for granted. The giant planets that orbit stars other than our sun tend to either hog the space we need or follow a wonky orbit that would kill us.[52]

■ *We have a working moon.* Our moon is not just a pretty sight in the sky. On account of its large size, it keeps earth's tilt stable (23 degrees), which reduces the temperature changes of seasons so that most life forms can adapt to them. Most planets do not have large moons like ours.[53] Mars has two insignificant moons, Deimos and Phobos. As a result, Mars has changed its tilt axis 45 degrees or more.[54]

> **Ya Gotta Have Principles. How About One of These?**
>
> ■ *Principle of Mediocrity* We must not assume that there is anything special about us or the earth. There are probably lots of planets like ours.
>
> ■ *Anthropic Principle* Many things worked together to bring us into existence, and we are entitled assume that we are special.
>
> ■ *Rare Earth Principle* Our earth is a prize, and we had better look after it.
>
> Which of these principles do you think will become the most widely accepted in the 21st century?

Our planet is in fact a prize.[55] The curious accident in the backwater turns out not to be the earth but the 20th-century view of the earth! You do not hear much talk of our insignificant position any more from the sciences, though you still hear plenty at the coffee bar.

Consequences

The evidence from science suggests that, if we have tickets in a lottery, it has been fixed in our favor. Or, perhaps the universe is not a lottery; perhaps, it is a gift. There may be aliens out there—we need not think that our universe is dark and silent—but instead of listening to the aliens' wisdom, maybe we should prepare to explain to them how we got to be so lucky. Who loves us?

But wait! Is it really so simple? How do we know that ours is the only universe? Maybe Tegmark is right. What if there are lots of universes? In fact . . . what if there is an infinite number of them?

ET, Phone Frank Drake

One outcome of the Copernican Principle was the assumption, strongly promoted by American astronomers Frank Drake and Carl Sagan (1934–1996), that we live in a crowded universe. Human beings and the earth we inhabit are nothing unusual … Therefore, a million intelligent civilizations must inhabit the Milky Way galaxy![56] The two astronomers' bold, happy speculation started as a serious scientific proposition, and ended as Sagan's sci-fi novel and movie, *Contact*.

In 1960, Drake conducted the first radio search for extraterrestrial intelligence, using microwaves. In 1961, he proposed the Drake Equation, to estimate the probability of life on other planets. The equation factors in conditions such as stars with habitable planets, the presence of water, and so on, to come up with the million civilizations who owe us a call.

One drawback of Drake's equation is that the estimates are necessarily a matter of choice. For example, astronomers estimate the number of stars that have planets as between 3% and 50%, which is pretty wide.[57] Sadly, there are few hard numbers to plug in.

Great Set. So, Where's the Cast?

NASA was interested in the search for extraterrestrial intelligence (SETI) in the 1970s, but dropped it in the 1990s, after an American politician ridiculed it as a search for "little green men."[58] Of course, the real problem was that the little green men were not returning our calls.[59] Indeed, in response to claims that sheer numbers of possible planets prove that alien civilizations must exist, physicist Enrico Fermi asked 50 years ago, "Where IS everybody? If the aliens exist, why aren't they here?"[60]

His question goes unanswered. Another question is whether extraterrestrial life would even be enough like us that we would recognize it as life. Paleontologist Simon Conway Morris argues in *Life's Solution* that aliens would have to be pretty much like us in order to even exist,[61] but Jack Cohen and Ian Stewart argue in *Evolving the Alien* that no, they needn't be like us at all.[62]

Of course, we may not be able to communicate with genuinely alien creatures or understand their signals.[63] Fred Hoyle, for example, who, among his many talents, wrote science fiction, described aliens as a Black Cloud of gas, floating slowly through space.[64]

(cont'd)

Real-World Searches for Life

Drake went on to serve as president of the SETI Institute, formed in 1984 as a privately funded independent agency that searches for life in space. In recent years, with the discovery of planets outside our solar system, the agency has shed its former "crop circles" image and emerged as a serious research agency.[65] Key SETI research interests today are finding simple life forms such as bacteria on other planets and understanding the origin of life.

Simple life forms are far more likely than complex ones, because most planets are much harsher than earth. Studies of this type are called *astrobiology* (or sometimes, exobiology), to distinguish them from the more fanciful concepts associated with "extraterrestrial life." Even if SETI does not find life, science benefits from establishing the specific reasons that life does not exist in a given environment.

Sagan, who became a popular-science communicator and prominent religious skeptic, continued to promote the idea that earth is not unique—except for the fact that we should care about it—to the end of his life. That was a key theme of his final book, *Pale Blue Dot.*

The Best Arguments for Chance

CHAPTER 2

As an individual, I myself feel impelled to fancy ... a limitless succession of Universes. Each exists, apart and independently, in the bosom of its proper and particular God.

—Edgar Allan Poe (1809–1849)[1]

Some universes would even be very close to ours, except that in some of them Elvis Presley would have kicked his drug habit, gotten involved in Tennessee politics, and would now be serving as the President of the United States.

—Fred Heeren, science writer[2]

Are there other universes—millions of universes that failed to be well designed for life? Could that be the answer to why our universe seems so well designed, to say nothing of our planet being particularly well suited?

In an internationally acclaimed short story, Canadian science fiction writer Robert J. Sawyer takes legendary detective Sherlock Holmes back to the scene of his death at the Reichenbach Falls. There he gives him a choice: He can satisfy the demands of readers by being brought back to life in this universe. In that case, this universe will continue as before. Or he can remain dead, and in that universe—in which he is dead—aliens from the direction of the star Altair will make contact with earth in 1907.[3] Holmes gets only two universes to choose from. As we shall see, some cosmologists argue that there is an infinite number.[4]

Many Universes?

Physicist Hugh Everett suggested in 1957 that the universe constantly splits into different futures. This happens each time a subatomic particle goes one way as opposed to the other. As Carl W. Giberson notes:

> Simple interactions, of the sort that are happening on your retina as you read these words, are splitting the entire universe, making multiple copies of everything that exists—every star, every galaxy, every television set.[5]

Think of it: new universes erupting inside the spider on the wall and the clouds in your coffee . . .

Although the concept is mind-boggling, the idea behind it is simple. If, thanks to the Big Bang and (maybe) the Big Crunch, our universe cannot be infinite in time, well, maybe it is infinite in space. In fact, maybe there is an infinite series of parallel universes in space. Each universe is a small bit of a larger "multiverse," in the way that each bubble in foam is a small bit of the foam.

Infinite Parallel Universes

In the May 2003 issue of *Scientific American*, physicist Max Tegmark puts forward an elaborate model of four different levels of multiverses.[6] According to him,

> The simplest and most popular cosmological model today predicts that you have a twin in a galaxy about 10 to the 10^{28} meters from here. This distance is so large that it is beyond astronomical, but that does not make your doppelgänger any less real. . . . In infinite space, even the most unlikely events must take place somewhere. There are infinitely many other inhabited planets, including not just one but infinitely many that have people with the same appearance, name and memories as you, who play out every possible permutation of your life choices.[7]

This is a Level I multiverse. We must take it on faith, because we will not see these other selves. They are simply too far away. The farthest we can observe is 14 billion light years, to the edge of our universe. So we cannot see into their universe, even if it exists. Level II multiverses, in Tegmark's view, can have different space, time, and laws of physics. We definitely cannot know anything about them. Level III multiverses are created every time you or anyone (or anything) takes one path instead of another in an infinite dimensional space. Don't ask if you can know anything about *them*! In the Level IV multiverse, all alternative realities exist at the same time, and mathematical concepts are real.

If you are tempted to question these ideas, Tegmark has a simple response: evolution. We are all evolved from lower life forms, and most of us are not adapted to comprehend the truth. He explains:

> Evolution provided us with intuition for the everyday physics that had survival value for our distant ancestors, so whenever we venture beyond the everyday world, we should expect it to seem bizarre.[8]

What if, for some reason, we suspect that our doubts are not based only on our failure to evolve? Well, now we come to the critical problem. Tegmark admits that the universe we live in appears to be fine-tuned. For example, the chart that shows the razor-thin chance that we could ever exist is captioned this way:

> Cosmologists infer the presence of Level II parallel universes by scrutinizing the properties of our universe. These properties, including the strength of the forces of nature and the number of observable space and time dimensions, were established by random processes during the birth of our universe. Yet they have exactly the values that sustain life. That suggests the existence of other universes with other values.[9]

In other words, the fact that our universe has "exactly the values that sustain life" proves that there must be other universes that don't. Otherwise our universe wouldn't be random.

So who decided that the origin of our universe *was* random? Tegmark's assumptions point to a problem that we will investigate throughout this book. What

History Channel: Are infinite parallel universes a new or old idea?

The ancient philosopher Epicurus (c. 341–271 BC) believed in an infinite universe that threw up worlds (equivalent to multiverses) randomly, following eternal laws (see Introduction). He also argued for parallel universes, saying: "Our particular cosmos . . . is only a temporary agglomeration of atoms, and it is only one of an infinite number of such cosmoi, which come into existence and then dissolve away."[11] So once again, he anticipated trends in modern physics by thousands of years.[12]

seems reasonable depends on prior commitments.[10] To Tegmark, this blizzard of four magnitudes of universes seems more reasonable than an intelligent design of one universe.

New Universes Sprout Only in Black Holes?

Cosmologist Lee Smolin is a bit more conservative than Tegmark. He speculates that new universes might erupt—but not just anywhere that a particle goes one way rather than the other. Perhaps only in the middles of cosmic black holes. The new universes are disconnected from our universe, because the laws of physics break down in black holes. That is why we don't know about them. Smolin believes that the eruption of new universes in black holes follows the principles of Darwinism (natural selection). He explains:

> It seemed to me that the only principle powerful enough to explain the high degree of organization of our universe—compared to a universe with the particles and forces chosen randomly—was natural selection itself. The question then became: Could there be any mechanism by which natural selection could work on the scale of the whole universe?[13]

In other words, natural selection (the outcome of law acting on chance), lurking in a black hole, organizes a complex universe, excruciatingly fine-tuned for life. Smolin does not claim that the black hole spouts millions of them.

Alternatively, he is attracted to the idea that the universe organizes itself:

> I believe more in the general idea that there must be mechanisms of self-organization involved in the selection of the parameters of the

Gamblers' Follies

Gamblers believe in chance. So of course it's a complete fluke that they just happen to get lots of wrong ideas, right?

One common wrong idea is the Gambler's Fallacy. The gambler thinks that, if he wins on the first throw of the dice, he was "meant" to be lucky. In reality, any number can come up on the first throw.

The other idea, just as wrong, is the Inverse Gambler's Fallacy. The gambler wins on a throw of the dice, and concludes that the dice must have been thrown many times before by others.

Not so. Dice have no memories.

We cannot be absolutely sure, either, that we earthlings were intended to be very lucky or that many others were not lucky *on only one throw*. It's the whole pattern of all the coincidences that work together in our favor that is called the Anthropic Principle, not a single instance of good luck.[15]

laws of nature than I do in this particular mechanism, which is only the first one I was able to invent.[14]

All these universes popping up in the clouds in our coffee, in the torment of a black hole, in the futility of an escaped balloon—their existence guarantees that our universe is a product of chance. If only they would exist . . . if only they would exist . . .

No Bang, ReBang, Pop Pop Bang Bang . . .

A number of new theories have been proposed that promise to restore our sense that we are nothing, or at least that we are not going anywhere. Let's look at some.[16]

- Some scientists continue to support No-Bang ideas. For example, physicist Eric Lerner champions "plasma cosmology." Collisions between vast clouds of charged particles are said to endlessly create the universe that we see.[17] Science writer Timothy Ferris comments that "this model has not yet made a prediction that can be tested observationally, and so remains too vague to be wrong."[18] However, these plasma scientists perform an important service in critiquing Big Bang cosmology, because science cannot afford to take anything for granted.

- ReBang? Each Big Bang is followed by a Big Crunch, one after another.[19] This scenario is usually called the Oscillating Universe. One problem is that there is no evidence that, after a Big Crunch, the universe would necessarily start up again. Anyway, recent evidence suggests that there will not be a Big Crunch. The universe will continue to expand because it does not have enough gravity to contract. The expansion may even be speeding up because of an antigravity force.[20] However, in 2002, a new theory suggested that a collision with a parallel universe, if one is available to collide with, might set off a ReBang.[21]

- The universe may have created itself out of nothing, simply by dividing from nothing into "positive" and "negative," which would equal zero. For decades now, cosmologists have been populating the void of nothing with a zoo of theoretical or imaginary particles. There is no way of knowing whether a universe can pop into existence in this way, from nothing to something, with no rest stops.

Is there an infinite number of universes? Only a few? Just ours? There is no more or less reason to believe in other universes than there is to believe that our universe was created by God, starting with the Big Bang. There is no eyewitness evidence in either case.[22] We must decide what sounds most reasonable, based on all the evidence.

But Do These Universes Exist?

Many cosmologists doubt that infinities of randomly created universes exist. For example, physicist Paul Davies says that it is one thing to assert that some regions of the universe lie beyond the reach of telescopes, but

> somewhere on the slippery slope between that and the idea that there are an infinite number of universes, credibility reaches a limit. As one slips down that slope, more and more must be accepted on faith, and less and less is open to scientific verification.[27]

So Where is it all going anyway? The Fate of the Universe, as of Friday . . .

The rate of the universe's expansion is said to be increasing. Current theory suggests that it will go on expanding forever. "Expanding forever" means just what it says. Even though there was a Big Bang, there will be no Big Crunch. The universe will run down. But not for another 100 trillion years. In theory, that leaves plenty of time to find another universe, if there is one.[23]

The rate of star formation is known to be slowing. That does not mean that we are facing a shortage of stars. There are about 10 times more stars than there are grains of sand on the planet earth, including all beaches and deserts. The slowdown is just a normal part of the aging of the universe.[24]

No, wait! In 2002, physicists Paul Steinhardt of Princeton and Neil Turok of Cambridge presented a new model in which the universe crunches and then restarts. The trick is that our universe is supposed to have been kicked off by a collision of parallel universes. When it runs down, lack of density will move our universe toward collision with another universe, destroying all matter and kick-starting a new cycle. According to Steinhardt, some clever beings might even survive, if they invent the right equipment.[25]

History check: This is a retread, not a new model. Traditional Hindu cosmology holds that the universe recreates itself every 8.62 billion years. The schedule has now been extended by scientists to a trillion years. Not surprisingly, astronomers have cautioned that the idea is still "very speculative, but nonetheless exciting."[26]

The schedule and program for the end of all things is, as we can see, subject to constant revision. Don't cancel your plans for the weekend.

He notes the similarity between discussions of multiverses and discussions of theology, arguing:

> Indeed, invoking an infinity of unseen universes to explain the unusual features of the one we do see is just as ad hoc as invoking an unseen Creator. The multiverse theory may be dressed up in scientific language, but in essence it requires the same leap of faith.[28]

We'll come back to the leap of faith in a moment.

But then maybe the universe is a wave function . . .

Stephen Hawking has tried his hand at designing a design-free universe, as well. In *A Brief History of Time*, he suggests:

> So long as the universe had a beginning, we would suppose it had a creator (the cosmological argument). But if the universe is really completely self-contained, having no boundary or edge, it would have neither beginning nor end: it would simply be. What place, then, for a creator?[29]

How can the universe both be finite and have no boundary? To make this work, Hawking relies on imaginary time, rather than real time. Chemists sometimes use the concept of time measured in imaginary numbers, such as the square root of minus 2, in order to solve equations.[30] He pictures the universe in imaginary time as being like a wave, with no one point that is the beginning.

The problem here is the reality check. When chemists use imaginary time to solve equations, they always have to convert back to real values. Once we get back to real time, the universe does have a beginning. Hawking acknowledges this, saying that "when one goes back to the real time in which we live, however, there will still appear to be singularities."[31] In other words, a beginning. He suggests:

> In real time, the universe has a beginning and an end at singularities that form a boundary to space-time and at which the laws of science break down. But in imaginary time, there are no singularities or boundaries. So maybe what we call imaginary time is really more basic, and what we call real is just an idea that we invent to help us describe what we think the universe is like.[32]

So ... what we call real is "just an idea we invent"? That is a leap of faith, a very different leap of faith from the belief that there is a God whose existence guarantees that what we observe in science experiments, however strange, is real and is happening. Which leap makes more sense for science?

Methodological and Metaphysical Naturalism

In Chapter 1, we noted an odd fact. Scientists such as Richard Dawkins are permitted to make a public case for atheism out of Darwinism, but the science community becomes very uncomfortable when anyone makes a public case for theism based on the anthropic coincidences. Why is that?

The most widely used way of thinking in science today is called *methodological naturalism*.[33] The scientist assumes that an intelligent designer—most would say God[34]—plays no role. For example, faced with the fine-tuning of the universe that seems to enable our existence, Tegmark assumes that his model of four levels of infinite universes, where every possible thing happens, is a more reasonable explanation than an intelligent designer, *precisely because* his model leaves an intelligent designer out of the picture.[35] The hailstorm of universes does not recommend itself on any other important ground.[36]

Many people argue that methodological naturalism is necessary because scientists who followed it have made valuable discoveries. That is true, but it is also true that scientists who did not follow it—Isaac Newton, who assumed that God was the designer, for example—have also made valuable discoveries.[37]

Scientists like ways of thinking that produce simple models. However, today's God-free model of the universe is not simple at all, in the way that Lucretius's eternal universe and Hoyle's Steady State universe were simple. For one thing, far too many universes, of which we can know nothing, are needed to get away from God. This complexity does not trouble Tegmark, who says: "Perhaps we will gradually get used to the weird ways of our cosmos and find its strangeness to be part of its charm."[38]

Well, charm is a matter of taste. There is nothing to choose between infinite, unresearchable universes and the assumption that this universe is fine-tuned for life because God intended it to be so. Tegmark's interpretations of quantum mechanics amount to an act of faith. Every faith imposes some costs on the believer.

Many people go on from methodological naturalism to the philosophy of *metaphysical naturalism*. Metaphysical naturalism is the view that there is in fact no God and that the universe came about by chance. In other words, this philosophy does not treat these ideas as a working science assumption but insists on them as a fact.

In addition, some people go way overboard and adopt a point of view called *scientism*. They think that anything that cannot be discovered through the scientific method cannot be true.[39] However, the scientific method was developed to enable scientists to research nature effectively. It was not intended to replace other methods of knowing, such as artistic or moral vision, for example.

Naturalism vs. Empiricism

Both types of naturalism, methodological and metaphysical, are sometimes confused with *empiricism*. Empiricism means making decisions based on evidence or developing a theory from the evidence. By contrast, naturalism is a philosophical assumption about how to look for evidence and what to accept as evidence. A metaphysical naturalist might say, for example, that the miracles portrayed in the Bible are impossible; an empiricist would simply want evidence that they happened.

Why do scientists leave God out of the picture?

A scientist might leave God out of the picture for one of these reasons:

Methodological naturalism Scientists assume that all events have natural explanations.

Metaphysical naturalism Nature is all there is; there is no supernatural. The scientist assumes that religious beliefs cannot be true. (Note: This is sometimes called "scientific naturalism.")

Scientism Truth can be discovered only through the scientific method. Anything that cannot be discovered in that way cannot be true. The scientist assumes that religious beliefs are a form of fraud.

Empiricism Scientists make decisions based on evidence. Such areas of life as faith, miracles, or answers to prayer are not easy to research, and may be ignored for that reason. This is unrelated to whether or not they are believed to be possible or true.

Metaphysical naturalism and scientism are modernist belief systems held by many people, including many scientists. Intelligent design advocate Phillip Johnson warns:

> It is easy to see why scientific naturalism is an attractive philosophy for scientists. It gives science a virtual monopoly on the production of knowledge, and it assures scientists that no important questions are in principle beyond scientific investigation. The important question, however, is whether this philosophical viewpoint is merely an understandable professional prejudice or whether it is the objectively valid way of understanding the world.[40]

Many scientists do not use any form of naturalism or scientism in determining ultimate reality for themselves. Nearly 40% of scientists identified themselves as religious believers in a 1996 poll, the same percentage as in a similar poll conducted in 1916.[41]

Faith or Reason?

It is important to note that 21st-century discussions of faith and science are *not* a debate between faith and reason, but between differing faiths.[42] You can believe in the hidden laws of infinite universes or in God. And both of these major positions are very old; there has not been a new discovery after all.

In the next chapter we will take a closer look at the aspect of the universe that concerns us most: life. It is here—no surprise!—that the controversy over design or chance burns hottest.

Which definition of faith makes the most sense to you?

Faith means belief in something concerning which doubt is theoretically possible.

—William James[43]

Faith means intense, usually confident, belief that is not based on evidence sufficient to command assent from every reasonable person.

—Walter Kaufmann[44]

Faith—an illogical belief in the occurrence of the improbable.

—H.L. Mencken, early 20th-century journalist[45]

Which definition would be of most help in science? In religion? Would the same definition work well for both?

The Best Arguments for Design

CHAPTER 3

> A common sense interpretation of the facts suggests that a superintel-
> lect has monkeyed with the physics, as well as with the chemistry and
> biology, and that there are no blind forces worth speaking about in
> nature. The numbers one calculates from the facts seem to me so over-
> whelming as to put this conclusion almost beyond question.
>
> —Fred Hoyle[1]

In 1868, Thomas Huxley, known as Darwin's "bulldog," had some good news to share with fellow supporters of Darwin's theory of evolution. While taking soundings for the telegraph cable, the exploration ship *HMS Cyclops* had dredged some strange mud from the sea floor. This "ooze," as the captain called it, was sent to Huxley for examination.

To Huxley, the substance was an organism so simple that it was somewhere between life and non-life. He named his not-yet-life form *Bathybius haeckelii*, after the embryologist Ernst Haeckel (1834–1919), who popularized Darwinism in Germany.

The timing of Huxley's find was perfect. For Darwin's theory of natural selection (1859) to work well, cells should be simple little units, like interlocking blocks of jelly. The jelly should form easily in the right chemical environment. It should also quickly reorganize itself, evolving under environmental pressure into a new and different life form. Just how such a simple life form would get started did not trouble Huxley. He wrote: "We need not trouble ourselves with any special hypothesis to account for the occurrence of a sheet of living matter in this position." All over but the shouting.

41

Writing to Haeckel about the find, Huxley said modestly: "I hope you will not be ashamed of your god-child."[2] Haeckel certainly had no reason to be ashamed; he himself believed that a cell is a "simple lump of albuminous combination of carbon."[3]

So, for the first time in history, Darwin's colleagues had solved the mystery of life. As it turned out, for the last time, too.

In 1872, another ship, *Challenger*, was sent out to explore, and collect more samples. When the results came back, *Bathybius* turned out to be a mixture of exoskeleton, preservative, and mud.[4] "My poor dear Bathybius appears likely to turn into a 'Blunderibus,'" Huxley moaned. Physicist Paul Davies, reflecting on the debacle, comments:

> In the 19th century, life was seen as a type of magic matter that emerged from the primordial ooze. The idea grew that this organic matter could be cooked up in the laboratory from a primordial broth if only the right ingredients were identified.[5]

Bathybius: The Sequel!

The sequel appeared a little less than a century later. In 1953, University of Chicago graduate student Stanley L. Miller and his PhD advisor Harold C. Urey put a mixture of gases that they believed were major components of earth's early atmosphere (methane, ammonia, hydrogen, and water) in a closed container and zapped them with the equivalent of lightning. A small quantity of amino acids, needed for life, formed.

The newborn acids were greeted by a publicity meltdown. Many people believed that Miller and Urey had finally discovered how life chanced to arise on the early earth.[6] Darwinism's triumph was complete because there was now an explanation for the origin of life. A later experiment in 1961 confirmed the finding.[7]

Artistically, it was perfect. Life itself from a zap of lightning! But art isn't life. Miller and Urey assumed that the early earth had little or no oxygen, and that it could provide the ingredients with a continuing supply of electricity. Neither of these conditions is considered likely today.[8]

A far more difficult problem is the sheer complexity of even the simplest *real* life forms. Davies explains what is wrong with Miller and Urey's approach this way:

The living cell is best thought of as a supercomputer—an information processing and replicating system of astonishing complexity. DNA is not a special life-giving molecule, but a genetic databank that transmits its information using a mathematical code. Most of the workings of the cell are best described, not in terms of material stuff—hardware—but as information, or software. Trying to make life by mixing chemicals in a test tube is like soldering switches and wires in an attempt to produce Windows 98. It won't work because it addresses the problem at the wrong conceptual level.[9]

Repeated zaps of lightning fry the chemical soup into goop. But can life forms organize (or self-organize) if there is no designer, nor even a principle of design, in the universe?

Origin of life researchers haven't given up. They now study high-temperature sites around thermal vents in the ocean, and areas deep underground, hoping to learn more clues. But, considering the size of the gap that really exists between life and non-life, they face a huge challenge in explaining how life can come into existence without any intelligent intervention at all.[10]

Jellies Sure Get More Respect Now

Huxley, like most scientists of his generation, had assumed that cells were simple. So did Miller and Urey, really. No scientist had looked, deep and in detail, inside a cell. They didn't look, because they couldn't.

Cells, including the trillions of cells in your body, build their machinery from molecules. As a result, most of their working parts are *below the wavelength of visible light*. They can be studied, but only by using advanced techniques such as X-ray crystallography.

The discipline of biochemistry, the study of the chemistry of life, started to provide answers in the 1950s,[11] nearly a hundred years too late for Huxley. No problem, Huxley would probably not have been happy with the answers anyway.

What did scientists find? That cells are not simple jellies but, as Davies suggests, more like supercomputers. We can also picture each cell as a factory, with hundreds of machines carrying out complex instructions.

So It All Just Sort of . . . Started to Happen One Day?

As we have seen, the universe has a beginning, and the numbers suggest that it is fine-tuned for life.[12] However, these facts are not the driving force behind the claim that the universe shows evidence of design. Rather, design advocates point to the sheer complexity of life forms as their strongest argument.

Within the 14 billion or so years that are the age of the present universe, does either chance or necessity produce the complex molecular machines that form cells, the building blocks of animals and plants? Or is there an element of design?

Fred Hoyle was one scientist who was aware of the problems that the origin of life presented to scientists' materialist worldview. He had to admit, against his preferences, that life forms look as though they are designed. He compared Darwin's belief that life just happened somehow to the hope that a tornado in a junkyard would somehow manufacture for us a Boeing 747.[13]

Hoyle did not *like* design, and, as we have seen, he continued to propose alternatives to the end of his life, as he did with the Big Bang. But he never found one that really worked.

Or Maybe It Is an Intelligent Design?

Some scientists, especially biochemist Michael Behe of Pennsylvania's Lehigh University, author of the controversial *Darwin's Black Box* (1996), have begun to argue that Darwinism—which explains everything in terms of law and chance—does not account for either the existence or the evolution of the complex machinery of cells. And we cannot talk about life without talking about cells. Every life form is either a cell or a highly organized, interconnected, indivisible nation of cells. Or, as Davies puts it: "Even a simple bacterium is a vast assemblage of intricately crafted molecules, many of them elaborately customized."[14]

Behe calls some of the machinery in cells "irreducibly complex." He means that there are no "simple" cell systems that could just arise by chance from the six organic elements (calcium, carbon, hydrogen, nitrogen, oxygen, and phosphorus) and then evolve into complex cell systems. That is because there is no simple way of doing the jobs that these systems do. A creature with a simpler arrangement could not live at all. A little malfunction here or there, and the cell does not evolve to a higher form of life; it dies. One reason that cells are complex is that they must use molecular machinery to force elements and chemicals to do things that they do not normally do.

The Bacteria's Motorized Propeller: An Example of Irreducible Complexity?

The flagellum is a rotary propeller used by bacteria to swim. Its method of propulsion was first identified in 1973. It comprises at least a paddle, a rotor, and a motor. Powered by acid, the flagellum is strikingly like a machine that a human being might design and build for such a purpose, though the whole thing is done with molecules.[15]

Darwinists and intelligent design advocates have gone to war over the flagellum. It is a good example of the new findings that force the issue of design versus chance out into the open.

Biochemist Michael Behe argues that the flagellum is an irreducibly complex design. The flagellum is not likely to arise from a series of lucky accidents for the bacterium, any more than a boat motor would arise from a series of lucky accidents for a stranded sailor.

The flagellum has become a logo for the intelligent design movement, with animated versions waving happily on Web sites devoted to popularizing intelligent design.[16]

Biochemist Ken Miller, author of *Finding Darwin's God* (1999),[17] has attacked the idea that the flagellum is irreducibly complex. He thinks that science will explain how it could happen by law and chance some day. He says:

> Living cells are filled, of course, with complex structures whose detailed evolutionary origins are not known. Therefore, in fashioning an argument against evolution one might pick nearly any cellular structure, the ribosome for example, and claim—correctly—that its origin has not been explained in detail by evolution.[18]

But does Darwinism have the answers? ID advocate Bill Dembski accuses Darwinism of "global disciplinary failure," charging that "Darwin's theory, without which nothing in biology is supposed to make sense, in fact offers no insight into how the flagellum arose."[19]

As Dembski's comment shows, the controversy between Darwinism and ID is fierce, accompanied by accusations of bad will on both sides. One reason is that the two sides have different standards of evidence.

The Darwinist knows that Darwinism must be the explanation, precisely because it rules out design. Therefore, he does not need to sketch out a complete explanation for a Darwinian pathway. He only needs to show that such a pathway may be theoretically possible.

The ID advocate disputes anything less than a completed pathway as an explanation because he accepts non-Darwinist answers as, in principle, possible. Therefore, he demands a more rigorous standard of evidence for Darwinism.

Bacteria are among the simplest life forms. Even so, increasing numbers of these minute creatures are discovered to have complex parts and behaviors. Barring a big breakthrough, this dispute between Darwinism and intelligent design is likely to be replayed many times over.

Behe is a key proponent of intelligent design theory. According to him, the cell works the way it does because at least some of its complex machinery was intelligently designed. Science cannot understand life as long as it excludes design.

Needless to say, Behe was soon roundly denounced by the Darwinist establishment. As Thomas Woodward puts it in *Doubts About Darwin: A History of Intelligent Design*, Behe's dissent was "the first time sophisticated skepticism of naturalistic evolution was brought to center stage in American society."[20] The reaction was predictable. One of the world's foremost philosophers of evolution, Michael Ruse, has said of Behe, "I think he is wrong, wrong, wrong . . . " Ruse directs his readers to Darwinist author Ken Miller to be rightly instructed.[21]

To understand Ruse's and other Darwinists' responses, we need to keep in mind that Darwinian evolution is not just a theory. Darwinism eliminates design, and to the Darwinist, eliminating design *is* science. The fact that Behe is not a creationist and accepts a role for evolution does nothing to turn aside shock and anger at his views.

The arguments on both sides are presented in more detail later in this book in the chapters on evolution and intelligent design. For now, let's look at the question addressed in the next chapter: What difference does it make who is right? What difference does design make?

Can life forms simply create themselves?

Stuart Kauffman, a leading thinker on self-organization, has asked this daring question: Can life forms self-organize—essentially creating themselves?

Although no friend to intelligent design, Kauffman makes clear in his book, *At Home in the Universe: The Search for the Laws of Self-Organization and Complexity*, that he is not pleased with Darwinism either.

As an alternative to both creationism and intelligent design, Kauffman proposes that matter self-organizes—essentially, he argues that design, like law and chance, is simply one of the three organizational pillars of the universe, in which case there need not be a designer.

He argues that "the existence of spontaneous order is a stunning challenge to our settled ideas in biology since Darwin."[22] Indeed, he enthuses, if self-organization is a principle of the universe, "what a revision of the Darwinian worldview will lie before us! Not we the accidental, but we the expected."[23] In other words, self-organization makes sense of the anthropic coincidences and vindicates the Rare Earth principle, proving that we do matter after all.

Kauffman's self-organization theory (also called complexity theory) has yet to break out of the realm of computer studies, but it has the potential to be a serious rival to intelligent design.[24] Perhaps it can be seen as a form of design theory that dispenses with the designer by identifying the organism itself, reflexively, as the designer: It organizes itself.

Currently, Kauffman is working on a concept of "the adjacent possible," which, as he explains it, is that "It just may be the case that biospheres on average keep expanding into the adjacent possible. By doing so they increase the diversity of what can happen next."[25]

Another complexity theorist is James Gardner, whose radical Selfish Biocosm hypothesis, originally presented in peer-reviewed scientific journals, proposes that life and intelligence have not emerged in a series of Darwinian accidents but are essentially hardwired into the cycle of cosmic creation, evolution, death, and rebirth. His thesis, like that of Kauffman, challenges both Darwinism and intelligent design because he accepts intelligent design—but not a divine designer.[26]   •

What About Life?
Did It Start by Design or by Chance?

───────── **PART TWO** ─────────

Why Design or Chance Matters So Much

CHAPTER 4

The overthrow of the "random universe" by contemporary science is the great unnoticed revolution of late-twentieth-century thought.

—Patrick Glynn, political scientist[1]

Anyone informed that the universe is expanding and contracting in pulsations of eighty billion years has a right to ask, "What's in it for me?"

—Peter De Vries[2]

In fact, the universe is *not*, according to current cosmology, expanding and contracting in pulsations of 80 billion years or so, as DeVries, quoted above, assumes. Current thinking is that it popped into existence a little over 14 billion years ago and won't just pop back again, ever. However, De Vries's question is still a good one: Why *should* we care how science understands the universe?

We should care because science—cosmology, physics, chemistry, biology, ecology—influences culture. And culture includes art, literature, architecture, politics, economics, and religion.[3] The world of art and literature today operates on the modernist assumption that the universe is an endless, meaningless void, in which life is a dismal accident. Whether that is true or not affects all of life.

So where did modernists get their ideas of what the universe is like? Modernists learned what they know about the universe from the science of the 19th and early 20th centuries. However, the news from science today is quite different. Current findings either do not support their views, or else they support

51

them only if you take a leap of faith into parallel universes or imaginary time.

There are many mysteries in science today for which there are no clear answers and no obvious places to look for answers. The main reason there are no clear answers is that modernism, which attempts to reduce everything to law, chance, energy, and matter, is never going to find the answers. Let's take a look at a couple of the mysteries.

Origin of Life Studies: A Fast Track from Nothing to . . . Where, Exactly?

Very little has been learned since Darwin's day about how life originated. Darwin wrote:

> It is often said that all the conditions for the first production of a living organism are now present, which could ever have been present. But if (and oh! what a big if!) we could conceive in some warm little pond, with all sorts of ammonia and phosphoric salts, lights, heat, electricity, etc. present, that a protein compound was chemically formed ready to undergo still more complex changes, at the present day such matter would be instantly devoured or absorbed, which would not have been the case before living creatures were formed.[5]

> **Modernist Perspectives on Life and the Universe**
>
> The more we know of the laws & nature of the Universe the more ghastly a business we perceive it all to be—& the non-necessity of it.
>
> —Thomas Hardy (1840–1928), British novelist, from a letter written in 1902
>
> Here we are, we're alone in the universe, there's no God, it just seems that it all began by something as simple as sunlight striking on a piece of rock. And here we are. We've only got ourselves. Somehow, we've just got to make a go of it. We've only ourselves.
>
> —John Osborne (1929–1994), British playwright
>
> If that's how it all started, then we might as well face the fact that what's left out there is a great deal of shrapnel and a whole bunch of cinders (one of which is, fortunately, still hot enough and close enough to be good for tanning).
>
> —Barbara Ehrenreich (1941–)[4]

That "big if" was as far as Darwin got with explaining the origin of life. He had the advantage that, in his day, the universe itself was held by many scientists to be eternal, which meant that an infinite amount of time was available for dunking things in ponds, somewhere, if not on earth. His successors must work within the finite amount of time following the Big Bang. They have not fared any better.

According to current theories, life on earth got started quickly about 3.8 billion years ago.[6] But after many years of study, researchers are far more aware of the size of the problem than of the explanatory power of any proposed solution.[7] In fact, John Horgan, senior writer for *Scientific American*, has called the origin of life "the weakest strut of the chassis of modern biology."[8]

The National Academy of Sciences puts the problem in an interesting way:

> The study of the origin of life is a very active research area in which important progress is being made, although the consensus among scientists is that none of the current hypotheses has thus far been confirmed.[9]

In other words, it is fair to say that we do not know how life originated.[10] That's not for lack of theories: For example, hot soup, cold soup, prebiotic pizza, RNA world, clay world,[11] silicon world, and self-organization[12] have all been tried.[13] Complicating the picture is the fact that the oldest, simplest life forms we know of, the one-celled *Archaea*, are not particularly simple.[14] In fact, there is no such thing as a simple life form.

Surveying the scene, Peter D. Ward and Donald Brownlee, authors of *Rare Earth*, argue, tongue-in-cheek, that

> the kind of origin of life theory a scientist holds to seems to depend on his/her field of specialty: oceanographers like to think it began in a deep sea thermal vent, biochemists like Stanley Miller prefer a warm tidal pool on the Earth's surface, astronomers insist that comets played an essential role by delivering complex molecules, and scientists who write science fiction part time imagine that the Earth was "seeded" by interstellar microbes.[15]

When we ask about the origin of life, what question are we trying to answer? Darwin was a materialist; that is, he saw life as made up only of material bodies. He wanted to know how such a body could form, with input only from the laws of nature acting on chance events.

In reality, life is mainly information. Our physical lives are not the sum of the chemicals that make up our bodies; they are also the staggering amount of information that governs the operation of the billions of molecular machines that manage all the chemicals. When we die, the chemicals are all still there, but the system of information that holds them together is lost.

Perhaps the question we should ask is not how does life form by chance, but what is the source of all the information that life requires?

Answering this question won't be easy, because information is not measured in the same type of units as matter or energy. It is a real quantity but not a material one.

The Human Genome

A classic example of the way that modernist thinking does not help us understand life has been the dance around the human genome. At first, researchers assumed that human beings would have more genes than anything else living. That would prove that we are just animals with more genes. Then it turned out that the common fern has way more chromosomes than we do. That proves that we are lower than the fern. Or does it? Does it prove anything except that we are not our genes?

Certainly, genes can provide some answers. But no simple, reductionist answers. If they had, you and I would still be hearing plenty from the stars of the Meat Puppet Show.

And here is the really interesting part: As we survey the ruins of materialism and reductionism, the mystery of human life persists. But there is a very big difference between the nature of the mystery today and the nature of the mystery thousands of years ago. Many things were a mystery then because people just didn't know. Many of those same things are a mystery today because we *do* know.

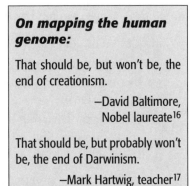

On mapping the human genome:

That should be, but won't be, the end of creationism.

—David Baltimore, Nobel laureate[16]

That should be, but probably won't be, the end of Darwinism.

—Mark Hartwig, teacher[17]

The Real Mysteries Are Fun!

Many more mysteries beckon us. The puzzles of the human brain and human evolution, the origin of human language and art, challenge us to think beyond the simple reduction of everything to law and chance and matter that was supposed to be the answer in the 20th century.

Today, a real mystery in science is not a "black box," a system whose workings are unknown. It is a cascade of intricate, interlocking systems where the challenge is to understand the design. The greatest mystery is life itself—not because we know nothing about it but because we know so much, and do not know how to understand what we know. We know so

Genes 'R' Not Us

When the Human Genome Project announced the completion of its map in 2000, one curious fact stood out. Fewer than 30,000 genes were responsible for organizing an entire human being, about one-third of previous estimates of 80,000 to 100,000. In other words, human beings were said to have about twice the number of genes of a fruit fly.

The modernist interpretation roared quickly through the mainstream media: This is quite a "comedown" for arrogant humans; just think how lowly we are—not a little lower than the angels but a little higher than the fruit flies.

As journalist Tom Bethell recalls the scene,[18] it took several days after the Human Genome press conference for the true meaning of the discovery to sink in. There followed a "kind of appalled silence," then whispers, alarms, and hastily revised explanations.

The true meaning of the discovery is that we are not our genes. If we have only a few more genes than a fruit fly, there are just not enough genes to enable us to be ourselves. Contrary to materialist expectations, we must look elsewhere to find out what a human being is.

Since then, there has been a great reduction in roaring from the mainstream media about what the human genome proves. The recent DNA hybridization studies of the chimpanzee showed estimates of 1% difference from the human genome. This might have been expected to lead to an overwhelming din of materialist lectures on the insignificance of humans, but it didn't. Again, that is because the similarity presents a problem to the materialist. Anyone can tell the vast, obvious differences between a human being and a chimpanzee.

Things got worse. In 2003, the number of human genes was revised downward to just fewer than 25,000, a few more than *Caenorhabditis elegans*, the tiny soil-dwelling roundworms that survived the destruction of the Columbia space shuttle and were returned to their owners.

And it gets even worse. Says David Thaler of Rockefeller University in New York City: "For now, we don't have any way even to quantify what fraction of all you'd like to know about an organism is in its genome."[19] Even deciding how to look for the missing information will present challenges for decades to come.

So what does this mean for society today? Gone are the hopes of finding a "violence gene," a "gay gene," or a "fat gene" that would take the hit for our behavior. After an endless run, the Meat Puppet Show, which portrays humanity simply as "meat puppets," is just about off the air.

Here is what we now know about the human genome: Our genes work together in complex combinations, talking to each other constantly as they direct the building of a bewildering variety of proteins, the machines that carry out the operations in each cell that keep us alive. The really tough part is that, instead of having only four building blocks, as genes do, proteins have 20. They are arrayed in three-dimensional machine-like structures of dazzling complexity, hundreds of molecules long. Plus, there are probably 10 times as many proteins as genes.

Anyone who wants to study DNA, the language of life that utters living beings, must learn the languages of the proteins, to see what genes translate into.

much that everything is a mystery that invites further investigation. We stand before an ocean of complexity, wondering where to start surfing.

Can We Ever Find Out the Truth About the Universe or About Life?

In the last sentence of his *A Brief History of Time* (1996), Stephen Hawking looked forward to a grand unified theory in physics that would enable us to know "the mind of God." However, by 2003, he dampened expectations by telling fellow physicists at a major Cambridge conference: "Maybe it is not possible to formulate the theory of the Universe in a finite number of statements." In other words, there cannot be a theory of everything.

In saying this, Hawking was recalling the work of Austrian mathematician Kurt Gödel. In 1931, Gödel showed that mathematical statements exist that are true but not provable. To demonstrate that, he created a mathematical statement that is the equivalent of the following sentence: "This statement cannot be proved true." If the statement is false, it can be proved true, but that is a contradiction. If the statement is true, then it cannot be proved at all.[20] Hawking is saying that perhaps the universe is like that statement. We cannot hope to prove everything. We must start by taking some things on faith, or we just can't prove anything.

It's not surprising that the old doctrines of modernism no longer fit. But how much, if any, of this has seeped through to the popular culture? To answer that we must return to Darwin.

Who Was Darwin?
What Did He Really Say?

CHAPTER 5

I see no good reasons why the views given in this volume should shock the religious feelings of anyone.

—Charles Darwin[1]

Although atheism might have been logically tenable before Darwin, Darwin made it possible to be an intellectually fulfilled atheist.

—Richard Dawkins, zoologist[2]

Charles Darwin (1809–1882) came from a well-to-do, well-educated English family. His grandfather, Erasmus Darwin, had developed a theory of evolution, though it was not widely accepted. His mother's father was the china entrepreneur Josiah Wedgwood.

At 22 Charles secured a place on an English survey ship, *HMS Beagle*, bound on a five-year scientific expedition around the world. From 1831 through 1836, he studied geology and biology, including fossils, in South America and other regions. He used this mass of information to develop his theory of natural selection.[3]

Most geologists prior to Darwin's day believed that plant and animal life had been created several times and then destroyed in catastrophes. The most recent catastrophe was believed to be a worldwide flood, assumed to be Noah's Flood as described in the Bible (Genesis 6–9). English geologist Sir Charles Lyell challenged this view in his three-volume work *Principles of Geology* (1830–1833), where he argued that the earth developed uniformly over long periods and was not subject to sudden, violent catastrophes. He proposed that the earth was perhaps 240 million years old.[4] Lyell was a major influence on Darwin. Darwin began to look for evidence of the accumulation of slow changes in biology as the explanation for the record of life on earth, as opposed to sudden catastrophes.

Generally, scientists in Darwin's day thought that species did not change. They assumed that species came into existence separately and that fossils represented species that had become extinct in catastrophes. Darwin, however, noted that each of the Galápagos Islands, off the west coast of South America near Ecuador, provided a habitat for a slightly different type of tortoise, mockingbird, and finch. He began to wonder about the relationship between distinct but similar species, and between present and fossil species. Were they really all separate creations or were they linked in some way? If so, what exactly was the link?

Darwin's Gradual Loss of Religious Conviction

As a young man in 1827, Darwin trained for the ministry at Cambridge, but lost interest. Over his lifetime, he gradually lost his faith as well, partly because of the implications of his theory of evolution and partly because of the death of his daughter Annie, who died of tuberculosis at the age of 10 in 1851. When he published *On the Origin of Species* in 1859, he seems to have been wavering. You can see this from the final paragraph. In the first edition, he wrote:

> There is grandeur in this view of life, with its several powers, having been originally breathed into a few forms or into one; and that, whilst this planet has gone cycling on according to the fixed law of gravity, from so simple a beginning endless forms most beautiful and most wonderful have been, and are being, evolved.

In the second edition, released several weeks later, he had changed the closing paragraph to read (note the words where emphasis has been added):

> There is grandeur in this view of life, with its several powers, having been originally breathed *by the Creator* into a few forms or into one; and that, whilst this planet has gone cycling on according to the fixed law of gravity, from so simple a beginning endless forms most beautiful and most wonderful have been, and are being evolved.

Some commentators have claimed that Darwin made this change because he was afraid of a religious backlash[5] and did not want to offend his believing wife. But it is just as likely that he himself was uncertain at that time whether or not there was a God behind it all. Toward the end of his life he described himself as an agnostic.[6]

(cont'd)

As for purpose behind the universe, he definitely didn't believe in it. He wrote to a friend:

> You would not probably expect any one fully to agree with you on so many abstruse subjects; and there are some points in your book which I cannot digest. The chief one is that the existence of so-called natural laws implies purpose. I cannot see this. Not to mention that many expect that the several great laws will some day be found to follow inevitably from some one single law, yet taking the laws as we now know them, and look at the moon, where the law of gravitation-and no doubt of the conservation of energy-of the atomic theory, &c. &c., hold good, and I cannot see that there is then necessarily any purpose. Would there be purpose if the lowest organisms alone, destitute of consciousness existed in the moon?[7]

Darwin was a vague sort of agnostic who could not rid himself of the idea that there must be some intelligence that started the universe, even though he wanted to dispense with the ideas of design or purpose. At one point, he wrote:

> Another source of conviction in the existence of God, connected with the reason and not with the feelings, impresses me as having much more weight. This follows from the extreme difficulty or rather impossibility of conceiving this immense and wonderful universe, including man with his capacity of looking far back wards and far into futurity, as the result of blind chance or necessity. When thus reflecting I feel compelled to look to a First Cause having an intelligent mind in some degree analogous to that of man; and I deserve to be called a Theist.[8]

Darwin could possibly be called a theist in the sense that, in the 20th century, many prominent theologians promoted ideas about God that were almost as vague as his. However, his "First Cause" should not be confused with the idea of God as a Creator. As ID advocate Phillip Johnson has pointed out: "A 'First Cause' who merely sets the natural mechanism in motion and then leaves everything to chance is not a Creator, just as a person who sets an automobile in motion downhill but neither steers nor brakes is not a driver."[9]

The Invisible Hand of Natural Selection

A turning point came for Darwin when he read *An Essay on the Principle of Population* (1798), by British economist Thomas Malthus. Malthus argued that human populations increase geometrically, given a chance, outstripping the food supply. Thus, human population growth could be checked only by famine, disease, war, or laws against poor people having children.

Darwin realized that Malthus's theories might be applied to animals as well. Animals always had more offspring than could survive. Competition for survival, which Darwin called natural selection, might be the means by which animal and plant species change, branch out, or go extinct over time.[10]

Another important influence on Darwin was British economist Adam Smith (1723–1790). Smith argued that if people are permitted simply to pursue their self-interest in a marketplace, the "invisible hand" of the market will produce the best possible economy. As Stephen Jay Gould puts it: "Darwin's theory uses the same invisible hand, but formed into a fist as a battering ram to eliminate Paley's God from nature."[11]

Darwin worked on his theory of natural selection for many years. He published it in 1859, when he risked being "scooped" because naturalist Alfred Wallace wrote to him with a similar idea. Darwin's *On the Origin of Species by Means of Natural Selection* was very popular and sold out in a few weeks, necessitating another printing.

Darwin described the evolution[12] of life as a competitive struggle over limited resources, in the shadow of predators and disease, as well as the risk of climate change. Here is how he thought it works:

- Individuals whose individual characteristics (variations) enable them to survive and reproduce in a given situation pass on those key survival traits.

- The number of individuals with these traits increases with each generation. Those that don't have the traits decrease.

- Under this pressure, some species evolve into new species; others go extinct.

Darwin's theory was right for its time. Many thinkers had been looking for a way to eliminate the idea of purpose or design from nature. Darwin's massive fact base, together with his theory, seemed to be the answer. As George C. Hunter writes:

> As early as the seventeenth century, almost two hundred years before Darwin published his theory of evolution, philosophers and theologians were calling for an intermediate process between God and creation. By the time Darwin came around this call had only increased in volume. What was needed was a credible explanation of how the process worked. This was Darwin's contribution, for he filled in the details.[13]

The discovery in 1861 of the feathered fossil *Archaeopteryx* convinced many that Darwin must be right. Archaeopteryx is the oldest fossil bird, and it has a full set of teeth. It was considered a transitional fossil, a reptile in the act of evolving into a bird.[14]

No Direction Is Up

The theory of natural selection is widely misunderstood. Many people assume that Darwinism teaches that the "best" creatures survive. Popular depictions of the "ascent of man," for example, show natural selection as a relentless series of improvements. From the monkey through the unshaven brute to (at last!) the movie idol.

But these popular depictions are mistaken. In Darwin's terms, no direction is up. A living creature inherits, at random, either fit or unfit characteristics. "Fit" does not mean "good." "Fittest" does not mean "best," only "best adapted" to a specific situation. The unguided course of nature enables well-adapted animals to breed and prevents others. Only those that breed

> **Darwinism and Racism**
>
> In his book *The Descent of Man*, Darwin made it quite clear that he considered blacks inferior to whites.[15] This was not an unusual view for his time, and he was, if anything, quite cautious in the deductions that he drew from it. While Darwinists today completely disclaim such views, in the 19th century they formed the underpinnings of "scientific racism"—supposedly more sophisticated than the garden variety of racism. The mapping of the human genome has shown, of course, that there is no relationship between social ideas about race and the facts of human heredity.[16] Today, no respected Darwinist, creationist, or ID advocate would subscribe to any form of racism.

continue to pass on their genes, for better or worse, at any given point. Darwin's selection is selection without any purpose at all. And that is all there is to life. In fact, Darwin originally called his theory "natural selection" rather than "evolution," in order to avoid the suggestion that the changes must be improvements.[17]

> **Natural Selection at Work**
>
> Picture two stallions. One is a magnificent animal; the other a swayback nag that hides in the scrub to avoid the stronger male. However, an equine epidemic sweeps through the grasslands. The superior horse is felled. The inferior one happens to be immune, due to the same accidents of genetics that produced his many physical problems. He breeds with all the surviving mares, passing on many undesirable traits before he is killed by a predator. As a result, the herd dies out. This is as much a story of natural selection as any account of gradual or sudden improvements. Only one in a thousand species that has ever lived is still with us.[18]

Back to the Slime, via *The Time Machine*

Science fiction writer H.G. Wells, at one time a student of Darwin's popularizer T.H. Huxley, understood clearly what Darwin meant. He underlined the blindness of natural selection in his science fiction novel *The Time Machine* (1895).

Wells depicts a world 800,000 years from now in which the human race has degenerated into two groups: the pretty but useless Eloi who are eaten by the monstrous, subterranean Morlocks. His purpose is to attack the British class system, but his understanding of natural selection governs his choice of metaphor. For him, no natural direction was up. However, he believed that socialism could change humanity's future through political intervention.

Why We Believed in Darwinism

Amazingly, by and large, despite its gloomy implications, Darwin's theory was accepted by most political and religious leaders of the late 19th century and through most of the 20th century. Let's have a look at some reasons why.

When I first learned about Darwin's theory of evolution in elementary school in the 1960s, it seemed the perfect explanation for the origin of life. It fit seamlessly into a scientific perspective inherited from the previous century. The teacher who explained to us that the eternal universe resulted from the spontaneous generation of hydrogen atoms also explained that life forms just naturally evolved in Darwin's "warm little pond"—and gobbled each other up for millions of years until only the fittest survived.

Indeed, popular Darwinism was part of our folklore. There was a fun side to it—for example the long-running Flintstones cartoons and the universally recognized "ascent of man" graphic that sold us politicians and rented us TVs.[19]

There was a sinister side as well. One of my teachers justified abortion on the grounds that the human embryo supposedly passed through "all the stages of evolution" and would, at a certain point, be "just a fish."[20] Similarly, a news commentator explained starvation during a political upheaval in Bangladesh by proclaiming that "man is a species that has overbred. Being human does not confer a right of survival."[21] The commentator's remark was not only phrased in Darwinist language but assumed that a civil war is best explained by the idea that human beings behave like rodents or grasshoppers, rather than by political explanations for conflict. Apart from Darwinism—

survival of the fittest—this assumption would be merely baffling to the hearer. Did the politics of the situation really mean nothing at all?

Of course, even as our teachers and commentators were chalking up the neat explanations, the scientific certainties behind them were collapsing. First, the general trend in science was away from the eternal universe and the accidental earth. Second, compared with other trends in science, Darwinism has not answered a lot of questions. As journalist Philip Gold notes:

> Evolutionary materialism—the belief that life arose and evolved by chance—is, after all, a mid-19th century notion. Since then, this paradigm has remained, by modern scientific standards, virtually stagnant. The missing links and vital fossil records have not been found. The list of things the paradigm can't explain, from the Cambrian Explosion and Chinese fossil records to the incredible and irreducible complexity of a single cell, keeps growing.[22]

It takes time, sometimes decades, for a popular culture to catch up. After all, far more people know about the Flintstones than about the Cambrian explosion.[23]

C.S. Lewis and "Man's Incorrigible Mind"

Some commentators became disillusioned with Darwinism early. C.S. Lewis (1898–1963), perhaps the most widely read Christian apologist of the 20th century, was careful to distinguish between evolution as a theory in biology and Evolution as an idea that came to dominate the politics and religion of his time. He noted that decades before Darwin's *On the Origin of Species*, poets and musicians had started proclaiming that humanity was inevitably evolving, onward and upward, to a glorious future.[24] "I grew up believing in this Myth and I have felt—I still feel—its almost perfect grandeur,"[25] he wrote.

However, there is a big difference between the myth of Evolution preached by poets and the theory in biology. Lewis made quite clear to his readers that the biological theory of Darwinism does not argue that there will be inevitable, continuous *improvements* over time. It only explains continuous *change* over time. The change can be degeneration or decline. Really, it is all the same to the biologist, especially if the subject is fossil lampreys or some other unattractive entity. But as applied to human society, the myth of evolution morphed from a *theory* about changes to a supposed *fact* about improvements. It became a powerful weapon for good or ill in the hands of social reformers and politicians. Lewis wrote:

To those brought up on the Myth nothing seems more normal, more natural, more plausible, than that chaos should turn into order, death into life, ignorance into knowledge.[26]

The reason continuous improvement without human effort seemed so plausible was that contrary examples in nature were simply ignored. For example, popular presentations of evolution typically feature the evolution of the modern horse from a bulgy little pawed creature. They do not highlight the evolution of an active, independent creature into a degenerate, disease-causing parasite, though that happens, too.

Much as Lewis admired the literature based on the Evolution myth, he didn't like the political version very much at all. About that, he wrote:

It has great allies,
Its friends are propaganda, party cries,
And bilge, and Man's incorrigible mind.[27]

Lewis was also well aware that Darwinism has often functioned as a religion in itself. It certainly functioned that way for Thomas Huxley, "Darwin's bulldog." Evolution was a religion for politically varied figures such as playwright George Bernard Shaw, philosopher Friedrich Nietzsche, and composer Richard Strauss. Popular understanding of evolution actually owes much more to them than to Darwinian biologists. Each of these thinkers had his own ideas about what evolution, specifically human evolution, was.[28] However, Shaw got it right at least once. He explained in *Back to Methuselah* that "if this sort of selection could turn an antelope into a giraffe, it could conceivably turn a pond full of amoebas into the French academy."[29] That, precisely, is what Darwin and his successors believe, and what everyone who can be described as a non-Darwinist disbelieves.

Lewis's views about Darwinism as a biological theory changed over time. In the 1940s and 1950s, a friend tried to get him to join a protest movement against it. However, he refused, fearing that association with anti-Darwinists would damage his reputation as a Christian apologist. "When a man has become a popular Apologist," he explained, "he must watch his step. Everyone is on the look out for things that might discredit him."[30] However, privately, by 1959 he had become increasingly skeptical of Darwinism and concerned about its social effects, especially on account of "the fanatical and twisted attitudes of its defenders."[31]

Did Most Religious People Oppose Darwinism?

Through most of the history of Western culture, science and religion were not in conflict. In the 17th century, when Newton published his laws of gravity, both science and religion participated in a common project called "natural philosophy." Only later, in the 18th century, did some atheistic philosophers see an advantage in pitting one against the other. However, theirs was not the common opinion, and many members of the clergy were enthusiastic amateur scientists. By the late 19th century, however, some academics created a great deal of publicity for a supposed warfare between science and religion.[32] Their works have affected modern education. A popular version of Darwinism suited it admirably.

As we have seen, when Darwin published his *On the Origin of Species* in 1859, he was by no means the first person to come up with a theory of evolution. Such theories had been proposed 50 years earlier, and the notion of evolution was widely accepted.[33] The significance of Darwin's theory was that, as noted earlier, it eliminated design from nature, leaving only chance and necessity (what *might* happen and what *must* happen). In other words, he argued that organisms just happened (chance), and those that were best adapted to a given environment survived (necessity). There need not be a design or a designer (and certainly not a Designer!).

Should Most Religious People Have Opposed Darwinism?

Darwin's ideas, first published in 1859 in *On the Origin of Species* and elaborated in 1871 in *The Descent of Man*, were well adapted to 19th-century science, but they became widely accepted by religious and political leaders as well, largely for cultural reasons. Darwin's materialist world is limited, but clearly defined. Many decisions are much simpler if you look at life strictly from the perspective of survival of the fittest.[34] Here is Darwin, writing in *The Descent of Man*, in defense of capitalism:

> In all civilized countries man accumulates property and bequeaths it to his children. So that the children in the same country do not by any means start fair in the race for success. But this is far from an unmixed evil; for without the accumulation of capital the arts could not progress; and it is chiefly thorough their power that the civilized races have extended, and are now everywhere extending, their range, so as to take the place of the lower races.[35]

The new competitive interpretation of life spread through society during the modern period. Traditional Christian and Jewish religion no longer provided an *intellectual* support for life, the way it had for Isaac Newton or Robert Boyle. The "real" world became the world of hard science and cold technology, which shared few important ideas with traditional religion. During the 20th century, religion slowly became, for many people, a venue for emotionalism, social causes, and therapy, and its intellectual life suffered gravely.

Of course, some religious groups did not accept their new, diminished role. The clash between Darwinism and creationism, championed by American fundamentalists in the Scopes trial in 1925 (see Chapter 7), is widely known, principally through the propaganda movie *Inherit the Wind*. What made the conflict between the creationists and the Darwinists so intense was the fact that, starting in Darwin's day, Darwinism functioned as something of a religion, competing for attention with the traditional religions. As physicist Stephen M. Barr has noted, what many take to be a conflict between religion and science is really something else. It is a conflict between religion and materialism.[36]

So who has cranked up the controversy today?

Actually, it was science, not religion. As we have seen in Part One, science has cranked up the controversy by slowly moving away from fundamental theories that promote atheism and toward theories that are easily compatible with belief in God. Today, Darwinism, an essentially atheistic doctrine of evolution that attempts to compete with traditional religions on their own turf, attracts increasing criticism and disbelief.

Some commentators write about the conflict over teaching Darwinism in the school system as if it were purely local or political. It is not local. It is not even, in isolation, political. It is cultural and philosophical, and it arises from the shift in the balance of power of theories in science.

Of the three grand old men of the 19th century (or dead white males, depending on your point of view) who dominated the thinking of the 20th century—Marx, Freud, and Darwin—only Darwin is left. Will he follow Marx and Freud into oblivion? Or will his theory be confirmed, eliminating design from biology at the very time when physics seems to imply design? Will something different happen altogether? Let's look a little deeper. First, how did different groups in society first react to Darwin's idea?

What effect do you think these changes will have on popular culture, once they sink in?[37]	
19th-Century Science View	*21st-Century Science View*
Universe is eternal.	Universe has a beginning (Big Bang).
Universe shows no evidence of design.	Universe is fine-tuned for life.
Earth is a mediocre, accidental planet.	Earth is unusually favorable to life.
Free will is impossible (determinism).	Universe is too unpredictable to rule out free will (quantum uncertainty).
Darwinism is a biological Theory of Everything.	Darwinism explains some things really well.
Theories that humans behave like machines explain everything.	The wheels keep falling off these theories.

Darwinism appeared, and, under the guise of a foe, did the work of a friend . . .

—Aubrey Moore, Anglican theologian, 1890

There is no objection, so far as faith is concerned, to assuming the descent of all plant and animal species from a few types.

—Joseph Knabenbauer, S.J.,
German Catholic theologian, 1877

It is atheism [and] utterly inconsistent with the Scriptures.

—Charles Hodge,
American Protestant theologian (Princeton),1874

Oh my dear, let us hope that what Mr. Darwin says is not true. But if it is true, let us hope that it will not become generally known!

—attributed to a 19th-century Anglican bishop's lady[1]

Who Loved Darwin?
Who Hated Him?

By 1865, Darwin's theory of natural selection was very popular and widely accepted. Scientists liked it because it had very great "explanatory power," which means that it shed light on many separate problems at once. For example, it explained why animals increased or decreased in size, shape, and attributes over millions of years, and why slightly different species can exist on different islands. It also explained why *very* different species such as the platypus and the kangaroo existed only in Australia.[2] If Darwinism could explain the origin of life as well, it would be a biological Theory of Everything, a grand unifying theory. Indeed, many people assumed it was that already, without inquiring too closely.

So, like all theories in science, Darwin's had some practical problems. The one that he and many other scientists regarded as the most serious was the fact that the timetable for the development of the earth proposed by prominent physicist Kelvin did not allow for more than about 100 to 200 million years for life to form by laws of nature acting on chance. That wasn't enough for Darwin.

The good news for Darwin was that later estimates revised the age of the earth upward, to the current approximately four billion years. The bad news was that the discovery of the complexity of life forms has ratcheted up the scale of the problem much more than that, worsening the problem.[6]

Here is how an early scientific opponent of Darwin, St. George Mivart, explained the problems as they existed in 1871:

What is to be brought forward (against Darwinism) may be summed up as follows: That "Natural Selection" is incompetent to account for the incipient stages of useful structures. That it does not harmonize with the co-existence of closely similar structures of diverse origin. That there are grounds for thinking that specific differences may be developed suddenly instead of gradually. That the opinion that species have definite though very different limits to their variability is still tenable. That certain fossil transitional forms are absent, which might have been expected to be present. That there are many remarkable phenomena in organic forms upon which "Natural Selection" throws no light whatever.[7]

Mivart's analysis of the problems has stood up well over the years. For example, consider his claim that "specific differences may be developed suddenly instead of gradually." The fossil record of larger, more complex creatures does not depict a gradual plod onward from the earth's formation four billion years ago. Instead, it shows a sudden, amazing burst of complex animal life forms about 525 million years ago, in the Burgess Shale[8] excavated at Field, British Columbia.[9] Plant life

Oh, Dear! Those Inconvenient Details ...

Why do some life forms, such as the 350-million-year-old coelacanth fish or the 300-million-year-old horsetail grass, survive largely unchanged? Darwin's theory of evolution argues that they are under no pressure to change because they survive in odd, difficult environments with few competitors.[3]

However, when the coelacanth was accidentally discovered in the Indian Ocean in 1938, it disappointed the scientists who thought that it would provide a living proof of Darwinism. The coelacanth, supposed to have been extinct for 70 million years, is a rhipidistian, a group of fish from which the ancestor of amphibians such as frogs and toads is thought to have come. So surely it would have a "transitional" anatomy. It didn't. It was all fish and no frog.[4] Similarly, the recent discovery of a well-preserved 425 million-year-old male shellfish (crustacean) showed that there have been no significant changes in crustacean body parts. One researcher called it "a demonstration of unbelievable stability."[5]

forms show similar bursts of unusual creativity as well, rather than plodding selection.

He also noted that very few transitional forms—animals in the process of becoming a different species—were found. Darwin said that the reason was that the fossil record was incomplete. But over a century later, Stephen Jay

Gould referred to the absence of anything like the expected number of transitionals as "the trade secret of paleontology."[10]

The evidence suggests that micromutation (small changes) are the kind that Darwinism produces, not macromutation (large changes).[11]

Another problem is that Darwinism depends on the formation of species: groups of animals that can breed with each other but not with other types of animals. The formation of new species usually takes a long time, which means that we cannot usually observe it and cannot be sure that Darwin's explanation is the correct one.[12]

Eugenics: Our Side Is the One That Is Up!

Many of Darwin's supporters were not deterred by these problems. They had bigger fish to fry. From what we can tell, Darwin failed to convince a number of his most ardent contemporary supporters of the inherent *purposelessness* of his natural selection. These supporters were adherents of Social Darwinism, a political philosophy that Herbert Spencer, who coined the term "survival of the fittest," developed from Darwin's theory. Social Darwinism argues that human society is a struggle in which the upper classes have emerged as superior. As a result, Social Darwinists promoted eugenics, a proposal to improve the human race by sterilizing the people they deemed unfit, generally the poor.

Darwin's cousin, Francis Galton, coined the term "eugenics" in 1883, and founded the eugenics movement. Darwin's son, Leonard Darwin (1850–1943), was president of the Eugenics Education Society from 1911 to 1928.

Monkey Don't See, Monkey Don't Do

Thomas Huxley (1825–1895) believed that if enough monkeys smashed typewriter keys for long enough, they would write Psalm 23, eliminating the need for design in the universe.

Would they write Psalm 23? Researchers at Britain's Plymouth University gave six Sulawesi crested macaque monkeys from the Paignton Zoo a room equipped with a computer and keyboards, and let them go at it for four weeks. Most monkeys did nothing, though one of them took to typing "s" repeatedly. Other monkeys used the keyboard repeatedly as a latrine.

Writer Lloyd Garver defends the monkeys' uninteresting performance by pointing out that few writers come up with good stuff on their first try.

Another problem is that they did not have a gorilla for a managing editor.

The purpose of the experiment was to study differences between animal life and computer programs that simulate animals (artificial life).[13]

Darwin's theory of natural selection does not provide a basis for the Social Darwinists' eugenic beliefs. Natural selection does not suggest any specific direction for evolution. Depending on the circumstances, for example, an abandoned slum child might be far better adapted for survival than a sheltered piano prodigy.[15] However, natural selection can be twisted to meet an existing social agenda. In a landmark decision in 1927, US Supreme Court Justice Oliver Wendell Holmes, a "Reform Social Darwinist,"[16] ruled in favor of compulsory sterilization, offering the judgment in the Buck v. Bell case that "three generations of imbeciles are enough."

In the United States, at least 60,000 people were subsequently sterilized, generally for reasons that would be rejected as racist or classist today.[17] As of this writing, there are ongoing lawsuits in North America over compulsory sterilization of the "unfit," as the "unfit" learn, often in old age, the true cause of their infertility.[18] Ideas in science do not inhabit an ethereal realm of pure neutrality, and Social Darwinism has led to many serious consequences.

> **A Social Darwinist on Helping the Poor**
>
> If the unworthy are helped to increase, by shielding them from that mortality which their unworthiness would naturally entail, the effect is to produce, generation after generation, a greater unworthiness.
>
> —Herbert Spencer, 1873[14]

Mainstream Religion Adapts to Natural Selection

Contrary to widespread belief, most Christian religious groups in Darwin's lifetime did not oppose the theory of evolution. One bishop, Samuel Wilberforce, clashed with Darwin's chief defender, T.H. Huxley, at the British Association for the Advancement of Science in 1860.[19] However, if anything, most Christians adjusted too comfortably and failed to ask the hard questions—for example, about the rapid growth of Social Darwinism.

Generally, in North America, the leading advocates of Darwin's theory were active religious believers. Christians in the sciences stressed that God creates through the process of evolution.[21] As science historian Del Ratzsch writes:

> Evolution, it was widely held, was simply the means by which God had produced his creatures, just as various planetary laws were the means by which he produced night, day and seasons...[22]

Most people who accepted evolution did not really understand that Darwin meant that evolution was purposeless and planless. They assumed that it was an assurance of continued progress toward a better life.

For example, in the 1880s, Asa Gray, an evangelical Christian biologist at Harvard, wrote textbooks in which he promoted evolution. True, many religious people were uncomfortable with the idea that human beings descended from a common ancestor with apes, but then, as now, paleontology—the study of old bones—was a fertile ground for controversy, and no one knew what would turn up one day.

Typical Mainstream 19th-century Christian Views of Evolution

God had a plan by which the race should steadily ascend, and the weakest become the strongest and the invisible become more and more visible, and the finer and nobler at last transcend and absolutely control its controllers, and the good in men become mightier than the animal in them.

—Henry Ward Beecher, American preacher (1885)[20]

The paleontological evidence before us today clearly demonstrates ordered progressive change with the successive development of new faunal and floral assemblages through the changing epochs of our earth's history. There should be no real conflict between science, which is the search for truth, and Christ's teachings, which I hold to be truth itself. It is only when scientists remove God from creation that the Christian is faced with an irreconcilable situation.

—Wendell Phillips (1811–1884), *Sheba's Buried City*

Neither of these optimistic views represents what Darwin understood as natural selection, but that misunderstanding was characteristic of the times.

Darwinism vs. Folk Evolution

In the 19th and 20th centuries, many Christians, and others, such as George Bernard Shaw, reinterpreted Darwinism so that it became a doctrine of progress. Folk evolution suited many popular religious and political points of view to which Darwinism was, in reality, irrelevant.

Concept	Darwinism	Folk Evolution
What evolution is	theory of change	theory of improvement
Type of change	changes may be gain or loss of functions	changes are improvements
Cause of change	some random variations work and others don't	changes lead to more and better functions
Purpose of change	no purpose proposed	purpose is to evolve into higher orders of life
Amount of change	current structure restricts types of change possible[23]	limitless possibilities
Direction of change	95-99% extinction; some survival with changes	ever onward and upward to new heights
Religious status	sometimes marketed by hardcore atheists[24]	often marketed as a new age religion, sometimes within orthodox religious groups

The Catholic Church accommodated evolution without much difficulty, viewing it as compatible with Catholic doctrine as long as Darwinists did not attempt to pronounce on moral or spiritual issues. However, Darwinists sometimes do just that. John Paul II continues to warn that, even if evolution is "more than a hypothesis," theories that deny that human beings are anything other than animals are "incompatible with the truth about man."[26]

Today, mainstream Catholicism and liberal Protestantism tolerate or encourage Darwinian evolution theory. As T.M. Berra notes:

Many evolutionary biologists are Catholic priests or nuns. Others are members of many of the world's other religions. They see evolution as God's plan, not as a denial of their belief in God, a view called theistic evolution. Most of the mainstream Protestant denominations such as Episcopalians, Presbyterians, and Methodists have also accommodated evolutionary theory. That they have . . . done so without compromise to basic beliefs or principles is reflected in the fact that the biology departments of the universities operated by these religions teach the same evolutionary theory as the major state universities. In liberal theological circles it has become a cliché to state that, "The Bible was written to show us how to go to heaven, not how the heavens go."[27]

> **Overall Mainstream Christian Views of Evolution in the 19th Century**
>
> Most scientists in the United States in the late 19th century were, themselves, believing Christians, and the ones who accepted evolution, and that would be the majority, simply took it as God's method of creation. So, although they may have wrestled with issues such as the mechanism of evolution, most of them didn't think it was necessary to reject evolution in order to salvage their Christian beliefs.
>
> —Ronald Numbers, American historian[25]

Of course, as we will see, the readiness with which mainstream Christianity adopted Darwin's doctrine raises some questions about what their "basic beliefs or principles" were, as they began to be elaborated in the 20th century.

General acceptance is not the whole story. Darwinism came to be clearly understood as a theory that, like the theories of Marx and Freud, eliminates both a benevolent God and human free will. London wits began to declare, "There is no God, and Herbert Spencer is his prophet." By the late 19th century, as well, some academics created a great deal of publicity for a supposed warfare between science and religion.[31] Their works have had a great influence on modern education. A popular version of Darwinism also suited them admirably. Some traditional religious believers tried to solve the problem just by outlawing Darwinism. How well did that work out?

Do you believe in "evolution"? What type?

Darwinism or, after about 1950, *neo-Darwinism* All life is explained by the survival of the fittest of random mutations,[28] acted on by the laws of nature.

emergent evolution Philosopher Henri Bergson (1859–1941) argued that evolution is creative, propelled from mud to man by a vital force (élan vital) that cannot be reduced to matter.

Lamarckism Changes that have proved useful in the lifetime of a creature are incorporated into the heritage that it passes on to its descendants. This belief is currently discredited in biology but widely used to explain the development of human culture and language.

naturalistic evolution Only natural causes, arising from within the universe, can explain changes over time. There is no divine direction or purpose. Darwinism is the most widely known type of naturalistic evolution.

Omega Point Paleontologist and theologian Pierre Teilhard de Chardin (1881–1955) argued that human beings draw evolution to a new, higher dimension, the noosphere or sphere of the mind. Evolution will continue until the material and the spiritual converge in an Omega Point.[29]

self-organization An organizing principle inherent in the universe enables life forms to self-organize and evolve. This is usually a form of naturalistic evolution, but it is not Darwinism.

theistic evolution The majority of religious believers who accept evolution today believe that God created life through the process of evolution.[30]

Note that Darwinism is one model of naturalistic evolution. Believing in Darwinism is not the same as believing in evolution.

The Scopes Trial: What Really Happened?

CHAPTER 7

The Darwinian theory represents man as reaching his present perfection by the operation of the law of hate—the merciless law by which the strong crowd out and kill off the weak.

—William Jennings Bryan, anti-evolution advocate[1]

Neanderthal man is organizing in these forlorn backwaters of the land, led by a fanatic, rid of sense and devoid of conscience . . .

—H.L. Mencken, literary journalist covering Scopes trial[2]

I n 2003, Celti Johnson of Kansas City, Missouri, was amazed to discover that her daughter's high school biology teacher had set aside three class periods to show *Inherit the Wind* (1960), a fictional Hollywood take on the 1925 Scopes trial. The movie teaches no biology whatsoever. It does, however, teach contempt for evangelical Christians.

As for the movie's faithfulness to history, one Calvin College professor has been in the habit of giving out a prize—a coconut—to the student who spots the most historical errors in the movie, after taking his "Monkey Trial" course, which includes reading the trial transcript. Over 70 errors have been identified so far.[3]

Celti Johnson and her family are evangelical Christians. She launched a complaint with the school board, and it soon hit the local media.

What happened in Dayton—nearly 80 years ago—broadcasts bent, distorted images even in 2003.

What Did Tennessee Reject and Why?

William Jennings Bryan, a progressive Democratic politician and former Secretary of State, was concerned about the growth of Social Darwinism, a philosophy that he blamed for the carnage of World War I. Bryan's view wasn't either unusual or unreasonable; many German intellectuals, influenced by the philosopher Friedrich Nietzsche, believed that violent Darwinian struggle benefited human society.[4] Bryan deduced that if Darwinism were taught in the school system, that belief would spread.

An important aspect of Darwinism, as it was understood at the time, was Social Darwinism, which included eugenics—essentially, people who were deemed inferior by Social Darwinists were to be prevented from having children. For example, of six well-known scientists who would have testified in favor of human descent from lower animals at the Scopes trial, none showed up, partly because they all favored forced sterilization and Clarence Darrow opposed it.[5]

In Bryan's day, biology textbooks reflected these scientists' view. In one edition, the text Scopes used (Hunter's *Civic Biology*) cheerfully announced, with regard to society's unfortunates: "If such people were lower animals, we would probably kill them off to prevent them from spreading."[6] Obviously, the social and moral conflict between orthodox religious beliefs and this sort of belief goes much deeper than controversies about whether earth was created in six days or billions of years.

On Bryan's advice, the Tennessee legislature enacted a statute on March 21, 1925, that banned the teaching that human beings were descended from lower animals. The statute did not forbid the teaching of evolution in general, and it applied only to tax-supported schools.[7]

When the General got hold of Darwin . . .

To get some idea why Bryan and his colleagues thought that Darwinism was a dangerous philosophy, consider the views of a top German general, Friedrich von Bernhardi (1849–1930), who was regarded as the outstanding military writer of his day: "War is a biological necessity of the first importance, a regulative element in the life of mankind which cannot be dispensed with, since without it an unhealthy development will follow, which excludes every advancement of the race, and therefore all real civilization. 'War is the father of all things.' (Heraclitus) The sages of antiquity long before Darwin recognized this."[8]

Bernhardi was a committed Darwinist. The popularity of views like his probably hastened World War I. His book was in the ninth printing when the war broke out.

The legislature ignored Bryan's warning against setting a penalty, and prescribed a $100 to $500 fine.

Dayton Grabs the Spotlight

By setting a penalty, the legislature also set the stage for a possible martyr and a show trial of the century. Sure enough, in the summer of 1925, Dayton, a small town in Tennessee, suddenly became a hub of intense international interest.

Science and physical education teacher John Scopes, the defendant, was charged with a misdemeanor: teaching human descent from lower animals. It is unclear whether Scopes ever did teach that. He had minimal qualifications to teach biology and had filled in for two weeks, preparing the students for exams, when the biology teacher was away. But that didn't really matter. The trial was not about Scopes's teaching; it was about a fundamental social conflict over the role that Darwinism should play in society.

The Real Life Cast of Characters

No one at the trial held the positions that they were represented as having in *Inherit the Wind* and similar literature.

- For example, most religious people thought that evolution and the Bible could be easily reconciled. As a result, evolution was not controversial in the United States until after World War I.[9] In fact, it became controversial *because of* World War I.

- Contrary to widespread belief—inspired in part by the play *Inherit the Wind* (1955) and the later movie version (1960)—Bryan did not believe that the earth was only 6000 years old. For years, Bryan had subscribed to the Day-Age theory, according to which the earth took perhaps hundreds of millions of years to create. In fact, almost all leading creationists in the 1920s believed in theories that reconciled the Bible with an ancient earth.[10]

- The prosecution was not originally spearheaded by famed defense lawyer Clarence Darrow, but by the American Civil Liberties Union. The ACLU, after losing out on various anti-patriotism efforts, was looking for an "individual liberty" platform and saw the Tennessee act as an opportunity. Darrow horned in on the ACLU case, seeing it as a chance to attack religion.

The ACLU wanted to dump Darrow, precisely because it wanted to avoid a confrontation over religion. But Darrow stuck to the case like a fly and took it over from ACLU.[11] Although Darrow did humiliate Bryan on the witness stand, he probably alienated the jury by doing so. That may have been the reason Scopes was convicted.

- Scopes was hardly a martyr. He was a well-liked science teacher cum football coach who agreed at a meeting with friends at the local soda fountain to be the one to be prosecuted. His way was paid to go to graduate school after the trial, an enormous benefit in those days.[12]

- Finally, Dayton was very far from the intolerant backwater portrayed by elite journalist H.L. Mencken, and later portrayed in *Inherit the Wind*. Dayton *reveled* in the case, seeing it as a marvelous chance to boost the prosperous "new South." Monkey dolls and paraphernalia were widely marketed as part of the publicity campaign.

> ### *The creation (or ... was it evolution?) of a vast commercial opportunity*
>
> A carnival atmosphere pervaded Dayton as the opening of the trial approached in July of 1925. Banners decorated the streets. Lemonade stands were set up. Chimpanzees, said to have been brought to town to testify for the prosecution, performed in a side show on Main Street. Anti-Evolution league members sold copies of T.T. Martin's book *Hell and the High School*. Holy rollers rolled in the surrounding hills and riverbanks.
> —From "An Introduction to the John Scopes (Monkey) Trial," one of the Famous Trials Web sites of the University of Missouri-Kansas City School of Law[13]

Nonetheless, the vast majority of townsfolk remained quite unconvinced by the theory of human descent from lower animals. One reporter quoted a student's remark about Scopes that probably captured the attitude best: "I like him, but I don't believe that I came from a monkey."[14]

Indeed, Edward J. Larson, author of a groundbreaking 1997 book[22] on what really happened at the trial, *Summer for the Gods*, offers a poignant observation. *Inherit the Wind* was written in reaction to the McCarthyism of the early Cold War. Not surprisingly, the "Bryan" character in the play has more in common with Joe McCarthy, who wrecked lives without apparent conscience during the 1950s than with the Christian progressive politician of the 1920s who offered to pay Scopes's fine. By the 1950s, the gentility of the 1920s—where Bryan understood the creation–evolution debate as an

The forlorn backwaters of Neanderthal Man?

It was Baltimore-based literary lion H.L. Mencken (1880–1956) who first suggested to Clarence Darrow that he volunteer to defend John Scopes. During the trial, Mencken, who was famous for his biting wit, did more than anyone to cast the Dayton debate as a contest between the clever and the backward. His dispatches[15] trashed Dayton, even though he also admitted that the town was much more pleasant than he had thought, full of "charm and beauty."[16]

What motivated him? Mencken was well known as a Social Darwinist, with little use for democracy (he termed the American public "the booboisie"). A new biography, *The Skeptic*, by Terry Teachout, which draws heavily from diaries, letters, and other material released after Mencken's death, reveals that he was also an anti-Semite and that he thought blacks were inferior.[17] He could hardly have been expected to see the point of Bryan's concerns.

Literary sources often defend Mencken, saying that he "wasn't really" a bigot; he just hated stupidity. If so, his hatred was selective, and his choice of targets was significant.[18] The 2002 PBS documentary *Monkey Trial*'s resource quotes historian Paul Boyer:

> Beneath Mencken's ridicule of the ignorant hayseeds of America was a very profound suspicion of Democracy itself. Mencken really believed that there was a small elite of educated and cultivated and intelligent human beings, and then there were the masses who were really ignorant and capable of nothing but being led and bamboozled.[19]

The documentary allowed the people of Dayton to tell their own story, to say that they were not the "servile rubes immune to shame"[20] depicted in Mencken's and other journalists' dispatches, and later in the play and movie *Inherit the Wind*.[21]

affair between gentlemen, to be conducted as a civilized discourse—was not even a memory. World War II and the Cold War put an end to that kind of thing, introducing a politics of raw power.

Scopes's conviction was overturned on appeal. He had not testified at the trial, and it was never clear that he had actually taught the descent of humans from lower animals. The Tennessee statute remained in force until the 1960s.

Goodbye Creationism? Hardly!

The issue did not go away when the law was dropped from the books. In fact, the 1980s saw a new round of pro-creation law cases in the United States, which has continued to the present day.

Seventy-five years later, American public opinion has remained divided on the issue. In a Gallup poll taken in 1999, 44% of Americans said that

The Scopes Trial vs. the Spin Cycle

There is a vast difference between what actually happened at the Scopes trial and the way the case was presented later, particularly in the stage play and movie, *Inherit the Wind*, which changed far more than the names of the title characters and the town.

Scopes Trial, 1925	Inherit the Wind, 1950s
Dayton was a circus, gleefully celebrating the trial, complete with live monkey and chimpanzees.	The town is an oppressive backwater populated by an ignorant mob.
Bryan was a progressive politician, concerned about the effects of Social Darwinism.[22]	The Bryan figure is a mindless reactionary.
Bryan thought evolution wasn't good science.	The Bryan figure denounces all science as Godless.
Bryan was fairly well-read on the subject of evolution.	The Bryan figure knows little or nothing about evolution.
Bryan, for the prosecution, was always courteous to witnesses.	The Bryan figure is abusive to the teacher's fiancée.
Bryan believed the earth was very old.	The Bryan figure interprets the Bible literally, in a rigid way, and without context.
Bryan did not want Scopes to face a penalty and offered to pay the fine.	The Bryan character rants that the fine is too small.
Darrow acted from acknowledged anti-religious motives.	The Darrow figure is concerned about freedom, justice, and progress.
Darrow was cited for contempt of the judge.	The Darrow figure is courteous.
Scopes offered to be prosecuted.	The teacher is the victim of a mob.
Scopes was never threatened with jail.	The teacher is jailed, and risks lynching.
Scopes and his lawyer admitted that he taught common descent but there are grounds for doubt.	The teacher's lawyer claims he is innocent.
Bryan, 65, died in his sleep five days after the trial, of unknown causes.	The Bryan figure collapses and dies in the courtroom in the midst of an incoherent rant.

The Jerome Lawrence and Robert E. Lee play, *Inherit the Wind*, was intended as a parable of the evils of McCarthyism[23] (anticommunist witch hunts), and they scripted it to that end.[24] But for generations of people who are unfamiliar with McCarthyism, it was a first, quite misleading, introduction to the debate around Darwinism. It also strengthened the myth of a war between science and religion.

they believed that God created humans in the last 10,000 years, 39% believed in evolution so long as it was understood as guided by God, and 10% believed that evolution occurred without God's help. Seven percent had no opinion.[25]

Times are changing. When Celti Johnson presented her case to the school board, she was not ridiculed. The members listened to the evidence she provided about the film vs. the history. They agreed with her unanimously that use of the video as an accurate resource for the science curriculum was not suggested, due to historical inaccuracies and dated material that might be potentially offensive.[26] Johnson saw their decision as a victory for science over propaganda. From Mencken's perspective, the booboisie had won.

Overall, it is quite likely that court cases over the teaching of human descent from lower animals, or Darwinism in general, have contributed to the high level of disbelief in both ideas in North America. Most people suspect that the winners and losers in a court case may bear no relation to truth or falsehood in reality. They form their own opinion based on what sounds reasonable.

What about evolutionists today? Where do they stand on Darwin?

How Modern Evolutionists
Have Evolved Away from Darwin

CHAPTER 8

The god hypothesis is rather discredited.

> —Francis Crick, co-discoverer of DNA structure in 1953[1]

God decided to create a species with whom he could have fellowship. Who are we to say that evolution was a dumb way to do it? It was an incredibly elegant way to do it.

> —Francis Collins, leader of Human Genome Project, 2003[2]

Although Darwin's theory of natural selection quickly won converts, many scientists raised objections, starting from the publication of *On the Origin of Species*. In fact, by the late 19th century, the theory was in eclipse, due to problems with the science.[3] These scientists believed in evolution, it's just that they doubted that Darwin's natural selection (chance sorted by law) explained it correctly.

Some objections were overcome by 20th-century findings. For example, there was the problem of Darwin's genetics. Darwin, like most scientists of his day, did not understand how genetics works. Paleontologist Niles Eldredge explains:

> Darwin had been but one of a long series of biologists who could make no real headway in understanding heredity. Indeed, Darwin's own ideas on the subject were far off the mark. He thought that hereditary factors were drawn from all parts of the body, in particles he called "gemmules," to be concentrated in eggs and sperm. German biologist Auguste Weismann had, by the late nineteenth century, disproved such

Darwinian pangenesis when he showed that whatever the controlling factors of inheritance might be, they are confined to what he called the "germ" tissues—ovaries and testes, for example, in vertebrate animals.[4]

Darwin believed that inheritance was a blend of the characteristics of the male and female parent. If so, most new traits will be blended into insignificance, whether they are favorable or not. How then can natural selection produce enough changes to create a new species?[5]

The rediscovery, in 1900, of Austrian monk Gregor Mendel's theory of inheritance provided a method for Darwin's natural selection. According to Mendel, inheritance is *not* blended; for example, either your mother's gene for a characteristic dominates, or else your father's does. Thus, an unblended trait can be inherited. In that case, significant change is possible, at least in theory.

However, other objections remain hotly disputed:

- *Biology*: In Darwin's scheme, detailed, complex structures must work immediately, in order to be useful enough to be preserved in the struggle for survival. How, then, can such structures be built up from scratch? For example, how safe is an evolving stick insect that still looks only one percent like a stick?

- *Paleontology*: The fossil record is a record of new species developing suddenly, not gradually, as Darwin thought.

  Some missing links have been found in the fossil record, but there is a persistent, large pattern of sudden, rapid evolution. Paleontologist Stephen Jay Gould has said: "The extreme rarity of transitional forms in the fossil record persists as the trade secret of paleontology. The evolutionary trees that adorn our textbooks have data only at the tips and nodes of their branches; the rest is inference, however reasonable, not the evidence of fossils."[6]

  Indeed, paleontologists sometimes call Canada's Burgess Shale, near Field, British Columbia, the "Big Bang" of biology.[7] There is also a Big Bang of birds[8] and an "explosion" of flowering plants,[9] among other dramatic events. Darwinists have invented several concepts to make these findings compatible with their theory, but the events are *not* what the theory would lead us to expect.

- *Earth sciences*: The earth was thought to be not more than 100 million years old, in Darwin's day. It was not enough time for his idea to work.

The earth is now thought to be over four billion years old. However, life forms have proved to be vastly more complex than Darwin thought, by orders of magnitude. More complexity is discovered every day. Is even four billion years enough, especially when the first 3.5 billion featured only bacteria?

The New Darwinism: Neo-Darwinian Synthesis

Mendel's genetics rescued Darwinism for the 20th century. However, genetics, systematics, paleontology, comparative anatomy, embryology, and other disciplines were all developing separate opinions about what evolution meant. In the mid-20th century, a series of interdisciplinary meetings enabled scientists to develop a coherent evolution theory based on Darwinism. This "evolutionary synthesis" came to be called neo-Darwinism. Today's Darwinist is (usually) a neo-Darwinian who blends modern genetic understanding with Darwin's theory of natural selection. That is the Darwinism you probably learned in school.

Timeline: Darwin's Theory of Evolution to Today

Various theories of evolution proposed.	1750–1850		
		1830	*Key geologist Lyell describes Earth as ancient.*
Earth found to be 100 million years old. (Too little time for Darwin.)	1846		
		1856	*Neandertal skull provokes human origins debate.*
Darwin publishes Origin of Species.	1859	1861	*Fossil bird* Archaeopteryx *found.*
		1880s	*Most religious leaders do not oppose Darwin's idea.*

Social Darwinism: Poor people are evolution's losers. Uproar follows.	1895	
		1896 — *Radioactivity discovered. Radioactive dating later suggests earth is 4.3 billion years old. (Maybe enough time for Darwin.)*
Mendel's heredity laws can support Darwin.	1900	
		1912 — *Piltdown Man said to prove Darwin right.*
Social Darwinism blamed for WWI; evolution questioned.	1914–1918	
		1925 — *Scopes trial; creationists go their own way.*
Neo-Darwinism blends Darwin with Mendel's genetics.	1940s	
		1950s — *Piltdown Man revealed as fake.*[10]
Miller-Urey experiment said to explain life's origin. DNA unlocked.	1953	
		1950s— *Biochemistry (chemistry of life forms) shows life is immensely complicated.*

Some paleontologists say evolution occurs rapidly (punctuated equilibrium).	1972	
	1975	*Sociobiology explains human culture as Darwinism.*
Dawkins explains human behavior as selfish genes.	1976	
	1982	*Gallup Poll reveals half of Americans doubt evolution.*
Burgess Shale, which shows complex life forms appeared suddenly, publicized.	1990s	
	1994	*Sociobiologists claim race determines IQ. Uproar follows.*
Gallup Poll shows 57% of Americans prefer creationism or ID.	2001	
	2002	*Human genome unravelled. Animal links explored.*
Darwin's key sexual theory trashed at major science meet.	2003	

Darwinism Becomes a Religion

For many 20th-century philosophers and scientists, Darwin's theory became far more than a description of the method by which life forms change over time. It became more like a Church of Darwin, as well as a source of folk beliefs. It is, in fact, the creation story of atheism, and it is often defended in the same way as a religious truth.

For example, prominent philosopher of science Daniel Dennett has come to believe that evolution is not only a good idea but the best idea anyone ever had.[11] Can this be right? After all, we have experienced the benefits of many good ideas in recent millenia—the wheel, human rights and the scientific method come quickly to mind—so why is Darwin's idea supposed to be the single best? Here is Dennett's explanation:

> In a single stroke, the idea of evolution by natural selection unifies the realm of life, meaning, and purpose with the realm of space and time, cause and effect, mechanism and physical law. But it is not just a wonderful scientific idea. It is a dangerous idea.[12]

Why is it a dangerous idea? Evolutionary biologist Douglas Futuyma provides some insight into that:

> By coupling undirected, purposeless variation to the blind, uncaring process of natural selection, Darwin made theological or spiritual explanations of the life processes superfluous. Together with Marx's materialist theory of history and society and Freud's attribution of human behavior to influences over which we have little control, Darwin's theory of evolution was a crucial plank in the platform of mechanism and materialism—of much of science, in short—that has since been the stage of most Western thought.[13]

Scientists who believe all this are following a modernist religion, and they are often very hostile to traditional religions. For example, James Watson and Francis Crick, co-discoverers of the double helix structure of our DNA in 1953, took the opportunity of the 50th anniversary of their discovery to lash out at them. Watson claimed that "every time you understand something, religion becomes less likely." Crick proclaimed that "the god hypothesis is rather discredited," stating that distaste for religion was a prime motivator in his work.[14] In case anyone missed the point, Watson went on to inform TV viewers in 2003 of how "'embarrassed' he is to meet scientists who believe in God, or indeed who take religion seriously." Not surprisingly, he was talking to ultra-Darwinist Richard Dawkins at the time.[15]

Of course, most scientists do *not* treat evolution as a source of meaning in life. Francis Collins, the medical doctor who succeeded Watson in 1993 as the head of the Human Genome Project that has mapped the human genetic code, is a devout Christian. He argues: "God decided to create a species with whom he could have fellowship. Who are we to say that evolution was a dumb way to do it? It was an incredibly elegant way to do it."[17]

Collins worries, with good reason, about the effect that some of his colleagues' hostility to other belief systems will have on the public view of evolution. He notes:

> **Downwind from Inherit the Wind: The Museum as Church**
>
> Evolution after Darwin had set itself up to be something more than science. It was a popular science, the science of the marketplace and the museum, and it was a religion—whether this be purely secular or blended in with a form of liberal Christianity ... When believers in other religions turned around and scratched, you may regret the action but you can understand it—and your sympathy for the victim is attenuated.
>
> —Michael Ruse[16]

It is not just the fringe elements of the Church that are demanding a Creationist view in order to prove that you are a true believer; it is also the scientific community fringe who are basically saying that evolution proves there is no God.[18]

He should worry. In the United States, Darwinists have obtained court decisions that, essentially, make Darwinism the established religion of the school system, daring anyone to preach some other gospel. Some are accepting the challenge.

As a religion, Darwinism is intolerant. The Darwinist assumes that what he believes is true. Therefore, only evidence that supports Darwinism can be valid evidence. Those who propose other theories must be silenced, for the good of society. We will encounter a number of examples of that attitude in the course of this book.[19]

While science strives to be objective, it is *not* done in a philosophical vacuum. The philosophical beliefs of neo-Darwinists can be just as important in shaping their views as the philosophical beliefs of creationists and ID proponents are in shaping theirs.

Where does the public currently stand in all this? In September 2001, polling firm Zogby International asked Americans what students should be taught about Darwinism.[20] Should it be Darwin only, or are dissenting theories allowed? Fifteen percent thought it should be Darwin only, but 71% thought that evidence against Darwin's theory should be allowed. Fourteen percent were not sure. Local polls have given similar results. The really interesting finding is that 80% of 18–29 year olds thought that teachers should include evidence against Darwinism, but only 59% of seniors 65 and older thought so.[21]

Most people believe in some sort of evolution, but there is growing dissatisfaction with Darwinism. The difference between young people's views and seniors' views illustrates this dissatisfaction. Meanwhile, modern Darwinists adhere strictly to naturalism, but they dissent from the traditions of their mid-20th-century elders in many other ways. Let's look at some of the reasons.

1. The Numbers Still Do Not Add Up

> The neo-Darwinist population-genetics tradition . . . will look ridiculous in retrospect, because it is ridiculous.
>
> —Lynn Margulis, biologist who developed a key theory of the origin of complex cells[22]
>
> We cannot expect to explain cellular evolution if we stay locked in the classical Darwinian mode of thinking.
>
> —Carl Woese, biologist who identified key early life forms[23]

Darwin's numbers did not add up in his own lifetime, because the earth was thought to be only hundreds of millions of years old. It is now thought to be over four billion years old. That gives Darwinism more time, but the life forms turned out to be vastly more complex, beyond anything Darwin imagined.

To restate the argument: Darwinism claims that the complexity we see around us in animal and plant life was produced by the laws of physics and chemistry acting on random fluctuations in the genomes of life forms over the last 3.7 billion years. This includes the immense complexity inside each cell of every diverse living creature, and the complexity of human brains, artifacts, and society. (Darwinists claim to explain all that, too.)

We have encountered this argument earlier, with respect to the universe as a whole. The question is, can random fluctuations—sorted by laws of nature—produce the complex and organized pattern that we see, within the time allowed?

A Mystery of the Natural World: A Worm Armed for War

Here is an example of the level of complexity the natural world produces.

Gordon Rattray Taylor was a well-respected British science writer, and Chief Science Advisor to BBC Television. Shortly before his death in 1981, he completed a book, *The Great Evolution Mystery*, in which he explained why he questioned Darwinism and neo-Darwinism. He relates, for example, the strange tale of the relationship between the pond hydra (*Hydra*) and the flatworm *Microstomum*.

The pond hydra is a tiny creature, shaped like a tube, with a mouth end and a foot end. It proceeds through life by rolling end over end. Some species of hydra hunt and protect themselves with a battery of poison guns: tiny stinging cells mounted on their surface that fire a coiled, poisoned hair, with a second hair serving as the trigger.

The hydra is usually safe from the flatworm, but every so often a flatworm seeks out and consumes a hydra. The worm somehow swallows the hydra's poison gun apparatus without digesting it, and then positions the guns on its own surface. It uses the guns for its own protection; one species actually fires them like rockets at assailants.

As long as the flatworm has ammunition from a previous meal, it ignores hydras. However, when it is low on ammunition, it finds another hydra, eats it, and repeats the cycle.

Taylor asks how a creature with no brain or complex nervous system learns this routine. How does it remember and pass it on? He writes: "The theory of evolution by natural selection is powerless to explain how chance variation could have evoked such a closely coordinated programme."[24]

Taylor believed that evolution occurs, and he also believed that natural selection played a role in evolution. However, he came to doubt Darwinism, the idea that natural selection and a few other naturalistic processes explain the life we see around us. Rather, he argued that "we seem to see a purposiveness of the kind which Darwinists refuse to believe in."[25] Taylor did not believe that this purposiveness—or purpose—was part of a divine plan. He thought it was implicit in the nature of life itself.

Hoyle's Tornado Watch

A number of mathematicians have doubted Darwinist claims for decades. They cannot add up the numbers and get a right answer for the complexity of life. In 1966, a symposium was held at the Wistar Institute, a research center at the University of Pennsylvania in Philadelphia, featuring leading mathematicians and evolutionary biologists. There, mathematician D.S. Ulam told the Darwinists that it was very unlikely that the eye could have evolved through a slow build-up of tiny, purely random changes, with the most survival-oriented changes preserved for the next generation. The number of needed changes was just too large for the time available.[26] The Darwinists' reaction was interesting. According to ID advocate Michael Behe:

> At the symposium one side was unhappy, and the other was uncomprehending. A mathematician who claimed that there was insufficient time for the number of mutations apparently needed to make an eye was told by the biologists that his figures must be wrong. The mathematicians, though, were not persuaded that the fault was theirs. As one said: "There is a considerable gap in the neo-Darwinian theory of evolution, and we believe this gap to be of such a nature that it cannot be bridged with the current conception of biology."[27]

A leading evolution theorist, Ernst Mayr, responded to the mathematicians, "Somehow or other by adjusting these figures we will come out all right. We are comforted by the fact that evolution has occurred."[28] But the question is not whether *evolution* has occurred; it is whether *Darwinism* is the best explanation for it.

The mathematicians accused the Darwinists of making their theory mean pretty much whatever they needed it to mean, in order to deal with the lack of clear evidence from nature. One said bluntly: "You can explain anything you want by changing your variables around."[29] The mathematicians were just not as willing to invoke the powers of randomness—Hoyle's fabled "tornado in the junkyard"—to produce life forms as Darwinian biologists were.

2. Is Darwinism the Only Possible Explanation?

Some biologists attack neo-Darwinism for a different reason. They think it is too narrow, rooted in a competitive and capitalist vision that satisfies Darwin's heirs but has nothing to do with how life really develops. One of these biologists is Lynn Margulis at the University of Massachusetts. Margulis is best known for her widely accepted theory that the power plants of animal and plant cells (mitochondria) were once free-living bacteria.[30] As far as she is concerned, "the benefit/cost people [neo-Darwinians] have perverted the science."[31] In other words, it is capitalism's science. She doubts that new species form from the fittest random mutations (changes), because almost all actual changes are entirely unfit, and cause the life form to die.

Memo to Life Forms

RE: Your long-term survival chances
MESSAGE: Quit blaming yourselves

It has come to our attention that University of Chicago paleontologist David M. Raup has bad news for you: No matter what your evolutionary strategy, sooner or later, you're doomed.

In *Extinction: Bad Genes or Bad Luck?* Raup, a specialist in the growing field of extinction, points out that there are currently about 40 million species. But estimates of the numbers that have ever lived range between 5 and 50 billion, depending on how species are counted.[32] "Thus, only about one in a thousand species is still alive—a truly lousy survival record," he comments.

Management does not blame you for the situation. This memo is for information only.

Because TV specials on evolution focus on the extinction of the dinosaurs, with amazing pyrotechnics, they ignore the depressing reality that extinction is normal. Just as individuals die, so do types. Despite the huge diversity of life forms, new species have kept ahead of extinctions by only a tiny fraction.[33]

Some facts, of interest to life forms, about extinction:

- Plant or animal species have lifespans averaging four million years.[34] "Long periods of boredom interrupted occasionally by panic," explains Raup.[35]

- There were five major extinctions (the Big Five), including the one that did in the dinosaurs, the K–T (Cretaceous–Tertiary) extinction. These major downsizings accounted for only five percent of all extinctions.[36] The rest happened in the normal course of events.

- Odds are that each year one species in four million goes naturally extinct, or about 10 a year. Biologists don't get to see natural extinctions at the moment they happen.[37]

- Life forms, do not blame yourselves! There is no obvious explanation for documented extinctions.[38] Darwin's idea that more adapted life forms extinguish less adapted ones is simply not supported by research.[39] Available data suggest that the answer is: "Time and chance happeneth to them all." (Eccles. 9:11, KJV)[40]

- Cockroaches have avoided extinction. The public relations value of their feat is much less than you might hope for. Please do not use that strategy.

Management continues to view human-caused extinctions as a very serious problem. Most natural extinctions occur over geological ages, during which other life forms can adjust. By contrast, human-caused extinctions are rapid, leaving a damaged ecology.

By departing from strict Darwinism, Margulis has come up with a plausible explanation for some features of the history of cells. Her example shows that strict adherence to Darwinism is just as likely to prevent new discoveries as to provide a path to them.

Anyway, if she's right, they're wrong. In that case, a number of theories of evolution that have long been suppressed or ridiculed may have to be reconsidered. This includes non-naturalist theories that consider the possibility of design.

3. Is There Really Only One Common Ancestor for Life?

A key assumption of modern Darwinism is *common descent*, the belief that every life form on the planet, including us, arose from a single cell that happened to get started nearly four billion years ago.[41] That belief, too, is under question, at least where microbes are concerned.

Carl Woese is a University of Illinois microbiologist. He discovered in the 1970s that the *archaea*, the simplest form of life on earth, are not bacteria. He believes that there must have been at least three types of cell in the beginning, and that these cells shared information about their separate inventions in order to proceed. His idea is not unreasonable, because simple life forms can share genes. He argues:

> We cannot expect to explain cellular evolution if we stay locked in the classical Darwinian mode of thinking. The time has come for biology to go beyond the Doctrine of Common Descent.[42]

Like Lynn Margulis, Woese is no armchair malcontent: He is a scientist whose findings have led him to question a key "doctrine" of Darwinism. Of course, we must ask, if one single common ancestor cell is highly unlikely to be produced by chance (Darwin's "big if"), what are the chances for several of them?

It is important to note that all these disagreements revolve around whether or not Darwinism (survival of the fittest of a number of random mutations) is a useful explanation for how all of life got started, changes, and develops. In

> **Definition**
>
> **Archaea** (ar-KEY-a) simple, one-celled creatures that can survive in very harsh environments, for example environments that are very hot, cold, or salty. Scientists believe that archaea are among the oldest life forms.

Did Darwin Explain Sex?

Charles Darwin believed that natural selection explains the sexual traits and behavior of animals. According to his theory of sexual selection, developed in *The Descent of Man* (1871), male animals fight among themselves for females. Female animals, by contrast, carefully choose the males with the best genes.

Darwin's theory enabled him to explain odd mysteries like the immense, beautiful—but useless and dangerous—tail of the peacock. His explanation was simple: the peacock's ladies prefer fancy feathers. Therefore, the peacock with the boldest display passes on his genes, which create his fancy feathers, even though the feathers are useless and dangerous.

Some of Darwin's followers (evolutionary biologists) take the argument a step further. They argue that males are promiscuous because they invest little in sperm, but females must carry and raise the offspring, so they are choosier and more responsible. However, a number of modern biologists have not found animal behavior to be as simple as this. For example, Stanford biologist Joan Roughgarden says: "The exceptions are so numerous they cry out for explanation."[43]

At the 2003 annual meeting of the American Association for the Advancement of Science, leading researchers and theorists in the evolution of sexual behavior presented growing evidence that Darwin's theory of sexual selection does not really explain the facts they deal with. A few animals, such as the whiptail lizard, exist only as females. Many animals change sex, as needed, to sustain their numbers. More important, animals often use sexual behavior for purposes that have nothing to do with passing on their genes. Homosexual behavior, which is genetically useless, was also identified in over 300 species. One researcher, Paul Vasey of the University of Lethbridge, sums the problem up by saying that "traditional evolutionary theories for sexual behavior are inadequate and impoverished to account for what is going on."[44]

These researchers support natural selection as an element in evolution, but they do not believe that it explains the sexual behavior of animals, as Darwin thought it did.

other words, the scientists discussed here are naturalistic evolutionists. They are not arguing that there is any design or purposeful path in nature, or that the order that we see in nature is a demonstration of God's work. Indeed, scientists who have little use for neo-Darwinism can also be quite hostile to the proponents of God-guided evolution or any type of intelligent design.

Some Scientific Objections to Darwinism[45]

Problem	Type of Problem	Why a Problem
Adaptation	Darwin's natural selection may not confer survival advantage.	Creatures that evolve the least seem to last the longest. (Taylor)
Antibiotic resistance	Appears to come from inbuilt mechanism.	Evolution is supposed to be blind. (Hunter)
Cambrian explosion	Darwinism assumes slow, gradual changes, *not* sudden appearance of over 30 animal phyla, then no more.	Sudden appearance of complex life forms about 525 million years ago. No major groups since then. (Gould)
Common ancestor	Darwinism requires that all life springs from a common ancestor.	Origin of life may be easier to understand if there is more than one ancestor. (Woese)
Competition	Darwinism requires survival of the fittest.	Cooperation is important in evolution. (Margulis)
Computer simulations of evolution	Large computer memory can mimic long evolutionary stretches of time.	Programmer often builds in assumptions that favor evolution. (Berlinski)
Convergence	Marsupial mammals occupy the same niches as placentals.	Patterns appear in nature that seem to exceed chance. (Wesson)
Falsifiability issue	Ultra-Darwinians like Dennett insist that something like Darwinism *must* be true.	A theory that cannot be falsified cannot be scientific. (Popper)
Few or no transitional forms	Darwinism requires gradual change from one form to another.	New life forms appear without long succession of obvious ancestors. (Patterson)

History problem	Darwinism wants to be like physics.	"Physics envy" causes Darwinism to risk sounding like sociology. (Eldredge)
Living fossils	Some creatures survive eons without evolving (cockroach, coelacanth).	Contrary to the theory, they mutate but do not evolve. (Grasse)
Major new developments	Complex structures such as lung of bird, eye of rock lobster, flagellum of bacteria must arise by chance.	No clear path exists for chance in most cases. (Denton)
Molecular clock (timetable of changes)	Computer calculations assume that more genetic divergence means earlier common ancestor.	There is no consensus on the rate at which mutations occur. (Maddox)
Natural selection's scope	Darwinism should be able to explain large changes.	Evidence for small changes via natural selection is common, but for large ones rare. (Patterson)
Positive selection	There is little evidence for it.	Darwinism should be able to explain it. (Kimura)
Probability issue	Darwinism means random evolution.	There isn't enough time for random evolution. (Yockey)
Punctuated equilibrium	Paleontology's "trade secret" is that it does not support strict Darwinism.	New life forms appear comparatively suddenly, not slowly, as Darwin thought. (Gould)
Selfish gene problem	Sexual reproduction means life forms transmit only half their genes.	Why would sex get started in a "selfish gene" world? (Eldredge)
Sexual selection	Sex is more complicated than Darwin thought.	To what extent does sex support natural selection? (Roughgarden)

Note: These objections are mostly raised by scientists who accept evolution in principle, and represent problems with Darwinian evolution in particular.

Alternatives to Darwinism?

One reason that biologists defend Darwinism is that no comprehensive theory has come forward to replace it. David Walsh suggests that it is sign of trouble when a scientific theory plays a greater role outside its field of application than within it. He notes:

> Darwinian evolutionism functions to such an extent as the overarching worldview of modernity that even its subjection to scientific analysis is treated with deep misgivings. Everyone is more comfortable if its examination is reduced to the stylized opposition between evolution and creationism. That way, no one has to pay serious attention to the minor consideration that neither of them can be taken seriously as scientific theories. They cannot be disproved because the theories are designed to accommodate all contrary or missing evidence against them.[46]

However, despite the many protestations to the contrary that we hear in the media, Darwin's theory is not really essential to biologists' work. As A.S. Wilkins writes:

> The subject of evolution occupies a special, and paradoxical, place within biology as a whole. While the great majority of biologists would probably agree with Theodosius Dobzhansky's dictum that nothing in biology makes sense except in light of evolution, most can conduct their work quite happily without particular reference to evolutionary ideas. Evolution would appear to be the indispensable unifying idea and, at the same time, a highly superfluous one.[47]

The reason evolution is "highly superfluous" is that, in reality, nothing in biology makes sense except in the light of biochemistry, which is what gives biology its place in the linked chain of sciences. Evolution is a form of history, a history that may or may not have happened as described in any current work on the subject.

So where are we now? Many biologists cling to Darwinism, not because it really works that well but because they dare not consider any other option; it is too scary.[48] However, some scientists continue to defend neo-Darwinism, convinced that it is still the answer. One of these is Richard Dawkins, and in the next chapter, we will look at why he thinks so. We will also look at his great antagonist Stephen Jay Gould, the man who dared to question strict Darwinism from within the science establishment, and paid the price.

Darwin's Quarreling Heirs:
Dawkins vs. Gould

CHAPTER 9

If you meet somebody who claims not to believe in evolution, that person is ignorant, stupid or insane (or wicked, but I'd rather not consider that).

— Richard Dawkins, Darwinist crusader[1]

If Dawkins's professional goal is "public understanding of science," he is a flop, seemingly trying his best to make worse what he is supposed to fix.

— Gregg Easterbrook, journalist[2]

. . . the brilliant and authentic native voice of modern evolutionary biology.

— John Tooby and Leda Cosmides,
evolutionary psychologists, on Dawkins[3]

. . . Gould himself has lent real strength to the creationist movement.

— Robert Wright, science writer[4]

The first self-consciously revolutionary scientist—the first scientist who set out to create a revolution at least in part because he felt that the field just needed one.

— Darwinian evolutionist H. Allen Orr on Gould[5]

R ichard Dawkins, a zoologist, author, and lecturer, is probably the British media's favorite scientist, a Carl Sagan equivalent who is good for pithy sound bites. In 1995, a chair was created for him at Oxford University, as Professor of Public Understanding of Science, endowed by American Microsoft billionaire Charles Simonyi. More than that, the elegant Oxbridge don is a cultural icon. As one of his editors explains:

> If you're an intelligent reader, and you read certain literary novels that everybody has to read, along with seeing Tarantino movies, then reading Richard Dawkins has become part of your cultural baggage.[6]

He is also the best-known promoter of "ultra-Darwinism"—more Darwinist than Darwin.[7]

Dawkins, an engaging popular writer, is the author of key modern concepts in Darwinism such as these:

■ *Selfish genes.* Why do some animals, or people, sacrifice themselves for others? Dawkins argues in *The Selfish Gene* (1976, 1989) that self-sacrifice is an illusion. Rather, genes scheme to acquire immortality by getting passed on. "We are survival machines," he has insisted, "robot vehicles blindly programmed to preserve the selfish molecules known as genes."[8] His view helped launch the sociobiology movement of the 1970s, an updated form of Social Darwinism.

■ *Blind Watchmaker thesis.* In his 1986 book, *The Blind Watchmaker: Why the Evidence of Evolution Reveals a Universe Without Design*, Dawkins argues that even astonishingly complex phenomena such as human DNA can gradually self-assemble via natural selection.

■ *Mount Improbable.* Dawkins's *Climbing Mount Improbable* (1996) continues the Blind Watchmaker theme. For example, in a famous response to Stephen Jay Gould's question, "What good is 5 per cent of an eye?" he said that six percent of an eye is better than five, and seven percent is better still.[9] In other words, an eye can self-assemble as long as each version is a little less near-sighted than the one before.

■ *Meme theory.* Powerful ideas are like genes or viruses that infect our minds. They reproduce and evolve, Darwin-style, irrespective of truth. Dawkins's favorite example of a meme is traditional religion.[10]

Dawkins on Religion

Although Dawkins is a science professor at Oxford,[11] he devotes a good deal of his professional energy to attacking religion. Religion, he says, is a "virus of the mind"[12] or a "'chain letter' that people are forced to pass on to others under the threat of eternal damnation."[13] He has probably done more than anyone to cement evolution as anti-traditional religion. He likes to say that "Darwin allows one to be an intellectually fulfilled atheist,"[14] and his latest book, *The Devil's Chaplain*,[15] hammers the theme pretty hard. Fellow Darwinist Michael Ruse calls him "the atheist's answer to Billy Graham."[16]

Yet Dawkins is hardly without a religious sensibility. In an interview on PBS's *Think Tank*, Ben Wattenberg quoted him as saying:

> Living organisms had existed on earth without ever knowing why for 3000 million years before the truth finally dawned on one of them. His name was Charles Darwin.[17]

Responding to this, Wattenberg charged that Dawkins's language is "near messianic," adding that "you are making the case that these other people have this virus of the mind. That tonality says, I found my God." Dawkins defended himself, saying: "It's not religious in any sense in which I would recognize the term."[18]

Despite not recognizing the term, Dawkins has made converts. His friend Douglas Adams (1952–2001), author of *The Hitchhiker's Guide to the Galaxy*, described reading *The Selfish Gene* as "one of those absolutely shocking moments of revelation when you understand that the world is fundamentally different from what you thought it was." He added: "I'm hesitating to use the word, but it's almost like a religious experience."[19]

Dawkins's (non)religion even finds room for things that no human can understand. Darwinism is one of them. He writes: "Human brains, though they sit atop one of its grandest peaks, were never designed to imagine anything as slow as the long march up Mount Improbable."[20] So, it turns out, Darwinism itself is the reason that many people don't believe in Darwinism.

Dawkins's religion also has a devil of sorts, in the form of mathematician David Berlinski, who, Dawkins suggests, might be a "genuine candidate for the wicked category," that is, those who deliberately withhold belief in evolution.[21] Berlinski has sinned repeatedly by publishing articles that criticize the mathematics behind Dawkins's theories.[22]

If making Darwinism into a religion sounds puzzling, here is, perhaps, a clue. Dawkins is a strong advocate of scientism, a philosophy that truth is discovered by the scientific method. A person who seriously believes in scientism, but nonetheless has a religious streak, must form a religion from the materials available, whether attractive or otherwise.

Dawkins's benefactor Charles Simonyi has urged him to "tame his militancy."[23] Whatever else might be said about the militancy, it isn't sweeping Britain. In April 2003, the British Vardy Foundation, started by evangelical Christian Peter Vardy who became wealthy through car dealerships, announced its intention to open six Christian academies in the north of England that provide quality education for poor students and, among other things, allow students to question Darwinism.

According to a Vardy spokesperson, "We don't reject Darwinism. We say it's a theory many people are committed to and some are not."[24] Dawkins calls the program "educational debauchery," but three times as many students apply as are accepted. The science education they receive has been accepted by the governing authority, OFSTED, but the controversy, of course, continues.

Why Teaching Evolution Is Controversial

Why, many people ask, do some religious people get upset about the teaching of evolution in the schools? After all, they do not similarly question the teaching of the Big Bang or quantum theory. Are they just trying to force religion on the schools?

As we have seen, it's a bit more complicated than that. Unlike Big Bang theory or quantum theory, Darwinism has always been tied into an explicitly anti-religious view of life. It started with Charles Darwin's own gradual loss of faith. Darwinist views have had social and political consequences as well, such as Social Darwinism, sociobiology, and evolutionary psychology. For example, they animate Professor Dawkins's widely publicized screeds against traditional religions. The Darwinist may be as committed to teaching his religion as any missionary.

Of course, religious scientists, such as genome mapper Francis Collins, accept evolution, at least in some form. But many Darwinists see Collins and his like as deluded, or even an embarrassment.[25]

Thus, the controversy is not between people who want to impose religion in the classroom and people who want to keep it neutral. A classroom that accepts evolution in the form of ultra-Darwinism is not "neutral"; it can easily become a conduit for intolerant views on religion and for a specific set of assumptions about human nature, society, and politics that most parents would oppose.

No doubt, it is possible to separate Darwinism in the classroom from the anti-religious zealotry in which it often arises.[26] In the same way, presumably, intelligent design theory or objections to Darwinism can also be taught without the religious views in which they often arise.[27]

Dawkins's Secular Critics

Although Dawkins sees his main enemies as religious figures, the secular world has not always treated him kindly. He has suffered from the unpopularity of sociobiology. His other main ideas have been strongly challenged within his discipline:

- *Selfish genes.* Evolutionary geneticist Gabriel Dover denies that genes have the role that Dawkins asserts. He notes that there are no one-to-one correspondences between genes and complex traits, so genes cannot really act in a "selfish" way.[28]

- *Blind Watchmaker/Mount Improbable* theses. Biochemist Michael Behe points out that the evolution of vision itself, never mind the role that the eye plays, is extraordinarily complex, and perhaps irreducibly so.[29] The real challenge is at the level of biochemistry, not just zoology—cells, not just animals. Phillip Johnson has pointed out that "5 per cent of an eye" is not the same thing as "5 percent of normal vision." Vision requires many complex parts to work together all at once.[30] Mathematician David Berlinksi has also taken issue with Dawkins's claim that an eye can evolve by a slow multitude of steps. Dawkins claimed in *River Out of Eden* (1995) that two biologists, Dan-Erik Nilsson and Susanne Pilger, had demonstrated in a series of calculations the random evolution of the eye, thus proving his thesis. However, in 2001, Nilsson told Berlinski that they had not in fact succeeded, commenting that "the genetic algorithms need a fair amount of work." In 2003, Berlinski labeled Dawkins's claim a "scientific fraud."[31]

- *Meme theory* Even the otherwise supportive Darwinist Jerry Coyne has blasted the "meme" theory of ideas as a tautology. True, ideas do spread from one person to another. But how does Dawkins's theory shed any light on the process?[32]

But one thing about Dawkins, he is as true a believer as they come. For example, discussing major mutations that can really change an animal, but are almost never beneficial, he writes:

> The argument over whether macromutations such as antennapaedia could ever be beneficial (or at least could avoid being harmful), and

therefore whether they could give rise to evolutionary change, therefore turns on how "macro" the mutation is that we are considering. The more "macro" it is, the more likely it is to be deleterious, and the less likely it is to be incorporated in the evolution of a species. As a matter of fact, virtually all the mutations studied in genetics laboratories—which are pretty macro because otherwise geneticists wouldn't notice them—are deleterious to the animals possessing them (ironically I've met people who think that this is an argument against Darwinism!).[33]

To Dawkins, it is inconceivable that anyone would think that a fact base that undermines Darwinism could actually be cited as an argument against it. Only a true believer writes this way.

Enter the Antagonist: Dawkins Squares Off with Stephen Jay Gould

For many years, Dawkins skirmished in print with the American paleontologist Stephen Jay Gould, whose evolution theory opposed his. Of Gould, Dawkins said: "I think the tendency of American intellectuals to learn their evolution from him is unfortunate, and that's putting it mildly."[34] He described Gould's key theory, called punctuated equilibrium, as "a sorry mess," set out in a "deeply muddled book."[35]

Gould replied in kind, and the hostilities became so fierce that the battle itself resulted in a book by Australian philosopher Kim Sterelny, *Dawkins vs. Gould: Survival of the Fittest.*[36] Gould, who died in 2002, was hardly an eccentric; he became a household name in North America on the subject of evolution, So what could he have done or said that upset Dawkins so much?

Stephen Jay Gould (1941–2002) filled the same role for North America as Richard Dawkins does for Britain. He was Darwinist-in-chief, the man who could explain to a secular culture where it came from, if not where it was going. However,

> We are glorious accidents of an unpredictable process with no drive to complexity, not the expected results results of evolutionary principles that yearn to produce a creature capable of understanding the mode of its own necessary construction.
>
> –Stephen J. Gould, American paleontologist[37]
>
> Nothing is more dangerous than a dogmatic worldview–nothing more constraining, more blinding to innovation, more destructive of openness to novelty.
>
> –Gould on Dawkins's selfish gene theory[38]

Gould and Dawkins were not friends. Indeed, according to a Dawkins profile in the *New Yorker*, "they would not want to be stuck in the same elevator."[39]

Gould was a Harvard paleontologist, and author of many popular works on evolution, as well as professional ones. He served as president of the American Association for the Advancement of Science in 1999–2000.[40] In popular culture, he was probably much better known for appearing as an animated character on *The Simpsons* in 1997.[41] His chief claim to fame was his challenge to Dawkins's ultra-Darwinism.[42]

In 1972, together with fellow paleontologist Niles Eldredge, Gould published a paper that addressed candidly the "trade secret" of paleontology, as he later termed it,[43] the fact that the fossil record does not show what Darwin hoped, that natural selection is "daily and hourly scrutinizing, throughout the world, every variation, even the slightest; rejecting that which is bad, preserving and adding up all that is good."[44] On the contrary, the record shows that species change very little for long periods of time, and then produce descendant species comparatively suddenly. Gould called this pattern "punctuated equilibrium" (sometimes dismissed as "punk eek").

Gould also doubted that "fitness" drives survival; he argued from the fossil evidence that life is a grand lottery in which survivors have merely been lucky enough to escape randomly occurring catastrophes.

His most famous book, *Wonderful Life: The Burgess Shale and the Nature of History*[45] (1989), enlarged this theme. He brought to the public's attention the fact that almost all the major body plans (phyla) of animals are found in a deposit in the mountains near Field, British Columbia, the famous Cambrian explosion dating from about 525 million years ago. Since then, few or no new phyla have arisen, though many old ones have gone extinct. A great increase in the number of new species within each surviving phylum has occurred, but nature is seemingly content to rework old patterns and has not set off in radical new directions.[46]

In keeping with this theme, Gould was convinced that human beings were a fluke, not an inevitable outcome of increasing mammal intelligence.

The Paleontologist and His Public

Gould was immensely popular, and with reason. He was an excellent communicator, but, more than that, he took the field against evolutionary psychology. A major reason for the unpopularity of Darwinism is its dark legacy of Social Darwinism, suspected of having made a comeback in the 1970s as sociobiology and, in its latest retro form, in the 1990s as evolutionary psychology.[47] This was the concern that motivated Bryan. Gould increased the overall public comfort level with Darwinian evolution among people who were not concerned about a common ancestry with apes but were concerned that science not be co-opted to support political agendas about race and class.[48] As Paul R. Gross put it in the *New Criterion*:

> To people outside the field, Stephen Jay Gould was the answer: a uniquely articulate scientist who spoke for fairness and decency, who fought dangerous denizens of society such as creationists, racists, economic oppressors, and who defeated them with science.[49]

Or, as Gould's obituary in the *Times of London* put it:

> Gould was a passionate opponent of attempts, conscious or otherwise, by scientists over the past century or so to justify or bolster the entrenched power of the well-educated Caucasian protestant male in Anglo-Saxon society.[50]

Gould and His Colleagues

Gould was much less popular with his colleagues. He was often derided by other Darwinists. For example, leading evolutionary psychologists John Tooby and Leda Cosmides charged: "We suggest that the best way to grasp the nature of Gould's writings is to recognize them as one of the most formidable bodies of fiction to be produced in recent American letters."[51] Similarly, John Maynard Smith, a leading evolutionary biologist, said of Gould:

> The evolutionary biologists with whom I have discussed his work tend to see him as a man whose ideas are so confused to be hardly worth bothering with, but as one who should not be publicly criticized because he is at least on our side against the creationists.[52]

Gould's critics lost no time in their efforts to minimize his legacy after his death. Indeed, evolutionary psychologist David P. Barash, reviewing Gould's major professional work, *The Structure of Evolutionary Theory*, described him as a "literate bio-terrorist" whose work was not for "anyone with anything else to do with his or her life."[53]

No doubt some colleagues were envious of his success with the public. Some were put off by the fact that his ideas were influenced by Marxism.[54]

And certainly, he scored no points with Richard Dawkins when he described Dawkins's selfish gene theory as "a hyper-Darwinian idea that I regard as a logically flawed and basically foolish caricature of Darwin's genuinely radical intent."[55]

A much bigger sin was his vocal criticism of evolutionary psychology, which most of his colleagues supported. Evolutionary psychology seeks to explain the whole of human life, even disbelief in Darwinism, as a category of Darwinism. Even an insider cannot expect to get away unscathed, after deliberately undermining a project as ambitious as that.[56]

However, the biggest problem Gould presented was probably this: He made it legitimate to criticize Darwin, or anyway, to criticize Darwinism. He argued that those who forbid any criticism are guilty of "Darwinian fundamentalism," of pushing their line "with almost theological fervor."[57] The mud sticks, too. Reading Darwinist literature, one cannot help noticing the way in which each writer stresses his or her own orthodoxy and total fidelity to Darwin, much like bishops discussing the encyclicals of a pope.[58] Science writer Robert Wright, who stresses that he himself is an orthodox Darwinian, puts this charge against Gould bluntly:

> Gould is not helping the evolutionists against the creationists, and the sooner the evolutionists realize that the better. Over the past three decades, in essays, books, and technical papers, Gould has advanced a distinctive view of evolution. He stresses its flukier aspects—freak environmental catastrophes and the like—and downplays natural selection's power to design complex life forms. In fact, if you really pay attention to what he is saying, and accept it, you might start to wonder how evolution could have created anything as intricate as a human being.[59]

EP, Phone Home?

Evolutionary psychology ("rebranded sociobiology," as Richard Dawkins terms it) argues that human nature and behavior is best understood as a constant replay of conditions that prevailed in the Pleistocene era, which lasted from 1.8 million to 11,000 years ago, and are now part of our genes. Its funniest episode is surely the EP interpretation of the eclectic, ungovernable world of art. In 1998, sociobiologist E.O. Wilson announced at a conference on postmodernism that evolution favors "a more traditionalist view of the arts." Unfortunately, it became apparent that, by "traditionalist" art, Wilson meant the swell scenery that finds its way into paint-by-number sets and jigsaw puzzles. A critic has described his view as "kitsch all the way down."[60] Gaffes like this, rather than perceived opposition to Darwinism, probably explain EP's persistent lack of headway in the social sciences and arts.[61]

That is the legacy that Gould's detractors are anxious to minimize. Gould never did explain what, exactly, was punctuating the equilibrium. What was disturbing the dark silences of the planet?

Gould and Religion

Unlike Dawkins, Gould avoided attacking religion directly. He had no doubt that traditional religion accorded to human beings an importance that they could not possibly possess. For example, in his Introduction to Carl Zimmer's *Evolution: The Triumph of an Idea*, he writes:

> Evolution substituted a naturalistic explanation of cold comfort for our former conviction that a benevolent deity fashioned us directly in his own image, to have dominion over the entire earth and all other creatures. Our favored and well-attested theory, Darwinian natural selection, offers no solace or support for these traditional hopes about human necessity or cosmic importance.[62]

Gould did not agree with Dawkins's assumption that the only reason that Americans did not accept Darwinism is that their brains are wired wrong. He thought that most of his fellow Americans understood but did not accept Darwinism because they feared that it would render both life and morality devoid of meaning. So he argued that, on the contrary, Darwinism was "ethically neutral and intellectually exhilarating."[63] For example, he believed, Darwinism can combat racism by showing that there is little difference among human groups. He also believed that "our quest for decency and meaning can emerge only from our own moral consciousness."[64] This was likely an important reason that he opposed evolutionary psychology's attempt to reduce morality to the functions of the selfish gene. He wanted to preserve morality, despite the implications of Darwinism.

Gould wanted to isolate traditional religions in a realm of values, as opposed to facts. He sought "a respectful, even loving concordat" in which science would attend to facts and religion to values.[65] However, as critics have noted, in his scheme, religion must make do with "values" that have no basis in fact.[66] What really happens in that case is that no values can be asserted, just empty platitudes and fuzzies.

No Debate with Creationists!

Gould and Dawkins clashed on Darwinism, but one thing they agreed on was that they would not debate creationists.[67] Gould felt that doing so was "politically stupid." He explained:

> This is a political struggle. It's not an intellectual struggle. Debate is absurd. It's dishonorable in science to think that an issue will be solved by rhetorical skill. Young-earth creationists want a sign of respectability they cannot have, because they are wrong.[68]

Gould's critics may have doubted his commitment to Darwinism, but the National Center for Science Education (NCSE), an American advocacy group for Darwinism in the schools, considered him a friend and supporter.[69] After his death from cancer in 2002, NCSE solicited the names of hundreds of scientists named Steve (or Stephanie) who say that they "support evolution."

NCSE raises money for its battles by warning against the influence of the creationists. In other words, as late as 2003, the creationists—far from disappearing, as expected—are a thriving bunch. How did they manage it? Who are their supporters and why? Let's look at that in the next few chapters.

In the Beginning, There Was … Creationism!

PART THREE

Creationism: Morphing into a Modern Movement

CHAPTER 10

If God's Word be true, evolution is a lie. I will not mince the matter: this is not the time for soft speaking.

—Charles Spurgeon, preacher, 1886[1]

If all the animals and man had been evolved in this ascendant manner, then there had been no first parents, no Eden, and no Fall. And if there had been no fall, then the entire historical fabric of Christianity, the story of the first sin and the reason for an atonement, upon which the current teaching based Christian emotion and morality, collapsed like a house of cards."

—H.G. Wells, science fiction writer[2]

For most of Western history, scientists accepted the biblical account of the origins of the universe and life, as given in Genesis 1 and 2. The heavenly bodies were studied and their movements predicted, but the details of their origins remained a mystery until modern times. As more and more new scientific information came to light from the 18th century onward, it became possible to construct histories of origins that did not require or even include information derived from the Bible.

Secularization in the Modern World

Vast amounts of new information about the earth coincided with major changes in the role of religion in the Western world. Secularization meant that traditional Christian religion slowly ceased to be part of the institutional apparatus of society. This change has had both good and bad effects on Christianity in North America. On the one hand, religion lost many privileges in the public square. On the other hand, it was also freed from the oppressive need to support the social and political establishment's policies.

Proportionately, many more active religious believers live in the United States, which does not have an established church, than in many European countries that do. As a result, in North America, intense spiritual revivalism and religiously based social justice activism have flourished right alongside the secularism and materialism of government, corporations, and universities. However, there is often simply no communication between religious and secular worldviews, and significant social tensions result.

Pretended vs. Real Conflicts Between Science and Religion

In addition to tensions based on real issues, many difficulties were created by people who marketed false ideas about conflict between religion and science. A number of works written around the turn of the 20th century promoted the idea of warfare between the two, including John William Draper's *History of the Conflict Between Religion and Science* and Andrew Dickson White's *A History of the Warfare of Science with Theology in Christendom*.[3]

These men's works gained a wide following, which was ironic because there was no significant contention between science and religion at the time. As historian Edward J. Larson notes, these widely read works

> neither reported the growing harmony between theologians and evolutionists nor noted that most great physical scientists of the period, from John Dalton and Michael Faraday to Lord Kelvin and James Clerk Maxwell, were devout Christians.[4]

Taking a cue from such works, much popular mythology portrayed religion as preventing advances in science. One outcome was that religious believers began to find themselves under attack at universities.

Evangelical Christian Opposition to Evolution

At the turn of the 20th century, most educated Christians had no opinion about evolution or vaguely supported it. It was quite easy to interpret Genesis as allowing for a long evolution of life forms. For example, A.H. Strong wrote:

If science should render it certain that all the present species of living creatures were derived by natural descent from a few original germs, and that these germs were themselves an evolution of inorganic forces and materials, we should not therefore regard the Mosaic account as proved untrue. We should only be required to revise our interpretation of the word *bara* in Gen. 1:21, 27, and to give it there the meaning of mediate creation, or creation by law. Such a meaning might almost seem to be favored by Gen. 1:11—"let the earth put forth grass"; 20—"let the waters bring forth abundantly the moving creature that hath life"; 2:7—"the Lord God formed man of the dust"; 9—"out of the ground made the Lord God to grow every tree"; cf. Mark 4:28 . . . "the earth brings forth fruit automatically."[5]

That said, few Christian clergy clearly understood what Darwin meant.

In *The Fundamentals*, a popular series of pamphlets published between 1910 and 1915 (from which the term "fundamentalism" is probably coined),[6] minister-geologist George Frederick Wright, who collaborated with Asa Gray, argued that the Bible taught "an orderly progress from lower to higher forms of matter and life." However, he also said that the first humans had come into existence "as the Bible represents, by the special creation of a single pair, from whom all the varieties of the race have sprung."[7] So Wright did not accept the origin of human beings from the same ancestor as the primate apes. But apart from that, he was comfortable with evolution. Like most people in his day, he assumed that Darwinian evolution meant progress from a lower to a higher, or improved, state.

As mentioned earlier, it was World War I that caused many North American evangelicals to question Darwinism. That was the first "modern" war, in the sense that industrial technology was used to inflict huge suffering on soldiers and civilians alike. Evangelicals attributed the war to the Germans' belief in Social Darwinism—and not without cause (see Chapter 7).

The critical event for evangelical Christians in the United States was the historic Scopes trial in 1925. As we saw in Chapter 7, almost nothing that is widely believed about the Scopes trial actually happened. The one important thing that did happen was largely ignored. Cut off from the university system and ridiculed by the establishment after Scopes, Christians who did not accept an account of evolution that left out God's creative action slowly began to beef up their own schools, colleges, publishing houses, and other organizations[8] and to amass their own story of the history of life. Far from subsiding, as was predicted, the creationists have prospered.

Young earth creationism, which argues that Genesis should be interpreted literally, grew slowly during the 20th century, and has a worldwide reach today. According to historian of science Ron Numbers, there are well-established YEC movements in Australia, Europe, Korea, Russia, and Turkey, as well as North America.[9] As a result, creationists have begun to demand equal time in the school system.[10] We will pick up their story in Chapters 11 and 12. But first, let's look at how the Scopes trial actually advanced creationism, when, by all accounts, it should have destroyed it.

> Evolution . . . a theory universally accepted not because it can be proved by logically coherent evidence to be true but because the only alternative, special creation, is clearly incredible.
>
> —D.M.S. Watson,
> British paleontologist, 1929[11]
>
> Science has proof without any certainty. Creationists have certainty without any proof.
>
> —Ashley Montague,
> anthropologist, 1984[12]
>
> Belief in evolutionary theory is a matter of sheer faith.
>
> —John MacArthur,
> creationist author, 2001[13]

Who is a creationist?

In Tennessee in 1925, during the Scopes trial, a creationist was someone who believed that God plays an active role in getting the universe and life started, and in guiding its development. *How active* a role was a point of controversy among creationists. Where and when and how can we see God's hand? How will we recognize it?

The majority of North Americans today are, in some sense, creationists. Eighty-three percent believe in God's intervention, according to a 1999 Gallup poll. Like their forebears, they differ as to the type and degree of intervention, but not on the main idea.[14]

However, there has been a significant change over the years in what the term "creationist" means. A creationist has come to mean primarily a person who believes that God created the heavens and the earth in six 24-hour

> **Four Common Ideas About How the World Came to Exist . . .**
>
> - There is no evolution, or if there is, it is not an important force.[15] Life was created in six days, as the Bible says (young earth creationism).
>
> - The "six days of creation" were vast ages in which God worked (old earth creationism).
>
> - God never intervened. Evolution is his instrument (theistic evolution).
>
> - There is no God. It all happened by law and chance (atheistic evolution).

days, and that the fossil record is best explained by Noah's Flood, described in the Book of Genesis as a worldwide flood.

Young earth creationism took root in the United States after the Scopes trial. It was exported worldwide and is now thriving in many countries. As North American education systems fragment, young earth creationism has become the alternative that many Christian homeschoolers and private school systems are offering to the atheistic evolution of Richard Dawkins or Stephen Jay Gould.

Essentially, creationists simply decided not to believe in the assumptions of materialist philosophy and the Darwinist biology that springs from it. Biochemist Stuart Kauffman, who is not a creationist, does not think they are entirely wrong to take this view:[16]

> We, who are heritors of Darwin, who see the living world through the categories he taught us more than a century ago, even we have trouble with the implications: man as the result of a chain of accidental mutations, sifted by a law no more noble than survival of the fittest. Creation science is no accident in late-twentieth-century America. Its proponents adhere to it in an ardent effort to forestall the feared moral implications of humans as descendants of a haphazard lineage branching from some last common ancestor more remote in time than the Cambrian explosion some 500 million years ago.

He goes on to argue that "the science in creation science is no science at all," but asks: "Is the moral anguish so foolish? Or should creationism be viewed rather more sympathetically?"[17]

Generally, the public does view creationism more sympathetically than do science organizations committed to Darwinism, probably because people sense, as Kauffman does, that the creationists know something that the Darwinists don't.[18]

Traditional Bible Interpretations That Accept Evolution

Young earth creationism was not always popular. In the 19th century, most North American Christians who were aware of developments in the sciences simply accepted evolution. Although many disputed the idea that humans descended from ape-like creatures, the churchgoing public associated evolution with exciting prospects for ongoing improvement in an already optimistic age.[19]

How Genesis 1 Describes the Origin of the Universe and Life

The Beginning

¹ In the beginning God created the heavens and the earth.

² Now the earth was* formless and empty, darkness was over the surface of the deep, and the Spirit of God was hovering over the waters.

³ And God said, "Let there be light," and there was light.

⁴ God saw that the light was good, and he separated the light from the darkness.

⁵ God called the light "day," and the darkness he called "night." And there was evening, and there was morning–the first day.

⁶ And God said, "Let there be an expanse between the waters to separate water from water."

⁷ So God made the expanse and separated the water under the expanse from the water above it. And it was so.

⁸ God called the expanse "sky." And there was evening, and there was morning–the second day.

⁹ And God said, "Let the water under the sky be gathered to one place, and let dry ground appear." And it was so.

¹⁰ God called the dry ground "land," and the gathered waters he called "seas." And God saw that it was good.

¹¹ Then God said, "Let the land produce vegetation: seed-bearing plants and trees on the land that bear fruit with seed in it, according to their various kinds." And it was so.

¹² The land produced vegetation: plants bearing seed according to their kinds and trees bearing fruit with seed in it according to their kinds. And God saw that it was good.

¹³ And there was evening, and there was morning–the third day.

¹⁴ And God said, "Let there be lights in the expanse of the sky to separate the day from the night, and let them serve as signs to mark seasons and days and years,

¹⁵ and let them be lights in the expanse of the sky to give light on the earth." And it was so.

¹⁶ God made two great lights–the greater light to govern the day and the lesser light to govern the night. He also made the stars.

¹⁷ God set them in the expanse of the sky to give light on the earth,

¹⁸ to govern the day and the night, and to separate light from darkness. And God saw that it was good.

¹⁹ And there was evening, and there was morning–the fourth day.

²⁰ And God said, "Let the water teem with living creatures, and let birds fly above the earth across the expanse of the sky."

²¹ So God created the great creatures of the sea and every living and moving thing with which the water teems, according to their kinds, and every winged bird according to its kind. And God saw that it was good.

²² God blessed them and said, "Be fruitful and increase in number and fill the water in the seas, and let the birds increase on the earth."

²³ And there was evening, and there was morning–the fifth day.

(cont'd)

> 24 And God said, "Let the land produce living creatures according to their kinds: livestock, creatures that move along the ground, and wild animals, each according to its kind." And it was so.
>
> 25 God made the wild animals according to their kinds, the livestock according to their kinds, and all the creatures that move along the ground according to their kinds. And God saw that it was good.
>
> 26 Then God said, "Let us make man in our image, in our likeness, and let them rule over the fish of the sea and the birds of the air, over the livestock, over all the earth,** and over all the creatures that move along the ground."
>
> 27 So God created man in his own image, in the image of God he created him; male and female he created them.
>
> 28 God blessed them and said to them, "Be fruitful and increase in number; fill the earth and subdue it. Rule over the fish of the sea and the birds of the air and over every living creature that moves on the ground."
>
> 29 Then God said, "I give you every seed-bearing plant on the face of the whole earth and every tree that has fruit with seed in it. They will be yours for food.
>
> 30 And to all the beasts of the earth and all the birds of the air and all the creatures that move on the ground—everything that has the breath of life in it—I give every green plant for food." And it was so.
>
> 31 God saw all that he had made, and it was very good. And there was evening, and there was morning—the sixth day.
>
> * 1:2 Or possibly "became"
> ** 1:26 Hebrew; Syriac "all the wild animals"
> New International Version

Comparing evolution with the Bible, Christians took one of two positions. They assumed

- *either* that the six Biblical days of creation (Genesis 1:1–2:4) were vast geological ages rather than 24-hour periods (the Day–Age theory);

- *or* that there was a vast gap of time between the creation of earth and the creation of the Garden of Eden, around 4000 BC.

Christians have found these assumptions reasonable because the Bible does not give an age for the earth. As Bible scholar P.A. Zimmerman notes:

> The Bible does not anywhere make an explicit statement in which the age of the earth is given. It tells us how long the Children of Israel were in Egypt, the length of time from the Exodus to the building of Solomon's temple, the duration of the Babylonian Captivity, etc. But

nowhere is there a statement of how many years it was from creation to the time of Abraham or any other date that can be correlated with secular history. It is important to remember this point. Any estimate of the age of the earth based on the Bible rests on deductions drawn from information contained in Holy Scriptures. If the deductions are valid, the conclusions are likewise valid. The reverse is true if the deductions are in error.[20]

So most Christians saw no clear reason for a conflict between an old earth and Genesis. Many Christians also didn't care whether Darwin saw purpose in evolution or not. *They* saw it. The aged poet Alfred Lord Tennyson (1809–1892) typified this view in "Lockesley Hall: Sixty Years After," where he described "Evolution" as "ever climbing after some ideal good."[21] Christians of the 19th and early 20th centuries saw plenty of progress in living standards, women's rights, anti-war efforts, and such, and they simply co-opted Darwin's theory to mean that the progress that they saw was part of a general, divine plan. Also, there was a fair amount of humor around the subject that suggested easy acceptance, for example the following lines by Victorian journalist Mortimer Collins:

> There was an ape in the days that were earlier,
> Centuries passed and his hair became curlier;
> Centuries more gave a thumb to his wrist—
> Then he was a Man and a Positivist.[22]

Not everyone took such a benign or light-hearted view of Darwin's idea, however. In 1874, Princeton theologian Charles Hodge, one of the dissenters, created a stir by saying Darwinism was atheism: "'What is Darwinism'? It is Atheism. This does not mean ... that Mr. Darwin himself and all who adopt his views are atheists; but it means that his theory is atheistic, that the exclusion of design from nature is, as Dr. Gray says, tantamount to atheism."[23] The famous Scofield Bible (1909) accommodated the controversy by promoting the gap theory and an ancient earth in its reference notes. Similarly, some of the authors of the early *Fundamentals* pamphlets (1910–1915) accepted evolution,[24] though others didn't. Overall, opposition to Darwinian evolution was not a defining mark of American evangelicalism before World War I.

A Bible Interpretation That Does Not Accept–or Even Need–Darwinian Evolution

World War I dampened many evangelical Christians' enthusiasm for evolution (and the idea of progress). After the Scopes trial, which the evangelicals thought they had won, they retreated from the mainstream to start their own colleges, societies, and journals. Organized creationism of any kind was assumed to be dead, though most North Americans continued to believe privately that God existed and had some role in the origins of life and the universe. Meanwhile, some creationists were developing a new point of view that they felt could reconcile the Bible and science while dispensing altogether with Darwin.

How Christians have understood the creation story in the Bible

No traditional Christian perspective has simply set Genesis 1 aside. Here are some basic ways in which Christians have understood the relationship between the age of the earth and Genesis.

Theory	Interpretation	How Genesis understood	When widely known	Scientist with this view
Traditional view	Creation took six days; earth 6000 years old	Genesis accepted as given	up to 18th c.	physicist Isaac Newton (1642–1727)
Day–Age interpretation (also called progressive or old earth creationism)[25]	Each Genesis day is read as a vast geological age (Ps. 90:4; 2 Pet. 3:8)	Evolution guided by God	19th c.	astronomer Hugh Ross (1945–)
Gap theory (also called ruin–reconstruction theory)	Between Gen. 1:1 and 1:2 (Garden of Eden) was a huge time gap	Evolution guided by God	19th c. to 21st c.	geologist Gaines Johnson[26] (no longer widely held)
Young earth creationism	Creation took six days; earth 10,000 years old. Noah's flood explains apparent evolution	Genesis taken literally	mid-20th c.	geophysicist John Baumgardner, Los Alamos Laboratory

In 1923, self-taught geologist George McCready Price published a book called *New Geology*, arguing that the earth really is only 6000 years old, as was traditionally believed. Price belonged to the Seventh-day Adventist religious sect, which emphasized the literal truth of Scripture. Ellen G. White (1827–1915).[27] a founder considered to be a prophet by many, believed that life on earth is only 6000 years old. This belief was especially important to Adventists like Price because Adventists saw themselves as champions of the divine inspiration of the Scriptures. At the time, Price's book received little attention in the sciences. He was mainly known as a writer for a leading fundamentalist magazine. However, in the 1930s, some evangelicals began to dust the book off and take a look at it.

One of these people was Henry Morris (1918–), the man who founded modern young earth creationism. A hydraulic (water) engineer, Morris had an enviable record in research, teaching, and practical engineering applications. In 1942, he began to question evolution while teaching civil engineering at Rice University in Texas. It seemed to him that God would

> **Definition**
>
> **Young earth creationism** a literal reading of chapters 1 and 2 of Genesis, the first book of the Bible, assuming that earth and the life forms on it were created by God in six 24-hour days, approximately 10,000 years ago.[28]

surely explain such crucial issues clearly in the Bible, rather than leaving them uncertain. After extensive Bible study, Morris became convinced that the Bible teaches that earth was created in six 24-hour days. That view conflicts with a modern account of the geology of earth, which shows many successive ages of changes. However, in 1943, Morris read Price's book, which attributed the changes to Noah's flood.

Possibly because he was a water engineer, Morris was immediately taken with Price's flood geology. He could see how a global flood would unleash effects so catastrophic as to equal great ages of lesser events. Together with theologian John C. Whitcomb, Morris set to work to explain the history of the planet in terms of a literal reading of Genesis, focusing on Noah's flood. The eventual result was *The*

> The standards of evidence supporting evolution seemed ridiculously trivial compared to the evidence on which engineers have to base their systems, and also compared to the tremendous evidences for the divine origin of the Bible (fulfilled prophecy, the resurrection of Christ, etc.).
>
> —Henry M. Morris, father of modern young earth creationism[29]

Noah's Flood, as Told in the Bible

Genesis 6

11 Now the earth was corrupt in God's sight and was full of violence.

12 God saw how corrupt the earth had become, for all the people on earth had corrupted their ways.

13 So God said to Noah, "I am going to put an end to all people, for the earth is filled with violence because of them. I am surely going to destroy both them and the earth.

14 So make yourself an ark of cypress wood; make rooms in it and coat it with pitch inside and out.

Genesis 7

1 The LORD then said to Noah, "Go into the ark, you and your whole family, because I have found you righteous in this generation.

2 Take with you seven of every kind of clean animal, a male and its mate, and two of every kind of unclean animal, a male and its mate,

3 and also seven of every kind of bird, male and female, to keep their various kinds alive throughout the earth.

4 Seven days from now I will send rain on the earth for forty days and forty nights, and I will wipe from the face of the earth every living creature I have made."

20 The waters rose and covered the mountains to a depth of more than twenty feet.

21 Every living thing that moved on the earth perished—birds, livestock, wild animals, all the creatures that swarm over the earth, and all mankind.

22 Everything on dry land that had the breath of life in its nostrils died.

23 Every living thing on the face of the earth was wiped out; men and animals and the creatures that move along the ground and the birds of the air were wiped from the earth. Only Noah was left, and those with him in the ark.

24 The waters flooded the earth for a hundred and fifty days.

(Note: These are excerpts from the New International Version translation. You can compare a number of different translations of Genesis 6 and 7 at www.gospelcom.net.)

Genesis Flood, published in 1961. The book immediately sparked interest in young earth creationism among conservative Christians.

The Beauty of Young Earth Creationism

The beauty of young earth creationism is that it is arrestingly simple, as a concept. It postulates not only that evolution did not happen but that it did not even *need* to happen, in order for the world to look the way it does.

On this view, God created the world in six days, and then inspired the Bible, which explains how he did it and why it looks older than it is.[30] In other words, mainstream science is simply wrong, because it has not heeded the Bible.

Over the years, the creation scientists, as they came to be called, have developed a series of basic beliefs.[31] They are listed below, with explanatory comments.

1. Sudden creation of the universe, energy, and life from nothing. (*On this point, creationists have a lot in common with Big Bang cosmology, though not with Darwinism, which emphasizes a slow accumulation of effects.*)

2. The insufficiency of mutation and natural selection in bringing about development of all living kinds from a single organism. (*Creationism rejects orthodox science's view that every life form originated in a single cell about four billion years ago.*)

3. Changes only within fixed limits of originally created kinds of plants and animals. (*Creationists do not deny that life forms can change, but they think that there are limits to the changes that mutation coupled with selection can achieve.*)

4. Separate ancestry for man and apes. (*Always a sore point for conservative Christians! Recall that the Tennessee law that Scopes was charged with violating forbade teaching human descent from lower animals; it did not forbid teaching evolution in general.*)

5. Explanation of earth's geology by catastrophism, including the occurrence of a worldwide flood. (*Noah's disastrous flood, described in Genesis 6–7, explains the geology we see.*)

6. A relatively recent origin for earth and living creatures. (*God created major animal groups separately, about 10,000 years ago. Most dinosaurs died in Noah's flood.*)

Contrary to widespread belief, creationists did not adopt the detailed chronology worked out for the Bible by Irish Archbishop James Ussher (1581–1656), which dated the creation of earth to noon on Sunday, October 23, 4004 BC.[32] As Morris and Whitcomb have noted, the archbishop's chronology did not really work out too well.[33]

Were the famous scientists of long ago young earth creationists?

William Provine, a prominent Darwinist, thinks so. In a recent online review, he complained that a National Academy of Sciences publication on how to teach evolution is flawed. He questioned the Academy's decision to cite Copernicus, Kepler, Galileo, and Newton as examples of thinkers whose views on physics and astronomy were vindicated because, as he put it: "Why would the National Academy have chosen this example in a book about evolution when all four were young-earth creationists?"[34]

Well, prior to about 1750, everyone was, in one sense, a young earth creationist! For example, the Venerable Bede (672?–735) wrote a history of the world, and so did Sir Walter Raleigh (1554?–1618). Both men began with "Creation," the origin of the universe, as described in Genesis 1 and 2. They assumed that Creation took place about 6000 years ago. But the two men could hardly have been more different! Bede was an English monk in the Dark Ages, and Raleigh was a skeptical English adventurer who lived nearly a thousand years later in the Elizabethan Renaissance.

Raleigh was rumored to be an atheist, holding forth in taverns, but his religious views had no impact on where he would begin his account of history. Prior to the development of geology as a scientific discipline in the 18th century, there was no widely accepted source of information about cosmic or human origins apart from the Bible. Raleigh would have to either begin with Genesis, or take the risk of resurrecting an account of origins written by a classical Greek philosopher. But the philosophers' accounts were not science-based; they were simply accounts that were not based on a Christian understanding of the universe.

So Copernicus and the others were not young earth creationists in the sense that Provine assumes. They accepted a traditional account of origins as an alternative to no account. They did not choose to read Genesis literally, as opposed to figuratively. Like most scientists of their day, they were principally concerned with astronomy and physics.

Armed with a complete theory of life that does not need evolution, the young earth creationists began to make converts rapidly among conservative Christians.[35] From the 1940s onward, belief in flood geology grew steadily as books were read and lectures delivered in church basements across North America. Contrary to alarms sounded by pundits that they would retreat to the Dark Ages, taking society with them, young earth creationists did the opposite. They began to get science degrees and gain employment in science-related fields.[36]

Rejection by Modernist Christians in Science

One group that the young earth creationists did not convince was the American Scientific Affiliation, an organization of Christians in science,

Religious Orientations That Are Not Creationist			
Theory	Interpretation	How Genesis understood	When widely known
Christian evolution	Evolution is how God creates. His work can't be detected.	interpreted symbolically	early 19th century[38]
Theistic evolution	Same as above	conformity with Bible not essential	same as above
Pantheistic evolution	The universe naturally moves toward life	Bible, at best, one of many sources	ancient

founded in 1941. Its members mostly accepted evolution as the way God created the universe. After some initial cooperation, the Christian evolutionists of ASA ridiculed and shunned the young earth creationists.[37] The two groups wrote each other off and proceeded on separate tracks.

So, ironically, the only type of creationism that is at odds with most current science findings—young earth creationism—is by no means the oldest type. It is actually the newest type, arising in the United States after Scopes.

Most Europeans took Genesis as a starting point for earth's history because it was the only source, prior to modern geology. They did not choose the account in Genesis over a contemporary one. By contrast, today's young earth creationist makes the decision to believe that Genesis should be interpreted literally and that modern research should use it as a starting point. And that is a decision with consequences, especially for scientists, as we will see in the next chapter.

Spin Cycle: Creationism and the Media

Screaming headlines or op-ed pieces warning against "creationism in the classroom" can be confusing. They can mean a number of different things, depending on what "creationism" means:

1. *God is behind it all somehow.* Some Darwinists describe anyone who believes that God had something to do with life on earth as a creationist.[39] In this broad sense, most North Americans are creationists. For example, this description would take in Christian evolutionists, who would disagree that they are creationists in any sense.

2. *Intelligent design.* Sometimes, intelligent design advocates (people who believe that the universe shows detectable evidence of intelligent design) are incorrectly called creationists. (See Chapter 14.) Intelligent design theory does not require a belief in creationism, as we shall see, though some ID theorists are also creationists.

3. *Progressive (old earth) creationism.* Many Christians believe that God intervened directly to produce life and human beings, and perhaps some other life forms. This is a form of creationism. However, given the absence of any science-based account of the origin of life and the poor quality of evidence for transitional fossils, progressive creationism does not conflict with current science findings. It does contradict the personal philosophy of scientists who are atheists.

4. *Young earth creationism.* Young earth creationists generally believe that the first two chapters of the Book of Genesis in the Bible should be taken literally as an exact account of earth's and life's origins, rather than as a figurative one. This belief conflicts with most current science findings. (Note: Not all young earth creationists are Christians; many are Muslims. Also, some belong to non-Western religions and accept a story of origins other than Genesis. See page 155.)

When "creationism" is attacked in the media, it is best to take a moment to identify the object of hostility before taking sides.

Can a Scientist Be a Creationist?

CHAPTER 11

Serious Christians haven't taken Genesis absolutely literally since Augustine, about 400 A.D.

—Michael Ruse, Darwinist philosopher[1]

As a Christian, I am interested in glorifying God; as a creation scientist I am interested in utilizing science to know God more so that I can glorify Him.

—Kurt Wise, young earth creationist paleontologist
and serious Christian[2]

Sir Julian Huxley, a famous scientist and the first Director-General of UNESCO, had momentous words for humanity during the Darwin Centennial in 1959:

In the evolutionary pattern of thought there is no longer either need or room for the supernatural. The earth was not created, it evolved. So did all the animals and plants that inhabit it, including our human selves, mind and soul as well as brain and body. So did religion.

Evolutionary man can no longer take refuge from his loneliness in the arms of a divinized father figure whom he has himself created, nor escape from the responsibility of making decisions by sheltering under the umbrella of Divine Authority, nor absolve himself from the hard task of meeting his present problems and planning his future by relying on the will of an omniscient, but unfortunately inscrutable, Providence.[3]

However, Huxley, as a cofounder of the American Humanist Association, didn't plan to leave humanity without a religion. He wanted to develop a new one. It would be based on Darwin's theory of evolution:

> Finally, the evolutionary vision is enabling us to discern, however incompletely, the lineaments of the new religion that we can be sure will arise to serve the needs of the coming era.[4]

Huxley, grandson of Thomas Henry Huxley, could be sure that this new religion would arise because he was in fact helping to found it. He was a major figure in directing the development of Darwinism as a sort of religion, to be propagated principally through the public school system, as well as through museums and other public works. The creationists, however, stubbornly refused to be converted.

The Road Less Traveled

Most stories about the creation–evolution controversy in the mainstream media implicitly assume that the statements made about creationists by their opponents are, without reservation, true. Here is a summary of what you can learn from mainstream sources:

1. Key young earth creationists hate and fear science.

2. They entirely lack science credentials.

3. No creationist works for any established science organization, and creationists cannot generate ideas worthy of scientific study.

4. Creationists know nothing about evolution.

5. Creationists have weird beliefs, compared with those entertained by current orthodox science.

6. Creationists accept alleged evidence for their beliefs uncritically, so they perpetrate hoaxes, unlike current orthodox science.

7. Creationists buy into a religious belief and their science positions follow from it, which is not the case with other scientists. Goodbye, brain cells.

Every one of these statements is incorrect, questionable, or hypocritical. The hypocritical part is that, as we shall soon see, the same charges can be leveled against Darwinists. While working on this book, I had to unlearn just about everything I thought I knew about contemporary young earth creationists, especially those who work in the sciences.

Creationism as a Reaction to Huxley's Religion of Evolution

The growth of young earth creationism during the 20th century is easier to understand once we grasp the way in which Darwinian evolution became, for many of its strongest exponents, an established religion of the scientific world. The tendency began long before Huxley; he was merely describing what many thought and some said.[5]

Scientists who were Christians reacted to this new religion in a variety of ways. Christian evolutionists assumed that Darwin was right about the facts, but that God was behind it all. They found that they could work quietly in science while ignoring the popular science-as-religion hype. However, as we saw in the previous chapter, a few scientists believed that Genesis should be read literally and that there was no place, or no important place, for evolution. They devoted their careers to researching the links between Genesis and the evidence. Some of these researchers have made creationism credible to millions of people. In this chapter and the next, we will look at why people listen to them.

1. Do Young Earth Creationists Hate and Fear Science?

Ronald Numbers, a historian at the University of Wisconsin, is one of the few professional historians who have studied creationism. He is not a creationist himself. However, in general, he found, the supporters of creationism were very far from hating or fearing science. On the contrary, he notes:

> Very rarely, in reading anti-evolution literature from the Christian community, will you find attacks on science. They loved science! In the Twenties, they viewed evolution as a "mere speculation that didn't deserve the name of science." They wanted to protect the good name of science.[6]

It is the same today, he says:

> Most people, I believe, who sign up with young earth creationism don't see themselves as rejecting science. They see themselves as choosing between two alternatives—and the one that they are choosing just happens to agree with the Bible.[7]

By the 1970s, after some scientists with impressive credentials had embraced creationism, the creationists changed their tack. They argued that creationism is scientific, too—specifically, that young earth creationism is a minority theory that deserves to be considered as an alternative to Darwinism. They continued to love science, and wanted to be a part of it, as long as God could be a part of it, too.

Can a creationist be a medical doctor?

Micah Spradling, who planned to become a doctor and specialize in prosthetics, had no problem in his Texas Tech classes with learning about the evidence for human evolution from lower animals. But he was surprised and concerned when his professor, Michael Dini, demanded in 2002 that he "truthfully and forthrightly" affirm it if he expected a letter of recommendation to medical school.[8] The language is reminiscent of creeds and religious revivals. Worse, Dini was the only professor whose recommendation would be relevant to Spradling's career plans.

When it comes to medicine, Dini argued, on his Web site: "How can someone who does not accept the most important theory in biology expect to properly practice in a field that is so heavily based on biology?" Acknowledging that all the needed information on human ancestry is not yet available, he said that if physicians do not accept common ancestry of humans and lower animals, it is easy to imagine that they can make "poor clinical decisions."

Several area doctors took issue with Dini's claims and said that evolution has nothing to do with clinical decisions. "That would be like Texas Tech telling him he had to be a Christian to teach biology," said one.[9] He asked: "How dare someone who has never treated a sick person purport to impose his feelings about evolution on someone who aspires to treat such people?"[10]

The university backed Dini, arguing that the decision to write a letter of recommendation was a personal one. An official also claimed in a letter released to a newspaper that Dini was a devout Christian who had studied for the priesthood and that his criteria "are not discriminatory against Christians." The university's Honors College had also named him Teacher of the Year in 1998–1999. Michael Duff, in his column in Universitydaily.net, described Dini as "defending his profession against barbarians who would tear it down."[11]

It came out that Dini was in the habit of talking about religion in his biology class. One student claimed that the professor wasn't "anti-religion" but that he "just believes that religion has no insight on evolution," a comment that gives more insight into the character of the class discussion than the student perhaps realized.[12]

Liberty Legal Institute, which specializes in religious freedom, contended that Dini is a state-paid official using a state-funded Web site to discriminate.[13] In January 2003, the US Justice Department investigated a complaint filed by the Institute.

After discussions between the university, the Liberty Institute, the Justice Department, and Dini, the professor changed his policy in 2003. He changed the wording slightly so that students must be able to explain the Darwinian theory of evolution in scientific terms, while not being required to explicitly profess a belief in it.[14] Justice department lawyer Ralph F. Boyd, Jr., assistant attorney general for civil rights, said:

(cont'd)

> The new policy rightly recognizes that students don't have to give up their religious beliefs to be good doctors or good scientists. A biology student may need to understand the theory of evolution and be able to explain it. But a state-run university has no business telling students what they should or should not believe in.[15]
>
> Micah Spradling was not in a position to wait for the mess to be sorted out the following year. He transferred to Lubbock Christian University. He almost didn't get in because the classes were full, but when LCU officials were shown Dini's original policy, they relented and made a place for him.
>
> This incident shows the extent to which Darwinism is a religion among academics. Consider the following. A likely influence on Darwin was Adam Smith's "invisible hand" of the free market economy.[16] Would the academics have been as complacent if the class were economics, and the student was punished for doubting the "invisible hand"? Certainly not, because even a full professor is permitted to doubt the invisible hand. To doubt Darwin is scandalous; to doubt Adam Smith is not. And yet there is probably far more evidence for Adam Smith's views.

2. Do Any YECs Have Science Credentials?

According to historian Numbers, in the 1920s, creationists depended for scientific expertise on very slender resources, "on a few teachers in Christian colleges (none with even a master's degree in biology or geology), on a physician or two, and on a medical-school dropout."

That situation slowly began to change toward mid-century. In 1963, when the Creation Research Society (the leading creationist organization of the late 20th century) was organized, five of 10 founders had earned doctorates in biology from major universities. Two had PhDs in science or engineering.[17]

By 1981, when Darwinists clashed with creationists over the teaching of creationism in Arkansas, the plaintiffs who opposed creation science overwhelmingly came from religious organizations. But, says Numbers, "virtually all of the experts testifying in support of creationism possessed graduate degrees in science."[18]

3. Do Any Creationists Work for Science Organizations or Generate Ideas Worthy of Study?

Kurt Wise: The Road Back to Dayton

Kurt Wise is associate professor of science and director of the Center for Origins Research and Education at Bryan College in Dayton, Tennessee. In

1989, after training under Stephen Jay Gould at Harvard, he moved—creationist position intact—to the original scene of the Scopes trial, to spend his career developing young earth creationist models of biology and biogeography.

No doubt because of his Harvard background, Wise has no time for those who want to "fight evolution." He asks—as all scientists do—where the scientific models are that would replace it.

Wise is unsparing about the current shortcomings of organized young earth creationism. Specifically, he denounces "kitchen table ministries," among whom he includes the giant Answers in Genesis and crusading hucksters of poor quality materials who target homeschooled students. In many cases, he laments, "the poor kids are being taught garbage."[19] "No one, in my opinion, is doing a good or even a fair job with primary or secondary school curricula," he also complained recently.[20]

However, he thinks things may be changing. In the fall of 2003, Broadman and Holman published a college textbook on baraminology, edited by one of his associates, Todd C. Wood. (Creationists divide animals into "kinds" or *baramins* rather than species. For example, wolves, dogs, and coyotes might be considered one baramin, rather than three separate species.[21])

So, what was it like working for Gould? "It was a fabulous learning experience," Wise recalls.

> Steve knew my views from the beginning and we spoke about it from time to time. Steve was what I called a heart libertarian—he believed that everyone has the right to believe whatever they want. Therefore he not only believed I had a right to believe anything I wanted about origins, but he even defended my right to be a creationist. His response to my position was usually to say something like, "Of course you know I think you are wrong." Steve always seemed to see me as an intriguing curiosity—probably wishing (as most of my professors did) that I was an evolutionist and not a creationist.

And what is it like for Wise to live in Dayton, forever notorious as the scene of the Scopes trial? There has been much hurt, he says, over what the media did to the town during the trial, and afterward in the movie *Inherit the Wind*.

> When I moved to Dayton in 1989 there was still a fair bit of anger and resentment about the issue throughout the town. As older members of the community have died off, however, the attitude seems to have gradually

shifted to somewhere between indifference and an opportunity to maintain a livelihood via tourism.

Wise, who calls himself a "neocreationist," is straightforward about the fact that a literal reading of the Bible motivates him. If you don't accept a literal reading, he says, "you are talking about 20 to 25 percent of the Bible you have to toss out immediately. But it doesn't stop there. The very doctrines we hold true become threatened."[23] In that respect, he is similar to Richard Dawkins, who feels that Darwinism enables him to be intellectually fulfilled as an atheist.[24]

Wise's search for a creationist model that validates the Bible has taken him to the Grand Canyon and Death Valley to study fossils. With geologist colleague Steve Austin, he has presented a poster session (1995) and a paper to the Geological Society of America (1999) on the boiling-water death of fossil nautiloids (ancient shellfish) in the region, which he attributes to the catastrophes associated with a comparatively recent worldwide flood.

He thinks that those who question his right to do science if he is a creationist are on the wrong side of history. "In the history of science, who cared where your idea came from?" he argues, as long as it results in useful findings.[25]

> **Kurt Wise on Creationism**
>
> Although there are scientific reasons for accepting a young earth, I am a young-age creationist because that is my understanding of the Scripture. As I shared with my professors years ago when I was in college, if all the evidence in the universe turns against creationism, I would be the first to admit it, but I would still be a creationist because that is what the Word of God seems to indicate. Here I must stand.[22]
>
> —Kurt Wise

John Baumgardner: Young Earth and High Tech

Geophysicist John Baumgardner has been hailed by *U.S. News and World Report* (1997) as a world-class expert in the design of computer models for planetary catastrophes.[26] He has worked as a technical staff member at Los Alamos (New Mexico) National Laboratory since 1984.

Baumgardner went to graduate school specifically to get professional credentials in order to study the impact of the worldwide flood of Noah, which he believes is responsible for present-day landforms and fossils. As part of his PhD research, he developed Terra, a three-D computer model of earth's interior, funded by NASA. NASA wanted models for catastrophic events, in order to study both Earth and other planets. Venus, for example, is thought to have been recently resurfaced in some sort of catastrophe.

Like Wise, Baumgardner is upfront about his religious convictions, telling the media: "I would say my primary goal in my scientific career is a defense of God's Word."[27] His views have never been a problem at Los Alamos, where he is part of Megaviews Forum, a group of mostly Christian scientists. Some of these scientists are young earthers, and he says that there are also young earthers at NASA.

Both Baumgardner and Wise have benefited from a gradually growing acceptance that catastrophes can explain changes in the planet's history. For example, it is now widely believed that an asteroid impact, rather than natural selection, killed off the dinosaurs.

Because they believe what they do, creationists like Baumgardner and Wise research ideas that no one else would research, and sometimes produce valuable information. In many enterprises, starting from a non-mainstream position can have that effect.

RATE Group

Given the importance they attach to a young earth, key young earth scientists, including Baumgardner, have devoted considerable energy to disproving the methods of dating that peg the age of the earth as about 4.5 billion years. They would like to see an age in the 6000–10,000-year range, but any age range in the thousands rather than the billions would probably be good news for them.

The RATE (Radioactivity and the Age of The Earth) group, a joint project of the Institute for Creation Research (ICR) and the Creation Research Society (CRS), has recently released a paper arguing that radioactive decay rates can be drastically accelerated. In a study of zircons, a decay rate expert (who apparently did not know that RATE was a creationist project) estimated the age of the sample submitted as between 4000 and 14,000 years, not the expected 1.5 billion years.[28]

Whatever the eventual fallout from the radioactive decay rate controversy, the young earth scientists will certainly force the others to ensure that their methods are reliable—something that would not be nearly as likely if everyone just assumed that the billion-year age was correct and suppressed dissent.

4. Do Creationists Know Nothing About Evolution?

In the mid-20th century, before many scientists were involved, young earth creationism often provided a refuge for folk beliefs that were irrelevant to the larger issues over which Bryan wrestled with Darrow in 1925. For example, in the 1960s, the Bible-Science Association's *Newsletter* and the CRS *Quarterly* provided a forum for geocentrists, people who continue to believe that earth is the *stationary* center of the universe—to the despair of most creationists.[29] In recent years, creation science organizations have tried to prevent the use of their movement to propagate these beliefs.[30]

Today's creationist is often well informed about the sciences. In fact, Cornell evolutionist William Provine warns that, far from knowing less about evolution than others, creationists typically know much more. He pictures the following scene:

> Biology class in a small high school starts the section on evolution. The Jehovah's Witnesses in class know far more than any other students in the class about evolution, and they are sure it did not occur. Witnesses begin thinking about evolution at a very early age. They are ready to talk about evolution in the class.[31]

The young Witness—or conservative Christian, for that matter—has good reason to think about evolution from a very early age. The creationist must think about evolution in order to remain a creationist. That said, creationism offers a different, but often surprisingly parallel, view of the universe and life on earth. The first verse of Genesis can be compared with the Big Bang theory.[32] The extinction of the dinosaurs by Noah's Flood can be contrasted with the extinction of the dinosaurs by an asteroid. The need to articulate and defend one's beliefs often results in retaining many scientific concepts that would otherwise be forgotten after high school, and learning many new ones as well.

5. Are Creationists' Beliefs Odder Than Mainstream Science Beliefs?

Creationists on the Origin of Death and Evil . . .

Some young earth creationist beliefs flow from and lead to fundamentally different assumptions about life than Darwinist ones. In particular, Christian creationists believe, based on their reading of key passages in the Bible, that death and decay entered the world because of human sin. Thus, the cruelty that the Darwinist attributes to the workings of blind laws and chance, the creationist attributes to the effects of human sin on nature.

If all creatures, including human beings, were created at about the same time—as the creationist insists—human sin may indeed be an obvious explanation for cruelty and waste in nature as well as in society. According to this view, the evil effects of sin in nature will only be eliminated when human beings are redeemed at the end of time.[33]

However, if the non-YEC geologists are right, and life on earth is billions of years old, human sin cannot be a simple explanation for all instances of death and evil. The relevant Bible passages can be read with profit, and a link can be made, but the whole subject requires more complex interpretation. So the creationists who defend a young earth have a great deal at stake: an apparently simple interpretation of the Christian faith vs. a more nuanced and complex one.[34]

Does "Many Universes" Cosmology Make Better Sense?

Young earth creationists are often ridiculed for their belief that life on earth is less than 10,000 years old. It is worth looking into the hidden assumptions that underlie the ridicule. Are creationist beliefs weirder than the beliefs of many non-creationist physicists? If so, why?

According to physicist Paul Davies:

> *A Key Bible Passage on the Origin and Redemption of Evil in the Natural World*
>
> The creation waits in eager expectation for the sons of God to be revealed. For the creation was subjected to frustration, not by its own choice, but by the will of the one who subjected it, in hope that the creation itself will be liberated from its bondage to decay and brought into the glorious freedom of the children of God. We know that the whole creation has been groaning as in the pains of childbirth right up to the present time.
>
> Romans 8:19–22, NIV

Many physicists now think that there are more than three spatial dimensions ... since certain theories of subatomic matter are neater in 9 or 10 dimensions. So maybe three is a lucky number that just happened by accident in our cosmic neighborhood—other universes may have five or seven dimensions.[35]

Now, these interesting ideas may be right or wrong, but they primarily support a theory of the universe that does not require a designer. As Davies puts it: "Perhaps these parameters were all fluke products of cosmic luck, and our exquisitely friendly "universe" is but a minute oasis of fecundity amid a sterile space–time desert."[36]

The creationists claim that earth cannot be more than 10,000 years old because that is the simplest way to understand Genesis. The cosmologists speculate on unobservable universes that are, they hope, design-free and creation-free. In the absence of evidence, both parties are making a philosophical choice. Both positions are subject to much ridicule.[37] And both parties want science that supports their beliefs, with neither accepting any substitutes.

6. The Hoax Watch: Jurassic Park–the Prequel! vs. the Feathered Fraud

One of the most controversial creationist beliefs is that human beings and dinosaurs have lived at the same time. This is often used as proof that creationist scientists are deluded compared with non-creationist scientists. Which leads us to the Wild West saga of the Paluxy mantracks.

In 1950, a creationist paleontologist named Clifford Burdick claimed that some tracks in the lower Cretaceous limestone along the Paluxy River near Glen Rose, Texas—previously considered to be odd dinosaur tracks—were actually human footprints. Obviously, if he was right, paleontology would detonate.

Creationists jumped at the possibility that the dinosaur tracks suggested that earth is not old.[38] In 1971, Eden Films (now called Films for Christ) distributed a movie on this theme called *Footprints in Stone*. Shown in hundreds of schools and churches, this documentary convinced many that dinosaurs and humans had once lived together. In 1980, John Morris, son of Henry Morris, published *Tracking Those Incredible Dinosaurs and the Men Who Knew Them*,[39] promoting the "mantracks," as Glenrose residents called them. By 1983, there was a Creation Evidences Museum (1983) near the

Dinosaurs in the Bible?

Some passages in the Book of Job, perhaps the oldest book of the Bible, refer to creatures known as Behemoth (Job 40:15–24) and Leviathan (Job 41:1–34). No one is sure just what these mysterious animals were.

A conventional interpretation is that Behemoth is a hippopotamus and Leviathan is a crocodile, though some of the details don't quite fit. Many young earth creationists argue that these creatures were late surviving dinosaurs. For example, about Leviathan we read, "Any hope of subduing him is false; the mere sight of him is overpowering" (Job 41: 9).

It's true that some people would describe their neighbor's undisciplined mutt that way, but Job clearly pictured something truly awesome, whatever it was.

Paluxy and Dinosaur Valley State Park.

Under pressure from investigators with less emotional investment in the story, a different explanation for the mantracks emerged. It seems that Cretaceous dinosaurs usually walked on their toes, like cats (digitigrade). However, for unknown reasons, they sometimes walked on the entire foot, like humans (plantigrade). When they did so, their tracks resembled human tracks. In 1986, John Morris began to retract the Paluxy claims, and the film was withdrawn.

Discredited claims can have unexpected implications, decades later. Stockwell Day, the newly elected leader of the Canadian Alliance conservative political party, lost a lot of support during the 2000 election campaign when the CBC (the government broadcaster) aired the accusation of an Alberta college professor that Day believed that "the world was 6,000 years old and that men walked with dinosaurs."[41] This was the first of a range of misfortunes that saw Day removed as party leader in 2002.

From a scientific perspective, the saga was not entirely a waste. As investigator Ronnie Hastings writes: "Our pursuit of the mantracks has led to new insights into dinosaur locomotion and, perhaps, dinosaurian behavior."[42] But the creationists, of course, were written off as hopeless, principally because they were accused of seeing what they wanted to see and did not consider other reasonable explanations. If so, are they the only ones who do this?

The Search for Noah's Ark

If Noah's Ark is ever found, many creationist claims can be tested. Creationists have been trying to find the Ark for a long time, suffering the ridicule of skeptics as a consequence. But the creationists are no longer the only ones looking for it. Currently, Robert Ballard, who found the *Titanic*, is also searching.

There was a huge rise in water levels in Western Asia about 7000 years ago, but most geologists have argued that the waters rose gradually. In 1997, however, geologists Walter Pitman and William Ryan published a study arguing that a sudden, catastrophic flood caused the Mediterranean to overflow into the Black Sea, raising water levels by 511 feet. Such a rise would, of course, eliminate non-marine life, except perhaps for human rescue efforts, such as the Ark.

Interestingly, Noah's Flood is taken for granted among Armenians, who often include the Ark in paintings of Mt. Ararat, where it is said to have come to rest. Many Armenians consider themselves descendants of Noah.[40]

And the hunt goes on.

It's a Bird! It's a Dinosaur! It's a. . . um . . . Fraud

Young earth creationists are often ridiculed for the mantracks episode, but other paleontologists have also been the victims of self-delusion in recent years and could do well to take a hard look in the mirror.

Consider the feathered dinosaur fraud. In November 1999, *National Geographic* published an amazing find: a fossil of a feathered dinosaur, dubbed "Archaeoraptor," appeared to prove that birds evolved from carnivorous dinosaurs. "Feathers for T. Rex?" was the coy title. In January 2000, the prestigious magazine quietly retracted its claim. The fossil turned out to be a composite of different animals cleverly joined—not dinosaur feathers, after all, but horsefeathers.[43]

Much worse, a wave of high-profile frauds in key sciences in recent years[44] has prompted Britain's Royal Society to rethink the way in which research results are publicized.[45]

Do Darwinists Have Any Advantage in Dealing with Fraud?

One troubling possibility is that a Darwinist might be less able, rather than more able, to avoid fraud than a creationist. Consider, for example, philosopher Michael LaBossière's musings on fraud in science.[46] In a spectacular display of Social Darwinism, LaBossière suggests that morality is a product of Darwinian natural selection. Scientists follow it because it advances their careers, not because there is actually a God-given truth that must be acknowledged. If morality does not advance a scientist's career, the scientist should not follow it. Except, he argues, what if everyone behaved that way? Then the system would collapse.

For some reason, LaBossière believes that people will avoid dishonesty, even under personal pressure, because they fear what would happen if everyone else is dishonest. That is naive. If everyone is dishonest, cheating is society's real value system and it is the only way to survive. And yes, the system will collapse. But . . . people who cheat may survive the collapse and start another cheat system. People who refuse to cheat while living in a cheat system will not likely survive.

In reality, people who refuse to cheat typically have a commitment to truthfulness that goes beyond Darwinian survival. Overall, if LaBossière is right, Darwinism provides much less incentive to avoid outright cheating than the fear a creationist is likely to have of the final judgment of God.[47]

Of course, however differently they might view deliberate fraud, the creationist and the Darwinist are equally subject to *self*-delusion. *National Geographic* staff were not dishonest; they believed in the feathered fraud for the same reason as the creationists believed in the mantracks. The find confirmed cherished beliefs. Self-delusion is difficult to avoid completely because the victim (oneself) is a consenting adult. Who gladly learns the truth of that old saying about things that seem too good to be true?

7. Are Creationists the Only Ones Whose Science Is Based on Prior Beliefs?

Darwinists are as likely as creationists to shut their ears to whatever conflicts with their prior beliefs. In an interesting passage in *The Blind Watchmaker*, Richard Dawkins asserts that, even if we were to see a statue of the Virgin Mary wave to us, we should not assume that we have witnessed a miracle but rather that the atoms somehow all moved in one direction at the same time.[48] In other words, we should reject the idea of a miracle in principle, *even if we see one.*

Dawkins's view is not surprising. What people think is reasonable always depends, to some extent, on their prior attitudes, values, and beliefs. Because Dawkins believes that miracles cannot occur, he advises anyone who sees such an event to ignore it.

Michael Behe, an intelligent design theorist, comments on Dawkins's advice about the statue:

> Most people who saw a statue come to life would tell Dawkins that there are more things in heaven and earth than are dreamt of in his philosophy, but they couldn't make him join the Church of England.[49]

No, indeed. If the litmus test for belief in Darwinism is the willingness to set aside contrary evidence, then Darwinism is no different in principle from creationism. In that case, the decision to support one over the other is a choice about beliefs, not about evidence.

Do Scientists' Religious Beliefs Make Any Difference to Their Views on Origins?

As noted earlier, most scientists have religious views similar to those of the general public. For example, 41% of American PhD scientists believe in a God to whom one can pray.[50]

However, the picture changes drastically when you consider those who belong to elite academies such as the American National Academy of Sciences (NAS). For example, when polled by historians Edward Larson and Larry Witham in 1996, only 7% of members expressed personal belief in

God and over 72% expressed personal disbelief. The remainder expressed doubt or agnosticism.[51]

The elite scientists' views are radically different from those turned up by typical public opinion polls that show, for example, that 95% of Americans believe in God. For that matter, more than 8 in 10 Americans believe in miracles, which means that most would not heed Richard Dawkins's advice about the statue.[52]

The pollsters' finding about NAS members is significant because organizations such as NAS promote Darwinism to the education system. In 1998, Bruce Alberts, then president of NAS, urged the teaching of Darwinian evolution in public schools, claiming that "there are many very outstanding members of this academy who are very religious people, people who believe in evolution, many of them biologists." Larson and Witham commented crisply: "Our survey suggests otherwise."[53]

It would be a mistake to assume that the scientific elite holds the views that it does simply because it consists of elite scientists. Quantum chemist Fritz Schaeffer III notes that

> whatever influences people in their beliefs about God, it does not appear to have much to do with having a Ph.D. in science. It is true in science, as well as in essentially all other professions, that after income levels reach perhaps $50,000 per year (in North America), further increases in salary may be correlated with higher percentages of agnosticism.[54]

In other words, the people who are most successful in the secular culture of modernism are most accommodated to its values. That is not really very surprising. Nor is it surprising that the cultural elite assumes that its beliefs should be taught in the school system as fundamental truths and that non-elite beliefs should be suppressed.

The Key Question That Is Never Asked . . .

Mainstream media usually report on the pronouncements of organizations like NAS as if they were neutral, objective sources of information or wisdom. In other words, the organization is given a free ride! The rude question about the *specifics* of religious belief—which would reveal that NAS is dominated by atheists—is just not asked. So the story never gets out, that NAS members may be right or wrong about Darwinism, but they are no more objective about it than the creationists are.

ASA: Between a Rock and a Hard Place

Sadly, the American Scientific Affiliation (ASA), an organization of Christians in science who mostly believe in Darwinian evolution,[55] learned this the hard way when it tried to mediate the creation–evolution controversy.

In 1984, the National Academy of Sciences printed a booklet called *Science and Creationism: A View from the National Academy of Sciences*, warning about the dangers of creationism. In response, under the leadership of Christian evolutionist Walter Hearn, the ASA put out its own work in 1986, *Teaching Science in a Climate of Controversy: A View from the American Scientific Affiliation*. It was an attempt to explore a middle way in which science and religion could coexist.

According to Ronald Numbers, ASA's peaceable attempt to replace controversy with constructive dialogue outraged many Darwinists. Apparently led by William J. Bennetta, they denounced the ASA for promoting "creationism in disguise."[56] Stephen Jay Gould, who was widely regarded as conciliatory toward religion, Niles Eldredge, and other Darwinists denounced *Teaching Science. The Science Teacher* raised the stakes by publishing a group of essays called "Scientists Decry a Slick New Packaging of Creationism."

Numbers comments: "Indeed, it was a strange world that could seem to turn Hearn, perhaps the most notorious and uncompromising evolutionist in the evangelical world, into a dangerous crypto-creationist."[57] The situation was all the more ironic because the ASA had abruptly dismissed the creationists, with insults, over three decades earlier.

ID advocate Phillip Johnson offers an explanation:

> Really zealous scientific naturalists do not recognize subtle distinctions among theists. To the zealots, people who say they believe in God are either harmless sentimentalists who add some vague God-talk to a basically naturalistic worldview, or they are creationists. In either case, they are fools, but in the latter case they are also a menace.[58]

The fact that ASA wanted to mediate made the ASA members appear to be a "menace," because their aspiration implied that people who believe in God could be reasonable. Overall, one thing emerged as perfectly clear: To many prominent Darwinists, no one who professed any form of belief in God was acceptable, even in a peacemaker role, not even if they also believed somehow in Darwinism.

Disbelief in or doubt about Darwinism, let alone subscribing to another view, is seen by many elite scientists as a profound act of disloyalty to modern Western civilization. One visiting Chinese professor described the situation succinctly, when talking to Darwinism critic Jonathan Wells: "In China we can criticize Darwin, but not the government; in America, you can criticize the government, but not Darwin."[59] In both hemispheres, the contention over the forbidden issue is more likely to increase than decrease.

Is There a Growing Split Within Creationism?

Creation scientists no more think alike than do evolutionists, though most of their controversies are too technical to enlighten anyone but the participants. However, one controversy is worth profiling for what it says about the future direction of creationism.

The young earth creationists are pushing the old earth creationists out of many Christian settings. Radio astronomer Hugh Ross, a major exponent of the day–age theory (old earth creationism),[60] operates a ministry called Reasons to Believe, which depends heavily on astronomy for the purpose of evangelizing scientists. Ross, who accepts that the earth is billions of years old, has criticized young earth creationism in his books, saying, for example:

> Few, if any, other issues today generate as much animosity between Christians and secularists as does this doctrine of a recent, 144-hour creation week. The idea that the beginning of the universe, Earth, and life on earth dates back only a few thousand years makes a mockery of all the sciences and infuriates scientists.[61]

Ken Ham, president of Answers in Genesis—probably the biggest and most successful of the young earth creationist organizations—has struck back with an extended attack on Ross, accusing him of both scientific and theological incompetence. Ham targeted first of all Ross's belief that the Bible is compatible with the findings of modern astronomy, such as an old universe and the Big Bang.[62] (Answers in Genesis does not like the Big Bang because, while it is instantaneous, it assumes billions of years of later evolution, not just a week.)

In mid-2003, the two sides were quarreling over the proposed terms of a debate. Characteristically, Ross wanted a debate at a science facility, in front of PhD-level astronomers, but young earth physicist Russell Humphreys wanted a debate in front of the supporters of both sides. While young earth creationism now boasts, as we have seen, a number of credentialed scientists, groups like Answers in Genesis remain principally lay movements.

For Ross, there is bitter irony in the current young earth creationist attacks on the Big Bang. As he told Humphreys in his letter:

> You describe astronomers, in particular, as "economically and religiously" committed to the big bang when, ironically, they have been pushed—by the preponderance of evidence—to accept it. For decades they fought against it, especially for its implications about the Creator. Billions of dollars have been invested in studying it—mainly for the sake of finding an escape from it! And each effort to find a loophole has served to tighten the case for it—which presents problems for those who dislike its consistency with biblical cosmology.[63]

Ross seems to be caught in the crossfire between scientists who are committed to atheism and those who are committed to a young earth. About scientists in the middle—the *traditional* old earth (OEC) creationists—he says:

> OEC is loudly drummed out when it is detected; so those who hold to an OEC view either lie low or find the rare church where it is not an issue. . . . Typically, these folks must keep a very low profile, as I mentioned above, or find a church where the topic is rarely mentioned, or seek Christian fellowship in groups outside the local church.[64]

A number of scientists in Ross's position have crossed over into the intelligent design camp, focusing on the question of whether design is detectable and avoiding religious controversy. About the intelligent design advocates, Ross says, "In a sense I consider myself as a partner with them. But they are hampered by their 'big tent' approach (an unwillingness to offend YEC or reject their model)."[65]

In any event, while scientists who believed in any model of divine design in nature argued among themselves, in the early 1980s, the science establishment woke up to discover that young earth creationism, far from disappearing as expected, was alive and well and coming soon to a large church nearby. What happened then? Well, let's see . . .

Why Has Creationism Been Growing?

CHAPTER 12

The rise of creationism is politics, pure and simple; it represents one issue (and by no means the major concern) of the resurgent evangelical right. Arguments that seemed kooky just a decade ago have reentered the mainstream.

—Stephen Jay Gould (1941–2002)[1]

Profound but contradictory ideas may exist side by side, if they are constructed from different materials and methods and have different purposes. Each tells us something important about where we stand in the universe, and it is foolish to insist that they must despise each other.

—Neil Postman, culture critic, 1995[2]

While researching this book in 2003, I searched on the terms "creationism" + "quotations." A vast well of anti-creationist sayings googled up. There seemed to be no pro-creationist sayings in the online treasuries of quotations.

This is hardly because creationism is universally disbelieved. The polls show otherwise, and the Internet boasts a number of well-developed young earth creationist sites from many countries. So young earth creationism thrives, despite complete dismissal by the punditocracy whose thoughts are collected for the treasuries of quotations. *How* does it thrive in such a hostile environment?

The Wild Cards

Recall that in the 1950s, Darwinism was experiencing a revival. Neo-Darwinism merged Mendelian genetics and Darwinism so that, for the first time, there was a plausible explanation for how changes can be passed on to future generations.

More, in 1953, Stanley Miller and Harold Urey showed how amino acids, needed for life, can be created in a test tube, suggesting that the problem of the origin of life was also nearly solved. It wasn't anywhere near to being solved,[3] but many pundits believed that it was. Because pundits wrote and acted accordingly, the public effect was the same as if the problem had been solved.

Then the double helix of DNA was discovered in 1953. Thousands of media sources trumpeted that, soon, complete control over human nature would be possible. The science elite would decide humanity's fate. Endless magazine articles and television programs hummed and burbled the theme. The future looked bright for Darwinists, and they were ready to take on new challenges.

In 1950, Pope Pius XII had weighed in with the view that Darwinism was a serious hypothesis. Liberal churches, of course, had already completely accommodated to Darwinism. By the time *Inherit the Wind* (1955) effaced or misrepresented the cultural issues that Bryan had campaigned on, the fundamentalists were still largely invisible to the mainstream. Few knew or cared what they thought.

The outcome of the Scopes trial, as opposed to the Scopes myth that developed later, was a draw, as far as education in the United States was concerned. Scopes was convicted of teaching common ancestry of humans and apes from a textbook (though his conviction was later overturned on a technicality). The message that textbook publishers gleaned was: *Stay away from the whole topic of evolution.* And they did.

Many students arrive in high school not knowing the fundamental differences between a worm and a snake, apart from the different superstitions that popular culture assigns to them. The challenge is getting the student to understand—not Darwin's answer, that's the easy part—but the question that Darwin proposed an answer to. Before the neo-Darwinian synthesis of the early 1950s, there was no consensus on exactly how Darwinism was supposed to work. So, many education systems simply rolled on without Darwin, for better or worse.

However, in 1947–1948, the US Supreme Court reinterpreted a long-standing ban on teaching religion in the schools. Originally, the ban had meant that one sect should not be favored over another. But, in a series of decisions, it came to mean that no religious expression should be permitted at all. Significantly, in North American culture, creationism was interpreted as a religion, but Darwinism, despite clear evidence of its religious tendencies, was not.

Wild Card 1: The Soviet Union

In 1957, the Soviets launched Sputnik, the first satellite, and left Cold War Americans feeling very insecure. Americans decided that the solution was more and better science education. The new curricula sponsored by biology teacher groups promoted Darwinism. But, as we have seen, young earth creationism was also thriving at that time, so the new emphasis on Darwinism in the schools was met by power surges of creationism in the church basements.[4] Henry Morris's widely read *Genesis Flood* (1961) introduced young earth creationism to large new audiences. One thing that certainly helped the creationists was that the case for Darwinian evolution is almost always overstated in the science literature, so they have gained strength over the years simply by pointing out the exaggerations and omissions of their foes.[5]

Meanwhile, at the Darwin Centennial in 1959, Sir Julian Huxley delivered his famous oration announcing that evolution would be the new religion, leaving no doubt at all in the minds of those who were paying attention that many Darwinists were not simply disinterested scientists; they were definitely presenting a new worldview. That worldview would now be taught through the compulsory school system and reflected in prevailing social assumptions.

Wild Card 2: Disillusionment with Science

Then, another wild card was played. In the 1960s and 1970s, there was widespread disillusionment with elite science. This was mainly because the close links between the science establishment and the defense industries were seen as perpetuating the Cold War. Young people started looking for answers from other sources.

Non-religious or indifferently religious North Americans tried to understand life

> Evolution after Darwin had set itself up to be something more than science. It was a popular science, the science of the marketplace and the museum, and it was a religion—whether this be purely secular or blended in with a form of liberal Christianity.
>
> —Michael Ruse, philosopher[6]

> A nontheistic religion of secular evolutionary humanism has become, for all practical purposes, the official state religion promoted in the public schools.
>
> —Henry M. Morris, hydraulic engineer and creation advocate[7]

through antirealist philosophies, usually based on Eastern teachings; many conservative Christians, by contrast, put their faith in young earth creationism, which had come to be known as scientific creationism or creation science. In 1963, scientists committed to young earth beliefs founded the Creation Research Society. In 1974, Henry Morris brought out a handbook for teachers, *Scientific Creationism*. At that point, the conservative Christians were in a position to operate their own educational systems, which they increasingly did.

The conflict continued to boil. In 1968, the US Supreme Court struck down laws against teaching evolution. However, if anyone thought that judicial rulings would stamp out young earth creationism, they were mistaken. During the 1970s and 1980s, it began to spread out of its heartland in the South and the Midwest, throughout the United States.

Some of the growth can be attributed to key changes in the religious landscape. Young earth creationism grew chiefly among vibrant new religious movements that believed that life-changing experiences cannot be separated from vital and orthodox belief (often called "saving faith"). The conservative churches that were creationism's natural home were growing, and the liberal churches that were hostile to it were shrinking.[8]

Wild Card 3: Retooled Social Darwinism Hits the Streets

The 1970s also saw a resurgence of Social Darwinism, rebranded as sociobiology.[9] As always, Social Darwinism enraged many social justice activists by attributing problems such as racial discrimination, sexism, and poverty to the inevitable outworking of Darwinian evolution.[10] Members of the public who had been trained in arts rather than sciences came to know Darwinism principally through Social Darwinism, which managed to be both unattractive and unconvincing at the same time.[11]

The Establishment Wakes Up

By the 1980s, when Darwinists woke up, creationists were demanding equal time in the schools. In 1987, the US Supreme Court ruled that equal time for creationism was unconstitutional, but it didn't matter much any more. By then young earth creationism was already gaining a worldwide following. This included branches in Canada, Australia and New Zealand, Korea, Holland, Germany, Russia, the Middle East, and pretty much anywhere with access to the Internet.[12] There has also been a wave of creationist publishing. A representative book in the genre is *Science Comes Closer to the Bible* by Arimasa Kubo, a Japanese science writer, who offers: "English-speaking countries brought God's Good News to Japan. This book is a token of return thanks to them and a kind of reversed export of the Gospel from Japan."[13]

Not All Creationists Are Christians

Organized creationism started among conservative Christians in the United States and spread out mainly through Christian networks. Most national creationism Web sites[14] are sponsored by Christian groups who combine a creationist view of the origins of life and humanity with evangelism. However, there are some interesting exceptions:

Muslim creationism American creationists such as Henry Morris and Duane Gish provided materials to Muslims, but the idea has spread through Muslim channels. The Turkish book, *Evolution: A Bankrupt Theory*, by Adem Tatli (1990), features a preface by its publisher Ubeydullah Küçük, who charges: "Darwinism and evolutionary theory have given answers to origin questions that are unscientific, pessimistic, absurd, not in keeping with human dignity, and entirely in contradiction with universal absolute truths, and have thus become the opposite of wisdom."[15]

American Indian creationism Indian creationism has helped to fuel the growing repatriation movement, a protest against archeologists' practice of treating Indian burial sites as a "found" treasure, to be disposed for the archeologists' own purposes. "We never asked science to make a determination as to our origins," said Sebastian LeBeau, repatriation officer for the Cheyenne River Sioux, a Lakota tribe based in Eagle Butte, South Dakota. "We know where we came from. We are the descendants of the Buffalo people. They came from inside the earth after supernatural spirits prepared this world for humankind to live here. If non-Indians choose to believe they evolved from an ape so be it. I have yet to come across five Lakotas who believe in science and in evolution."[16]

Unlike the Muslims, who revere Jesus as a prophet, North American Indian creationists can be strongly anti-Christian.[17] This type of creationism was given a voice by Vine Deloria, Jr., in *Red Earth, White Lies: Native Americans and the Myth of Scientific Fact.*[18]

As mentioned in Chapter 9, by 2002, Richard Dawkins found himself embroiled in a controversy over the decision of a British religious charter school to teach creationism as a valid alternative "faith position" to evolution.[19] According to the *Guardian*, 10% of biology students in Britain hold creationist beliefs, with the proportion higher among Muslims.[20]

Timeline: Young Earth Creationism During Decades of the 20th Century

1850s–1920s		Christians mostly accept evolution
1920s–1950s		fundamentalists dissent; start own colleges, journals
	1930s	Scopes myth stereotypes Christians
	1940s	Neo-Darwinism grows; so does YEC
	1950s	YECs spurned by Christian science group, but launch massive campaign
1960s–1970s		widespread disillusionment with elite science
	1960s	growth of young earth creationism
1970s–1980s		creationism grows through US (spread associated with new religious movements)
1975–1980s		Darwinists attack YEC
1980s–2000s		YEC gains worldwide following

Timeline: Key Events in Creationism in the 20th Century

Scofield Bible promotes ancient earth	1909		
		1910–1915	*The Fundamentals* pamphlets guardedly accept God-guided evolution
			first sign of Young Earth Creationism
		1918	fundamentalists cite Darwinist beliefs for WWI carnage
US anti-evolution bills pass	1923		*New Geology* claims life on earth only 6000 years old
		1925	Scopes trial

(cont'd)

1938 Deluge Geology Society (DGS) founded	1938	
	1941	ASA founded; members are Christian scientists
ASA ridicules creationists Flood geology	1949	
Inherit the Wind misrepresents Scopes trial	1955	
Geoscience Research Institute founded	1957	
	1957	Sputnik spurs teaching of Darwinism
Darwin Centennial; Huxley's speech	1959	
	1961	*Genesis Flood* sparks young earth creationist revival
Creation Research Society founded	1963	
	1968	US Supreme Court strikes laws against teaching evolution
	1974	*Scientific Creationism*, Henry Morris's handbook for teachers
New Social Darwinism angers many	1975	
	1981	creationists seek equal time in schools
US National Academy of Sciences defends evolution	1984	
	1986	ASA mediates dispute but is attacked by atheistic Darwinists
equal time for creationism unconstitutional in US	1987	
	2002	Some British charter schools teach creationism as well as evolution

The Internet: A Boon for Creationism?

The Net has been praised or vilified by thousands of commentators, to no effect. Its size and power as an information democracy grows every year.[21] The most significant difference that the Internet makes to the creation–evolution debate (and to every debate) is its fundamental principle: *Every linked computer is the peer of every other linked computer.*[22] That's not just technobabble. As an outcome of the peer principle, the Internet eliminates the distinction between big and small, between establishment and underdog. Both can be found by search engines. On the Internet, it is nearly impossible for establishment organizations to ban—or even police—non-establishment ones. The establishment is forced to compete on the power of its ideas, together with its ability to convey them in a wired world. Some establishments make this adjustment successfully, and some don't.

Technology drives key changes in society, and the Internet has encouraged a huge practical democracy of ideas. Put another way: A creationist Web designer can put up a site that draws much more traffic and convinces many more people than a large, establishment science organization that embraces naturalistic evolution, spurns effective communication, and attempts to shut down discussion by threatening dissenters with lawsuits, failing grades, career oblivion, or a diagnosis of idiocy.

> The central lesson of technology in our time is this: "The Internet Changes Everything."
> —Reed Hundt, former Chairman, Federal Communications Commission[23]

The threats, even if carried out, will not achieve the desired goal of shutting down the communication of creationism, or of any other subject. In fact, the threats themselves join the communication buzz, a sort of cyberspace street drama in which the establishment organization is, inevitably under the circumstances, cast as the villain—or worse, the buffoon.

A further outcome of the wired world is that mainstream media no longer have a stranglehold on the *interpretation* of information of public interest. For example, it would be nearly impossible for modern media to get away with what H.L. Mencken got away with in 1925: portraying Dayton, Tennessee, as the last refuge for Neanderthal Man, when the town was in fact coping intelligently with a difficult issue, and doing so in a gracious, creative, and civic-minded way.

Today, the Daytons of the world have access to the Internet. If they are targeted by disinformation from elite journalists, equal time is as near as the nearest linked terminal. They can instantly broadcast corrections to all who care.[24] A person who questions the slant of a local opinion leader on evolution, for example, can access pages from around the world that offer alternatives. Those who cannot afford to subscribe to journals can at least read the abstracts online. They can buy an article of special importance or interest online. They can enter the names of the author or subjects in a search engine. They can write to the authors for more information, and may very well get a reply.

The Google search engine alone accesses more than 3.3 billion Web pages, as of this writing. In theory, everyone on earth could have a Web page by the end of the century.[25] There has never been a communications medium like the Internet before, and the world will never be the same. The establishment media have largely lost the power to simply suppress dissident information and simply deny legitimacy to its purveyors. They can still publish only what they wish, of course, but multiple different takes are available for no more trouble than entering a few key words in a search engine.

Overall, the Internet has been a significant boon to organized creationism. It greatly reduces the costs of providing information to the public, including a growing network of homeschoolers. That in turn reduces the amount of money that creationists need to raise in order to get their message out. Creationists are generally aware of the advantages the Net provides. For example, Creation Science Resource ministry, an online Web host for creationists established in 1995, notes: "The world wide web is readily accessible today in developed countries, and has become the first choice of information for the average person."[26]

The quality of the information provided is, of course, a separate question. The successful Internet user must be a discerning critic, here as elsewhere. But the main difference between the Internet and the *New York Times* is that the Internet gives you the tools and information to question the story you are reading. All you need to supply are the critical thinking skills.

A Who's Who of Major Creationist Organizations

Name	When founded	Founder	Location	Function	Key features
Answers in Genesis (www.answersingenesis.org)		Ken Ham	offices in seven countries	ministry	aims at worldwide reach
Bible-Science Association (www.creationsafaris.com)	1963	Walter and Valeria Lang	San Fernando, CA	local branches, aimed at families	field trips (creation safaris)
Creation Research Society (www.creationresearch.org)	1963	10 creation scientists	St. Joseph, MO	research institute	voting members are scientists
Geoscience Research Institute (www.grisda.org)	1958	Seventh-day Adventists	Loma Linda, CA	main interest is geology; old earth is allowed	raised bar for creationist research
Institute for Creation Research (www.icr.org)	1970	Henry Morris, father of YEC creationism	near San Diego, CA	graduate school on creationism	creationist museum, on-line courses
Reasons to Believe (www.reasons.org)	1986	astronomer Hugh Ross	Pasadena, CA	aimed at scientists	old earth creationists
Revolution Against Evolution (www.rae.org)	1984	Webmaster Douglas B. Sharp	Lansing, MI	online database, TV show	many creationist resources

Note: Many additional creationist organizations are listed by Revolution Against Evolution at http://www.rae.org/revevlnk.html.

How Many Young Earth Creationists Are Out There?

It is difficult to be sure how many YECs there are or whether their movement is still growing. Poll questions often offer simple options. The 1997 Gallup poll offers these three: God created humans pretty much in their present form in the last 10,000 years (44%), evolution was guided by God

(39%), and evolution was unguided by God (10%).[27] Anyone who checks off the first option is considered a young earth creationist.

Recorded human history—the humanity that most of us identify with—is almost entirely compressed into the last 10,000 years. How many respondents who checked the first option meant only that known human history is an outcome of God's will, or perhaps that "humans" means creatures we can identify as human, rather than furry hominids shrieking in the treetops?[28]

To identify young earth creationism, poll questions must be more explicit. For example, does the respondent believe that the creation of the earth took place in a single creation week of six 24-hour days? Were Adam and Eve individual humans who were directly created by God 6000 years ago, and do not share a common ancestor with chimpanzees? Was there no such thing as death before humanity succumbed to sin? Did Noah's Flood account for the extinction of most dinosaurs? These are key specific beliefs that characterize young earth creationists and distinguish them from those who merely believe that God directed or played a role in the origin of the universe, life, and humanity.[29]

The Strength of Creationist Beliefs

Creationists who take their stand on the literal truth of the Bible know that the Bible is true from personal experience, *not* from theological argument. Often, the personal experience is a life-changing one, to which contrary argument is irrelevant. One is reminded of US president George W. Bush, who makes his personal religious faith quite clear, alongside his struggle with a drinking problem for which he required the strength that faith gave him. Bush is skeptical of evolution and thinks that students should learn both creationism and evolution.[30] Incidentally, Ronald Reagan was another popular American president who took the same position.[31] His views had no apparent impact on his electoral chances; he was elected president twice.

It is interesting to contrast the drubbing that Stockwell Day received in the Canadian media over his support for creationism with the relative indifference of

> For the growth of the creationist movement has been fuelled by a sense of outrage at the way atheist beliefs and secular values are often presented as if they were part of biological science. To put it in the vernacular: if someone says "my science shows that your religion is bunk," the natural reaction is "well then there must be something wrong with your science."
>
> —D. Young,
> *Australasian Science*,
> April 2002[32]

Americans to Bush's views on the same subject. This is partly a cultural difference between the two countries. Canadians demand that their politicians support current establishment beliefs. Even those leaders who are expected to be agents of reform must reform the system while protecting the establishment and its beliefs.

Essentially, any science that appears to deny the power of a life-changing experience is itself likely to be denied outright. The conservative Christians of the United States respond not by banishing science but by seeking a different science, one that can accommodate what they know from experience to be true. The conflict between the fundamentalist and the metaphysical naturalist on a subject like this cannot be settled by judgments in law courts or statements from mainstream science bodies. It is hard to see how it can be settled at all.

Michael Ruse, for example, compares Darwinism to young earth (scientific) creationism, and says that

> even if Scientific Creationism were totally successful in making its case as science, it would not yield a scientific explanation of origins. Rather, at most, it could prove that science shows that there can be no scientific explanation of origins. The Creationists believe the world started miraculously. But miracles lie outside of science, which by definition deals only with the natural, the repeatable, that which is governed by law. Hence, Creationism can aspire only to a Pyrrhic victory: that the evidence of nature and the methodology of science show that no natural laws explain the ultimate past.[33]

In other words, it wouldn't matter to Ruse if Baumgardner and the RATE group turn out to be right about the age of the earth. What they are doing cannot be science in principle, even if it is correct.

So where are we? A science that cannot accommodate evolution denies evidence that most scientists are convinced is both real and vital. But a science that cannot accommodate the power of the Bible to change lives denies the experience of many millions of people. It may be too much to hope for an answer to this dilemma. But there is clearly a need for new directions.

Can Intelligent Design Provide Answers?

The young earth creationists disapprove of intelligent design theory just as Darwinists do, and for much the same reasons: ID is a different tack. It does not concern itself with Genesis. It simply extends the anthropic coincidences that we looked at in earlier chapters to biology. It keeps evolution while discarding Darwinism, by reintroducing the idea of design. Can that work? Let's see.

Design …
the Picture Is Coming In

PART FOUR

Intelligent Design: Why So Controversial?

CHAPTER 13

> Just when it seemed that natural causes might suffice to account for all natural phenomena, there were breakthrough discoveries in both mathematics and biology.
>
> —Charles Thaxton, biochemist[1]

> Intelligent design is not creationism and it is not naturalism. Nor is it a compromise or synthesis of these positions. It simply follows the empirical evidence of design wherever it leads. Intelligent design is a third way.
>
> —William Dembski, mathematician[2]

A guy doesn't take phone calls when he is parachuting into a forest fire. But Washington state biology teacher (and summertime smoke jumper) Roger DeHart happened to be pulling weeds, awaiting a fire call in the summer of 1997, when he was paged to line 1. It was his superintendent. And the news was amazing. The American Civil Liberties Union (ACLU) was threatening the school board with a lawsuit over the way DeHart taught evolution.

"I have always taught evolution. That has never been a question for me,"[3] he recalls. Throughout the 1990s, Roger DeHart had taught high school biology and environmental chemistry at Burlington-Edison High School near Seattle. He was, by all accounts, a popular teacher. Because he was interested in the new theory of intelligent design, he began bringing materials about it to the classroom. Although he is a Christian, he did not talk about God or religion; in fact, he tried to ensure that students could not tell what his position was.[4] He insisted that they argue the case for both sides, and encouraged them to think.

However, in 1997, one of his students and the student's parents complained to the ACLU that teaching about the intelligent design controversy amounted to teaching religion. Hence the threat of a lawsuit.

The superintendent investigated, and found no impropriety.

Angry letters from the ACLU and the Darwin lobby poured into the Board. Then, in 1998, the ACLU went to the media.

To his amazement, DeHart became a cover story in the *Los Angeles Times* and the subject of an attack ad signed by 350 people in his home town[5], as well as of dishonest journalism[6] and of gag orders from his principal. All stemming from his interest in intelligent design.

Students tried to defend him. One senior wrote a letter, supported by other students, saying in part:

> I am writing in response to the quote by the administration that the complexities of the evolution/creationism issue were "far above" the level of high school freshmen. My fellow students and I take personal offense at this comment and believe it is typical of this administration . . . We grapple with such concepts as Shakespearian literary analysis, foreign languages, advanced algebra, and in biology, concepts such as deoxyribonucleic acid, cloning and genetic engineering. This curriculum design which paints the student body as "unsophisticated" and below the level of mainstream publications stands in stark contrast to the higher education Burlington students pursue after graduation. . . . These comments are an insult to the intelligence of the student body of Burlington-Edison High School, and I believe an apology is necessary.[7]

The administration did not apologize; it bailed. Faced with the threat of a costly lawsuit from ACLU, the Board told DeHart to teach nothing but the text, which provided a standard overview of Darwinism. This overview included material that appears to support Darwinism but is in reality questioned or discredited in the science literature.[8] DeHart was forbidden to provide articles from *Nature* or *American Biology Teacher* that corrected the errors in the textbook. In his own words, DeHart "was told not to teach anything but the text even if it is wrong."[9]

When DeHart moved to a new school district, the controversy followed him, including four front page stories in the local paper. His new administration continued to be besieged by media and by angry letters from the Darwin lobby. Even before he took his new job at Marysville High, he was threatened with reassignment. Later, in 2001, after 23 years of distinguished teaching in biology, he was reassigned—to Earth Science. His place was taken by a physical education teacher with no experience in biology.[10] He finally gave up on public education and now teaches at Oaks Christian High School in Westlake Village.[11]

Another area teacher, Doug Cowan, who teaches at Curtis High School in University Place, admitted to the media in 2001 that for the past nine years he had also been exploring the intelligent design hypothesis. He told the *Tacoma News*: "I'll probably be under attack by the ACLU too. But that's the nature of science. It's always controversial."[12]

But why this controversy? Why now? Why so intense? What *is* the modern intelligent design hypothesis, and why is the Darwin lobby so anxious to suppress any discussion of it?

What Is Really at Issue?

DeHart had run afoul of the establishment by encouraging his students to ask about the big question we considered earlier: Can science consider the possibility that the universe was designed by an intelligent creator? Or is such an idea intrinsically beyond what science can consider? Must we accept Darwinism, in the face of mounting problems, merely because it makes the big question unaskable?

There are two important differences between creationism[13] and intelligent design. First, unlike creationists, intelligent design advocates accept evolution—but they doubt that it can do everything that Darwinists claim. Second, their purpose is not to support Genesis, but to follow the evidence wherever it leads.[14] ID advocate Phillip Johnson puts it like this:

> The question for now is not whether the vast claims of Darwinian evolution conflict with Genesis, but whether they conflict with the evidence of biology. To make that question visible, it is necessary to distinguish between the dictates of materialist philosophy and the inferences that one might legitimately draw from the evidence in the absence of a materialist bias. So I put this simple question to the Darwinian establishment: What should we do if empirical science and materialist philosophy are going in different directions?

Suppose, for example, that the evidence suggests that intelligent causes were involved in biological creation. Should we follow the evidence or the philosophy?[15]

But why should evidence and philosophy be at loggerheads? Part of the answer may lie in the history of design arguments.

Traditional Design Arguments

For 2000 years, most Western scientists assumed that the universe was designed. They did not think that, as a consequence, they should cease to try to understand it. But they assumed that design underwrites the idea that a rational explanation exists. Everyone wondered whether some things could have been designed better—but that was the province of theology, not science.

The most widely known traditional argument for design is "Paley's watch." It is often used to warn students away from arguments for design, which are called "natural theology."

Eighteenth-century Anglican theologian William Paley (1743–1805) argued

> This most beautiful system of the sun, planets, and comets, could only proceed from the counsel and dominion of an intelligent and powerful Being.
>
> —Isaac Newton, developer of laws of gravity[16]

that the existence of God can be demonstrated from the apparent design of the universe. In *Natural Theology* (1802), he argued that if you found a watch out in a field, you would assume, because of its complex nature, that it was a designed object. The universe was a similar object, in Paley's view. A reasonable person would assume, based on its complexity, that it was designed. Paley's audience would find this particular example compelling because the pocket watch was just coming on the market in his day.[17] Paley argued not only for the existence of a designer, but for God, as presented in the Bible. He felt that the universe was as good as it could be.

Skeptical philosopher David Hume (1711–1776) is often said to have refuted Paley's idea of design. In fact, Hume, who published *Dialogues Concerning Natural Religion* 23 years before Paley, does not present arguments against design. Rather, Hume shows that the design of the universe does not obviously support the idea of God, as presented in the Bible. The universe shows evils and imperfections. For that matter, it could have been designed by one god or many.[18] Hume was skeptical about the nature of the designer, but, contrary to widespread assumptions, he did *not* attempt to demonstrate that there is no design.

Traditional No-Design Arguments

The idea that design might not be necessary for life forms was first advanced in modern times by Darwin.[19] As we saw earlier, after the publication of *Origin of Species* (1859), Darwin and his followers argued that what looks like design is only an appearance created by the operation of natural selection on chance variations. In fact, "no design" was the beauty of natural selection. It was a theory that could eliminate design and a Designer, which simplified the concepts that scientists needed to consider.[20]

In 1986, Richard Dawkins introduced the term "designoid" to a broad public to describe this "appearance of design," when in reality there is no design. However, the new discoveries about the complexity of life, as a result of biochemistry, mean that Dawkins has a great deal more to explain than Darwin ever did. And, starting in the 1980s, some scientists quietly began to look for answers other than "no design."

Modern Design Arguments

In the early 1980s, a group of English-speaking, mostly Christian, scientists and intellectuals, including Charles Thaxton, Walter Bradley, and Dean Kenyon, would meet to talk about how best to understand the origin and development of life, in view of the new

The Real Core of Darwinism?

"The real core of Darwinism . . . is the theory of natural selection. This theory is so important for the Darwinian because it permits the explanation of adaptation, the "design" of the natural theologian, by natural means, instead of by divine intervention.

–Ernst Mayr, evolutionary biologist[21]

The functional design of organisms and their features would seem to argue for the existence of a designer. It was Darwin's greatest accomplishment to show that the directive organization of living beings can be explained as the result of a natural process, natural selection, without any need to resort to a Creator or other external agent. . . . Darwin's theory encountered opposition in religious circles, not so much because he proposed the evolutionary origin of living things (which had been proposed many times before, even by Christian theologians) but because his mechanism, natural selection, excluded God as the explanation accounting for the obvious design.

–Francisco Ayala, former president of the American Association for the Advancement of Science[22]

discoveries of barely fathomable complexity. In their view, the old arguments for design were too bound up with an old-fashioned kind of theology that sought to prove that all design was perfect. Still, the "no-design" option was increasingly unbelievable.[24] They began to construct modern arguments for design.

Modern design arguments are not a rehash of Paley. They stem from 20th-century science findings about the complexity of life that Darwin and his followers did not expect, any more than Hume or Paley did. Life processes are very much more complex than an 18th-century pocket watch, and new systems that are essential for life are being discovered all the time.

Design and Information Theory

The modern case for design is based on information theory. Information theory provides a tool for distinguishing between mere order, which can occur without design, and complex order, which probably cannot.

> **Richard Dawkins on "Designoids" Created by Natural Selection:**
>
> I think that the distinction between accident and design is clear, in principle if not always in practice, but this chapter will introduce a third category of objects which is harder to distinguish. I shall call them designoid (pronounced design-oid not dezziggnoid). Designoid objects are living bodies and their products. Designoid objects look designed, so much that some people—probably, alas, most people—think they are designed. These people are wrong. But they are right in their conviction that designoid objects cannot be the result of chance. Designoid objects are not accidental. They have in fact been shaped by a magnificently non-random process which creates an almost perfect illusion of design."
>
> –from *Climbing Mount Improbable* (1996)[23]

Life differs from non-life by the vast amounts of information it embodies. Every cell, for example, is full of tiny machines made of molecules, performing a variety of complex tasks. The molecules of life contrast sharply with the regular, simple, and repetitive patterns seen in non-living substances such as salt crystals. How does all this information organize and develop itself?

A complex form of information that we experience in our daily lives, such as a book, is created by an intelligence—ours. Rather than search for a means by which complex information would somehow organize itself by chance, Thaxton, Bradley, and their colleagues decided to assume that the information was not organized by chance, but by a designing intelligence. Apart from that, they would follow the evidence wherever it led.[25]

It is easier to understand the ID case for design if we look at the types of structure that surround us from the perspective of information theory.[27] Consider:

Simple Repetitive Structure (Periodic and Specified Order)

A periodic and specified order repeats a specific pattern over and over.[28] There is little information in these patterns, and only a few instructions are needed to specify (explain how to create) them.

A checkerboard pattern is an example of a simple, repetitive structure, exhibiting periodic (repeated) and specified (specific) order. You can create the pattern with few instructions: "First black square. Then white square. Repeat."

> Information theory is a special branch of mathematics that has developed a way to measure information. In brief, the information content of a structure is the minimum number of instructions required to describe or specify it, whether that structure is a rock or a rocket ship, a pile of leaves or a living organism. The more complex a structure is, the more instructions are needed to describe it.
>
> —Charles Thaxton, biochemist[26]

Random Structure (Aperiodic and Unspecified Complexity)

A pile of pebbles has a random structure. A random structure is the simplest type of complexity. There is great complexity, but no order. This is the opposite of the simple repetitive structure of the crystal or checkerboard, where there is great order but little complexity.

The pile, like the crystal or checkerboard, contains little information because few instructions are needed to specify it. "Pick up any pebble. Dump in pile" would be sufficient instruction. Pebbles can pile up randomly in this way as the result of the movement of water or ice.

High Information Content, No Simple Instructions (Aperiodic and Specified Information)

The truly puzzling type of information is the type that is characteristic of human artifacts, and is also written in our DNA. It does not follow a repetitive pattern (aperiodic). But it has a pattern that relates it to other information (specified), and it is complex (no simple instructions can create it). For example, the DNA in a cat embryo is a complex series of instructions for a kitten that the embryo is carrying out.[29] Complete instructions for creating the DNA would be as long as the DNA itself.

The only experience we have of complex, aperiodic, and specified information is the artifacts that are designed by intelligent agents: artworks and computers, for example. So the nub of the conflict between the intelligent design advocates and the Darwinists is this: The intelligent design advocates think that it is reasonable to assume that such complex artifacts as living creatures are not the product of either law or chance. Rather, they can be assumed to be designed, if they meet the criteria for design.

> Experience shows many examples of specified complexity, e.g., books, paintings, artifacts, produced by intelligence and none produced by natural processes. Living organisms are characterized not by order but by specified complexity, i.e., information. This dramatic development has profound implications for the design argument.
>
> —Charles Thaxton[30]

The Types of Information We Encounter

Type	Description	Agent	Example
Periodic and specified order	simple repetitive structure, simple instructions	law	checkerboard, crystals
Aperiodic and unspecified complexity	random structure, no simple instructions	chance	pile of pebbles
Aperiodic and specified information	high information content, no simple instructions	intelligent agent	novel, computer program, DNA

Note: An intelligent agent can produce a law-like repetitive pattern with few instructions (knitting) or a random mess (litter). But, according to ID theory, the process does not work in reverse. Law or chance do not produce complex, specified information.

The Darwinist argues that we must assume that life forms are not designed, and seek an explanation from natural law and chance alone. But perhaps what we must do instead is look at the evidence.

Living organisms embody a variety of features. Some could arise from natural causes. The origin of many is unclear. Some would be best explained by design. How can we tell?

Can Design Be Detected?

Several sciences today are organized around the detection of intelligent design. Was a suspicious fire the result of arson? Is an odd-looking stone just a rock, or is it a primitive tool? Could a pattern of radio waves be a signal from a distant galaxy? Forensics, archaeology, and the SETI search for extraterrestrial life all depend on discovering a pattern that cannot be the result of natural law or chance, and therefore must be a result of intelligent design. So, if design cannot be detected, these sciences should not exist.

But can design be detected in nature? Michael Behe's concept of irreducible complexity—"A biological system is irreducibly complex when its operation requires the cooperation of numerous parts, none of which performs a useful function unless all are present"[32]—is proposed by ID advocates as a starting point for detecting design.

As we saw earlier, an irreducibly complex system cannot arise from a simpler system—which in turn arises from a still simpler system, which in turn arises from non-life, as Darwin hoped—precisely because no simpler system answers the need at all.

> ### How Can One Detect Design?
>
> One can detect the past action of an intelligent cause from the presence of an information-intensive effect, even if the cause itself cannot be directly observed. Since information requires an intelligent source, the flowers spelling "Welcome to Victoria" in the gardens of Victoria harbor in Canada lead visitors to infer the activity of intelligent agents even if they did not see the flowers planted and arranged.
>
> —Stephen C. Meyer, design theorist[31]

The obvious analogy is between living systems and complex machines. A car cannot be understood as a tricycle that sprouted a four-stroke engine and an extra wheel; it cannot be understood at all except as a product of an intentional design. In the same way, your computer did not evolve from a typewriter by a long, slow series of steps. Most of the steps that separate your computer from a typewriter were the product of intelligent design.[33] The intelligent design advocate asks, to what extent are life forms best understood in this way?

Design and Science: Where Do We Put the Bar?

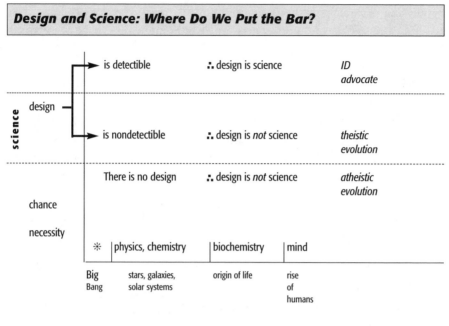

If you are an ID advocate, you assume that design is detectable and researchable. Therefore, design is part of science, and methodological naturalism (law and chance only) is mistaken in excluding it. So you place the bar in the higher of the two positions (dotted line).

If you are a theistic evolutionist, you assume that design is there but is not detectable or researchable. Only law and chance are detectable; design must be seen by faith. Therefore, design is not part of science, and methodological naturalism (law and chance only) is correct in excluding it. So you place the bar in the lower of the two positions (dotted line).

If you are an atheistic evolutionist, you assume that design does not exist. Only law and chance are detectable because that is all there is. Therefore, design is not part of science, and methodological naturalism (law and chance only) is correct in excluding it. So you place the bar in the lower of the two positions (dotted line).

Thus, theistic and atheistic evolutionists use the same bar, but ID advocates use the higher one. That is why theistic evolutionists join atheistic evolutionists in attacking ID.

Note: This explanatory diagram, which was developed by Ontario physics teacher Elizabeth Dunning, does not deal with the question of miracles, which are assumed to be direct interventions by God.

Is Design a Miracle?

It is important to understand that intelligent design is *not* a claim that miracles occur. Rather, (1) design is an actual feature of the universe, one that cannot be duplicated by the effects of natural law and chance, and (2) design is researchable, and therefore a valid part of science.[34]

Design may be frontloaded into the universe, so that no miracles or interventions are ever needed. But such a design is real, not an illusion, as Dawkins would have it.

Behe is arguing that irreducible complexity is a marker for design, in the same way that constantly repeating patterns, such as in natural crystals, are a marker for law.

If design is accepted, what happens to methodological naturalism?[35] Well, it becomes a three-legged stool (law, chance, design) as opposed to a two-legged stool (law, chance). Remember, the ID advocates propose design as a real and researchable explanation.

A miracle would be a direct intervention by God, in order to give a message of some kind. It is not law, chance, or design, in the usual sense.

In other words, to ID advocates, design is not a miracle, but a researchable fact. Of course, intelligent design, unlike metaphysical naturalism, does not rule out miracles in principle. For that matter, an ID advocate can easily accept Dawkins's notion that some things look designed but are not. However, other things look designed because they are.

Lastly, ID is not Christian evolutionism. A Christian evolutionist agrees that design is real, but insists that it can be seen only through the eyes of faith, and is therefore not science. Hence, Christian evolutionists are among the strongest opponents of the design hypothesis.

How Complex Is a Cell, Really?

Biochemistry has demonstrated that any biological apparatus involving more than one cell (such as an organ or a tissue) is necessarily an intricate web of many different, identifiable systems of horrendous complexity. The "simplest" self-sufficient, replicating cell has the capacity to produce thousands of different proteins and other molecules, at different times and under variable conditions. Synthesis, degradation, energy generation, replication, maintenance of cell architecture, mobility, regulation, repair, communication—all of these functions take place in virtually every cell, and each function itself requires the interaction of numerous parts.

—Michael Behe, biochemist[36]

So yes, a cell is really complex.

Early History of the Intelligent Design Movement

A number of scientists who were not Christians were beginning to ask the same questions as Thaxton and Bradley. For example, biochemist Stuart Kauffman advocated that complex systems on the boundary between order and chaos can evolve by themselves.[37] Astronomer Fred Hoyle, who professed atheism, wrote *The Intelligent Universe* (1984), contending that there was a quality of mind in space/time itself that can produce the nearly unfathomable complexity of life forms.

In 1984, chemist-historian Thaxton and engineering professor Bradley published *The Mystery of Life's Origin*,[38] drawing on information theory to challenge Darwinism. Thaxton also organized conferences and debates around this theme and, in 1988, came up with the term "intelligent design" to describe the intuition—too vague at this point to be called a hypothesis—that intelligence comes first.

Darwin, of course, would have been shocked by this idea. In his view, and that of all Darwinists, intelligence is an accidental by-product of the development of an upright-walking, ape-like creature, perhaps a hundred thousand years ago. The very quality that enables us to comprehend the complexity of nature is itself a product of the process. It happened to have evolved, by chance.

For example, when Alfred Wallace, who hit on natural selection at about the same time Darwin did,

> ## What Major ID Advocates (e.g., Behe, Dembski) Are Saying:
>
> - Nature consists of law, chance, and design.
> - Design can be detected in nature.
> - Some features of nature ("irreducibly complex" features) illustrate design.
> - Studying design will help us understand nature better.
> - Evolution occurred, but law and chance cannot do everything by themselves.
>
> ## What They Are Not Saying:
>
> - The earth was created in six 24-hour days.
> - Noah's Flood explains the geology we see.
> - Evolution did not occur.
> - Evolution should not be taught in school. (They think that it should be taught, but that current problems should be confronted.)

suggested in an article in 1869 that natural selection could not account for the mental attributes of human beings, Darwin's response was, "I hope you have not murdered too completely your own and my child," and scrawled "No!!!" in the margin, underlining it three times.[39]

Darwin and his contemporaries had little idea how complex all life forms really are, or how complex human mental faculties are. Recall that in 1868, Thomas Huxley, Darwin's "bulldog," believed he had found an organism so simple that it was halfway between life and non-life.[40] If scientists in Darwin's day had expected the complexity that really exists in even the smallest life forms, Huxley would not have made this error.

An Intellectual Hobby?

Intelligent design might have remained an intellectual hobby that justified summer conferences for academics in pleasant surroundings. In the 1980s, Darwinism was everywhere entrenched as an orthodoxy, and battled only by young earth creationists. For example, in 1976, Cynthia Russett wrote, in *Darwin in America*: "For many years, it was possible to doubt the validity of Darwin's theory, but skepticism is not a tenable position today."[41]

Besides, questioning Darwin out loud could also be a career setback, as some intelligent design theorists discovered. Kenyon, for example, was briefly removed from teaching introductory biology when some students complained that he criticized Darwinism. He was reinstated by the Academic Senate.[42] No doubt, some of Kenyon's students were raised to regard Darwinism as a religion, in which case criticism of Darwinism at an American university would be as unthinkable as going to Mecca to criticize Islam.

Or a Pent-up Torrent of Well-Earned doubt?

Then in the late 1980s, law professor Phillip Johnson, a former California criminal prosecutor, started to make his voice heard. Johnson had clerked for chief justice Earl Warren, and had been a satisfied agnostic until a failed marriage set him thinking about life. He experienced a religious conversion in 1980.

However, Johnson did not begin to think seriously about design issues until 1987–1988, while on sabbatical in England. There he read Dawkins's *The Blind Watchmaker* (1986) and Denton's *Evolution: A Theory in Crisis* (1985).[43] Denton argued, contra Dawkins, that Darwinism was simply not answering the questions that many scientists were asking about evolution.

Unlike most writers on Darwinism, Denton did not soft-pedal the problems with Darwinism. He said:

While most evolutionary biologists who have written recently about evolution concede that the problems are serious, nearly all take an ultimately conservative stand, believing that they can be explained away by making only minor adjustments to the Darwinian framework. In this book I have adopted the radical approach. By presenting a systematic critique of the current Darwinian model, ranging from paleontology to molecular biology, I have tried to show why I believe that the problems are too severe and too intractable to offer any hope of resolution in terms of the orthodox Darwinian framework, and that consequently the conservative view is no longer tenable.[44]

Denton took issue with some of the strongest arguments in favor of Darwinism, for example, the pentadactyl (five-digit) limb. Essentially, vertebrate limbs have five digits, regardless of whether they are wings, hands, or flippers. This establishes common ancestry beyond reasonable doubt. Except for one thing. You should then reasonably expect that the limbs would develop from the same body parts of the embryo. If so, the case would be closed. Yet that is precisely what embryologists do *not* see. According to Denton, "The forelimbs develop from the trunk segments 2, 3, 4 and 5 in the newt, segments 6, 7, 8 and 9 in the lizard and from segments 13, 14, 15, 16, 17 and 18 in man."[45] This finding is more consistent with a design hypothesis, in the sense that a design is put into effect in each case, from whichever materials are most convenient. Johnson decided that Denton was either "very, very wrong, or very, very important."[46] But he did not make up his mind right away.

Johnson also spoke to openly skeptical paleontologist Colin Patterson, curator at the British Museum of Natural History in London. Patterson would challenge scientists to tell him one thing they knew about evolution.

> I tried it on the members of the Evolutionary Morphology Seminar in the University of Chicago, a very prestigious body of evolutionists, and all I got there was silence for a long time and eventually one person said, "I do know one thing—it ought not to be taught in high school."[47]

Patterson was also blunt in his assessment that there are no true transitional forms—animals obviously turning into other animals—in the fossil record.[48] Thus, it is difficult to prove that evolution has occurred. As Johnson said later:

Absent an explanation of how fundamental transformations can occur, the bare statement that "humans evolved from fish" is not impressive. What makes the fish story impressive, and credible, is that scientists think they know how a fish can be changed into a human without miraculous intervention.[49]

At that time, Johnson began a draft of a book that examined Darwinism, using a legal standard of evidence. He did not publish the book, *Darwin on Trial*, until 1991. By that time he had met a number of ID scientists, who helped him refine his argument.

It is important to be clear about what his accusation in *Darwin on Trial* actually was:

> The question is not whether natural selection occurs. Of course it does, and it has an effect in maintaining the genetic fitness of a population.... These effects are unquestioned, but Darwinism asserts a great deal more than merely that species avoid genetic deterioration due to natural attrition among the genetically unfit. Darwinists claim that this same force of attrition has a building effect so powerful that it can begin with a bacterial cell and gradually craft its descendants over billions of years to produce such wonders as trees, flowers, ants, birds and humans.[50]

Johnson pronounced Darwinism failed, on the evidence. A furor ensued. Most Darwinists assumed that Johnson was arguing for creationism, not because he argued for it but because they did not consider a scientific alternative to Darwinism possible.

A Low Road? A Bad Book?

Darwin on Trial was trashed in all the major science journals, a fact that in itself signified that things are changing. After all, if *Darwin on Trial* had been merely the eccentricity of an aging, addled law professor, why would the highly competitive science journals even bother to accord it a denunciation? Stephen Jay Gould announced in *Scientific American* that "Johnson has taken a low road in writing a very bad book," essentially because Darwinism should not be expected to conform to legal standards of evidence.[51] This must have come as news to parents who saw Darwinists regularly apply to the courts to get legal rulings that forced students to learn Darwinism in school. *Scientific American* did not allow Johnson the right of reply.

The scientists' outrage stemmed partly from Johnson's prosecutorial style. Having mastered the art of breaking down dubious tales propounded by felons from the witness stand, he applied his art to weaknesses in the reasoning of major scientists. "You had to meet intimidation with counterintimidation in order to move the discussion forward," he told journalist Larry Witham later. "Now that perhaps was a lawyer's contribution."[52]

Are Christian Evolutionists Just Theistic Naturalists?

Johnson was really the first ID advocate to address the central role that the philosophy of naturalism plays in the favor granted to Darwinism by the establishment, despite its meager showing on actual evidence, *and* the central role that Darwinism plays in return in propping up naturalism.[53] As a result, he angered not only atheistic scientists, but also the many Christian scientists who have made their peace with naturalistic evolution, and have no use for intelligent design concepts.

Calling these Christian Darwinists "theistic naturalists," Johnson challenged them to show how their position differs from soulful atheism, adding:

> I do not think that the mind can serve two masters, and I am confident that whenever the attempt is made, naturalism in the end will be the true master and theism will have to abide by its dictates. If the blind watchmaker thesis is true, then naturalism deserves to rule, but I am addressing those who think the thesis is false, or at least are willing to consider the possibility that it may be false.[54]

He also came to Michael Behe's defense:

> Behe says at one point that he is not a creationist, at least if that term means someone who is concerned about supporting the creation account in the Bible. He also does not challenge evolution, if that term means "common ancestry." Then why isn't Behe classified as a theistic evolutionist? He would be if that term meant a theorist who does not rely on the Bible or other religious authority, and accepts gradual development of organisms over long periods of time, but who sees the need for some guiding (i.e., designing) intelligence.[55]

But, says Johnson, that is not what theistic evolutionism really means:

> The defining characteristic of theistic evolution, however, is that it accepts methodological naturalism and confines the theistic element to

the subjective area of "religious belief." It is (barely) acceptable in science to say, "As a Christian, I believe by faith that God is responsible for evolution." It is emphatically not acceptable to say, "As a scientist, I see evidence that organisms were designed by a preexisting intelligence, and therefore other objective observers should also infer the existence of a designer." The former statement is within the bounds of methodological naturalism, and most scientific naturalists will interpret it to mean nothing more than "It gives me comfort to believe in God, and so I will." The latter statement brings the designer into the territory of objective reality, and that is what methodological naturalism forbids.[56]

In taking this position, Johnson finds himself with some interesting company. Physicist Steven Weinberg, emphatically not a supporter of design theory, has said:

Wolfgang Pauli was once asked whether he thought that a particularly ill-conceived physics paper was wrong. He replied that such a description would be too kind—the paper was not even wrong. I happen to think that the religious conservatives are wrong in what they believe, but at least they have not forgotten what it means really to believe something. The religious liberals seem to me to be not even wrong.[57]

The Wimp's Way Out?

Johnson also angered creationist scientists like Kurt Wise, who said of *Darwin on Trial*: "You do not propose an alternative. This is a wimp's way out."[58] So to the creationists, intelligent design is creationism without a face; to the Christian evolutionists, it is creationism without a label.

Johnson always refused to say where he stood on creationism. No doubt he wanted to avoid alienating potentially useful creationists. But his reticence is likely an outcome of his "prosecutor" stance as well: The prosecutor forces the other guy to defend himself and does not suggest that he even needs a position of his own; his only object is to establish the defendant's guilt. By angering so many establishments at once, Johnson guaranteed that, within a few short years, the science community knew plenty about the concept of intelligent design.[59]

Darwin's "Black Box" Is Opened

In 1996, as noted earlier, Michael Behe, a biochemist at Lehigh University in Pennsylvania, published *Darwin's Black Box*, arguing that cells could not arise entirely by chance. Behe, a Roman Catholic, was comfortable with evolution. However, as a biochemist, he began to doubt that the bewilderingly complex machines that drive every cell of a living body could arise by chance. When he surveyed the literature on evolutionary biology, he did not find satisfactory answers. He decided that natural selection by chance does not account for the complexity of the cellular machines that keep us alive, and that life is more appropriately seen as a product of intelligent design. This view was directly contrary to Darwin's view, and that of the science establishment.

As we saw in Chapter 3, Behe introduced the concept of "irreducible complexity" to the public. Irreducible complexity describes a system that cannot work if any part is missing or malfunctioning. Without directed design, no irreducibly complex system arises. Natural selection cannot select a system that does not yet exist.

Behe challenges Darwinists to show rigorously how a system such as the blood clotting mechanism or the flagellum that the bacterium uses to move around can originate by chance. His conclusions and challenges were widely denounced in the science establishment, but his position as a working biochemist has enabled him to continue to make his case. He has since been joined by mathematician William Dembski, who makes the case for intelligent design based on information theory.[62]

Darwin's Challenge

If it could be demonstrated that any complex organ existed, which could not possibly have been formed by numerous, successive, slight modifications, my theory would absolutely break down. But I can find out no such case.

—Charles Darwin[60]

Although it sounds at first as though Darwin was providing a means to falsify his theory, he was really protecting it from falsification. No one can demonstrate a universal negative such as "could not possibly have." (In a given life form? In any life form? In this universe? In any universe?) Evidence in science is based on the balance of probabilities here and now. Thomas Kuhn, for example, writes, "All historically significant theories have agreed with the facts, but only more or less."[61] The problem for any theory begins when it is not more (and more) but less (and less).

Behe Changes the Focus of the Debate

Most past arguments about evolution have depended on data from long extinct organisms. Sometimes the data that survive apparently support Darwinism (the whale series, for example) and sometimes they don't (the Cambrian explosion[64]). No one knows what difference the lost evidence would make.

> **Definition**
>
> **irreducible complexity** a biological system is irreducibly complex when its operation requires the cooperation of numerous parts, none of which performs a useful function unless all are present.[63]

In contrast, as a biochemist, Behe argues from existing organisms. If we are talking about existing organisms, then either we have all the information or we can get it through present-day research. Increasingly, academic contentions focus on biochemistry or artificial life computer programs, not on the vagaries of what has been preserved from the ruins of half a billion years of prehistory.

The reason Behe called his book *Darwin's Black Box* is that, in Darwin's day, as the anecdote about Huxley's "half-alive" creature shows, cells were a *black box*, an object whose inner workings are unknown.[65] No one had much idea what went on inside a cell until biochemistry came into its own after World War II.

Intelligent Design vs. Methodological Naturalism

As we have already seen, the fact that some features of life forms may be irreducibly complex does not necessarily mean that a miracle was required to produce them.[66] It means that design is a real feature of the universe, one that cannot be duplicated by the effects of natural law and chance. Design may well be frontloaded into the universe, so that no miracles are necessary—the concept of intelligent design includes that possibility.

However, a frontloaded design is still real, not illusory. It is not an outcome of law and chance, as methodological naturalism would require. That is the real conflict between intelligent design advocates and Darwinists. The former would research design, while the latter would explain it away as an illusion.

Not surprisingly, *Darwin's Black Box* suffered the same fate as *Darwin on Trial*. Trashed in the science media, it found a steady audience among educated lay readers.[67] Behe himself was subjected to an extraordinary amount of vitriol. For example, an article in *Biology and Philosophy* compared him to Stalin or Osama bin Laden.[68] Neither Behe nor anyone else had a precise idea of what they meant by intelligent design in the beginning. But they have been forced to refine their arguments in the storms that followed. They have had to demonstrate that intelligent design can be a scientific idea, and that it can in fact function as a "third way," a way out of the impasse between blind evolution and young earth creationism.

Fired with enthusiasm, the ID advocates fanned out to speak at university campuses, wherever they were welcome. As we will see in the next chapter, however, their critics in the science establishment struck back, charging that intelligent design cannot be, even in principle, a scientific idea.

Is ID Good Science?
Is It Science at All?

CHAPTER 14

The argument from design dons yet another set of clothes. However,…
these new duds are almost as transparent as the Emperor's, scarcely
hiding the naked creationism that lies below.

—Victor J. Stenger, Darwinist philosopher[1]

I predict that within twenty years people will look back on the present
and wonder how so many seemingly smart people could have believed
in Darwinian evolution.

—Jonathan Wells, embryologist[2]

Once it has achieved the status of paradigm, a scientific theory is
declared invalid only if an alternate candidate is available to take its
place.

—Thomas Kuhn, philosopher of science[3]

For a science writer, it was the opportunity of a lifetime. On the
plane to New York, in May 1989, Forrest Mims, III, 46, prepared to be interviewed by the editors of the elite science magazine, *Scientific American*.

The Texan freelancer's credentials were pretty good. He had written
many books and published several hundred articles in a huge variety of science venues. He was probably best known for the books and lab kits on elec-
tronics projects that he had developed for Radio Shack over the years. He
even had a claim to minor historical fame as a co-founder of MITS, Inc.,
which introduced the Altair 8800, the first microcomputer, in 1975.[4]

Mims had offered to write the column "Amateur Scientist" for *SciAm*. His offer was gladly accepted in principle, pending an interview to discuss the details with editor Jonathan Piel. Mims canceled his current assignments and boarded a plane.

It should have been a great meeting. And it was, at first. Piel liked Mims's proposed topics. The deal was pretty well sewn up—until Mims happened to mention, in a list of publications for which he had written, some Christian magazines, where he wrote about how to take kids on long distance bicycle trips.

Piel asked bluntly: "Do you believe in the Darwinian theory of evolution?"

Mims said no.

Suddenly, the temperature plunged below freezing.

Incredibly, Piel insisted that, if *SciAm* published Mims, everything he wrote for publications *other than SciAm* would have to be reviewed by *SciAm* before publication. Otherwise, *SciAm* would dock his pay or dismiss him. Given that freelance writers are, by the very nature of their profession, accustomed to freedom, this was a heavy restriction, to say the least.

In the months that followed, *SciAm* editors pestered Mims about his religious beliefs, and even about his opinion on abortion. The magazine grudgingly assigned him a trial column. Editors liked it. More assignments were ordered. Maybe things would work out after all, Mims thought. Maybe he had finally passed all of the Darwinists' tests.

However, during one phone call, Piel again raised the subject of Mims's Christian beliefs. He professed worry that, if word got out that Mims was a Christian, a "public relations nightmare" might ensue.

By then Mims had realized the sad truth: *SciAm* was not simply going to assign him a column and move on to some other, more realistic concern.

So often, people bring about the thing they fear the most. A public relations nightmare indeed threatened Piel, but not the one he had anticipated. The *Houston Chronicle* broke a story about *SciAm*'s incredible treatment of Mims. The *Wall Street Journal*, the *New York Times*, and the *Washington Post* picked it up.

Most media people are Darwin fans. That is not because they have necessarily given the matter much thought. They merely believe that they *ought* to be Darwin fans, *Inherit the Wind*–style. Thus, on the issues alone, they would likely sympathize with *SciAm*.

However, the media, like any industry, have certain unwritten rules. Here is one: No one who writes for a living should have to face a prolonged inquisition on personal beliefs or lifestyle just to get an assignment. The way *SciAm* tried Forrest Mims terrified the average journalist.

So, when the story became public knowledge, the media could hardly afford to support *SciAm*. Almost the entire industry considered its practices in this area unprofessional and undesirable. The media promptly dumped on the prestigious science magazine. Science organizations were not amused by the *SciAm* editors' antics either, and the magazine's conduct was censured.

SciAm publisher John Moehling then precipitated a media meltdown by refusing to talk about what happened. He claimed: "We don't discriminate in our pages among the people who work here or write for us."[5] Unfortunately, two *SciAm* editors had already told reporters that Mims was dropped because he was thought to be a creationist.

In the context, the *SciAm* editors meant that Mims was not a Darwinist. Mims told AP that he had not ever written about creationism. When asked, he told the media: "I don't know how old the earth is." As a man who calibrates instruments, he is dissatisfied with some aspects of current radiometric dating. Asked about this in 2003, he said: "I'm reasonably familiar with the science on both sides of this issue, and, frankly, I have not fully made up my mind."[6]

Based on criteria used in this book, he wobbles between young earth creationism and old earth creationism or, possibly, intelligent design. Nonetheless, he asked me to place him in the intelligent design camp rather than the creationist camp. No matter. He is not a Darwinist, and that is what counted for *SciAm*.

Editor Piel added fat to the fire by denying discrimination against Mims, when questioned by the *Wall Street Journal*. However, Mims had been advised by a lawyer friend to tape a key phone call with Piel, so Mims played the tape for the *Journal*. The *Journal* was satisfied that Mims had, in fact, been dumped because he was assumed to be a creationist, contrary to Piel's protestations. That didn't help *SciAm*'s credibility much. Worse, *Harper's Magazine* published "Science's Litmus Test" in March 1991, an article based on the infamous tape.

Mims did not cry over spilt milk. He simply went back to the type of assignments he had canceled in order to meet with *SciAm* personnel. "At first I was very hurt and disappointed," he admits. "Then I decided to pursue serious science using the instruments that I built for the column that was never published."

Within a year, his daily measurements of the ozone layer, using a home-made instrument that he designed and built, found a significant error in

NASA's ozone satellite, which led to his first paper in *Nature*, one of the world's leading science journals.[7] His ozone project also won a 1993 Rolex Award, the money from which allowed him to work with a friend to design a microprocessor-controlled version of the instrument. That instrument was later commercialized by Solar Light Company and is now the standard handheld ozone instrument used by ozone scientists around the world.

Mims's story shows how deeply any concept such as intelligent design challenges a Darwinist establishment.

What Is the Intelligent Design Controversy Really About?

The intelligent design controversy is a conflict about how to interpret unexpected findings in science. However, some scientists are concerned that acknowledging "intelligent designership" will stall the progress of science. How valid is this concern?

Darwinism has been treated by many as a biological Theory of Everything. Recall that Darwin thought that if anyone could show that any complex organ "could not possibly have been formed by numerous, successive, slight modifications, my theory would absolutely break down."[8] The ID advocates have dedicated themselves to finding just such evidence in the bewilderingly complex world of biochemistry, a science unknown before 1950 that provides a promising field for their search.

Not surprisingly, intelligent design theory has garnered the unremitting hostility of Darwinists. As far as the Darwinists are concerned, ID cannot be science at all, let alone good science. What are their major objections?

Objection 1: ID Is Merely "Stealth Creationism"

Opponents of ID often claim that ID is "stealth creationism."[9] In other words, ID is a front put up by the religiously based young earth creationists to advance their claims, particularly in the school system.

However, key ID proponents such as Michael Behe and William Dembski are not young earth creationists and do not reject evolution. For example, Michael Behe says:

> For the record, I have no reason to doubt that the universe is the billions of years old that physicists say it is. I find the idea of common descent (that all organisms share a common ancestor) fairly convincing,

and have no particular reason to doubt it. Although Darwin's mechanism—natural selection working on variation—might explain many things, however, I do not believe it explains molecular life.[10]

And William Dembski says:

> Intelligent design is not a form of anti-evolutionism. Intelligent design does not claim that living things came together suddenly in their present form through the efforts of a supernatural creator. Intelligent design is not and never will be a doctrine of creation.[11]

In Dembski's view, young earth creationism is essentially a religious position, whereas intelligent design disputes Darwinism on the scientific evidence alone. Behe and Dembski argue that design, as well as chance and law, are a part of nature, and that Darwinism has not explained all design away.

It is also worth noting that opposition to Darwinism does not arise solely from religious communities. Over the years, a number of atheists and agnostics have checked out of Darwinism, mainly because of problems with the evidence.

The charge that Behe, Dembski, and other ID advocates are creationists in disguise will likely continue to be made.

Astronomer Arthur Eddington once gave the following as an example of the difficulty of understanding the limitations of one's chosen rules for evidence. A researcher into fish (ichthyologist) uses a net with two-inch mesh holes. After sorting his catch, the ichthyologist states that no sea creature is less than two inches long. If an observer objects that the two-inch net would not catch the smaller fish:

> Although I have referred to the ID people in the past as "creationism lite," I think that's a mistake. The interesting thing is that many of the ID people are certainly prepared to buy into some kind of evolution, maybe a fairly major kind.
>
> —Michael Ruse,
> Darwinist philosopher[12]

> The ichthyologist dismisses this objection contemptuously. "Anything uncatchable by my net is ipso facto outside the scope of ichthyological knowledge. In short, "what my net can't catch isn't fish." Or—to translate the analogy—"If you are not simply guessing, you are claiming a knowledge of the physical universe discovered in some other way than by the methods of physical science, and admittedly unverifiable by such methods. You are a metaphysician. Bah!"[14]

For the fish researcher in this illustration, his theory does not interpret the facts so much as *it determines what facts may be considered*. Anyone who

Opposition to Darwinism That Is Not Based in Traditional Religion:			
Scientist/ Mathematician	Point of view	Specialty	Proposals
David Berlinski	skeptic	mathematics, author of *A Tour of the Calculus* (1996), many anti-Darwinist articles	doesn't know what works, but knows what doesn't work
Michael Denton	agnostic	biochemist, author of *Evolution: A Theory in Crisis* (1985)	cosmos itself pre-destined for life
Fred Hoyle	atheist	astronomer, author of *The Intelligent Universe* (1984)	life seeded from elsewhere in eternal universe

Note: Hoyle was primarily skeptical of the idea that Darwinism can originate life. Denton and Berlinski are also generally skeptical of the vast changes in life forms that Darwinism is supposed to make possible.[13]

identifies a weakness in his theory is assumed to be making a religious claim, not a scientific one, because the claim deals with facts he is not willing to allow. This is a characteristic response of Darwinists to criticism. Irreducible complexity, for example, simply cannot exist because it is outside Darwinism.

One source of confusion here is that many Darwinists see any deviance from strict Darwinism as, by definition, "creationism."[15] Thus, when they say that intelligent design is stealth creationism, many of them sincerely believe their own accusation. The public, however, assumes that creationism means young earth creationism (in other words, rejection of evolution); or else it means a general attempt to teach an explicitly Christian doctrine of origins in science classes.[16] During public debates, the confusion works to the advantage of all Darwinists, so even those who understand the difference are not in any hurry to clear it up.[17]

Many key young earth creationists such as Kurt Wise and the Answers in Genesis ministry oppose intelligent design theory. If ID is really helping them, they do not express much gratitude.[18] We will look at their views of intelligent design in the next chapter.

Objection 2: ID Is a Science Stopper

Another common theme among scientists who attack intelligent design theory is that ID is a science stopper. It would cut the ground out from under science. The answer to any question would simply be "God did it," and no one would do any more research.

In his essay in *Darwinism Defeated?* geologist Keith B. Miller spells this out: "Using an intelligent design approach, the inference of intelligent design would be made, and any motivation for further research would end."[19]

Similarly, Eugenie Scott of the National Center for Science Education, a Darwinist education lobby, argues that design theorists say: "'Well, gee, I can't understand it. Therefore I'm saying God did it.' . . . and once you say God did it, you stop looking for a natural cause. It's what we call a science stopper."[20]

Historically, there is no basis for this assumption. Many of the greatest scientists of previous centuries, for example, Copernicus, Galileo, Kepler, Pascal, Newton, Faraday, and Kelvin, believed that the universe was intelligently designed, and that its design was detectable.[21] So great was the influence of these men that key terms or units of science measurement are named after them (e.g., the Galilean moons of Jupiter, the Copernican solar system, and units of measurement such as the pascal, newton, farad, and kelvin.)[22] Newton, who died in 1727, is widely regarded as the greatest Briton who ever lived.[23] If belief in detectable divine design was a science stopper, it seems that no one told *these* scientists where to stop.[24]

In the mid-19th century, Darwin and his contemporaries introduced the idea that there was no design. Later, it became mandatory to assume that there is no design. Today, many people mistakenly believe that *science* depends on this assumption. In reality, only *Darwinism* depends on the assumption of no design. When examining systems that may be irreducibly complex, it is just as much of a science stopper to say "evolution did it somehow" as to say "God did it somehow."

Of course, a scientist who accepts design is more likely to focus on some questions than others. For example, a scientist who assumes that the many different versions of the eye are a product of intelligent engineering rather than chance will not spend time trying to figure out how the eye arose or changed purely by chance. That is a project for Darwinists. The ID advocate would be more likely to focus on identifying the patterns that govern the eye's origin and development. In an intelligently conceived system, a detectable pattern must exist. Whether such a line of research is fruitful remains to be seen. But if it is fruitful, science must live with the ID scientist's choice of projects.

So if there is no design, ID is a science stopper. But if there is design, Darwinism is a science stopper. Only research—in both directions—will determine which is true.

Objection 3: If It Is Not Strict Darwinism, It Cannot Be Science

The main impetus behind the Darwinist's belief that ID is a science stopper is the assumption that Darwinism is the only appropriate view for a scientist today. To the Darwinist, science *means* methodological naturalism, which in turn *means* eliminating design.

Lawrence Krauss, a professor at Case Western Reserve University, spells this out: "They're trying to make it appear like they're scientists who just disagree with other scientists."

Can Science Survive a Design Inference?

A NASA spacecraft going into orbit suddenly begins to separate into two parts. From your seat inside, you have no idea why. You attribute the separation to laws of nature or chance—and doubt your own chances of survival.

However, suppose you are familiar with the engineering requirements faced by the mission planning team. You know why the craft is separating. The craft must separate now to allow your special purpose space vehicle to proceed beyond earth's gravitational field.

Law and chance, by themselves, won't accomplish this reliably, so NASA doesn't leave it to law and chance. NASA programs the separation components into the craft's design before the launch.

The separation and the components can be studied in any level of detail you wish. In this way, design is not a problem for science.

But if you tried to explain the successful launch as a result of random movements of molecules or the workings of the laws of nature alone, and ignored any input provided by the mission planning team, you would face many problems with the evidence.

ID Gets Off to Rocky Start at Christian University

Bill Dembski was hired in 1998 by Baylor University's visionary president, Robert Sloan, Jr. Sloan wanted to make the Waco, Texas, university the "Notre Dame of Protestantism," and he was looking for new ideas that might help him put Baylor on the map.

Dembski's credentials were pretty good. After a rigorous peer review, Cambridge University had published his book, *The Design Inference*, on means of detecting intelligent design. His task was to assemble the first American academic center for the study of design theory at Baylor. He named it the Michael Polanyi Center, after the Hungarian scientist and philosopher.[25]

The high point was 2000, when the Center's Nature of Nature conference on naturalism in science attracted well-known scientists such as Simon Conway Morris (paleontology), Alan Guth (inflation theory), John Searle (philosophy of mind), and Nobel Prize–winner Steven Weinberg (physics), as well as design theorists.

Soon afterwards, things went downhill. Christian evolutionists at the university viewed the intelligent design center as a threat and an embarrassment. The fact that Sloan had used his authority to hire Dembski directly did not help matters. Faculty attempted to discredit the Center academically, and the faculty senate voted overwhelmingly to ask Sloan to dissolve it. At least one prominent faculty member left.[26]

As the conflict grew, Sloan hired outside experts to evaluate the Center. The outside experts recommended more oversight and a cosmetic change (changing the name) but disappointed many faculty members by agreeing that intelligent design was indeed worthy of study.

At that point, Dembski made an incautious remark, announcing in an e-mail that his critics had "met their Waterloo." Refusing to apologize for shouting back, he was fired from his own Center, and he gradually dropped out of Baylor affairs.

He quickly made up for the setback by founding the International Society for Complexity, Information, and Design (ISCID) in 2001, an online community of scientists that explores issues that bear on design.

Dembski's contract with Baylor finishes in May 2005. He does not expect to stay. He says: "All the indications are that my contract will not be renewed. The sort of center and nucleus of scholars that I had envisaged for Baylor seems unlikely to happen there and will probably require a free-standing institute."[27]

David Berlinski summed the matter up as follows: "Those who have benefitted from the change from a fundamentally religious society to a fundamentally secular one are reluctant to relinquish their power."[28]

In an unrelated controversy, Sloan himself survived an effort to dump him in 2003.[29]

A number of them have scientific credentials, which helps, but in no sense are they proceeding as scientists."[30]

Essentially, a Darwinist can determine who is and who is not a scientist quite apart from credentials and contributions to science disciplines. It's easy. A scientist must be a Darwinist.

Darwinism as a Faith Position

Steven D. Schafersman of Texas Citizens for Science, testifying in 2003 in favor of retaining questionable examples of Darwinism in textbooks in his state, said much more than he realized when he argued that "Michael Behe, Jonathan Wells, Stephen Meyer, Paul Nelson, and William Dembski . . . are certainly knowledgeable about science and all have doctorates, but these individuals are not scientists because they do not behave like scientists." He went on to spell out that they are not scientists because they do not follow methodological naturalism—that is, they do not rule out design in advance.[31]

This is not something the Darwinist has discovered by evidence. It is something he *knows by faith*. The lack of transitional fossils that Stephen Jay Gould called attention to, for example, has never been seen as a problem because the Darwinist knows that the fossils must be there.

In addressing a criticism of Darwinism, for example, philosopher Daniel Dennett spells out clearly what it takes to be a Darwinist. Many have wondered why a creature that is on its way to becoming a stick insect would be more likely to survive if it looked five percent like a stick rather than four percent like a stick.

> If you are a Darwinist you know the necessary ancestors and transitionals had to exist, regardless of the lack of fossil evidence. If you doubt that their absence is an artifact of the fossil record, you are not a Darwinist.
>
> —Phillip Johnson,
> skeptic of Darwinism[32]

Surely a purely random process could not fool a predator by generating so small a difference? Dennett quotes philosopher Kim Sterelny in response:

> I do think this objection is something of a quibble because essentially I agree that natural selection is the only possible explanation of complex adaptation. So something like Dawkins' stories have got to be right.[33]

Essentially, Dennett is saying that we must accept the Darwinist explanation for the evolution of a stick insect *not* because it is an especially good explanation, but because we must consider other explanations impossible.

In the same way, Franklin Harold, professor emeritus of cell biology at Colorado State University, and author of *The Way of the Cell*, admits that Darwinism is not producing answers, but nonetheless argues:

> We should reject, as a matter of principle, the substitution of intelligent design for the dialogue of chance and necessity; but we must concede that there are presently no detailed Darwinian accounts of the evolution of any biochemical or cellular system, only a variety of wishful speculations.[34]

We must soldier on with the improbable in order to protect Darwinism. Darwinism will repay our faith in the end.

The line of reasoning of eliminating the impossible and accepting the improbable worked well for Sherlock Holmes in the famous detective stories. After all, Sir

> It is an old maxim of mine that when you have excluded the impossible, whatever remains, however improbable, must be the truth.
> —Sherlock Holmes[35]

Arthur Conan Doyle had *already* built in an improbable solution for Holmes to find. Although Holmes didn't know it, his cases were a product of intelligent design. But the Darwinist, by the very nature of what he believes, rules out an intelligent designer as the "author" of nature. He knows by faith that there is no such author. He may end up stuck with improbabilities, and no place to go. The idea that scientists must, in virtue of being scientists, buy into Darwinism is certainly a science stopper in itself, and makes the Darwinists' position on ID hypocritical.

No Debate with ID Advocates

One outcome of the Darwinists' faith in their system is a reluctance to debate ID advocates lest they give publicity to their objections.[36] Darwinist philosopher Michael Ruse explains:

> I think it's a bit of a crap shoot which way you go. I was very conscious of the fact that around about 1980, we evolutionists had been sneering at and ignoring the creationists, and we found ourselves with a court case on our hands, so basically, the position I take is that at some level it is my obligation. I have a certain sympathy with Dawkins and the late Steve Gould. These people far more than I have major positions in society so of course the creationists can't wait to fight it out with the visiting gunman. . . . At a certain level, if Dawkins gets involved with the

debate, he is giving the whole thing a certain air of intellectual respectability of some sort.[37]

Ruse himself has not taken Gould and Dawkins's approach. He is collaborating with ID advocate William Dembski on a book of essays, *Debating Design: From Darwin to DNA*, to be published by Cambridge University Press in 2004. No doubt, he is wise. A refusal to debate may be seen as evidence of strength in the beginning, but beyond a certain point it can also be interpreted as evidence of weakness.

Is Evolutionary Biology a Form of Mathematics or History?

Some sciences, like physics, can be seen as a form of mathematics. Physics deals with inanimate objects that do not have individual stories. Evolutionary biology, however, is a lot messier than mathematics. It is really a hybrid of mathematics and history. This is part of the problem when we are evaluating Darwinism or intelligent design.

Theories about the origins of life or prehistoric life are a form of "prehistory." "Prehistory" is, after all, just the history of a time before written documents.

Evolutionary biology is the study of specific events in the history of life that we reasonably believe to have happened. The trouble with any type of history is that it refers to specific people, animals, places, and events. Therefore, it cannot usually be deduced backwards from general laws.

For example, there is no law that we can state in the present time which would enable us to deduce that, say, the rise of Egypt or the fall of Rome must have taken place or could not have taken place. For any type of history, we have evidence, sound or flimsy. Showing that something "might have" happened a certain way is not proof; it merely transfers one's thesis from the realm of unfounded speculation to the realm of speculation founded on some (perhaps flimsy?) basis.

Unfortunately, many Darwinists have assumed that, because they can identify a way, however improbable, that their speculative history may have occurred, they have solved the problem of understanding what happened. They have not solved the problem. They have merely provided an explanation that needs to be evaluated against other explanations. If their explanation is only very remotely possible (as opposed to very probable), perhaps it should not receive special weight simply because it leaves intelligent design out of the picture.

The job of the historian or prehistorian is to record, so far as is possible, the way in which the events occurred and to make some sense of it. Often, there is not enough documentation to do the job properly. Hence there is a tendency to rely on grand theories such as evolution and to posit them as "laws" that must come true. But the grander the theories, the further removed they may be from the desperate messiness of individual facts.

The historian does not discover order, he imposes it. As a result, the writing of history, including natural history, is at least part literature as well as part science. The most any historian can hope for is that later historians will judge his lifetime's work to have been more non-fiction than fiction.

ID Advocates as Post-Darwinians

Most ID advocates are probably best described as post-Darwinians.[38] They do not, as a rule, doubt that natural selection occurs and explains many features of nature. If they doubted that, they would be anti-Darwinians, like the young earth creationists. However, unlike Darwinists, they do not believe that natural selection eliminates the need for design.

Objection 4: ID Is Not Testable

A theory in science should be testable. The Steady State theory, for example, was testable. In fact, it did not pass the tests. However, it remains a respectable theory because it is at least testable. It even has respectable adherents who hope that one day it will be vindicated.

Some critics have complained that intelligent design is not a testable theory. Physicist Lawrence Krauss told Ohio education authorities in 2002:

> Intelligent design is definitely not science. First of all, it doesn't actually make any predictions. It makes a claim, but it doesn't make any predictions that are testable, or falsifiable, and if it isn't falsifiable, it isn't science.[39]

Actually, it is possible to test for design. One way is by statistics. In forensics and archaeology, scientists routinely look for occurrences in which a defensible explanation in terms of law and chance is low, suggesting that design played a role. Another way is by looking for patterns that suggest language or communication.

It's worth noting that there is no real test for Darwinian evolution. Darwinists explain that it is impossible to observe because it happens over millions of years. Also, they claim, the fossil record does not show most of the transitions because the record is poor.[40] In any event, well-known apparent examples of Darwinism in action, such as the peppered moth studies, have not borne up well under scrutiny.[41]

Objection 5: ID Cannot Be Falsified by Evidence

One important question must be asked of any theory in science: What evidence would show that the theory is not correct?[42] A theory that cannot be disproven is more like an act of faith than a theory in science.

Some have claimed that intelligent design is a theory that cannot be disproven. For example, *The Skeptic's Dictionary* asserts: "If by 'empirical' one means capable of being verified or disproved by observation or experiment then ID is not empirical."[44]

The skeptics are mistaken. ID is empirical and can be disproven. Demonstrate that there are no irreducibly complex systems, and you have falsified ID. For example, when asked what he thought would dis-

> Darwinists will often compare their theory favorably to Einstein's theory of general relativity, for instance, claiming that it is just as well established. But how many physicists will claim that general relativity is as well established as Darwin's theory? Zero.
>
> —William Dembski, mathematician and ID advocate[43]

prove ID, Dembski replied: "Show me in detail how a nonpurposive natural process can bring about molecular machines like the bacterial flagellum."[45]

The Darwinists are admittedly at a disadvantage here. If even one aspect of life shows evidence of design, then—as Darwin himself pointed out—Darwinism is disproven.[46] But that was Darwin's own challenge, after all. It is an inevitable consequence not of a stacked deck but of the Darwinist's claim to eliminate design *altogether* from nature, to create a biological Theory of Everything.

In practice, Darwinists have responded by continually changing the theory in the face of adverse results[47]—and by hounding those who dissent from it.[48] As Phillip Johnson says:

> If we assume that Darwinism is basically true then it is perfectly reasonable to adjust the theory as necessary to make it conform to the observed facts. The problem is that the adjusting devices are so flexible that in combination they make it difficult to conceive of a way to test the claims of Darwinism empirically.[49]

Thus, it is just as reasonable to accuse Darwinism of being unfalsifiable as ID.

Talking Through Each Other?

As philosopher of science Thomas Kuhn has pointed out, most scientists hang on to their theories throughout their careers. Thus, discussions between schools are often unproductive or counterproductive, no matter what the findings are. He explained:

> To the extent, as significant as it is incomplete, that two scientific schools disagree about what is a problem and what a solution, they will inevitably

talk through each other when debating the relative merits of their respective paradigms. In the partially circular arguments that regularly result, each paradigm will be shown to satisfy more or less the criteria that it dictates for itself and to fall short of a few of those dictated by its opponent.[50]

In other words, even if the ID advocates found an Operations Manual, Programming Notes, and a Read Me First file in the human genome, a Darwinist would say that they evolved there by natural selection. If ID is going anywhere as a science theory, it will simply have to advance scientific knowledge—and outlast its vocal opponents.

Karl Popper: Falsification and Science

How do we know whether an idea is scientific or not? Karl Popper (1902–1994), a philosopher of science, pondered this question deeply. Popper grew up in early 20th-century Vienna, when Freud dominated psychiatry and Marx dominated politics. These two towering figures had one thing in common: Supporters insisted that their theories were science, and that any dissent was unscientific.

Talking to the proponents of Freud and Marx was a waste of time, Popper discovered. Anyone who pointed out that there was no hard evidence for Freud's theories was told that he "unconsciously" rejected them because he needed mental help. Anyone who pointed out that there was no hard evidence that Marx's "scientific" economics had produced anything but starvation was told that she belonged to the smug middle classes. Popper recognized these evasions as intellectual short circuits. But how could he explain clearly what was wrong with them?

One day, he attended a lecture by Albert Einstein and was struck by an important difference between Einstein, and Freud or Marx. Freud or Marx could provide evidence that supported their theories. Lots of people proclaimed that Freud had cured them or that Marx had liberated them.

But Einstein did better than that. He provided evidence that, if found, would disprove his theories. In other words, his theories were falsifiable. This, Popper realized, is the key factor that identifies a scientific theory. As it happens, Einstein's theories were verified—shown to be correct, in the terms of the experiments. In science classes, we study Einstein today, not Marx or Freud, because Einstein took that risk.[51]

Objection 6: ID Does Not Subject Itself to Peer Review

Bill Dembski's *The Design Inference* (1998) was peer reviewed and published by Cambridge University Press. But in general it is true that design theories have not been much published in the science press. In a world governed by Darwinism, advocacy of intelligent design is a quick route to career oblivion.

Right now, ID scientists routinely counsel young postdocs who are interested in studying ID-related issues *not* to reveal that fact until they are in a secure position.[52] However, Canadian Kirk Durston, who has degrees in physics, engineering, and philosophy, is unusually forthright about his goals. He told a reporter for a national magazine:

> I am currently working on a paper dealing with functional information, under the guidance of a professor in bioinformatics who wants to see my work published. It will be very low-key, mentioning nothing about ID, yet laying the groundwork for some major advances in this field— if it is, by some miracle, accepted for publication.[53]

He may indeed need a miracle of some kind. Some sense of the atmosphere in which ID scientists must test their ideas against those of others can be gained from the curious case of John Staver's workshop scheduled for the American Association for the Advancement of Science meeting in Seattle in February 2004.

Staver, who is opposed to ID, is doing a workshop, "The Challenge of Intelligent Design: New Science or Old Rhetoric?", along with two other nonsupporters, historian Ronald Numbers and lawyer Steven G. Gey. In the synopsis of the workshop, Staver's team says of ID scientists: "They present impressive academic credentials and possess substantial financial backing, yet rarely venture into established scientific discourse." Asked in an interview how he justified holding a workshop on ID without including a single supporter, given that his specific complaint is that they do not address the scientific community enough, he explained: "The proponents of one side don't feel any responsibility to present the arguments of the other side." He then went on to deny that there is even a controversy in science, arguing:

> For example, within the context of this controversy, first of all, there is no scientific controversy. There is quite a bit of social controversy, but the scientific community is about as unanimous as it ever gets at this point in time that evolution or biological evolution if you want to get more specific is the single theory or theoretical framework that explains the broad expanse of phenomena that we see today, the diversity across the realms of the life sciences, and also explains the underlying unity of that.[54]

The primary reason that there is any "social" controversy is the behavior of organizations like AAAS in, for example, having Staver give the workshop on ID instead of a scientist who represents the ID viewpoint. The remarkable thing is that Staver and presumably responsible parties at AAAS actually think that they are dealing with the issues appropriately, and that the controversy will just go away.[55]

The Book-Writing Vice

ID scientists are accused of publishing their ideas in books rather than peer-reviewed journals, where their work would be critiqued by other scientists before publication.

In reality, the book-writing vice—if it is a vice—is as widespread among Darwinists as ID advocates. Charles Darwin started the trend with *On the Origin of Species*. He first published his idea in a journal, but no one paid him any attention. When the book appeared in 1859, it was a bestseller.[56] As paleontologist Niles Eldredge has pointed out:

> Books have always proven to be important turning points, fulcra in evolutionary history. The "modern synthesis" in evolutionary biology owed its genesis in no small part to seminal founding documents—books—by many of its most important contributors.[57]

He gives as examples Ronald Fisher's *The Genetical Theory of Natural Selection* (1930), Theodosius Dobzhansky's *Genetics and the Origin of Species* (1937), Ernst Mayr's *Systematics and the Origin of Species* (1942), and George Gaylord Simpson's *Tempo and Mode in Evolution* (1944).[58]

The most likely reason for battles of the books (instead of journals) is the sheer weight of supporting evidence needed to advance a new thesis about evolution. Journals are appropriate for a narrowly focused subject in an established field, but to unpack a genuinely new idea, a book must be written.

Peer Review: Meal Ticket or One-Way Ticket to Mediocrity?

Frank J. Tipler, relativity physicist at Tulane University and author of *The Physics of Immortality*, argues that the peer review process is not really suitable for assessing the validity of ID concepts. He charges that peer review today works primarily to suppress new ideas. It makes geniuses accountable to mediocrities whose main concern is the enforcement of orthodoxy.[59]

Intelligent Design: Some Key Books That Shape the Controversy

Thaxton's *The Mystery of Life's Origin*	1984	
	1985	Denton's *Evolution: A Theory in Crisis*
Dawkin's *The Blind Watchmaker*	1986	
	1991	Johnson's *Darwin on Trial*
Behe's *Darwin's Black Box*	1996	
	1998	Dembski's *The Design Inference*
Wells's *Icons of Evolution*	2000	
	2002	Dembski's *No Free Lunch*

Tipler, while controversial, is not alone in his concerns. Britain's Royal Society, an elite science organization, has started to examine the process of peer review. Society vice president Sir Patrick Bateson acknowledges that "peer review has been criticized for being too secretive, conducted behind closed doors and assessed by anonymous referees," with the overall effect that it is used by the establishment to "prevent unorthodox ideas, methods and views, regardless of their merit, from being made public,"[60] which sounds pretty much like what Tipler is saying.

When Einstein submitted three papers to the German physics review *Annalen der Physik* in 1905, there was no formal peer review process. None was needed. The editor-in-chief was Max Planck (inventor of Planck's constant), and the editor for theoretical physics was Wilhelm Wien (inventor of Wien's Law). Neither of these men was averse to new ideas; they had enough of their own to contend with. Both won Nobel Prizes in physics, as did Einstein.

However, one consequence of the explosion of science and science funding after World War II, was bureaucratization.[61] Tipler notes:

> If one reads memoirs or biographies of physicists who made their great breakthroughs after, say, 1950, one is struck by how often one reads that "the referees rejected for publication the paper that later won me the Nobel Prize."

One wonders how Einstein's papers would have fared under modern peer review. At the time he was publishing his works, only a handful of physicists grasped the concept of relativity.[62]

On the other hand, is it really true that new ideas in science are censored? ID opponents Dawkins and Gould have provided new ideas in evolution, such as the selfish gene and punctuated equilibrium. However, their new ideas were developed specifically in support of the current model of a design-free universe, which they vigorously defend. Gould became an embarrassment to many

> All great advances in science have by definition the effect of reducing the prestige of the "experts" in the field in which the advance is made. The expert's expertise is necessarily invalidated by a radical change in the underpinnings of a scientific discipline.
>
> —Frank Tipler, relativity physicist[63]

Darwinists precisely because, in spite of his best efforts, his ideas helped make it legitimate to question Darwinism. In the words of Phillip Johnson, he was the "Gorbachev of Darwinism,"[64] unable to understand that the forces he was setting in motion could overwhelm his system. It may be that new ideas suffer under peer review if they support a new model; not otherwise. In any event, it is worth mentioning that Gould took no chances on this; he was no fan of peer review of his own work.[65]

Under Bill Dembski's direction, the ID online journal, *Progress in Complexity, Information, and Design*,[66] has adopted Tipler's proposal that the *Annalen der Physik* approach be revived. Papers by junior scholars will be published on the recommendation of a senior scholar, not as a result of a peer review.[67] Time will tell whether this is a fruitful idea. Perhaps it only works for a publication that is as top-heavy with geniuses as *Annalen der Physik* was.

Following the Evidence

In response to all these issues, the battle cry for intelligent design has become "follow the evidence wherever it leads!" The background to this slogan is, of course, the fact that the science establishment generally follows the evidence that supports Darwinism because Darwinism upholds a widely held philosophy of methodological or metaphysical naturalism. Many simply do not "see" any other evidence. They can't, because their methodological naturalism (MN) glasses filter it out.

In the end, intelligent design will stand or fall on whether it provides new insights in science. All of the objections above are the objections of an old system against a new one. Of course, many other objections to intelligent design theory have been put forward. Objections of a religious character are addressed in Chapter 15. Some further scientific objections will be addressed in Chapter 16, which discusses the current state of ID research.

Does Forrest Mims, III, regret the fact that *Scientific American* jilted him? Not at all. "Losing the *Scientific American* column was the best thing that ever happened to my science career," he says. "It changed me from a mere science writer to a citizen scientist with many peer-reviewed papers."[68] And he has been busy. His major interest is actually the environment. He offers:

> I am very troubled by both the destruction of the environment and duplicity by government scientists and officials. For example, the same EPA that wants to sanction San Antonio for air quality violations does absolutely nothing about the 500,000 acres of sugar cane fires in Louisiana that contributed to the violations. Moreover, the EPA allows millions of acres of timber to be burned in prescribed fires, even though such burning produces ground level ozone and depletes stratospheric ozone.[69]

His column, "The Skeptical Environmentalist," addresses these issues for a state publication, just as it might have done for a national one, but for a smaller audience.

Mims notes that, curiously, when he was in conflict with *SciAm*, one of the *least* helpful bodies was his own religious denomination, the Southern Baptists. He thinks that they would support him today because they have become more "theologically conservative." But why wouldn't they support him when it counted? Why do many intelligent design theorists find that their most dogged opposition comes from Christian evolutionists?[70] Let's look at that next.

Is ID Good Theology?
Is It Theology at All?

CHAPTER 15

Having a wholehearted commitment to the historic Christian doctrine of creation does not in any way commit a Christian to favoring the mode of extranatural assembly that the concept of intelligent design entails.

—Howard Van Till, astronomer[1]

Once the intelligent design of some structure has been established, it is a separate question whether a wise, powerful, and beneficent God ought to have designed a complex information-rich structure one way or another.

—William Dembski, mathematician[2]

The intelligent design controversy is not a conflict between science and religion. As we have seen, there are scientists of many religious persuasions on both sides. And, as we have also seen, the whole notion of a conflict between science and religion has been greatly overblown. The hype has distorted public understanding of the conflict brewing around Darwinian evolution.[3]

First, the intelligent designer is not a proxy for God. Those who believe in the Judeo-Christian God will, of course, assume that he is the designer. But the method does not work backwards. Intelligent design could arise from an unknown god or from a self-organizing principle of the universe, for example, as Kauffman or Gardner believe.[4] The design does not tell us who the designer is.

However, the concept of "intelligent designership" has a powerful impact on theology. In some ways, it is more of a concern for theology than for science. Science will get on with any explanation that consistently sheds light on findings. But, in the Western world, theology is wedded to a particular concept of God. Does the "intelligent designer" add to or detract from that concept?

Many creationists and Christian evolutionists would say that intelligent design detracts from the idea of God, though they have very different reasons for their conclusions. Let's start with the creationists.

"Genesis Is the Only Intelligent Design!"

Many members of the young earth creation movement emphatically do *not* think that intelligent design is good theology. They are sharply critical of the ID advocates, even though they sometimes adopt the arguments that the latter advance. From the YEC point of view, ID is almost as wrong as evolution, and for the exact same reason: IDers do not start with the Bible, and their science is not driven by a need to provide support for a literal reading of Genesis. That is the express purpose of young earth creationism, as we have seen.

The most support that the biggest popular creation organization, Answers in Genesis, offers ID is to say that "we neither count ourselves a part of this movement nor campaign against it," according to spokesman Carl Wieland, CEO of Answers in Genesis, Australia. He also notes: "God, who used even the pagan king Cyrus for His purposes, may use the IDM in spite of the concerns we have raised,"[6] which, considering that Cyrus was a famous old tyrant, is hardly a ringing endorsement. Kurt Wise adds: "Being compatible with virtually all worldviews, ID gives very little insight into God, thus gives very little (to no) glory to Him, and is thus of very little use to me."[7]

> I don't think much of the ID movement. The basic goals of ID are to argue for a designer without defining what that designer is. Such a perspective only really excludes pure naturalism, permitting the flourishing of all other beliefs.
>
> —Kurt Wise, creationist paleontologist[5]

Of course, many young earth creationists, such as Paul Nelson, Marcus Ross, and John Mark Reynolds, dissent from these views. They enthusiastically support ID as advancing their goals. Overall, however, intelligent design is not "stealth creationism."[8] It asserts that design, like law and chance, is a fundamental fact about the universe. But is it really just a bad old idea about how God works, often called the God of the Gaps?

The "God of the Gaps": The Fading Smile of the Cheshire Cat

During the last few centuries, a curious idea grew up about the relationship between God and the universe. God was no longer seen as creating and sustaining the universe. Rather, God's sphere of action was considered to be only those areas that were a complete mystery to human beings. Whenever human beings discovered how a given process worked, that was one less job for God. Eventually, many people saw the role of science as banishing God altogether, and the role of religion as helping people to adjust to that fact.

God was the Cheshire Cat who, in *Alice in Wonderland*, vanishes "quite slowly, beginning with the end of the tail, and ending with the grin." The grin remains, as a sort of ritual, after the substance has gone. In science, this curious feline is called the "God of the Gaps." It inhabits the gaps that science has not yet filled in, and is forced to vacate by each new finding, until it gradually goes extinct.

Some theologians see intelligent design theory as a God of the Gaps theory. That is, design is assumed to exist only in those areas that are not understood or improperly understood. For example, Canadian evolutionary biologist Denis Lamoureux warns:

> Operationally, God is beginning to resemble not a ruler but the last fading smile of a cosmic Cheshire Cat.
>
> —Julian Huxley (1957)[9]
>
> "All right," said the Cat; and this time it vanished quite slowly, beginning with the end of the tail, and ending with the grin, which remained some time after the rest of it had gone.
>
> —Lewis Carroll (1865)[10]

> Once natural processes are discovered to account for the creation of a once acclaimed irreducibly complex structure, God's purported intervention is lost to the advancing light of scientific research. A serious consequence of filling these gaps (once believed to be the sites of God's active hand) is that God appears to be forced further and further into the dark recesses of our ignorance; and yes, the dangerous notion arises that maybe human ignorance is in effect the "creator," a resident only of our minds.[11]

This is a mistake. The scientists who believe that intelligent design is a part of the universe are well aware of the nature of the life forms that they study. They believe that the many intricate, interlocking systems that they encounter are most likely the result of an intelligent design. For example, philosopher of biology Stephen C. Meyer says:

> Design theorists infer design not merely because natural processes cannot explain the origin of such things as biological systems but because these systems manifest the distinctive hallmarks of intelligently designed systems—that is, they possess features that in any other realm of experience would trigger the recognition of an intelligent cause.[12]

In the case of the bacterial flagellum or the eye, it is what scientists *do* know—rather than what they do *not* know—that makes them look to an intelligent designer as the explanation. As discussed, Charles Darwin and Thomas Huxley could dispense with design because they thought that the cells that are life's most basic forms were simple little jellies and crystals.[13]

Of course, the ID scientists may be wrong. Intelligent design *is* falsifiable. It could turn out that what they now think is intelligent design is somehow only an illusion.[14] However, either way, the ID scientists are not proposing a God of the Gaps. They are proposing that God's actions in designing nature are in fact detectable in the same way as the computer software engineer's actions in designing a software program are detectable. In other words, the life forms or artefacts are the outcome of design and decisions, not only of necessity and chance. Of course, certain theological risks accompany this view, as we will see.

In any event, the biggest gaps right now are in the fossil record and in the understanding of origins generally. So it is just as plausible to accuse Darwinism of promoting "Transitions of the Gaps."

When these transitions come, they will reveal all things, yes? To be a good Darwinist, you must be very patient.

"The God I Worship Wouldn't Do It That Way!"

Since the mid-19th century, Christian scientists in the Western world have largely accepted Darwinism as the way God worked. Many of these scientists are members of organizations, such as American Scientific Affiliation (ASA)[15] and Canadian Christian and Scientific Affiliation (CSCA), that promote Christian evolutionism.[16] Young earth creationism has become a significant force in evangelical Christian circles, but the majority of Christians in science are still solidly with Darwin. And *not* with intelligent design.

Generally, Christian evolutionists argue that God's work in creating and sustaining the universe cannot be distinguished from the natural forces of law and chance and can be recognized only by the eye of faith. They are deeply skeptical of the intelligent design movement because they believe that it is wrong both scientifically and theologically. One of their strongest spokesmen is Howard Van Till, professor emeritus of physics and astronomy at Calvin College, who has often argued against intelligent design.[17] He says:

> If the universe is a creation, as . . . Christians profess, then its natural capabilities are part of its God-given nature. That being the case, I am more inclined to look for the Creator's signature in the generosity with which the creation's formational gifts have been conferred.[18]

In other words, God gifted the universe to create the life forms we see, apparently by law and chance, but we know by faith that that is not true. Essentially, Van Till is arguing the reverse of Richard Dawkins. Dawkins, as we have seen, argues that the universe arises by law and chance and only appears to be designed. We know by Darwinism that design is not true. Van Till argues that the universe was designed and only appears to arise by law and chance. We know by faith that law and chance alone is not true.

Van Till's view means that we must accept purely on faith that God intentionally gifted the universe, in the same way that Dawkins accepts purely on faith that there is no God and no design.[19] By contrast, ID advocates would insist that the design exists and is detectable, and need not be accepted on faith.

Theologian Rikki E. Watts of Vancouver's Regent College is skeptical of the invisible god of Christian evolutionism, challenging Denis Lamoureux on this precise point:

> I am at a loss to understand how the presence of design could be evident to all and yet those points at which guidance intervened be inherently inaccessible always and forever except to the eyes of faith. My question to Lamoureux is straightforward: in what observable respect does his theistic teleological evolution through guided natural processes differ from an atheistic purposeless evolution through unguided natural processes?[20]

Phillip Johnson has angered many Christian evolutionists by his repeated attacks on their invisible God. He charges that they "embrace evolution with all its randomness as much for its theological merits as for its scientific standing" because evolution undergirds modern movements in theology, such as the idea that God does not really know what will happen in the future and does not really work miracles.[21] Johnson notes:

> I have observed that in some Christian academic circles it is considered far more offensive to deny the theory of evolution than it is to deny the divinity of Jesus or even the existence of God.[22]

Of course, disbelief in Darwin is far more likely to result in banishment from polite society in general than is disbelief in Jesus.

Generally, theology has proven itself very adaptable to science findings over the centuries. The difficulty with arguing that "God wouldn't do it that way" is that one would need the proverbial hot line to God to know for sure. In the end, intelligent design will succeed or fail on its explanatory power in science, not on its popularity among Christian or other academics.

> My main problem with Intelligent Design is that I think it's so much against the spirit of modern science, and personally I would want to say that it's not very helpful theologically either. I just don't think that God, if God exists, works that sort of way.
>
> —Michael Ruse,
> Darwinist philosopher[23]

"But the Designer Does Not Even Have to Be God!"

That is true. The designer does not have to be God. Intelligent design does not require an omnipotent or omniscient designer; only an intelligent one. This may be the single thorniest problem that intelligent design theory poses. To their credit, the ID advocates do not back away from it. For example, Michael Behe has said:

> I am always quite careful to point out that, although most people will conclude that the designer is God, the fact of design itself doesn't demand that conclusion. Whether the designer of life was God or space aliens is not easily settled by scientific arguments.[24]

Michael J. Denton is even blunter:

> Even if we could prove that an adaptation was so improbable that it must be the result of intelligent design, the most we can argue for is an intelligent designer. But we cannot infer that the intelligence behind the design is the creator of the universe—God. There are other candidates; living things might themselves be intelligent or, as James Lovelock has

proposed the biosphere as a whole might be an intelligent being—Gaia, the Earth Goddess. Another candidate might be an extra terrestrial race who could conceivable have been involved in terraforming the earth over the past several billion years.[25]

In fact, Denton adds: "All purposes and designs in the cosmos that are not the result of natural law can never be safely attributed to God."[26] In other words, just because a system may show evidence of intelligence does not mean that it is authored directly by God. Intermediaries or self-organization may play a role. William Dembski says: "Intelligent design requires neither a meddling God nor a meddled world. For that matter, it doesn't even require that there be a God."[27]

What about Panspermia?

Remember that Francis Crick has proposed that life was seeded from elsewhere in the universe, a theory sometimes called panspermia. His idea doesn't really resolve the problem, but his reasoning is worth considering.[28]

First, let's pause and note the drastic change that has come about since the Miller-Urey experiment in 1953. As Thomas Woodward puts it:

> When a leading authority in biology deals with the festering problems of abiogenesis [origin of life] by turning to panspermia, it signals skeptical observers that the conditions are right to organize a comprehensive attack.[29]

Crick proposed his "outer space" theory because mainstream answers do not work. He should not be compared with the crop circles cults that refuse to accept natural explanations for their observations and insist that NASA is hiding space aliens.

Now back to Crick's reasoning. Life in the universe shows intelligent but not perfect design. The easiest explanation is that it is the product of a lesser god, a demiurge such as Plato proposed in the *Timaeus*. An intelligent designer, yes, but not a perfect one.[30] The demiurge was intelligent, but free to make mistakes.[31] We observe plenty of apparent mistakes. Space aliens are an obvious modern candidate for the role of demiurge because they are gods only in terms of superior technology. They need not be thought of as morally superior, and certainly not as commanding obedience to a higher moral code.

There are two key arguments against Crick's specific view. One is the lack of evidence. The other is that Crick's proposal simply ships the whole problem back in time or off to another galaxy, long ago or far away, rendering it unresearchable. The net effect is similar to saying, `twas a miracle. It amounts to proclaiming a miracle *without* founding a church.

So the designer could be—but does not have to be—God. That's the risk of following the evidence wherever it leads.

Of course, it is true that Christian scientists like Behe and Dembski believe that the intelligent designer is the God that they worship. They attribute less-than-perfect design to evil, in the traditional religious sense, or inevitable limitations.[33] But that is a private act of faith. It is not compelled by evidence of design.

The seriousness of this problem is often obscured by the fact that many American opponents of intelligent design argue that ID is just a way of sneaking the Judeo-Christian God into the school system. For example, *Church & State*, the publication of Americans United for Separation of Church and State, terms the intelligent design scientists "Religious Right activists" and intones:

> According to Greek philosophy the world maker is not necessarily identical with God, as first and supreme source of all things; he may be distinct from and inferior to the supreme spirit, though he may also be the practical expression of the reason of God, the Logos as operative in the harmony of the universe . . . a world-maker distinct from the Supreme God.
>
> –from The Catholic Encyclopedia Online[32]

Everyone knows the "designer" Religious Right activists are referring to is God. Opponents of religious neutrality in public schools are simply seeking official imprimatur for their theological beliefs on human origins.[34]

It is fair to say that Americans United members probably believe their own arguments. And they are mistaken. If intelligent design proves to be a viable approach to science, defending the Judeo-Christian God as the intelligent designer will *not* be a foregone conclusion; it will be a growth area in Christian apologetics. ID scientists who are Christians appear to believe that Christian apologetics is up to the challenge, but that remains to be seen. Virtually any theistic religion or, for that matter, any point of view that assigns meaning to the universe can make use of the idea of intelligent design. It is in the public domain.

One way of understanding the situation is to picture a funnel. Christians and Jews picture God as eternal, omnipotent, omnipresent, and omniscient.

They stand at the wide end of the funnel, and look down through the narrow end, which is intelligent design of life forms. Being the intelligent designer presents no problem for such a God. However, a person who stands at the narrow end of the funnel and looks into the wide end, cannot assume that everything that would fit in the wide end would also go through the narrow end.

The qualities of God cannot, for the most part, be defended simply by the notion of intelligent design. They are usually defended by reference to the history contained in the Bible. To summarize: In the Western tradition, God is the most reasonable identity for the designer, but not the only available or possible one.

"Imperfection and Evil Prove That There Is No Intelligent Design!"

In 1860, American botanist Asa Gray, a devout Christian who popularized evolution in the United States and arranged for the publication of *On the Origin of the Species* there, asked Darwin what the book had to say about God. He was hoping to hear some good things. But Darwin replied honestly, saying:

> I had no intention to write atheistically, but I own that I cannot see as plainly as others do, and I should wish to do, evidence of design and beneficence on all sides of us. There seems to me too much misery in the world. I cannot persuade myself that a beneficent and omnipotent God would have designedly created the Ichneumonidae with the express intention of their feeding within the living bodies of Caterpillars, or that a cat should play with mice.[35]

Darwin thought that design must be accompanied by "beneficence," that is, design must be either perfect or at least harmless. Failing that, he preferred to assume that there was no design. He could get away with that because he—and everyone else—assumed that the origin and development of life were simple. Therefore, no design was really needed anyway; law and chance could do it all. However, if life is irreducibly complex, we are back to the question of design.[36]

Dembski has noted that the confusion that Darwin displayed is still common. For example, when he debated Darwinists on PBS in 2000, they thought that anything less than perfect design could not be true design. The universe we live in is finite, limited, and transient. Therefore, it is unlikely that any actual design—whether divinely ordained or not—meets all needs or prevents all problems.[37] So, conveniently, in the Darwinists' all-or-nothing view, there is no place for actual design. Dembski notes:

> The problem of design in biology is real and pervasive, and needs to be addressed head on and not sidestepped because our presuppositions about design happen to rule out imperfect design. Nature is a mixed bag. It is not William Paley's happy world of everything in delicate harmony and balance. It is not the widely caricatured Darwinian world of nature red in tooth and claw. Nature contains evil design, jerry-built design, and exquisite design. Science needs to come to terms with design as such and not dismiss it . . .[38]

If design exists in nature, it can be inadequate for a number of reasons. This is not a problem for science because science can work with whatever evidence is available. It is a problem for philosophy or theology because, in those disciplines, inadequacy must be explained. Evil design, especially, cries out for explanation today, as much as in Darwin's day. And that is the major theological challenge that ID theory poses. It restores design of all kinds, including evil design. It is no problem for a theology that grapples with evil anyway, but it is bad news for a theology that hopes to get by on warm fuzzies.

"Worst of All: What If the ID Scientists Are on to Something?"

> No real designer attempts optimality in the sense of attaining perfect design. Indeed, there is no such thing as perfect design. Real designers strive for . . . the art of compromise between conflicting objectives. This is what design is all about.
>
> —William Dembski, ID advocate[39]

The issue of origins is inescapably philosophical as well as scientific. Where humanity has any vested interest, "objective" science does not really exist.[40] Darwinists such as Richard Dawkins and Stephen Jay Gould are just as invested in atheism as Michael Behe and William Dembski are in Christianity.[41]

And ID is indeed perilous. What if the ID scientists have stumbled onto something? Suppose they find unambiguous evidence of God's action in the universe. In other words, what if God *is* there, and he *isn't* what we think? In the last century, North American religious denominations were able to shape God to be pretty much whatever they needed. But if God is factual, then some doctrines may simply be disproven.

It's not hard to see why a science movement like ID would be unwelcome to some theists. It forces them to deal with evil design, an unwelcome task, to be sure. Not surprisingly, most of what we currently hear in the popular media about intelligent design is the rhetoric of attack and denunciation.

On the other hand, ID may also betray the ID advocates. After all, what if the intelligent designer is not God, as the ID advocates understand God? Will they still want to go where the evidence leads? Historically, few scientists have really done that.

Where will the ID scientists go from here? What will they do? We'll look at that in the next chapter.

The Future of Design

CHAPTER 16

The desire to escape Darwin is a common theme in contemporary thought. Its spreads far beyond creationist circles into the strongholds of secular rationalism.

—David Papineau, naturalist philosopher[1]

A new scientific truth does not triumph by convincing its opponents, but rather because its opponents die, and a new generation grows up that is familiar with it.

—Max Planck, physicist[2]

It's up to ID proponents to demonstrate a few incontrovertible instances where design is uniquely fruitful for biology.

—William Dembski, ID advocate[3]

A t the end of March 2003, readers of the *Harvard Crimson*, Harvard University's campus newspaper, woke up to a death notice to enjoy over their morning latte. It was not a conventional death notice. It was a *fatwa*. Columnist Jonathan H. Esensten, a biochemistry student, declared "Death to Intelligent Design," in much the same manner as certain Middle Eastern extremists declare death to sinners in theology or politics.[4]

Esensten was incensed because Harvard's Kennedy School of Government had hosted a debate the previous November between Jonathan Wells, a textbook critic and ID advocate, and Harvard biology professor Stephen Palumbi. The debate was uneventful, according to Esensten, with both parties agreeing that current evolutionary biology features many outstanding problems.

So why then was Esensten incensed? He explained: "Simply by debating them, scientists lend respectability to 'intelligent design' proponents."[5] And that is, apparently, a Bad Thing. He went on:

> This dalliance with the irrational must stop. The proponents of "intelligent design" must be denied any legitimizing platform for their views. They must be exposed for abusing scientific criticisms of evolution in their push for a theory straight out of orthodox religion. And this unmasking should begin at Harvard.[6]

Why are the ID proponents' views such a problem?

> First, it is an attack against contemporary evolution theory. This theory has been overwhelmingly successful in explaining observations from genetics and paleontology, despite its being a work in progress. Second, "intelligent design" seeks to argue that the observed complexity of living things could not have emerged by chance—that there must be some force that designed the various forms of life.[7]

In reality, the current state of Darwinism is "overwhelmingly successful" only to the extent that it retreats to trivial truisms when confronted with problems or failures—or worse, advocates apply political muscle to opponents.[8] Those activities certainly may be "successful," but they are not science.

Not everyone at Harvard politely ignored the invitation to a witch hunt. The following week, philosophy and government student Richard Halvorson, a regular columnist, responded with a vigorous defense of the intellectual life.[9] He asked: "Does our culture, like many others, have an unpardonable heresy?" Indeed it does, he argued, explaining:

> In Medieval Europe, the peasant was forbidden to question the truth of the Church. Under Communism, comrades doubting the Party were thrown in gulag labor camps. Now, citizens must recite principles of Darwinism through compulsory schooling.[10]

Halvorson pointed out that antireligious prejudice stalled scientific advance for decades during the 20th century because so many scientists were afraid to acknowledge the Big Bang, on account of its theological implications. Now biology seems to be incurring the same cost, he argued, charging that "academic McCarthyism" prevents Darwinists from even reading, let alone considering, the work of ID theorists such as Behe, Dembski, Denton, or Wells. Then he asked an interesting question:

> Biologists continue to recite the worn credo, "the central unifying principle of biology is the theory of evolution." But where would physics be if Einstein had been forced to chant, "The central, unifying principle of physics is Newtonian theory," until he could not see beyond its limitations?[11]

Halvorson closed by saying that "we must refuse to bow to our culture's false idols. Science will not benefit from canonizing Darwin or making evolution an article of secular faith." Then he added the words that form the epigraph of this book: "The most important question for any society to ask is the one that is forbidden."[12]

For the moment, let's overlook the merely political attempts of Darwin lobbies to stifle intelligent design theory. If ID is going anywhere as a theory in science, it must face the implications of both its past and its future. Its past is in a traditional Christian environment, and its future is in an environment of implacable hostility to the very idea of design. Most political opponents of ID hope for great gains by exposing its Christian roots. Let's look at the evidence.

Will Conservative Christian Backing Compromise ID Projects?

The intelligent design movement originated in the early 1980s as a discussion group of Christians in science who were interested in the relationship between biology and information theory. In the 1990s, when lawyer Phillip Johnson began to challenge Darwinists directly, using the strategies and tactics of a prosecutor in the law courts, the ID advocates gained a great deal of publicity. They also attracted the attention of an American organization called the Discovery Institute. The Seattle-based institute was founded in 1991 by public policy analyst Bruce Chapman.[13] Its wide-ranging interests include technology, law reform, national defense, economy, environment, transportation, and science and culture. Like most institutes, it promotes the views that it favors through books, reports, legislative testimony, articles, public conferences, and debates. Its annual budget is about US$4 million.

Key Discovery members saw that the concept of intelligent design was a good fit with the institute's overall cultural renewal goals. Specifically, they saw that the philosophy of metaphysical naturalism (nature is governed by law and chance, without purpose or design) had got such a hold on the sciences in the 20th century that the distinction between the philosophy of metaphysical naturalism and science (following the evidence) was almost lost.

Harvard zoologist Richard Lewontin denied the distinction between the two explicitly when he wrote:

> We take the side of science *in spite* of the patent absurdity of some of its constructs, *in spite* of its failure to fulfill many of its extravagant promises of health and life, and *in spite* of the tolerance of the scientific community for unsubstantiated just-so-stories, because we have a prior commitment, a commitment to materialism. It is not that the methods and institutions of science somehow compel us to accept a material explanation of the phenomenal world, but, on the contrary, that we are forced by our *a priori* adherence to material causes to create an apparatus of investigation and a set of concepts that produce material explanations, no matter how counter-intuitive, no matter how mystifying to the uninitiated. Moreover, that materialism is an absolute, for we cannot allow a Divine Foot in the door.[14]

Ironically, many religious leaders would rejoice to find Lewontin's level of faith common among their congregations. The average believer in a traditional religion demands more benefits in relation to his faith than Lewontin does, if only because a Divine Foot is actually thought to *be* in the door, for better or worse. But, more to the point, Lewontin's comments demonstrate the real problem that intelligent design faces. As Phillip Johnson puts it:

> There are two definitions of science at work in the scientific culture, and a concealed contradiction between them is beginning to come out into public view. On the one hand, science is dedicated to empirical evidence and to following that evidence wherever it leads. That is why science had to be free of the Bible, because the Bible was seen to constrain the possibilities scientists were allowed to consider. On the other hand, science also means "applied materialist philosophy." Scientists who are materialists always look for strictly materialist explanations of every phenomenon, and they want to believe that such explanations always exist.[15]

Materialism means law and chance, with no design. Thus, the near loss of the distinction between metaphysical naturalism and science explains Harvard student Esensten's demand that his university begin a persecution of intelligent design, in order to protect Darwinism.

The near loss also underlies the oft-heard claim that ID isn't science.[16] Actually, ID *is* science. What it *isn't* is metaphysical naturalism.[17] Many opponents of ID simply cannot make—and probably cannot even understand any longer—the distinction between science and metaphysical naturalism, though Galileo, Copernicus, and Newton would have grasped it immediately.

In 1996, Discovery founded the Center for Science & Culture,[18] with a $1.2 million budget, in order to promote intelligent design. Many key ID advocates accepted Discovery's invitation to become fellows, for example, Michael J. Behe, David Berlinski, William Dembski, Dean Kenyon, Stephen Meyer, Scott Minnich, Paul Nelson, Henry Schaefer III, Charles Thaxton, and Jonathan Wells. Phillip Johnson is an advisor. Having Discovery as an institutional backer enabled the ID advocates to make headway more quickly. However, two aspects of Discovery's relationship with intelligent design have become a source of controversy.

The Law of Moses?

One of several backers was a California savings and loan multi-millionaire, Howard F. Ahmanson, Jr., who had also given money to a movement called Christian Reconstructionism, which aimed to make the Law of Moses the basis of American law and government. This, of course, provided plenty of ammunition for groups such as Americans United for the Separation of Church and State who have invested a fair amount of time in opposing intelligent design theory.[19]

Ahmanson does not seem to have given an interview to the media since 1985 and has not been connected to Christian Reconstructionism since 1995. Rousas Rushdoony, the CR point man, died in 2001, and his cause never caught on with any large evangelical Christian constituency.[20]

While the Ahmanson connection never amounted to a scandal in itself, it served as a proxy for another, more troubling issue: A number of Christian academics have quietly raised concerns about ID's failure to publicly distance itself from young earth creationism (YEC), as the American Scientific Affiliation did 50 years ago.[21] Some wonder whether Discovery funding plays a role. Certainly, the association with YEC has created no benefits for

ID, because, quite apart from the bad publicity, the YECs do not usually return the favor. Some YECs routinely attack ID as just another example of a failure to follow the Scriptures.[22]

Whatever Keeps You Honest

Dembski defends his practice of associating with those young earth creationists who will have him—as well as pantheists, New Agers, and even that scourge of science boffins, Phillip Johnson[23]—saying:

> Actually, I rather like having unsavory associates, regardless of friendship or loyalty. The advantage of unsavory associates is that they tend to be cultural pariahs (Phillip Johnson is a notable exception, who has managed to upset countless people and still move freely among the culture's elite). Cultural pariahs can keep you honest in ways that the respectable elements of society never do . . .[24]

Inevitably, prominent ID advocates such as Dembski and Behe distance themselves from the young earth creationists simply by promoting different research initiatives. Public disputation with YECs would not advance their science goals.

The "Wedge" Document Devours Bandwidth

In 1998, an inhouse draft document was stolen in some way from the Discovery Institute.[25] It became known as the "Wedge" document because it outlined a strategy that followed up on Phillip Johnson's use of the term "the Wedge" in the mid-1990s.

Johnson had described himself as a wedge because he was trying to open doors for younger scientists whose dissent from Darwinism raised career obstacles. One biologist explained it this way: "Phil is the 'sharp edge' and the rest of us are the ever-widening shank."[26]

The document, a list of the sort of unrealizable goals that are typically generated by think tanks,[27] was never published or formally accepted by Discovery, but it created a furor among Darwin pressure groups. For example it stated:

> Discovery Institute's Center for the Renewal of Science and Culture seeks nothing less than the overthrow of materialism and its cultural legacies. Bringing together leading scholars from the natural sciences and those from the humanities and social sciences, the Center explores how new developments in biology, physics, and cognitive science raise

serious doubts about scientific materialism and have reopened the case for a broadly theistic understanding of nature.[28]

Of course, most North Americans have never given up a "broadly theistic" understanding of nature, as polls consistently show. Discovery's real target is the metaphysical naturalism and narrow Darwinism of the current science establishment, which the author of the document hoped to replace within two decades by intelligent design theory.[29]

That is a pretty ambitious project. Thoughtful critics, including Dembski, have pointed out that design advocates have spent entirely too much time in recent years quarreling with Darwinists at school board meetings and in the op-ed pages of newspapers, and not enough time doing the hard science research needed to advance their perspective.[30]

In any event, there is no conspiracy. Johnson's book, *The Wedge of Truth*, provides a public statement of his own social goals for the Wedge. For example:

> The Wedge has important things to say about science, but it has much more important things to say about the nihilism that infects intellectual life outside of experimental science. . . . Technology is at the flood tide of rationalist optimism, whereas the fields we call "the humanities" are at the ebb tide of nihilism.[31]

Following a stroke in July 2001, Johnson has been much less prominent in intelligent design advocacy.[32]

Bill Dembski, Michael Behe, and others are moving to put their approach to science on a solid disciplinary footing, and attract younger scientists to research problems on which ID might shed light.

A War of Religions?

Lobby groups such as Americans United for the Separation of Church and State (AU) frequently obsess about the religious beliefs of ID advocates such as Behe and Dembski, who declare themselves to be Christians.[33] AU does not seem similarly anxious to explore the beliefs of non-Christians associated with ID, such as David Berlinski, or Jonathan Wells, both of whom are also fellows of the Discovery Institute.

That is an interesting choice on AU's part. In response to the angry letters following one of his articles in the April 2003 edition of *Commentary*, a Jewish intellectual magazine, Berlinski commented on his personal beliefs. (As so often, Berlinski's sin was to show up the inimitable Richard Dawkins.

Dawkins had claimed in print that a computer simulation of the evolution of the eye existed, but it didn't.) Berlinski replied majestically to his Darwinist critics:

> As I have many times remarked, I have no creationist agenda whatso-ever and, beyond respecting the injunction to have a good time all the time, no religious principles, either.[34]

Berlinski's philosophy of life would scandalize a typical middle-American school board, but nonetheless Americans United can't really afford to call attention to it when attacking ID. The same officials who would label Berlinski's views scandalous would also realize that ID is not a stealth religious project, contrary to AU's overheated claims.

In fact, when the subject of religion comes up, one often encounters a curious disconnect in the writings of Darwinists. Microsoft billionaire Paul Allen funded the PBS *Evolution* series, which "wallows in religion"—of a sort designed to create support for Darwinism.[35] Microsoft billionaire Charles Simonyi funded Richard Dawkins's chair in the Public Understanding of Science at Oxford, which has enabled Dawkins to promote atheism to a bored, offended, and disbelieving public (disbelieving in atheism, that is) for nearly a decade. Likewise, the Templeton Foundation, started by wealthy investor John C. Templeton, finances many theistic evolution projects that interest mainly academics. Obviously, these wealthy investors are no different from the Discovery Institute in principle: they fund what they believe in, using their own money.[36] The public is either better or worse off, or perhaps merely more flummoxed, on account of their efforts. Western world taxpayers should be glad that this entire controversy is funded by billionaire high rollers, not by governments.[37]

The "disconnect" referred to above is the Darwinists' failure to admit—or perhaps a failure even to *see*—that all parties to the controversy, including themselves, have a philosophical investment. It is true that Michael Behe and William Dembski both see ID as furthering their Christian beliefs. But how do they differ from Richard Dawkins and Daniel Dennett, who see Darwinism as furthering their atheist/metaphysical naturalist beliefs? There are no "objective" players on the field, nor should we expect any, given the stakes.

This disconnect probably isn't doing Darwinism any good. By continually harping on some (but not all) ID advocates' beliefs, for example, the

Darwinists invite people to choose sides based on religion.[38] That is unwise. Far more people on this planet believe what Behe and Dembski believe than what Dawkins and Dennett believe.

"Becoming a Disciplined Science"

In October 2002, information theorist Bill Dembski, who has replaced Phillip Johnson as the point man for intelligent design, delivered a blunt talk to the RAPID Conference (Research and Progress in Intelligent Design) at Biola University in La Mirada, California. In "Becoming a Disciplined Science: Prospects, Pitfalls, and a Reality Check for ID," he demanded that the participants take a good hard look in the mirror—and he warned that it wouldn't be pretty.

He began by quoting a well-known intelligent design sympathizer—who had begun to lose interest—as saying:

> Too much stuff from the ID camp is repetitive, imprecise and immodest in its claims, and otherwise very unsatisfactory. The "debate" is mostly going around in circles. The real work needs to go forward. There is a tremendous ferment right now in the "evo/devo" field, for instance. Some bright postdocs sympathetic to ID (and yes, I know how hard a time they would have institutionally at many places) should plunge right into the thick of that. Maybe they are at this very moment: I hope so![39]

If impassioned and widely publicized school board hearings are any indicator, ID has been a victim of its own success with a broad public. Many people wanted to be liberated—and to liberate their local science curricula— from the suffocating spirit of Darwinism. They chose the forum that they could at least try to deal with: huge, contentious meetings. These well-meaning people impede the progress of the science they love by making ID disproportionately well known to the public, in relation to its actual accomplishments. They give more ammunition to its institutional enemies than to its advocates.

However, in Dembski's view, the problem with the seekers after liberation is not that they pursue school board politics. The problem is that they treat intelligent design as a tool. They do not ask if it is true. In his view, everything depends on whether it is true:

Smashing the Icons of Evolution

In 2000, biologist Jonathan Wells published *Icons of Evolution* and became a star overnight. A death star. His book was a withering, well-documented attack on the conventional examples of Darwinism in the leading high school and university textbooks. Most of these examples, he charged, are outright false or misleading.

In some cases, the text claimed or implied that the example proved things that it really didn't. In this category, top honors went to the famous peppered moth studies, which are still recycled in textbooks as an example of Darwinism in action, even though the science behind them now swirls in a huge cloud of uncertainties.[40]

Also, textbooks represent the Miller-Urey experiment as showing how life might originate on the early earth, even though current models of the early earth don't typically support the conditions that Miller-Urey would require.[41]

But at least one case that Wells analyzed can only be described as a fraud that has been perpetuated for generations.

Ernst Haeckel distorted many drawings of vertebrate embryos (fish, turtles, humans) in order to make them look more alike, to demonstrate that they all come from a common ancestor. Altered in this way, the drawings obviously support Darwinism.

In reality, according to Wells, embryos start out looking different from each other, look a bit alike at a middle stage, and then diverge dramatically later. While correct embryology does not disprove Darwinism, it also does not provide obvious support for it.[42]

Apparently, Stephen Jay Gould knew about this problem for many years. He did nothing to correct the situation until another biologist complained. Gould then blamed the textbook writers and also charged that the biologist who complained was a "creationist."[43] Wells responded:

> Who bears the greatest responsibility here—textbook-writers who mindlessly recycle faked drawings, people who complain about them, or the world-famous expert who watches smugly from the sidelines while his colleagues unwittingly become accessories to what he himself calls the "academic equivalent of murder"?

Wells tried grading the books and gave three of them a D. The rest received an F.

Textbook publishing is a lucrative industry dominated by a few prominent authors. Many of them were shocked by the idea that anyone would dare to critique their work in public. Iconoclast Wells quickly became the object of blistering ad hominem attacks. Wells is an easy target because he is a member of the Unification Church, though he is not active in the church. He has been attacked by both Darwinists ("loonie Moonie") and Christian zealots ("Satanic") on this account. He also spent a year and a half in prison rather than be recalled to active duty during the Vietnam war, a fact that would turn off many conservatives who might otherwise support him. All he says about that side of things is: "As a former Berkeley anti-war radical and ex-con, I am pretty thick-skinned."[44]

(cont'd)

Wells is often derided by his critics as a young earth creationist, but he isn't. He is comfortable with an ancient earth. However, his years spent researching the misrepresentations in textbooks have made him into a skeptic. In the end, he says: "After a witness has been caught in several lies, it is reasonable to doubt everything that comes out of his mouth. I prefer to reserve judgment until such time as I can see the evidence for myself."[45]

Currently, he is working on a critique of DNA-centered thinking in favor of an organism-centered approach, a book that he began while he was a post-doc in biology at Berkeley in the mid-1990s. Meanwhile, his exposé of Darwinist icons has made school trustees squirm uncomfortably at board meetings around the United States. Slowly, grudgingly, publishers of some recent editions of biology textbooks have started to remove information in support of Darwinism for which there is little evidence or questionable evidence.[46]

Intelligent design must not become a "noble lie" for vanquishing views we find unacceptable (history is full of noble lies that ended in disgrace). Rather, intelligent design needs to convince us of its truth on its scientific merits. Then, because it is true and known to be true, it can become an instrument for liberation from suffocating ideologies—ideologies that suffocate not because they tell us the grim truth about ourselves but because they are at once grim and false (Freud's psychic determinism is a case in point).[47]

Dembski was clearly unhappy with Phillip Johnson's "Wedge" and strove to distance himself from it. The street drama of rejection by a Darwinist establishment played well in the 1990s, but it became a liability because "wedges break things rather than build them up." Design needs to succeed as a scientific concept before it can succeed as a social or cultural concept, he warned.

By 2002, intelligent design had actually got somewhere. It had begun to set the terms of debate over origins, according to Karl Giberson and Donald Yerxa's new book, *Species of Origins*, which argues:

Since its inception in the early 1990s, the intelligent design movement has attracted so much attention that it has succeeded in dominating the origins debate. By this we do not mean that it is triumphant. Far from it. While design has made some modest inroads in the academy, it is frequently seen . . . as a more attractively packaged variety of creationism. But design has succeeded in setting the agenda for much of the debate.[48]

Giberson and Yerxa are not friendly to design, but they realize that the design advocates' questions cannot just be put off indefinitely, on the assumption that the forward–backward wobble of Darwinism is certain to overtake them.

To that end, Dembski introduced a number of science projects for ID advocates to begin to work on, including:

- *Catalog of Fundamental Facts (CFF)*, a rigorously developed list of specific examples of irreducible complexity in nature, for example, the mammalian visual system. Such a catalogue would force the science world to pay attention to problems that Darwinists have ignored or put off for decades.

- *Catalog Correcting Misinformation (CCM)*. Much information is cited in defense of Darwinism worldwide that would collapse under serious scrutiny.

This project would extend the work done by Jonathan Wells in *Icons of Evolution*, which identified the major errors in biology textbooks that promote Darwinism.

- *Network of Researchers and Resources (NRR)*. Dembski, together with Micah Sparacio and John Bracht, founded the International Society for Complexity, Information, and Design (ISCID) in 2001, to enable scholars interested in design who now work in isolation to benefit from live chats and videoconferences with peers. Their online journal is called *Progress in Complexity, Information, and Design*. ISCID keeps its costs down by operating economically from its site, www.iscid.org. The Web board requires, and receives, active moderation.

> **What ID Advocates Need to Do**
>
> If they could use their theories and come up with some interesting, surprising predictions, of a kind that people wouldn't expect, then I think people would start to take them seriously, just as people started to take Einstein seriously when he made some predictions about the perihelion of Mercury. Unless and until this happens, I'm not holding my breath.
>
> —Michael Ruse, Darwinist philosopher[49]

> A shift in prevailing scientific orthodoxies will come only when the objections to Darwinism . . . accumulate so forcefully that they can no longer be ignored.
>
> —David Berlinski[61]

The Monarch–Viceroy Mystery: What's Behind the Similarity?

An example of the type of misinformation that is frequently cited in defense of Darwinism is the simple explanation offered for the similarity in appearance of the Monarch and Viceroy butterflies.[50]

For decades, the relationship between the Monarch butterfly (*Danaus plexippus*) and the Viceroy butterfly (*Limenitis archippus*) was considered a clear textbook example of the evolutionary strategy of Batesian mimicry.

Batesian Mimicry?

In 1862, Henry Bates, an English naturalist and explorer of the Amazon, suggested that non-toxic species might evolve over time to look like toxic species. The non-toxic species would benefit because predators would avoid it as well as the toxic species.[51]

During the mid-20th century, Batesian mimicry was widely accepted as an explanation for the very close resemblance between the Monarch and the Viceroy. That was principally due to the studies of Jane Van Zandt Brower, published in *Evolution* in 1958.[52] The Monarch was assumed to be toxic, due to the fact that the caterpillars eat milkweed plants (*Asclepiadaceae*) and absorb the toxic cardiac glycosides. The Viceroy was assumed to be non-toxic. Its caterpillar feeds on willow family members.

For example, the United States Geological Survey gave the following information in the summer of 2003: "The Viceroy butterfly (*Limenitis archippus*) is edible, but mimics the poisonous Monarch in order to gain protection from predators."[53] Similarly, the University of Kentucky Agriculture Department's Entomology Web page stated in the same month that "by looking like a monarch butterfly (which tastes terrible to predators and makes them sick!), the viceroy (which is a tasty prey) is avoided by predators who have had a bad experience with monarchs in the past."[54]

However, research of 12 years earlier had cast doubt on any such simple relationship between the two butterflies, leaving a large mystery in its wake. In 1991, David Ritland and Lincoln Brouwer fed only the abdomens of Monarchs, Viceroys, and Queens to red-winged blackbirds, a frequent butterfly predator. (The Queen—*Danaus gilippus*—is a southern relative of the Monarch, with a darker wing shade.)

Presented with abdomens only, the birds would not be able to identify butterflies by their wing patterns and would have to rely on smell and taste alone. The birds found Monarchs and Viceroys about equally unpalatable (40% eaten), and Queens more palatable (70%). They ate 98% of the non-toxic controls.[55] Clearly, the Viceroy does not reduce its chance of being eaten by looking like the Monarch. Predators do not like either species much. Batesian mimicry was considered to be disconfirmed, although many popular sources continue to offer it as an explanation.

(cont'd)

A Comparison of the Two Butterflies

There are detectable differences between the Monarch and the Viceroy. The Viceroy has a black band running horizontally across the hind wings, which the Monarch lacks. Also, the Viceroy flutters, whereas the Monarch, usually a much bigger butterfly, flaps and then glides. There are some slight differences on the undersides as well. (In southern regions, the Viceroy is closer in color to the Queen.)

The resemblance is not the result of a close genetic relationship. The Monarch (*Danaus*) and the Viceroy (*Archippus*) belong to different subfamilies of the order Lepidoptera (butterflies and moths).[56] Their habits are also very different. The Monarch migrates over three to five generations between summer sites in the northern United States and Canada, and overwintering sites in Mexico. The Viceroy, which is territorial, overwinters in its home environment at the first and second growth stages (instars) of the caterpillar, in a form of hibernation (diapause).

The caterpillars are not at all similar. The Viceroy caterpillar resembles a bird dropping; the Monarch is striped orange, yellow, and black, with horns on both the head and tail.

Mullerian Mimicry?

Researchers then proposed another explanation for the resemblance of the adult Monarch and Viceroy: Mullerian mimicry. In 1878, German zoologist Fritz Muller, an Amazon naturalist like Bates, had suggested that a number of toxic species may adopt the same warning pattern (an *aposematic* pattern). The predators would learn faster if they had to learn only one signal to avoid, so, overall, fewer of all the prey species in the group (mimicry complex) would be eaten.

However, both the feeding habits and the toxicity of the Monarch are more complex than was originally supposed. While the caterpillars feed only on milkweed plants, the adults drink nectar from members of the composite flower family *Asteraceae*, producing pyrrolizidine alkaloids. Also, in the overwintering sites, major predators such as birds and mice are not affected by the poisons. Some predators eat only the less toxic parts, others do not absorb the toxic substances well, or are simply immune to them. In any event, northern milkweeds are less toxic than southern ones, and older butterflies are less toxic than younger ones.[57]

Ritland, based at Erskine College in South Carolina, has shown that Viceroys in the Southeast vary little in how tasty they are to predators, but Monarchs and Queens vary between 6% and 85%.[58] It may well be asked, if the Monarch displays warning coloration when many Monarchs are not poisonous, does the predator learn to avoid—or seek out—Monarchs? The kill rate of Monarchs is very high, especially in the overwintering sites. Why mimic such an ambiguous signal?

While studying another butterfly mimicry complex, Akira Saito remarked in *Forma* in 2002 that "during the 100 years following discovery of mimicry, not only has little been discovered about mechanisms of mimicry, but little evidence has been found to even verify the function of mimicry."[59]

(cont'd)

An Open Question

Another complicating factor is that in Canada, the Viceroy and other members of *Limenitidinae*, commonly called Admirals, hybridize to some extent.[60] The other members found in Canada are Red and White Admirals, and Red-spotted Purples, none of which resemble the Viceroy in wing pattern.

How can natural selection produce such similar wing patterns as those of the Monarch and Viceroy by a slow process of adaptation when the regional situation varies, the toxicity level is constantly changing—making the signal ambiguous or dangerous—and the Viceroy species does not appear to have strayed very far genetically in the process of acquiring the similarity?

Cataloguing instances where a Darwinist explanation has been too easily accepted is a first step to looking for better answers.

Where Will They Go from Here?

One of Dembski's goals is to codify the process by which intelligence is recognized, using the inferences of fields such as forensics and archeology, so as to apply them to biology. This explanatory filter is his chief contribution to the intelligent design movement, as well as his claim to fame. If chance and laws of nature can be ruled out as explanations, what is left is design.[62]

Meanwhile, Michael Behe has recently been investing time preparing articles for scholarly journals in biochemistry, based on the premise of intelligent design.

The key to a scientific understanding of design is not theology, but information theory.[64] If design is a part of nature, then the design is embedded in life as information. But many people are not used to thinking in terms of an immaterial quantity like information. As G.C. Williams writes:

> Information doesn't have mass or charge or length in millimeters. Likewise, matter doesn't have bytes. You can't measure so much gold in so many bytes. It doesn't have redundancy, or fidelity, or any of the other descriptors we apply to information. This dearth of shared descriptors makes matter and

> Johannes Kepler thought the craters on the moon were intelligently designed by moon dwellers. We now know that the craters were formed naturally. It's this fear of falsely attributing something to design only to have it overturned later that has prevented design from entering science proper. With precise methods for discriminating intelligently from unintelligently caused objects, scientists are now able to avoid Kepler's mistake.
>
> —William Dembski[63]

information two separate domains of existence, which have to be discussed separately, in their own terms.[65]

Yet the two separate domains unite in life forms. In an article in *Scientific American* in 2003, Jacob D. Bekenstein noted: "Ask anybody what the physical world is made of, and you are likely to be told 'matter and energy.' Yet if we have learned anything from engineering, biology and physics, information is just as crucial an ingredient."[66] He continues:

> The robot at the automobile factory is supplied with metal and plastic but can make nothing useful without copious instructions telling it which part to weld to what and so on. A ribosome in a cell in your body is supplied with amino acid building blocks and is powered by energy released by the conversion of ATP to ADP, but it can synthesize no proteins without the information brought to it from the DNA in the cell's nucleus. Likewise, a century of developments in physics has taught us that information is a crucial player in physical systems and processes.[67]

He also notes that a current trend, initiated by John A. Wheeler of Princeton University, is to regard the physical world as made of information, with energy and matter as incidentals.[68]

If information is considered a real, not an artificial "designoid" category of life, there are many research opportunities for intelligent design. ID might help to determine the questions that seem interesting. For example, instead of trying to figure out how the entire genome can arise "by chance," with vast amounts of DNA that is merely "junk," an ID advocate might suspect that the "junk" is not really a trash heap. It may be a library, a history, or a research centre. Studying it would be of more interest than explaining it away.

As a matter of fact, contrary to widespread earlier claims, some of the "junk" is turning out to have critical functions in repairing working parts of the DNA.[69] Older ID scientists now recommend molecular biology to younger ones, for good reason. If there is a language of life that is a product of intelligent design, it is as likely to be found in the DNA as anywhere.

Perhaps there is more openness now than there used to be. In any event, there are advantages and disadvantages to an ID perspective. If intelligent design exists, the ID scientist will learn a number of interesting and perhaps useful things. If it doesn't, the ID scientist is wasting time. This, of course, is the perennial problem of the road not taken. We rarely reflect much on the road not taken if the one we are on is interesting and profitable.

Don't Junk That "Junk DNA"

More than one-third of the human genome consists of repetitive elements, formerly classified as "junk DNA" because they had no known function. These elements include nearly two million transposable elements (retrotransposons, also called L1s), which make up 17% of total DNA. According to John V. Moran, assistant professor of human genetics and internal medicine at the University of Michigan Medical School, that is changing. "Until now, everyone thought L1s were just intracellular parasites in our DNA—leftovers from the distant evolutionary past. The big question in the field is: Are they still there because we can't get rid of them or do they have a function?

In a May 13, 2002, paper published online by *Nature Genetics*, a research team that included Dr. Moran reported that these mobile pieces of DNA may provide a repair service for the genome.

Retrotransposons can move around in the genome and produce copies of themselves by a process similar to copy and paste in word processing. This quality is useful when a double-stranded break in the DNA occurs. A double-stranded break, due to stress or contamination of the cell by chemicals, can lead to cell death. The retrotransposons move through the genome and look for such breaks; when they find one, they insert themselves and knit the region back together.

However, they also sometimes cut the genome themselves and insert themselves into it. Usually, according to Mark Batzer, professor of biological sciences at Louisiana State University, their intrusion makes no difference, but sometimes, as in the case of hemophilia A and muscular dystrophy, it can be disastrous.

For many years, the assumptions scientists made about evolution prevented the "junk" from being studied. As one researcher explains: "Although catchy, the term 'junk DNA' for many years repelled mainstream researchers from studying noncoding DNA. Who, except a small number of genomic clochards, would like to dig through genomic garbage? However, in science as in normal life, there are some clochards who, at the risk of being ridiculed, explore unpopular territories. Because of them, the view of junk DNA, especially repetitive elements, began to change in the early 1990s."[70]

Humans have more of these retrotransposons than any other species.[71]

Afterword

While writing this book, I tried to listen to everyone, a habit learned over three decades of journalism. Usually, I do not know what to think when starting the research for a story. This one was no exception. However, after two years, I have formed some opinions.

On the Big Bang

Many scientists dislike the Big Bang because we cannot go behind it. These scientists want to go behind the set—and get the stage carpenter to explain the play! Talking to the playwright would be more instructive. However, playwrights do not "explain" their plays. Art obviates explanation. Still, we want to know more, so we, necessarily, default to science again, perhaps a little wiser in the questions we ask.

On the Big Bang and God

Does the Big Bang compel belief in God? No. Nothing *compels* belief in God. Belief is a matter of drawing reasonable conclusions from the available evidence.[1]

On Evolution

I am probably best described as a post-Darwinian. I believe that evolution happened but that Darwinism is an inadequate explanation.[2] The reason is simple: Darwin did not anticipate the complexity of the problems, so his theory, in whatever rebrand it now appears, is not likely the solution.

Evolution has been hijacked by Darwinism. Current controversies over the teaching of evolution and the role of design stem from the fact that more and more people are aware of the problems of Darwinism, and they are looking for alternatives.

The Darwinists have mainly themselves to blame for the low esteem in which Darwinism is currently held by much of the public, compared with other theories in science.

First, there is the problem of their need to see Darwinism as a biological Theory of Everything. Darwinists insist on the implausible origin of life from non-life for the same reason as many of them insist on Social Darwinism: If there were any aspect of life that was not explained by Darwinism or other naturalistic, no-design theories, Darwinism would have to base its claims on evidence. And the state of the evidence is not good.

Then there is the problem of their bad behavior. For example, Richard Dawkins, the world's best-known living Darwinist, claims—on behalf of his Oxford chair as Professor of the Public Understanding of Science—that "if you meet somebody who claims not to believe in evolution, that person is ignorant, stupid or insane (or wicked, but I'd rather not consider that)."[3]

What is the public supposed to understand from this remark? That becoming a professor can make a man more didactic and self-righteous than is good for him? True, but hardly news. If I had to convince an auditorium of thoughtful Christians that evolution has happened, I could probably convince 90%, provided that (1) Richard Dawkins never opens his mouth again in public, and (2) the other ultra-Darwinists go back to studying insect colonies. As it is, I doubt I could convince 50%, and the number may be dropping.

Compounding the problem of bad behavior is the frequent rumble from the science press that the public does not know enough about science to understand why Darwinism must be true. Sorry, folks, you'll have to do better than that. Granted, much of modern science is hard to grasp. But lacking technical information is not the same thing as lacking good judgment about the probability that a very broad explanation is correct. More to the point, we are being asked to discount any explanation other than Darwinism, and to persecute dissenters. That is too much to ask.

The more I began to understand the issues, the more I realized that Darwinian evolution probably isn't the right explanation for the development of life, but that biologists don't have anything better right now. As Phillip Johnson puts it: "we cannot turn ignorance into information by calling it evolution."[4]

I sympathize. No, I really *do* sympathize. But I refuse to be bullied. And there is plenty of that going on right now, as this book documents.

The biggest problem of all is the growth of politics around the issues. Darwinism has significant problems as a theory in science. These problems originate in nature, not in the church basement. Of course, by themselves, problems are not necessarily fatal. Models in science always have problems. Darwinism has more problems than most. Still, scientists must work with a model. Perhaps they can work with Darwinism until another model replaces it.

However, just as some American pressure groups have attempted to out-law Darwinism, others have taken to the courts and to politics to protect it from criticism, alternative theories, or rejection. They have hassled and persecuted dissenters. Their constant use of legal and political muscle makes me think that Darwinism's problems are insurmountable. Perhaps not. Time will tell.

Here's a thought: What would happen if the Big Bang theory were similarly "protected" from skepticism? No doubt, steady state universes, umpteen-decker multiverses, and imaginary time scales would pop up on Web sites everywhere. They would be vastly more popular with the public than they are now.

That is because most people know what to make of intellectual bullying. The Darwinists have brought about the thing they fear the most: widespread assessment of their theory as *failed*.[5]

Third, there is the problem of underlying agenda. I have never heard such hardline, aggressive promotion of atheism under the guise of science as I have heard from the Darwinists. It is, at best, amusing to hear Darwinists charge that the creationists have an underlying religious agenda, when the Darwinists' own anti-religious agenda is pretty obvious.

Let's face it, everyone starts from a point of view, and what seems reasonable always depends to some extent on one's presuppositions.

For the record, I am an evangelical Anglican.[6] That fact undoubtedly helps shape my views, but I should add that my church requires no opinion, so far as I know, on Darwinian evolution, and professes little interest in the subject.

Fourth, Social Darwinism (sociobiology, evolutionary psychology, and whatever the next rebrand will be called) is a Bad Idea that should just be abandoned. Every time Social Darwinism rears its ugly head, many people learn about Darwinism for the first time. They discover that learned professors think that less educated people are inferior. Large numbers default to any alternative point of view—young earth Christian creationism, Native

American creationism, Muslim creationism, whatever—and oppose Darwinism in the schools to which they pay taxes. In other words, they are *not* as dumb as the professors think. They are not going to *pay* to be insulted.

The chief danger from compulsory teaching of Darwinism is that any dissenting view may begin to sound reasonable by default. However, a view cannot be assumed to have merit simply because it is not Darwinism.

On Theistic Evolution

The problem for theistic evolution (Darwinism with a slight glow of faith) is to explain how it differs from atheistic evolution, except in the hopes of its adherents.

Surely it was more honorable for Charles Darwin to lose his faith over the cat playing with mice than for Catholic Darwinist Ken Miller to cheerfully announce that perhaps it is not a problem after all. In *Finding Darwin's God*, he explains: "Evolution cannot be a cruel concept if all it does is reflect the realities of nature, including birth, struggle, life, and death."[7] As if these categories do not include every mortal evil that human beings can imagine! Some aspects of nature are just evil. The challenge of any theology, philosophy, or grand scheme of life is to explain that.

On Young Earth Creationism

Young earth creationism short-circuits the problem of evolution by declaring that Genesis is to be taken literally and that therefore the evidence is wrong. YEC functions as the answer to a problem that the YECs have created for themselves, in my view: the problem of taking Genesis 1 and 2 literally.

Their solution cannot have much appeal outside religious circles that encourage their way of interpreting Scripture. However, scientists working within this constraint will likely continue to come up with interesting information nonetheless. It is wrong for other scientists to ridicule or harass them.

Overall, young earth creationism is attacked as an antirealist belief system. However, given that the supposedly realist belief systems are not true to the nature of life, people inevitably look elsewhere for answers.

On "Mainstream Science"

The fact that a majority hold certain views has never been a guarantee of their interpretation of reality. The ability of Darwinism to interpret reality is precisely the point at issue. Hence the sheer uselessness of appeals to the fact that most scientists support it. Most scientists supported the earth-centered universe, spontaneous generation of life forms, and luminiferous ether in their day.

If the Darwinist is determined that natural selection is the only possible mechanism for the development of life, he must live with whatever explanation it provides, however improbable. That is his right. Forcing his theory on society and the school system is another matter.

On What Should Be Taught in Schools

Darwinism has become the Political Correctness of science, demanding loyalty to dubious propositions as a demonstration of faith in the system. The Darwin lobby accuses teachers who discuss intelligent design of promoting a religion. However, just as Julian Huxley intended it to be long ago, organized Darwinism is itself a religion, one that operates through science and education establishments.[8] Thus, for the Darwinist, there can be no neutral questions where biology is concerned and alternatives to Darwinism must be systematically suppressed. For the rest of us, there can be no serious thinking until academic freedom is re-established in this area.

What should students be told? They should be taught Darwinism, but teachers should acknowledge problems and not defend it as if it were a religion.

However, it is important to bear in mind that, after decades of educational fads, many students struggle with literacy and motivation, even in the upper grades. The teacher who has students who are even aware of higher-level issues is probably uncommonly lucky. Still, the exception tests the rule. Students who are smart enough to think for themselves must be allowed to do so.

On Textbooks and "Teaching the Controversy"

As a textbook editor myself, I know intimately the process whereby books are painstakingly improved from one edition to the next—or allowed to slide, unimproved, from one edition to the next, because the publisher will profit in any case from adoption by a large jurisdiction. The student has no power, and the teacher is hampered by budget constraints, politics, or a small, tight group of suppliers. Thus, there is no natural constituency for improvement.

However, for those who have the will, *improvement is still as near as the next edition of any given book!* All textbook units on evolution should be scrutinized for outworn or questionable arguments. Haeckel's embryo drawings, for example, should not be reproduced. However, some current evolution problems can be reworked to provide teaching value. For example, the peppered moth/peppered myth controversy can generate an excellent sidebar on the difficulties of field research in the complex world of insects.[9]

Should schools "teach the controversy," as intelligent design advocates want? That is, teach evolution but identify problems and encourage students to be aware of alternative theories such as intelligent design? As far as I can see, students can be introduced to the current debate *without* a swamp of controversy, provided the issues are investigated, but not politicized, legislated, or litigated.

For example, the "irreducible complexity" debate would make an excellent independent research project for a senior high school or first-year university student. The same goes for computer simulations of evolution. A computer-savvy student can be challenged to study evolution programs, and evaluate the relationship between the way they work and known facts of biology.

By contrast, backing away from the whole area for fear of controversy, or worse yet, under threat of lawsuits by Darwin lobbies, creates a worst-case scenario for education: The school system ignores headline issues and demands that discredited material be learned merely because it is in the textbook, then falls back on legal rulings. Consider the following dialogue:

Student: Mr. Mahmoud, what do you think about the intelligent design controversy?

Teacher: I am not legally allowed to discuss that with you.

Student: (to himself) Just like I thought. These clowns are all too stupid to do the math.

For the sake of education, let's be warned by the prescient comments of Thomas Huxley on the future of Darwinism:

> History warns us . . . that it is the customary fate of new truths to begin as heresies and to end as superstitions; and, as matters now stand, it is hardly rash to anticipate that, in another twenty years, the new generation, educated under the influences of the present day, will be in danger of accepting the main doctrines of the "Origin of Species," with as little reflection, and it may be with as little justification, as so many of our contemporaries, twenty years ago, rejected them. Against any such a consummation let us all devoutly pray; for the scientific spirit is of more value than its products, and irrationally held truths may be more harmful than reasoned errors.[10]

In the age of the Internet, institutions can no longer insulate themselves from challenge without losing credibility with their stakeholders. School systems may as well bite the bullet and discuss the issues responsibly.

On Intelligent Design

The question is not whether the universe shows evidence of design. Of course it does. The question is how to interpret the evidence. The most reasonable explanation is design. But what does that mean? It means that we are back where we always were, but now we recognize more landmarks. Recognizing design may give us a handle on the awesome complexity. That may or may not help. The human race has a history, and design is a part of it.

The current intelligent design controversy is a struggle within science between empiricism (what the evidence shows) and naturalism (the belief that no evidence that shows design can be admitted). Just as the young earth creationists created a problem for themselves by insisting that Genesis 1–6 must be interpreted literally, the naturalists created a problem for themselves by insisting that science must proceed as if there is no design. When Julian Huxley introduced the world to his new religion of Evolution in 1959, he could not have envisioned a conflict between evidence and naturalism. Surely all the evidence must support naturalism! Unfortunately, many in science today seem incapable of a rational discussion of the problem of what happens when the evidence doesn't support it. Contrary evidence piles up, increasingly strained interpretations are invoked, the issues are politicized in order to gain time, and dissenters (real or imagined) are persecuted and suppressed.

Who knows? Perhaps an informed public (key alumni, for example, or civil rights bodies) will eventually have to step in and point out that, as a society, we do *not* owe the Darwinists the right to set the terms by which we all understand life and reality. Nor have we given them the right to suppress all dissent from their religion/philosophy in the sciences, by whatever means they choose.

And Lastly. . . Everybody Is in It for the Philosophy

The issue of origins is inescapably philosophical as well as scientific. The notion of "objective" science is nonsensical, as we have seen. Many Darwinists, such as Richard Dawkins, Stephen Jay Gould, or William Provine, are just as invested in atheism as many (though not all) ID scientists are in Christianity.

If you are an atheist, you may find the case for Darwinism compelling because no other explanation would suit your view of the world.

If you are an ID sympathizer, you need to consider the danger of the idea that design is real. So many questions that are merely deferred to "everybody has a different opinion" become researchable questions. What if you don't like the design you find?

If you are a creationist, you may find ID almost as objectionable as atheism, and for the same reason: ID does not even attempt a defense of Scripture, which is the only reliable source of truth for you.

If you are a Christian evolutionist, you have made a precarious peace with a science whose backdrop is there is no real design in the universe, which is pretty much the opposite of what traditional Christianity teaches. Unlike Francis Schaeffer, who sought a "God who is there," you must be content with a God who is *not* there, except as an emotional experience.

All the above groups have their own good reasons for attacking each other, which is why we hear so much rhetoric of attack and denunciation, and so little discussion of the key issues.

On the Future

Most people in North America do not believe the ideas that lead to Darwinism. Those who have not started to believe those ideas are not likely to start now. Europe, where people do believe them, is waning in influence. We have only begun to see the effects of the death of modernism, for better or worse. But the big news is—design is back, to stay.

Notes

Introduction (Pages 1–12)

[1] Quoted in Henry F. "Fritz" Schaefer, III, "Stephen Hawking, the Big Bang, and God," a public lecture available at http://www.origins.org/articles/schaefer_bigbangandgod.html.

[2] There were, of course, disputes about the age of the earth, but that is a different matter. The earth could be finitely old in an infinite universe.

[3] Quoted in Henry F. "Fritz" Schaefer, III, "Stephen Hawking, the Big Bang, and God," a public lecture available at http://www.origins.org/articles/schaefer_bigbangandgod.html. According to Hugh Ross (H.N. Ross, *The Creator and the Cosmos: How the Greatest Scientific Discoveries of the Century Reveal God* [1993] (Colorado Springs, CO: NavPress, 1994), 3rd printing, p. 51), Eddington originally said: "Philosophically, the notion of a beginning of the present order of Nature is repugnant. . . . [I] should like to find a genuine loophole." A.S. Eddington, "The end of the world: from the standpoint of mathematical physics," Nature (1931), 127: 450. His infinitely elastic time scale for evolution was proposed in 1930: "We [must] allow evolution an infinite time to get started." A.S. Eddington, "On the instability of Einstein's spherical world," *Monthly Notices of the Royal Astronomical Society* (1930), 90: 672. The notion that we must allow evolution an infinite amount of time to get started says more about Darwinian evolution than about the age of the universe.

[4] See Wikipedia's Timeline of the Big Bang for more details, http://www.wikipedia.org/wiki/Timeline_of_the_Big_Bang. Stephen Hawking's *A Brief History of Time* provides a lucid explanation (New York: Bantam, 1996).

[5] *Journal* (1868).

[6] Quoted in *The Columbia World of Quotations*, 1996. This is a clear statement of ultra-Darwinism. Originally from R. Dawkins, *The Blind Watchmaker* [1986] (London: Penguin, 1991, reprint), p. 5.

7 For a useful discussion of this worldwide trend, see Peter L. Berger, ed., *The Desecularization of the World: Resurgent Religion and World Politics* (Grand Rapids, MI.: Eerdmans, 1999).

8 You can read more about Georges Lemaître at the online encyclopedia, Wikipedia, www.wikipedia.org/wiki/ Georges Lemaître, with links to many key concepts.

9 The Steady State model of the universe still has respected supporters, such as plasma cosmologist Eric Lerner. See Eric Lerner, *The Big Bang Never Happened: A Startling Refutation of the Dominant Theory of the Origin of the Universe* (New York: Random House, 1991).

10 If you do not have a Bible handy, you can fire up your browser, go to www.gospelcom.net, and read Genesis 1 through 9 online. This will be most helpful for understanding young earth creationism.

11 Readers may wish to visit the Web site of the "brights," where they will discover that two of the world's most prominent Darwinists, Richard Dawkins and Daniel Dennett, have helped found a movement to unite atheists under the banner of "Brights." See http://www.the-brights.net/ where, we are informed, "A Bright is a person who has a naturalistic worldview." "Naturalism" means approximately what Dawkins or Dennett believe, that nature is all there is.

12 David Simpson, *Internet Encyclopedia of Philosophy*, http://www.utm.edu/research/iep/, accessed January 11, 2003. See "Lucretius."

13 The views of Lucretius and Epicurus were not universally accepted. The Christian philosopher Augustine (354–430 AD) disagreed with them; he believed that God created the universe, and time along with it. See Stephen Hawking, *A Brief History of Time* (New York: Bantam, 1996), p. 13. However, like Christianity, Epicureanism was intended to be a true philosophy of life for the average person. As J. Gaskin says: "Epicurean ideas were never intended to be difficult or esoteric, the preserve of the learned. They were addressed to mankind almost as widely as St Paul addressed his letters on Christianity. Indeed, in some ways the content of the Epicurean Philosophy— the 'Philosophy of the Garden' as it was often called—has a more apparent relevance to the world we now know than Christianity itself. The Epicurean idea of an infinite universe of matter and space, indifferent to human hopes and concerns but whose workings can be understood, is the predominant scientific idea with which we now live." J. Gaskin, ed., *The Epicurean Philosophers* (London: J.M. Dent, 1995), p. ix.

14 March 12, 1978. Quoted in Henry F. "Fritz" Schaefer, III, "Stephen Hawking, the Big Bang, and God," a public lecture available at http://www.origins.org/articles/schaefer_bigbangandgod.html.

Chapter 1: By Design or By Chance? (Pages 15–30)

1 Robert Jastrow, *God and the Astronomers* (New York: W.W. Norton, 1978), p. 31.

2 Quoted in "The 'Just So' Universe" by Walter L. Bradley, in William A. Dembski

and James M. Kushiner, eds., *Signs of Intelligence: Understanding Intelligent Design* (Grand Rapids, MI: Baker House–Brazos Press, 2001), p. 168. An expanded version of the same idea is "It is true that we emerged in the universe by chance, but the idea of chance is itself only a cover for our ignorance. I do not feel like an alien in this universe. The more I examine the universe and study the details of its architecture, the more evidence I find that the universe in some sense must have known that we were coming." (F.J. Dyson, *Disturbing the Universe*, New York: Harper & Row, 1979, p. 250.)

3 Hubble identified this shift as Hubble's law, according to which galaxies are moving apart at a rate that increases with their distance. He discovered the motion as a result of the uniform shift of galaxies to the red end of the color spectrum, when light is broken up (in a process called spectrography). The red shift indicates that the galaxies are moving away from us.

4 You can read more about Olbers' Paradox at http://www.wikipedia.org/wiki/Olbers'_paradox.

5 Lemaître himself had called the beginning of the universe a "primeval atom," or, worse, a "dense egg," so we should be glad that Hoyle, who had a genius for popular communication, named the theory. For Hoyle's role, see "Fred Hoyle," Wikipedia, www.wikipedia.org. Hoyle also used the term "the Big Bang" in his radio talks on astronomy for the BBC in the 1950s; that is probably how it entered popular language. Science writer Timothy Ferris recalls in *The Whole Shebang: A State of the Universes Report* (New York: Simon & Schuster, 1998), p. 323n, that he served as one of the judges in a contest in the early 1990s to come up with a better name, but failed. Technically, scientists call the Big Bang a "singularity," meaning that it does not follow the usual laws that govern matter and energy.

6 Fred Heeren recounts this anecdote in *Show Me God: What the Message from Space Is Telling Us About God*, rev. ed. (Wheeling, IL: Day Star Publications, 2000), pp. 102–3. It apparently originated in John D. Barrow and Joseph Silk, *The Left Hand of Creation: The Origin and Evolution of the Expanding Universe* (London: Heinemann, 1983), p. 13. I have not been able to find out which 1940s potboiler the trio of physicists saw.

7 The idea of a Steady State universe wasn't totally new, according to Fred Heeren in *Show Me God: What the Message from Space Is Telling Us About God*, rev. ed. (Wheeling, IL: Day Star Publications, 2000), p. 102. Various modern Steady State theories had been proposed from 1918 on. However, the group that coalesced around Hoyle was by far the best known and most important.

8 According to J. Gribbin, in *In Search of the Big Bang: Quantum Physics and Cosmology* (London: Heinemann, 1986), p. 130, Lemaître's "primeval atom" of the universe was a hefty rock, "about thirty times bigger than our Sun." Today, physicists tend to think of it as a point of zero volume; thus, it has lost bulk but not significance.

9 Stephen Hawking, *The Illustrated A Brief History of Time* (New York: Bantam, 1996), p. 63. Hawking points out that such a small quantity of atoms at a time would

NOTES

not be in conflict with science experiments, which always have a plus or minus factor. That was an important consideration in the theory's favor.

[10] Fred Heeren, *Show Me God: What the Message from Space Is Telling Us About God*, rev. ed. (Wheeling, IL: Day Star Publications, 2000), p. 104.

[11] A lucid account of Steady State cosmology can be found in ibid., pp. 102–6.

[12] Timothy Ferris, *The Whole Shebang: A State of the Universes Report* (New York: Simon & Schuster, 1998), says (p. 111) that Hoyle et al. disliked Big Bang theory because "it implied an origin to the universe that remained shrouded in mystery if not mysticism." Scientists often have "religious" objections to scientific theories, even if they are atheists or otherwise not conventionally religious. For example, Albert Einstein, who is widely assumed to have been an atheist or pantheist, rejected quantum mechanics because he argued that "God" does not play dice with the universe. In the last sentence of his *A Brief History of Time*, Stephen Hawking, who shows no signs of being a conventional religious believer, argued that coming up with a grand unified theory in physics would enable us to know "the mind of God." Cosmology affects scientists that way. They start to talk about God even if they don't believe in him. Many resent this fact, but they certainly have not got God out of the picture.

[13] Robert Jastrow, *God and the Astronomers*, 2nd ed. (New York: W.W. Norton, 1992) p. 107.

[14] Stephen Hawking, *The Illustrated A Brief History of Time* (New York: Bantam, 1996), p. 62.

[15] The Steady State theory predicted only about 3% of hydrogen to be converted to helium. The Big Bang allows for a huge amount of energy to start the universe, and therefore suggested 25%. A lucid account of Steady State cosmology can be found in Fred Heeren, *Show Me God: What the Message from Space Is Telling Us About God*, rev. ed. (Wheeling, IL: Day Star Publications, 2000), pp. 102–06. See also Stephen Hawking, *The Illustrated A Brief History of Time* (New York: Bantam, 1996), pp. 62–63, for an account of efforts to make the Steady State theory work.

[16] Fred Hoyle, *The Intelligent Universe* (New York: Holt, Rinehart and Winston, 1983), p. 176.

[17] See, for example, "'Big bang' astronomer dies," *BBC News*, August 22, 2001, http://news.bbc.co.uk/1/hi/uk/1503721.stm.

[18] Timothy Ferris, *The Whole Shebang: A State of the Universes Report* (New York: Simon & Schuster, 1998), pp. 112–14.

[19] Thomas Kuhn, *The Structure of Scientific Revolutions*, 2nd ed., enlarged (Chicago: University of Chicago Press, 1970), p. 147.

[20] Proofs can be found in mathematics, but not in science. Mostly, scientists do not look for proof; they look for a model that fits most of the evidence.

[21] Absolute zero means that there is no heat at all. Strictly speaking, this never hap-

pens, because quantum particles won't allow it. (Both the position and velocity of particles could then be measured, and they do not allow themselves to be measured in this way.) However, absolute zero temperature is pegged theoretically at –273.16° C (–459.69° F), or 0° on the Kelvin scale (0 K). You can find out more about absolute zero at http://www.sun.rhbnc.ac.uk/~uhap057/LTWeb/Absolute.html. The story of Penzias and Wilson's discovery is amazing, and you can read about it in B. Bryson, *A Short History of Nearly Everything* (London: Doubleday, 2003). "They had found the edge of the universe, or at least the visible part of it, 90 billion trillion miles away. They were 'seeing' the first photons— the most ancient light in the universe though time and distance had converted them to microwaves, just as Gamow had predicted.", pp. 11–12).

22 See, for example, www.panspermia.org, a Web site that advances these views.

23 Timothy Ferris, *The Whole Shebang: A State of the Universes Report* (New York: Simon & Schuster, 1998), p. 20, attributes the statement that the discovery was like "looking at the face of God" to George Smoot. *The San Francisco Chronicle*, May 25, 1992, p. 35. Richard Isaacman, quoted by John Boslough, *Masters of Time: Cosmology at the End of Innocence* (New York: Addison-Wesley, 1992), p. 45, is quoted in Heeren, p. 159, as saying: "I felt like I was looking God in the face." No doubt there was plenty of religious excitement to go around.

24 *Nature* (1989), 340: 425. Incidentally, intelligent design advocate Michael J. Behe notes in *Darwin's Black Box: The Biochemical Challenge to Evolution* (New York: Free Press, 1996), p. 250, that Maddox has also said (in "Defending science against anti-science," *Nature* (1994), 368: 185) that "it may not be long before the practice of religion must be regarded as anti-science." Likewise, Geoffrey Burbidge of the University of California at San Diego somewhat uncharitably taxed his colleagues with rushing off to join "the First Church of Christ of the Big Bang." Hugh Ross recounts this jibe in *The Creator and the Cosmos* (Colorado Springs: NavPress, 1993), quoting from Stephen Strauss, "An innocent's guide to the big bang theory: fingerprint in space left by the universe as a baby still has doubters hurling stones," *Globe and Mail*, April 25, 1992. Burbidge has made clear that his own quasi-Steady State view supports Hinduism rather than Christianity. Hinduism is much more comfortable with a Steady State universe. You can read about Burbidge's current quasi-Steady State theory at http://cosswww.ucsd.edu/personal/gburbidge.html. Researching this subject, one is struck by the extent to which reactions to the Big Bang (and in some cases, even views on civil liberties) depend on religious or anti-religious commitments.

25 The latest figure on the age of the universe since the Big Bang is 13.7 billion years (http://www.gsfc.nasa.gov/topstory/2003/0206mapresults.html). This figure may be adjusted up or down, but current cosmology assumes an age range in this area.

26 Quoted in Henry F. "Fritz" Schaefer, III, "Stephen Hawking, the Big Bang, and God," a public lecture available at http://www.origins.org/articles/schaefer_bigbangandgod.html.

NOTES

[27] Carl Sagan, *Pale Blue Dot: A Vision of the Human Future in Space* (Ballantine Books, 1997), p. 12.

[28] Arno Penzias, quoted in Walter L. Bradley, "The 'Just So' Universe," *Signs of Intelligence: Understanding Intelligent Design*, William A. Dembski and James M. Kushiner, eds. (Grand Rapids, MI: Baker House–Brazos Press, 2001). The original source is A. Penzias, "Creation Is Supported by All the Data So Far," in H. Margenau and R.A. Varghese, eds., *Cosmos, Bios, Theos: Scientists Reflect on Science, God, and the Origins of the Universe Life, and Homo Sapiens* [1992] (La Salle IL: Open Court, 1993), Second Printing, p. 78.

[29] Quoted in Patrick Glynn, "Beyond the death of God," *National Review*, May 6, 1996.

[30] Useful information about black holes is available from NASA at http://imagine.gsfc.nasa.gov/docs/science/know_l2/black_holes.html. Despite the disclaimers, black holes are likely weirder than anything we imagine.

[31] See "Black hole snacks," September 5, 2001, http://science.nasa.gov/headlines/y2001/ast05sep_1.htm; See also "Star clinches case for Milky Way's supermassive black hole," *Scientific American* (October 17, 2002).

[32] *Oxford Dictionary of Thematic Quotations*, 2000.

[33] This is described in some sources as a legend, but we may hope that it is true. A thoughtful gesture of this sort was certainly possible. See *The Catholic Encyclopedia*, http://www.newadvent.org/cathen/04352b.htm.

[34] See, for example, "Natural adversaries?", an interview with historian David Lindberg in *Christian History* (Fall 2002), http://www.christianitytoday.com/ch/2002/004/17.44.html.

[35] "Contrary to popular belief, the centrality of the Earth in this scheme is a mark of its imperfection, not its importance. To place the Sun at the center would be to elevate the Earth to the status of a heavenly body. The notion that the Copernican Revolution dethroned humankind from the heart of things is largely a modern idea." Philip Sampson, "Victim of spin?" *Third Way* (June 1998): 24. See http://www.facingthechallenge.org/greeks.htm. Medieval philosophers largely took over traditional Greek and Roman views.

[36] "Copernicus" and "Kepler," *Encarta* 2003.

[37] See "Copernicus," *The Catholic Encyclopedia*, http://www.newadvent.org/cathen/04352b.htm.

[38] Guillermo Gonzalez and Hugh Ross, "Home alone in the universe," *First Things* (May 1, 2000), www.arn.org/docs/gonzalez/gg_homealone_.htm.

[39] Galileo (1564–1642) was later tried by the Inquisition for espousing the theory, principally, it seems, because he made fun of the Pope in the process. See Dava Sobel, *Galileo's Daughter* (New York: Walker, 1999), for an interesting and detailed

account of Galileo's troubles, seen in part through the letters of his daughter Suor Marie Celeste, a nun.

[40] Guillermo Gonzalez and Hugh Ross, "Home alone in the universe," *First Things* (May 1, 2000), www.arn.org/docs/gonzalez/gg_homealone_.htm.

[41] As per J.D. Barrow and F.J. Tipler, *The Anthropic Cosmological Principle* (Toronto: Oxford, 1988). The Principle of Mediocrity is sometimes called the Copernican Principle, but it really has little to do with the Polish astronomer Copernicus (1473–1543), who first proposed that earth revolved around the sun. Copernicus most likely would not have endorsed the "Copernican" view.

[42] *Scientific American* (May 2003). You can read the article online at http://www.sciam.com/article.cfm?chanID=sa006&articleID=000F1EDD-B48A-1E90-8EA5809EC5880000.

[43] Astronomer Hugh Ross covers many of these examples in "Design and the anthropic principle" at www.reasons.org.

[44] An interesting discussion of the unique (and amazing) properties of water can be found in Michael Denton, *Nature's Destiny* (New York: Free Press, 1998) pp. 15–46.

[45] Stephen Hawking, *The Illustrated A Brief History of Time* (New York: Bantam, 1996), p. 160.

[46] Paul Davies, "The Synthetic Path," in John Brockman, ed., *The Third Culture* (New York: Simon and Schuster Touchstone, 1996), p. 308.

[47] *First Things* (June/July, 2001).

[48] Quoted in Patrick Glynn, "Beyond the death of God," *National Review* (May 6, 1996).

[49] Ibid. You can read the article at http://catholiceducation.org/articles/science/sc0011.html.

[50] Max Tegmark, *Scientific American* (May 2003). See http://www.sciam.com/article.cfm?chanID=sa006&articleID=000F1EDD-B48A-1E90-8EA5809EC5880000.

[51] Peter D. Ward and Donald Brownlee, *Rare Earth: Why Complex Life is Uncommon in the Universe* (New York: Copernicus Springer-Verlag, 2000), p. 28.

[52] Ibid., pp. 240, 242, 269.

[53] "There was a time when the Earth was alone in space but it was not our Earth. Without the moon our world would not have developed the way it did. The Indians of North America have a saying, 'No moon, no man,' and in a way they are right." D. Whitehouse, *The Moon: A Biography* (London: Headline, 2001), p. 237.

[54] Peter D. Ward and Donald Brownlee, *Rare Earth: Why Complex Life is Uncommon in the Universe* (New York: Copernicus Springer-Verlag, 2000), p. 223.

[55] A recent article available on the NASA Web site provides a slightly different take on the Rare Earth principle, the "Goldilocks Zone." The Goldilocks Zone is the zone

in which life as we understand it can thrive. So far, that means an environment on earth, but it can be a pretty extreme one. For an interesting discussion of extreme life forms and their environments, see http://science.nasa.gov/headlines/y2003/02oct_goldilocks.htm.

[56] Drake developed the equation. Sagan (1934–1996) popularized the search for ET through his writings.

[57] See http://www.msnbc.com/modules/drake/default.asp. For more resources on the Drake Equation, see the page sponsored by Students for the Exploration and Development of Space http://www.seds.org/~rme/drake.htm. Also see Life Beyond Earth—Is Anyone Listening?, a PBS Web site, http://www.pbs.org/lifebeyondearth/listening/drake.html. You can calculate your own values for the Drake Equation and otherwise have lots of fun, even if the aliens never show up.

[58] See http://www.msnbc.com/modules/drake/default.asp.

[59] Whatever the politics, it is hard to imagine dropping the program if the little green men *had* returned our calls. In any event, NASA has started funding some projects in this area again; it gave a five-year grant to the SETI Institute in 2003. Dennis Overbye, "Search for life out there gains respect, bit by bit," *New York Times* (July 8, 2003). The new search is looking for habitable planets.

[60] This question is called Fermi's Paradox. Fermi asked it during a lunchtime discussion over napkin calculations at the Los Alamos observatory, 50 years ago. A recent book offers 50 reasons why we haven't heard from the aliens, assuming they exist. *If the Universe Is Teeming with Aliens . . . Where Is Everybody? Fifty Solutions to the Fermi Paradox and the Problem of Extraterrestrial Life* by Stephen Webb (Copernicus, 2002).

[61] Simon Conway Morris, *Life's Solution: Inevitable Humans in a Lonely Universe* (Cambridge: Cambridge University Press, 2003). You can read a sample chapter at http://books.cambridge.org/0521827043.htm. Morris believes that life comes into existence by a divine plan. See, for example, "Divining nature's plan," a review of Morris's book by Thomas Hayden, *U.S. News & World Report* (September 29, 2003), where Hayden notes: "A generation after his pioneering work in the Burgess Shale, Conway Morris is convinced that far from being a random, directionless process, evolution shows deep patterns, and perhaps even a purpose." http://www.usnews.com/usnews/issue/archive/030929/20030929041701_brief.php. A fee is charged to view the article.

[62] Jack Cohen and Ian Stewart, *Evolving the Alien: The Science of Extraterrestrial Life* (London: Ebury, 2003).

[63] Martin Rees, England's Astronomer Royal, makes this point in "Our greatest quest," *New Scientist* (July 9, 2003), www.newscientist.com/news/news.jsp?id=ns99993924.

[64] Fred Hoyle, *The Black Cloud* (London: Heinemann, 1957). This is now a rare book. It belongs to an older genre of science fiction, where science concepts are

explained in much detail, sometimes at the expense of storytelling technique.

[65] See, for example, Dennis Overbye, "Search for life out there gains respect, bit by bit," *New York Times* (July 8, 2003). The SETI site, www.seti.org, is a valuable source of information about the conditions needed for the existence of life.

Chapter 2: The Best Arguments for Chance (Pages 31–40)

[1] Edgar Allan Poe, "Eureka [Section 7]" from *The Works of the Late Edgar Allan Poe*, vol. 2, 1850, pp. 180–92.

[2] Fred Heeren, *Show Me God: What the Message from Space Is Telling Us About God*, rev. ed. (Wheeling, IL: Day Star Publications, 2000), p. 236. Heeren, of course, does not take the idea of multiple universes very seriously. Ain't nuthin but a hound dog.

[3] Holmes chooses to remain dead and forego the lame sequels. Sawyer's story, "You See But You Do Not Observe," in Pamela Sargent, ed., *Nebula Awards 31* (New York: Harcourt Brace, 1997), won Le Grand Prix de l'Imaginaire, France's top sci-fi award, as well as CompuServe SF Forum's Homer Award for Best Short Story of the Year. It is a good literary introduction to the concept of many universes.

[4] The theory is often called "many worlds" rather than "many universes." This book uses the latter term, or otherwise, multiverse/multiverses.

[5] Carl W. Giberson, "The Goldilocks universe," in *Books & Culture* (January/February 2003): 30–31.

[6] Max Tegmark, *Scientific American*, May 2003. See http://www.sciam.com/article.cfm?chanID=sa006&articleID=000F1EDD-B48A-1E90-8EA5809EC5880000.

[7] Ibid.

[8] Ibid.

[9] Ibid.

[10] An article on Tegmark's theories in *New Scientist* helpfully underscores this point: "But the main reason for believing in an ensemble of universes is that it could explain why the laws governing our Universe appear to be so finely turned for our existence… This fine-tuning has two possible explanations. Either the Universe was designed specifically for us by a creator or there is a multitude of universes—a multiverse." From "Anything goes," *New Scientist* (June 6, 1998), vol. 158, no. 2137: 26–30, available from the archives at www.newscientist.com.

[11] "Epicurus," Internet Encyclopedia of Philosophy, http://www.utm.edu/research/iep/e/epicur.htm. Epicurus did not deny the existence of the gods, but he thought they had no effect in the universe. His view can be compared with the idea that God started the Big Bang but has not influenced the universe in any way since then.

[12] For a thoughtful discussion of this theme, see Benjamin Wiker, *Moral Darwinism: How We Became Hedonists* (Downer's Grove, Il: InterVarsity Press, 2002). He

notes, "… modern science was designed by an ancient Greek, Epicurus," and provides valuable background. You can read the Introduction online at http://www.gospelcom.net/ivpress/title/excl/2666-I.pdf.

[13] Lee Smolin, "A Theory of the Whole Universe" in John Brockman, ed., *The Third Culture* (New York: Simon and Schuster Touchstone, 1996), p. 293, http://www.edge.org/documents/ThirdCulture/z-Ch.17.html. Interestingly, the author whom Smolin credits as being most helpful in this matter is Richard Dawkins. For more on Dawkins, see Chapter 9 of this book.

[14] Lee Smolin, "A Theory of the Whole Universe" in John Brockman, ed., *The Third Culture* (New York: Simon and Schuster Touchstone, 1996), p. 294.

[15] You can find out more about gamblers and their fallacies from Wikipedia, http://www.wikipedia.org/wiki/Inverse_gamblers_fallacy.

[16] See Carl W. Giberson, "The Goldilocks universe," in *Books & Culture* (January/February 2003), pp. 30–31. The whole subject of quantum theory, of which the "many universes" idea is a part, is very complex, but is ably dealt with by Timothy Ferris in *The Whole Shebang: A State of the Universes Report* (New York: Simon & Schuster, 1998).

[17] See, for example, Eric Lerner, *The Big Bang Never Happened: A Startling Refutation of the Dominant Theory of the Origin of the Universe* (New York: Random House, 1991). Lerner's work would be much more convincing if he stuck to cosmology. He spends much effort arguing that the Big Bang theory is part of a conservative trend, exemplified in politics and society. Many would dispute that the trends of the last 40 or so years have been conservative.

[18] Timothy Ferris, *The Whole Shebang: A State of the Universes Report* (New York: Simon & Schuster, 1998), p. 66.

[19] For an example of this view, see Faye Flam, "Seeing big bang with fiery finish and sequels," *Philadelphia Inquirer* (April 26, 2002).

[20] See, for example, *Time* (June 25, 2001).

[21] For an opposing view, see Faye Flam, "Seeing big bang with fiery finish and sequels," *Philadelphia Inquirer* (April 26, 2002).

[22] When cosmologists use the expression "other universes," they sometimes mean other regions inside our own universe where different laws of physics may apply. We do not know whether these regions exist or how we could study them. Current science assumes that the laws of physics are universal.

[23] *Time* (June 25, 2001). The "accelerating universe" was *Science* magazine's Discovery of the Year for 1998.

[24] Helen Briggs, "Dark future for universe," *BBC News* (August 14, 2003), http://news.bbc.co.uk/1/hi/sci/tech/3148041.stm.

[25] Faye Flam, "Seeing big bang with fiery finish and sequels," *Philadelphia Inquirer* (April 26, 2002).

26 Ibid.

27 Paul Davies, "A brief history of the multiverse," *New York Times*, April 12, 2003.

28 Ibid.

29 Stephen Hawking, *The Illustrated A Brief History of Time* (New York: Bantam, 1996), p. 181. Hawking first published this idea in 1984 in work with James Hartle, a physicist at the University of California, Santa Barbara. See *Ibid.* p. 175.

30 Henry F. "Fritz" Schaefer, III, discusses the use of imaginary numbers in "Stephen Hawking, the Big Bang, and God," a public lecture available at http://www.origins.org/articles/schaefer_bigbangandgod.html. The square root of a minus number is called imaginary because it cannot exist in nature; no natural number, whether positive or negative, yields a minus result when multiplied by itself. However, imaginary numbers can be used in calculation. For more information, go to, for example, the University of Toronto Mathematics Network page on imaginary numbers, at http://www.math.toronto.edu/mathnet/answers/imaginary.html.

31 Hawking, *The Illustrated A Brief History of Time* (New York: Bantam, 1996), p. 179. Schaefer notes: "A case can be made that the Hartle-Hawking 'no boundary proposal' is only of marginal scientific interest. The reasons for this conclusion might include: (a) the theory is a mathematical construct that has no unique empirical support; (b) the theory makes no verifiable scientific predictions that were not achieved earlier with simpler models; (c) the theory generates no significant research agenda. The primary purpose of the theory seems to be an attempt to evade the cosmological argument for the existence of God, via the claim that nature is self-contained and effectively eternal."

32 Ibid., pp. 172–77. In recent years, Hawking has backed away from any easy theory of everything. See, for example, a talk he gave at the Davis Inflation Meeting, May 29, 2003, Astrophysics, abstract astro-ph/0305562, "Cosmology from the top down," available at http://xxx.lanl.gov/abs/astro-ph/0305562. There, he notes: "So even when we understand the ultimate theory, it won't tell us much about how the universe began." He also doubts that string theory, the hottest new idea, predicts the state of the universe. For more on string theory, see "The future of string theory: a conversation with Brian Greene," *Scientific American* (October 13, 2003), http://www.sciam.com/print_version.cfm?articleID=000073A5-C100-1F80-B57583414B7F0103. Greene tells *SciAm*: "To me that suggests what a fundamental discovery is. The universe in a sense guides us toward truths, because those truths are the things that govern what we see. If we're all being governed by what we see, we're all being steered in the same direction. Therefore, the difference between making a breakthrough and not often can be just a small element of perception, either true perception or mathematical perception that puts things together in a different way." Note that the universe is here seen as one that "guides us toward truths."

33 According to American historian Ron Numbers, the phrase *methodological naturalism* was coined by philosopher Paul de Vries, who first used it in 1983 at a conference,

and later in a paper, "Naturalism in the natural sciences," *Christian Scholar's Review* (1986), 15: 388–96. See his essay, "Science Without God: Natural Laws and Christian Beliefs" in *When Science and Christianity Meet* (University of Chicago Press, 2003).

[34] Most religious believers will assume that the intelligent designer is God. This is not required by the assumption of intelligent design. For some, God is merely a First Cause. For others, God is the deity of an established religion. Some well-known scientists such as Francis Crick argue that life may have been seeded from interstellar space. See for example, Maddox's comment, "The co-originator of the structure of DNA, put the argument more specifically: 'The chances that the long polymer molecules that vitally sustain all living things, both proteins and DNA, could have been assembled by random processes from the chemical units of which they are made are so small as to be negligible, prompting the question whether the surface of the Earth was fertilized from elsewhere, perhaps from interstellar space.' 'Panspermia' is the name for that." J. Maddox, *What Remains to Be Discovered: Mapping the Secrets of the Universe, the Origins of Life, and the Future of the Human Race* [1998] (New York: Touchstone, 1999, reprint), p. 131. Some have argued for design as a concept only, like law or chance, or for self-design. For practical purposes, in this book, "God" and "design" are generic terms, except where qualified in context.

[35] It is certainly possible to believe that there is an infinite number of universes without disbelieving in God. Don Page of the University of Alberta is a Christian scientist who considers it possible. Similarly, Stephen M. Barr writes in *First Things* (June/July 2001): "If some kinds of universe exist while others do not, it would seem to suggest that Someone has made choices. Far from destroying the case that a cosmic Designer exists, the many-universes idea only strengthens it." Barr is assuming that only some kinds of universes would exist. However that may be, Tegmark's theory, as set out in *Scientific American*, seems designed explicitly to get around the need for God.

[36] Nonetheless, Tegmark's multiverses, if they existed, could be drafted into service as heavens and hells for traditional religions. As one correspondent, Anita Brubaker, wrote to *Scientific American*: "If Tegmark's multiverse theory is true, then one of the many existing universes has no pain, no death and no suffering. On the other hand, one universe's inhabitants experience maximum pain. Has Tegmark demonstrated the existence of what are usually called heaven and hell?" Well, at least it is an economical theory. A universe that was heaven for dogs could conveniently double as a hell for cats. However, don't hope for too much; this idea is probably not coming soon to a church near you. Still, see Brubaker's comments, http://www.sciam.com/article.cfm?articleID=000302B0-3E8F-1F30-9AD380A84189F2D7.

[37] See Chapter 13 for pre-Enlightenment scientific assumptions.

[38] Ibid.

[39] A century and a half ago, Charles Dickens made fun of this approach to knowl-

edge in *Hard Times*, where the inspector for Mr. Gradgrind's school makes a child who lives and works with horses look like a fool compared with another student who can merely recite printed facts about horses but has no actual experience. You can read an excerpt at http://www.mtholyoke.edu/acad/intrel/hardtime.htm.

[40] Phillip E. Johnson, *Darwin on Trial* (Downer's Grove, IL: InterVarsity Press, 1993), pp. 123–24.

[41] You can read an excerpt from the research done by Edward J. Larson and Larry Witham, "Scientists still keeping the faith: comparing scientists in 1916 and 1996," at www.beliefnet.com/story/1/story_193.html. The original research was done by James Leuba, who predicted in 1916 that religious belief would decline. In both surveys, belief in God was defined as belief in a God "to whom one may pray in expectations of receiving an answer." Interestingly, the number of scientists who believed in personal immortality declined from 51% to 38%. The number who even wanted immortality "intensely" declined from 34% to 10%.

[42] It is no accident that, partly as a result of new cosmology, religion has become a much more important political presence, for better or worse. See, for example, Peter L. Berger, ed., *The Desecularization of the World: Resurgent Religion and World Politics* (Grand Rapids, MI: Eerdmans, 1999). After the collapse of major atheistic systems (communism, fascism, etc.), no one seems to be looking for salvation outside faith now.

[43] From Laurence J. Peter, *Peter's Quotations: Ideas for Our Time* (New York: William Morrow, 1977).

[44] Ibid.

[45] Ibid.

Chapter 3: The Best Arguments for Design (Pages 41–47)

[1] "The universe: past and present reflections," *Engineering and Science* (November 1981). Another source is "From 1953 onward, Willy Fowler and I have always been intrigued by the remarkable relation of the 7.65 Mev energy level in the nucleus of 12C to the 7.12 Mev level in 16O. If you wanted to produce carbon and oxygen in roughly equal quantities by stellar nucleosynthesis, these are the two levels you would have to fix, and your fixing would have to be just where these levels are actually found to be. Another put-up job? Following the above argument, I am inclined to think so. A common sense interpretation of the facts suggests that a superintellect has monkeyed with physics, as well as with chemistry and biology, and that there are no blind forces worth speaking about in nature." (F. Hoyle, "The Universe: Past and Present Reflections," *Annual Review of Astronomy and Astrophysics*, Vol. 20, 1982, pp. 1–35, p. 16).

[2] Charles Blinderman, Professor of English and Adjunct Professor of Biology, and David Joyce, Associate Professor of Mathematics and Computer Science, Clark University, provide information on the whole affair at http://aleph0.clarku.edu/huxley/guide9.html.

NOTES

[3] M.J. Behe, *Darwin's Black Box: The Biochemical Challenge to Evolution* (New York: Free Press, 1996), also www.id.ucsb.edu/fscf/LIBRARY/BEHE/MM.html.

[4] You can read the original article Huxley wrote, "On some organisms living at great depths in the North Atlantic Ocean," *Quarterly Journal of Microscopical Science* (1868), vol. 8, new series: 203–12, http://aleph0.clarku.edu/huxley/SM3/bathy.html, a page created by Charles Blinderman, Professor of English and Adjunct Professor of Biology, and David Joyce, Associate Professor of Mathematics and Computer Science, Clark University. They also provide information on the whole affair at http://aleph0.clarku.edu/huxley/guide9.html. For an interactive look at how complex cells really are, see http://www.intelligentdesign.org/menu/cell/cell_life.htm.

[5] Paul Davies "How we could create life," *The Guardian* (December 11, 2002). http://www.guardian.co.uk/comment/story/0,3604,857635,00.html.

[6] Miller and Urey were acting on a suggestion made by Russian scientist A.I. Oparin and British scientist J.B.S. Haldane in the 1920s that lightning, striking through the atmosphere of earth, could produce the chemistry needed for life.

[7] In 1961, Juan Oro found that one of the nucleotides, adenine, could be formed in an atmosphere that did not have much oxygen (a reducing atmosphere).

8 See, for example, *Cruising Chemistry*, written by Diane Szaflarski and Robert and Melanie Dean from the University of California, San Diego, Extension School's Program for Teacher Enhancement in Science and Technology and John Simon of the University of California, San Diego's Department of Chemistry and Biochemistry. http://www.chem.duke.edu/~jds/cruise_chem/Exobiology/miller.html. Their diagram of the experiment is quite helpful. Cells exclude oxygen from processes where it creates a problem. Of course, the cells have to do this at the right time in the right way. According to B. Bryson, "Scientists are now pretty certain that the early atmosphere was nothing like as primed for development as Miller and Urey's gaseous stew, but rather was a much less reactive blend of nitrogen and carbon dioxide. Repeating Miller's experiments with these more challenging inputs has so far produced only one fairly primitive amino acid." *A Short History of Nearly Everything* (London: Doubleday, 2003), p. 253. In other words, when it comes to creating life, the luck is worse now than it was back in the Fifties.

[9] Paul Davies "How we could create life," *The Guardian* (December 11, 2002). http://www.guardian.co.uk/comment/story/0,3604,857635,00.html.

[10] To get some idea what they are doing now, look at David W. Deamer, "Tracking the course of evolution: how did it all begin?" *The Self-assembly of Organic Molecules and the Origin of Cellular Life.* http://www.ucmp.berkeley.edu/education/events/deamer1.html.

[11] See Michael J. Behe, *Darwin's Black Box: The Biochemical Challenge to Evolution* (New York: Free Press, 1996), pp. 10–12.

[12] We can, of course, default to Tegmark's suggestion that there is an infinite num-

ber of universes, but that is really a faith position at present. See n 35 and n 36 for Chapter 2.

[13] In Fred Hoyle, *The Intelligent Universe* (London: Michael Joseph, 1983), p. 19.

[14] Paul Davies, "How we could create life," *The Guardian* (December 11, 2002). http://www.guardian.co.uk/comment/story/0,3604,857635,00.html.

[15] See Michael J. Behe, *Darwin's Black Box: The Biochemical Challenge to Evolution* (New York: Free Press, 1996), pp. 70–72, especially the illustration on p. 71. Much about the flagellum is not well understood. What is understood is daunting. For example, "More so than other motors, the flagellum resembles a machine designed by a human (Figure 1 a). The flagellar filament (propeller) is a 10 μm-long, thin, rigid, cork screw-shaped structure, with a helical period of about 2 μm. The filament is connected to the hook by two junctional proteins. Named according to its shape, the flexible hook acts as a universal joint permitting the filament and motor to rotate about different axes. The filament, junction, hook, and drive shaft all appear to have a common helical design. The remaining flagellar parts are rings. The L and P rings are believed to act as a bushing through which the rotating drive shaft passes. These two rings are anchored in the outer membrane and peptidoglycan, respectively. ... In the periplasm, the drive shaft inserts in a socket just above the S ring. The M ring is a 25 nm disk, which traverses the cell's inner membrane. Extending into the cytoplasm from the extended M ring is the C ring, a 45 nm annulus. A ring of about 10 membrane particles known as studs surround each flagellar motor. These probably sit in the L-shaped shelf made by the M and C rings." D. J. DeRosier, "The Turn of the Screw: The Bacterial Flagellar Motor," *Cell*, Vol. 93, April 3, 1998, p. 17.

[16] You can see one at http://www.arn.org/docs/mm/flagellum_all.htm.

[17] Kenneth R. Miller, *Finding Darwin's God: A Scientist's Search for Common Ground Between God and Evolution* (New York: HarperCollins, 1999). In the book, Miller does not address the flagellum in detail but simply says that Darwinists need more time to study it. Later, he offers a rebuttal in "The flagellum unspun: the collapse of 'irreducible complexity,'" at http://www.millerandlevine.com/km/evol/design2/article.html.

[18] See Miller, *ibid.* http://www.millerandlevine.com/km/evol/design2/article.html.

[19] In ID advocate Bill Dembski's reply, "Still spinning just fine: a response to Ken Miller," at http://www.designinference.com/documents/2003.02.Miller_Response.htm. Dembski's comment is worth quoting in full, to get the gist of ID's charge against Darwinism: "The problem is that Ken Miller and the entire biological community haven't figured out how those systems arose. It's not a question of personal incredulity but of global disciplinary failure (the discipline here being biology) and gross theoretical inadequacy (the theory here being Darwin's). Darwin's theory, without which nothing in biology is supposed to make sense, in fact offers no insight into how the flagellum arose. If the biological community had even an inkling of how such systems arose

by naturalistic mechanisms, Miller would not—a full six years after the publication of *Darwin's Black Box* by Michael Behe—be lamely gesturing at the type three secretory system as a possible evolutionary precursor to the flagellum. It would suffice simply to provide a detailed explanation of how a system like the bacterial flagellum arose by Darwinian means. Miller's paper, despite its intimidating title ('The Flagellum Unspun') does nothing to answer that question."

[20] Thomas Woodward, *Doubts About Darwin: A History of Intelligent Design* (Grand Rapids, MI: Baker, 2003), p. 15.

[21] Michael Ruse, *The Evolution Wars: A Guide to the Debates* (Santa Barbara, CA: ABC-CLIO, 2000), p. 285. See Note 17 above for a reference to one of Miller's topical works.

[22] Stuart Kauffman, *At Home in the Universe: The Search for the Laws of Self-Organization and Complexity* (New York: Oxford University Press, 1995), p. 8.

[23] Ibid. Kauffman adds: "The revision of the Darwinian worldview will not be easy. Biologists have, as yet, no conceptual framework in which to study an evolutionary process that commingles both self-organization and selection."

[24] Indeed, it would be interesting to compare Kauffman's principle of self-organization with the intelligent design hypothesis. You can learn more about his theories at ISCID, http://www.iscid.org/stuartkauffman-chat.php, where he participated in a live chat with the ID folks.

[25] "It may be that biospheres, as a secular trend, maximize the rate of exploration of the adjacent possible. If they did it too fast, they would destroy their own internal organization, so there may be internal gating mechanisms. This is why I call this an average secular trend, since they explore the adjacent possible as fast as they can get away with it. There's a lot of neat science to be done to unpack that, and I'm thinking about it." For more, see "The adjacent possible: a talk with Stuart Kauffman," http://www.edge.org/3rd_culture/kauffman03/kauffman_index.html.

[26] See the International Society for Complexity, Intelligence and Design page on Gardner, http://www.iscid.org/james-gardner.php, where you can read a transcript of an online discussion with him, and also his Biocosm home page, http://www.biocosm.org/.

Chapter 4: Why Design or Chance Matters So Much (Pages 51–56)

[1] Quoted in Patrick Glynn, "Beyond the death of God," *National Review* (May 6, 1996).

[2] *The Glory of the Hummingbird* (Boston: Little Brown, 1974). Quoted at www.creativequotations.com/one/2526b.htm.

[3] The reverse is also true, of course: What scientists learn from their culture greatly influences how they do science. Only the most gifted scientists, Newton or Einstein for example, pioneer a new way of understanding reality. The others effectively apply the

existing theories, and typically resist any change. Thomas Kuhn provides valuable insights on this process in *The Structure of Scientific Revolutions* (Chicago: University of Chicago Press, 1970). Not surprisingly, younger scientists adapt more readily to new ideas. Or, as Max Planck says: "A new scientific truth does not triumph by convincing its opponents, but rather because its opponents die, and a new generation grows up that is familiar with it." See T.S. Kuhn, *The Structure of Scientific Revolutions* [1962] (Chicago: University of Chicago Press, 1970), p. 151.

[4] Barbara Ehrenreich, "Blocking the Gates to Heaven," in *The Worst Years of Our Lives* (1991). First published in 1986. From *The Columbia World of Quotations*, Columbia University Press, 1996.

[5] Charles Darwin, in a letter written in 1871 to Joseph Hooker, in F. Darwin, ed., *The Life and Letters of Charles Darwin* (London: John Murray, 1888), vol. 3, p. 18, quoted in Robert Shapiro, *Origins: A Skeptic's Guide to the Origin of Life* (Summit: New York, 1986), p. 185. Shapiro, a professor of chemistry at New York University, notes: "This quote is often reproduced in texts and articles on the origin of life. Many workers would prefer to replace the word 'protein' with 'nucleic acid,' as we have seen. Otherwise, it is remarkably current today, which is a tribute either to his foresight or to our lack of progress."

[6] Encarta 2003. See also S.J. Mojzsis, G. Arrhenius, K.D. McKeegan, T.M. Harrison, A.P. Nutman, and C.R.L. Friend, "Evidence for life on Earth before 3,800 million years ago," *Nature*, Vol. 384, 7 November 1996, pp.55–56 and S. J. Mojzsis and T.M. Harrison, "Vestiges of a Beginning: Clues to the Emergent Biosphere Recorded in the Oldest Known Sedimentary Rocks," *GSA Today*, April 2000.

[7] Klaus Dose, "The origin of life: more questions than answers," *Interdisciplinary Science Reviews* (1988), vol. 13, no. 4: 348.

[8] John Horgan, *The End of Science: Facing the Limits of Knowledge in the Twilight of the Scientific Age* (London: Little, Brown, 1997), p. 138.

[9] *Science and Creationism: A View from the National Academy of Sciences*, 2nd ed., 1999.

[10] For example: "Determining how the first DNA molecules appeared on Earth has been a very difficult scientific problem, and it is still far from solved. No one has yet discovered how to combine various chemicals in a test tube and arrive at a DNA molecule." From Peter D. Ward and Donald Brownlee, *Rare Earth: Why Complex Life Is Uncommon in the Universe* (New York: Copernicus Springer-Verlag, 2000), p. 62.

[11] For an interesting article on this theme, see "Study suggests life sprang from clay," CNN.com (October 25, 2003), http://edition.cnn.com/2003/TECH/science/10/25/clay.life.reut/index.html. Despite what the title implies, Szostak stressed, "We are not claiming that this is how life started."

[12] Hot soup, cold soup, prebiotic pizza, RNA world, clay world, silicon world, and self-organization: Many of these theories are discussed and critiqued at Intelligent Design and Evolution Awareness (IDEA) Club

http://www-acs.ucsd.edu/~idea/origlife.htm, a student intelligent design site.

[13] In "Row erupts over 'life-starter vents,'" a recent online article from the BBC, Paul Rincon notes that the ancient hydrothermal vents that are considered a possible home of the earliest life may only be a few thousand years old. Awkward discovery. See http://news.bbc.co.uk/2/hi/science/nature/3220633.stm.

[14] Information about the *Archaea* is available at http://www.ucmp.berkeley.edu/archaea/archaea.html. The *Archaea* have not provided anything like a straightforward picture of evolution. For example, J.L. Howland writes: "Here is a paradox: Archaea are undeniably prokaryotic, yet they exhibit many eukaryotic features concerning the manner in which they manage genetic information. Indeed, their genetic systems appear to include a rather complicated mix of prokaryotic and eukaryotic strategies for information handling. How is this situation consistent with what we know of their evolutionary history? Archaea and Eubacteria branched apart early in the course of evolution. Their divergence, occurring well over two billion years ago, can be called the first major event in the history of life after its origin; only much later did Eukarya appear on the scene. But, on examination of their genetic systems—the ways that they organize and express the information encoded in their DNA—Archaea often much more closely resemble eukaryotic organisms, those greatly more complex organisms whose cells contain nuclei and other membrane-bounded organelles. At the same time, archaeal cells have some features in common with those of the prokaryotic Eubacteria. So which is it? Are the real archaeal affinities with the other prokaryotes or with the more advanced eukaryotes? The answer turns out to be 'both,' so we must now ask how such a thing is possible." J.L. Howland, *The Surprising Archaea: Discovering Another Domain of Life* (New York: Oxford University Press, 2000), p. 157.

[15] Peter D. Ward and Donald Brownlee, *Rare Earth: Why Complex Life is Uncommon in the Universe* (New York: Copernicus Springer-Verlag, 2000), p. 69. The science fiction writer the authors refer to is the late Fred Hoyle.

[16] Quoted in Mark Hartwig, "The end of creationism?" *Citizen Magazine* (August 2000), reprinted at http://www.arn.org/docs/hartwig/mh_endofcreationism.htm.

[17] Mark Hartwig, "The end of creationism?" *Citizen Magazine* (August 2000), reprinted at http://www.arn.org/docs/hartwig/mh_endofcreationism.htm.

[18] Tom Bethell, "A map to nowhere: the genome isn't a code and we can't read it," *American Spectator* (April 2001).

[19] *Wall Street Journal* (May 30, 2003).

[20] See Michael Brooks, "How much can we ever know about the Universe?" *New Scientist* (April 5, 2003). Hawking was addressing the Dirac centennial celebration. Helen Joyce gives a readable introduction to the concepts behind Hawking's ideas in "Tying it all up" at online math magazine *Plus*, http://plus.maths.org/issue21/features/strings/

Chapter 5: Who Was Darwin? What Did He Really Say? (Pages 57–67)

1 *On the Origin of Species* (1859).

2 *The Blind Watchmaker* (1986).

3 The information concerning Darwin's life is from Microsoft® Encarta® Reference Library 2003.

4 The belief that the earth was 6000 years old was based on chronologies worked out by scholars who studied the Bible. The Bible does not say how old the earth is, and the scholars start with certain assumptions. See pp. 123–24.

5 For example, see Chris Mooney, "Darwin's sanitized idea," in *Slate* (http://slate.msn.com/id/115965/), September 24, 2001. Mooney argues that the PBS series *Evolution*, aired that year, was "an exercise in Creationist appeasement." Few creationists agreed with him.

6 Mooney, September 4, 2001.

7 Charles Darwin, letter to W. Graham, July 3, 1881, in F. Darwin, ed., *The Life and Letters of Charles Darwin*, vol. 1 [1898] (New York: Basic Books, 1959) p. 285. Interestingly, he goes on to say: "But I have had no practice in abstract reasoning, and I may be all astray. Nevertheless you have expressed my inward conviction, though far more vividly and clearly than I could have done, that the Universe is not the result of chance." Darwin sometimes flirted with a vague sort of theism, but note that in this case, the context is the explicit denial of purpose.

8 Charles Darwin, in N. Barlow, ed., *The Autobiography of Charles Darwin, 1809–1882: With Original Omissions Restored* [1958], New York: W.W. Norton,1969) pp. 92–93. (See also Note 35 for Chapter 15 for a key factor in his loss of faith, along with further resources.)

9 Phillip E. Johnson, "Comparing Hostage-Takers," Founder's Lecture at Trinity Evangelical Divinity School, 1992, http://www.arn.org/docs/johnson/pjcht.htm.

10 Darwin was not the first person to suggest an idea like natural selection. Apparently, Scottish geologist James Hutton, known as the father of modern geology, had floated a similar idea in 1794. However, Darwin had a much larger fact base, a clearer grasp, and an elegant writing style. See "The original theory of evolution . . . were it not for the farmer who came up with it, 60 years before Darwin" by Steve Connor, *The Independent* (October 16, 2003), http://news.independent.co.uk/world/science_medical/story.jsp?story=453801. This story is available for a fee. Also, as a letter from geologist William L. Abler of the Field Museum of Natural History to *Nature* (426, 759 (18 December 2003)) points out, William Paley proposes (and rejects) a concept of natural selection in chapter 5 of his *Natural Theology* (1803). Darwin claimed to know Paley's work well.

11 Stephen Jay Gould, "Darwin and Paley Meet the Invisible Hand," in *Eight Little*

Piggies: Reflections in Natural History (London: Jonathan Cape, 1993), pp. 148–49. Rhetoric like this should be borne in mind when one encounters the claim that there is no conflict between evolutionary biology and traditional religious beliefs. While Gould was usually much less intemperate than Richard Dawkins, he held similar views. See also D. J. Depew and B.H. Weber, *Darwinism Evolving: Systems Dynamics and the Genealogy of Natural Selection* (Cambridge, MA: MIT Press, 1997), p. 8.

12 Darwin called it "descent with modification." The term "evolution" was popularized by Herbert Spencer in his *Principles of Biology*, first published in 1864. Darwin first used it in a later book, *The Descent of Man* (1871).

13 C.G. Hunter, *Darwin's Proof: The Triumph of Religion over Science* (Grand Rapids, MI: Brazos Press, 2003), pp. 10–11.

14 For a description of Archaeopteryx, go to http://www.ucmp.berkeley.edu/diapsids/birds/archaeopteryx.html. See also Jonathan Wells's discussion of controversies around this and other feathered finds in *Icons of Evolution* (Washington: Regnery, 2000).

15 Pamela Winnick, writing in the *Pittsburgh Post-Gazette* (September 23, 2001), http://www.arn.org/docs2/news/winnickpbsevolution92301.htm, expresses impatience with the PBS series, *Evolution*, for glossing over these established facts. It seems that, contrary to Mooney, Note 5 above, creationists were not the main targets of appeasement. For more on the racism that prevailed in Darwin's day, see Michael Ruse, *The Evolution Wars: A Guide to the Debates* (Santa Barbara, CA: ABC-CLIO, 2000), p. 57.

16 See Jonathan Marks, "A feckless quest for the basketball gene," *New York Times* (April 8, 2000), http://www.uncc.edu/jmarks/pubs/feckless.html for a clearly written explanation of the modern understanding of how genes work and why race functions mainly as a social category.

17 See, for example, Leesa Blake et al., *Biology 12* (Toronto: McGraw-Hill Ryerson, 2002), p. 347.

18 See, for example, David M. Raup, who writes, in *Extinction: Bad Genes or Bad Luck?* (New York: W.W. Norton, 1991), p. 3: "There are millions of different species of animals and plants on earth—possibly as many as forty million. But somewhere between five and fifty billion species have existed at one time or another. Thus, only about one in a thousand species is still alive—a truly lousy survival record."

19 According to the "Flintstones" entry in the online compendium *Yesterdayland*: "Bedrock was essentially straight out of 1960's suburbia, but with rocks as the essential resource, dinosaurs as the favored pets, and technology that was crude at best." As the longest-running cartoon on prime time in the 1960s (1960–1966), *Flintstones* took for granted a popular folklore around human evolution. Without that, the humor would have been meaningless. Yesterdayland is no longer online, but you can read similar information at www.topthat.net/webrock/. It is unlikely that a similar theme could be exploited today; different social groups would assign radically different meanings to every possible comic situation.

[20] This was a pop version of Ernst Haeckel's discredited theory of embryology, according to which "ontology recapitulates phylogeny." That is, the embryo undergoes all the stages of evolution from the beginning of life, as a fish, amphibian, apelike ancestor, etc. In reality, an embryo, from the first cell, is only an embryo of its own species and undergoes only the development of its own body, according to species-specific genes. But Haeckel's theory was too good for many to pass up. It has survived today in the otherwise inexplicable early claim of abortion rights groups that "the fetus is not a human being." Cultural absorption of Haeckel's theory enabled the statement to appear to make sense in the 1960s. Later, it was amended to "the fetus is not a person," as courts declared that the unborn human was not entitled to legal protection.

[21] The author recalls this statement vividly from a news broadcast in 1971.

[22] Philip Gold, "End of Darwinism?" *Washington Times* (October 25, 2000), www.menssana2000.com/darwin.htm.

[23] In the Cambrian explosion, all or almost all modern phyla (large classifications) of animal life forms appeared together about 525 million years ago. See also p. 86.

[24] By way of example, Lewis cites Keats's *Hyperion* (1818), Wagner's *Ring of the Nibelung* cycle (1869–1876), and Shaw's *Back to Methuselah* (1921). Interestingly, he notes, the "onward and upward" Evolution theme is so old by the time of *Back to Methuselah* that it can be treated as comedy rather than tragedy or philosophy. C.S. Lewis, "Funeral of a Great Myth," in *Christian Reflections* (Glasgow: William Collins Sons, 1980), p. 112. This collection appears to have first been published in 1967.

[25] Ibid., p. 117

[26] Ibid., p. 112.

[27] Ibid., p. 122. This is a burlesque of William Wordsworth's sonnet "To Toussaint L'Ouverture (1807)": "Thou hast great allies;/Thy friends are exultations, agonies,/And love, and Man's unconquerable mind." L'Ouverture was a Haitian freedom fighter. Lewis had far more respect for people like L'Ouverture than for the politicians and propagandists who inevitably followed in their wake. (*Note*: You can read the whole sonnet at http://www.brycchancarey.com/slavery/wordpoems.htm#overture.)

[28] Shaw was an ardent socialist, and Nietzsche provided much of the theoretical basis for fascism. Both promoted the idea of evolution from Man into Superman, but of the two, Nietzsche seems to have understood Darwin's theory better, in general. See the table comparing Darwinism with typical evolution folklore, on p. 74.

[29] George Bernard Shaw, *Back to Methuselah: A Metabiological Pentateuch* (New York: Brentano's, 1929), p. xlvi. That Darwinism in fact demands this is sometimes disputed, but consider the following comment from the late American astronomer Carl Sagan: and A. Druyan, in *Shadows of Forgotten Ancestors: A Search for Who We Are* [1993] (London: Arrow, 1993, reprint), pp. 63–64, 428n: "Some of the underlying emotional reasons for rejecting natural selection were later vividly expressed by the playwright George Bernard Shaw: '[T]he Darwinian process may be described as a chapter

of accidents. As such, it seems simple, because you do not at first realize all that it involves. ... if this sort of selection could turn an antelope into a giraffe, it could conceivably turn a pond full of amoebas into the French academy.' ... George Bernard Shaw, *Back to Methusaleh: A Metabiological Pentateuch* (New York: Brentano's, 1929), p. xlvi. The last sentence is in fact the modern evolutionary point of view."

[30] Ronald L. Numbers, *The Creationists: The Evolution of Scientific Creationism* (New York: Random House, 1992), pp. 153, 391*n*. Numbers's note (28) indicates that Lewis's views on evolution are known from letters written to Bernard Acworth, a creationist friend. This letter was written October 4, 1951. Copies of all of Lewis's letters to Acworth have been deposited in the Marion E. Wade Collection, Wheaton College, Wheaton, IL.

[31] Ibid.

[32] Ronald Numbers, Hilldale and William Coleman Professor of the History of Science and Medicine and chair of the Department of the History of Medicine at the University of Wisconsin-Madison, interviewed at www.counterbalance.net/bio/numbody.html.

[33] For earlier evolutionists, see Del Ratzsch, *Battle of the Beginnings: Why Neither Side Is Winning the Creation–Evolution Debate* (Downers Grove, IL: InterVarsity Press, 1996), pp. 19–21, and, for a more extensive discussion, Michael Ruse, *The Evolution Wars: A Guide to the Debates* (Santa Barbara, CA: ABC-CLIO, 2000), pp. 1–27.

[34] Many people have pointed out that Herbert Spencer, not Charles Darwin, coined this expression, but Darwin does not appear to have objected to it. For example: "The expression often used by Mr. Herbert Spencer, of the Survival of the Fittest, is more accurate, and is sometimes equally convenient." (*On the Origin of Species, iii*, quoted in *Dictionary of Quotations and Proverbs*, London: Octopus Books,1982).

[35] Charles Darwin, *The Descent of Man* (London: John Murray, 1871, pp. 1, 169), quoted in Michael Ruse, *The Evolution Wars: A Guide to the Debates* (Santa Barbara, CA: ABC-CLIO, 2000), p. 56.

[36] "Retelling the story of science," *First Things* (March 2003): 16–25. http://www.firstthings.com/ftissues/ft0303/articles/barr.html.

[37] Ibid.

Chapter 6: Who Loved Darwin? Who Hated Him? (Pages 69–76)

[1] Stephen Jay Gould provides this attribution in Introduction to *Evolution: The Triumph of an Idea* by Carl Zimmer (New York: HarperCollins, 2002).

[2] The platypus is an unusual mammal that lays eggs. See http://www.dpiwe.tas.gov.au/inter.nsf/WebPages/BHAN-53573T?open for information. The kangaroo, like many Australian mammals, is a marsupial. It gives birth to

embryos that finish their development in a pouch. For more information about marsupials, see http://www.ucmp.berkeley.edu/mammal/marsupial/marsupial.html.

3 To learn more about coelacanths *Latimeria chalumnae*, go to http://www.ucmp.berkeley.edu/vertebrates/coelacanth/coelacanths.html. To learn more about horsetail grass *Equisetum arvense*, go to http://www.ucmp.berkeley.edu/plants/sphenophyta/sphenophyta.html.

4 Michael Denton, *Evolution: A Theory in Crisis* (Bethesda: Adler & Adler, 1986), pp. 157, 179, 180. You can learn more about the coelacanth at www.dinofish.com, a coelacanth conservation project. One intriguing bit of information: Coelacanths do not lay eggs. They give birth to a couple of dozen live "pups."

5 The researchers knew it was a male because the penis was preserved. For more information on *Colymbosathon ecplecticos*, see *BBC News*, December 5, 2003, http://news.bbc.co.uk/2/hi/science/nature/3291025.stm.

6 Benjamin Wiker explains the scope of the problem, "For the first half-billion years of the earth's history, no evolution would be possible, because no life was possible until the earth cooled sufficiently and a suitable climate developed. Moreover, approximately 85 percent of geologic time occurred in the Precambrian period where the comparatively few life forms fossilized were quite primitive. With the Cambrian period came the sudden appearance of a multitude of complex life forms, an 'explosion' that occurred beginning, not four billion years ago, but approximately five hundred and fifty million years ago. Even more difficult to explain, the explosion itself actually did occur within a few million years, thereby reducing the evolution of all the major animal groups in biology to Kelvin's calculated time span (albeit for different reasons than Kelvin's). We note that Darwin himself agonized over the Cambrian explosion (although he did not call it that): 'the difficulty of assigning any good reason for the absence of vast piles of strata rich in fossils beneath the Cambrian system is very great.... The case at present must remain inexplicable; and may be truly urged as a valid argument against the views here entertained.'" (Benjamin Wiker, *Moral Darwinism: How We Became Hedonists* (Downers Grove IL: InterVarsity Press, 2002), p. 229.

7 St. George Mivart, *On the Genesis of Species* (London: Macmillan, 1871), p. 21, quoted in Michael J. Behe, *Darwin's Black Box: The Biochemical Challenge to Evolution* (New York: Free Press, 1996). (*Note*: Mivart was not a saint, as far as we know. "St. George" was his given name. He was excommunicated towards the end of his life, as his opinions became increasingly unorthodox. See the account in the Catholic Encyclopedia Online, http://www.newadvent.org/cathen/10407b.htm.)

8 Go to http://www.burgess-shale.bc.ca/menu.htm for more information about the incredible array of life forms found in the Burgess Shale. Essentially, there were more different types of basic body plans half a billion years ago than there are today, and no one knows why.

9 There are some earlier bursts of complex life forms, for example a spate of crea-

tures found on the Avalon Peninsula of southern Newfoundland in Canada and dated to about 570 million years ago. You can read more about them at http://www.ucmp.berkeley.edu/vendian/mistaken.html. Most of the organisms have not been found anywhere else in the world as of 2003, and "defy identification with any known living organism." Some have not yet received scientific names (2003). There is also a remarkable discovery from the same era at Cheng-jiang, in southern China. See http://geology.about.com/library/weekly/aa022899.htm for details. Very old organisms show a sudden explosion of life, not a slow ascent from non-life to semi-life to more-like-life to life.

[10] Stephen Jay Gould, "Evolution's erratic pace," in *Natural History* (May 1977), vol. 136 (5): 14.

[11] See Phillip E. Johnson, *Darwin on Trial* (Downer's Grove, IL: InterVarsity Press, 1993), pp. 26–28 for a lucid summary of this problem.

[12] The definition of a species has changed over the years, so the subject is complex. Now, animals that *do not* mate are considered to be separate species, as well as animals that *cannot* mate. See, for example, "Observed instances of speciation" by Joseph Boxhorn, 1995, online at http://www.talkorigins.org/faqs/faq-speciation.html. As a result, sometimes biologists may be inclined to jump the gun a bit in declaring that a new species has been created. For an example of this, see Jonathan Wells, "Darwin's Finches," in *Icons of Evolution* (Washington: Regnery, 2000), pp. 159–76. Also, some life forms cannot even be classified as species. See, for example, "Corals defy species classification," *Science Daily* (February 19, 2003), online at http://www.sciencedaily.com/releases/2003/02/030219080258.htm.

[13] The experiment is part of the Vivaria Project, which will install computers in zoos across Europe. For more information, see Brian Bernbaum, "Monkeys and Typewriters," http://www.arn.org/docs2/news/monkeysandtypewriters051103.htm. For interesting comments, see Lloyd Garver, http://jewishworldreview.com/0503/garver1.asp and Dennis Prager, "Monkeys and atheists," http://jewishworldreview.com/0503/prager1.asp. The author agrees with Garver that the monkeys needed a gorilla for a managing editor. Then they would at least have got out an acceptable edition of *Monkeyhouse News*.

[14] Quoted in Michael Ruse, *The Evolution Wars: A Guide to the Debates* (Santa Barbara, CA: ABC-CLIO, 2000), p. 75.

[15] This does not mean that no Darwinist saw moral significance in what happens to the slum child or what he becomes. But moral significance is not the province of natural selection; passing on one's genes enables one to be an ancestor, and thus be relevant to natural selection.

[16] See "Social Darwinism" in *Encarta Encyclopedia* 2003.

[17] See www.eugenicsarchive.org for more information on eugenic sterilization in North America.

18 For example, see "B.C. faces lawsuit over sterilizations" (WebPosted Feb 7 2003 08:01 AM PST at http://vancouver.cbc.ca/template/servlet/View?filename=bc_lawsuit20030207.

19 Michael Ruse, *The Evolution Wars: A Guide to the Debates* (Santa Barbara, CA: ABC-CLIO, 2000), pp. 59–60.

20 Quoted in *ibid.*, pp 107–08.

21 For example, see Edward J. Larson, *Summer for the Gods: The Scopes Trial and America's Continuing Debate over Science and Religion* (New York: Basic Books, 1997), pp. 14–30, and Michael Ruse, *The Evolution Wars: A Guide to the Debates* (Santa Barbara, CA: ABC-CLIO, 2000), pp. 59–109, for a brief history of religious responses to evolution.

22 Del Ratzsch, *Battle of the Beginnings: Why Neither Side Is Winning the Creation–Evolution Debate* (Downers Grove, IL: InterVarsity Press, 1996), p. 55.

23 What biologists mean when they say that current structure restricts the types of change possible is that not every desirable change can happen. For example, your cat could chase birds much more effectively if equipped with a pair of wings as well as four legs. But, as a four-legged vertebrate, he cannot evolve an extra set of limbs nor can he afford to give up two of his legs for the purpose. Also, the feline body would need complete redevelopment. For most struggling species, extinction is a far more likely fate than a grand new evolutionary strategy.

24 See especially, the Brights movement, www.the-brights.net, for an example of this.

25 Ronald Numbers, Hilldale and William Coleman Professor of the History of Science and Medicine and chair of the Department of the History of Medicine at the University of Wisconsin-Madison, interviewed at www.counterbalance.net/bio/numbody.html.

26 See, for example, "Catholics and Evolution" in *Catholic Encyclopedia*, http://www.newadvent.org/cathen/05654a.htm, and "Apes 'R' not us: Catholics and the debate over evolution" at Catholic Educator's Resource Center, http://catholiceducation.org/articles/science/sc0038.html.

27 T.M. Berra, *Evolution and the Myth of Creationism: A Basic Guide to the Facts in the Evolution Debate* (Stanford: Stanford University Press, 1990), p. 124.

28 In Darwin's day, the changes were called "variations," but after the rise of the neo-Darwinian synthesis, they came to be called "mutations," which referred to random changes in genetic material. Genetics was unknown to most scientists in Darwin's day.

29 This type of evolutionism is sometimes called "convergent evolution." I have not called it that here because the term *convergent evolution* also has a more conventional meaning: the tendency of unrelated life forms such as the Australian echidna, the North American porcupine, and the European hedgehog to evolve similar structures, in this case, protective spikes. For more on convergent evolution, see

http://www.wikipedia.org/wiki/Convergent_evolution.

[30] There is also such a thing as deistic evolution, which is somewhat different from theistic evolution, even though the two terms both make use of an old word for God (*deus* vs. *theos*). M.J. Erickson explains in *Christian Theology*: "Although the term is rarely heard, deistic evolution is perhaps the best way to describe one variety of what is generally called theistic evolution. This is the view that God began the process of evolution, producing the first matter and implanting within the creation the laws which its development has followed. Thus, he programmed the process. Then he withdrew from active involvement with the world, becoming, so to speak, Creator emeritus. The progress of the created order is free of direct influence by God. . . . God is the Creator, the ultimate cause, but evolution is the means, the proximate cause. Thus, except for its view of the very beginning of matter, deistic evolution is identical to naturalistic evolution for it denies that there is any direct activity by a personal God during the ongoing creative process. Deistic evolution has little difficulty with the scientific data. There is a different story with respect to the biblical material, however. There is a definite conflict between deism's view of an absentee God and the biblical picture of a God who has been involved in not merely one but a whole series of creative acts." M.J. Erickson, *Christian Theology* [1983] (Grand Rapids, MI: Baker, 1988), 5th printing), pp. 480–81. Actually, some people who call themselves theistic evolutionists are more appropriately called deistic evolutionists, because they see God as little more than a First Cause of events.

Chapter 7: The Scopes Trial That Really Happened (Pages 77–83)

[1] Edward J. Larson, *Summer for the Gods: The Scopes Trial and America's Continuing Debate over Science and Religion* (New York: Basic Books, 1997), p. 27.

[2] Ibid., p. 201.

[3] The professor is Del Ratzsch, who occasionally teaches a course called "The Monkey Trials" at Calvin College, which requires students to read the transcript of the trial, as well as some recollections of participants. The coconut award is given on the last day of class, when the movie is shown.

[4] Edward J. Larson, *Summer for the Gods: The Scopes Trial and America's Continuing Debate over Science and Religion* (New York: Basic Books, 1997), p. 40. Rickard Weikart, Associate Professor of Modern European History at California State University, will shortly publish *From Darwin to Hitler: Evolutionary Ethics, Eugenics, and Racism in Germany* (New York: Palgrave Macmillan, 2004). According to a summary, the book "is scheduled to appear in 2004 with Palgrave Macmillan in New York, a major publisher of historical scholarship. In this book Richard Weikart explains the revolutionary impact Darwinism had on ethics and morality. He demonstrates that many leading Darwinian biologists and social thinkers in Germany believed that Darwinism overturned traditional Judeo-Christian and Enlightenment ethics, especially the view that human life is

sacred. Many of these thinkers supported moral relativism, yet simultaneously exalted evolutionary 'fitness' (especially intelligence and health) to the highest arbiter of morality. Darwinism played a key role in the rise not only of eugenics (a movement wanting to control human reproduction to improve the human species), but also euthanasia, infanticide, abortion, and racial extermination. This was especially important in Germany, since Hitler built his view of ethics on Darwinian principles. In the final chapter Weikart argues that Hitler was not amoral, but upheld a consistent ethic that rested on Darwinian foundations." You can read more at http://www.csustan.edu/History/Faculty/Weikart/FromDarwintoHitler.htm.

5 Edward J. Larson, *Summer for the Gods: The Scopes Trial and America's Continuing Debate over Science and Religion* (New York: Basic Books, 1997), p. 135. Many people who believe in Darwinism strongly oppose eugenics. They point out, quite rightly, that Darwinism is about the survival of the actual fittest, not of those that we think are most worthy. While this argument does not solve all problems, it enables a Darwinist to oppose eugenics. For an enlightening series of essays along these lines, see Hilary Rose and Steven Rose, *Alas, Poor Darwin: Arguments Against Evolutionary Psychology* (London: Vintage Random House, 2000).

6 Edward J. Larson, *Summer for the Gods: The Scopes Trial and America's Continuing Debate over Science and Religion* (New York: Basic Books, 1997), p. 27.

7 House Bill No. 185 actually says: "That it shall be unlawful for any teacher in any of the Universities, Normals and all other public schools of the State which are supported in whole or in part by the public school funds of the State, to teach any theory that denies the story of the Divine Creation of man as taught in the Bible, and to teach instead that man has descended from a lower order of animals." It does not prohibit the teaching of animal or plant evolution.

8 The entire text of Friedrich von Bernhardi's book, *Germany and the Next War* (New York, 1914, transl. by Allen H. Powles), pp. 16–20, 85–105, 114, 167–82, can be read at Humanities and Social Sciences Online, http://www2.h-net.msu.edu/~german/gtext/kaiserreich/bernhardi.html.

9 Edward J. Larson, *Summer for the Gods: The Scopes Trial and America's Continuing Debate over Science and Religion* (New York: Basic Books, 1997), p. 40.

10 Ronald L. Numbers, "Creationism," Microsoft® Encarta® Reference Library 2003. 1993–2002.

11 Larson gives a very detailed account of the runup to the trial in the second part of *Summer*.

12 He taught algebra, physics, and chemistry at Central High School in Dayton. Edward J. Larson, *Summer for the Gods: The Scopes Trial and America's Continuing Debate over Science and Religion* (New York: Basic Books, 1997), pp. 200–01. Scopes used the opportunity to study geology at the University of Chicago, and he worked as a geologist until his retirement in 1963. Interestingly, according to Doug Linder's

Scopes Trial page, http://www.law.umkc.edu/faculty/projects/ftrials/scopes/SCO_SCO.HTM, he was baptized in South America, and got married there. He died in 1970. He also thought highly of Bryan, arguing that he was the greatest American since Thomas Jefferson. See http://groups.yahoo.com/group/CreationEvolutionDesign/message/7964.

[13] An Introduction to the John Scopes (Monkey) Trial, http://www.law.umkc.edu/faculty/projects/ftrials/scopes/evolut.htm, accessed March 16, 2003, p. 2. This is one of the Famous Trials Web sites of the University of Missouri-Kansas City School of Law.

[14] Edward J. Larson, *Summer for the Gods: The Scopes Trial and America's Continuing Debate over Science and Religion* (New York: Basic Books, 1997), p. 200.

[15] You can read some of Mencken's wit at the expense of Dayton at the Scopes Trial Home Page, sponsored by the Famous Trials project by Doug Linder. http://www.law.umkc.edu/faculty/projects/ftrials/scopes/menk.htm. You can also read about *Hell and High Schools* and other exotic Americana at the site.

[16] Edward J. Larson, *Summer for the Gods: The Scopes Trial and America's Continuing Debate over Science and Religion* (New York: Basic Books, 1997), p. 93: "I expected to find a squalid Southern village, with darkies snoozing on the horse blocks, pigs rooting under the houses and the inhabitants full of hookworm and malaria. What I found was a country town of charm and even beauty." Mencken's expectations say more about him than about Dayton.

[17] See, for example, Roger K. Miller, "New bio debunks Mencken myths," a review of Terry Teachout, *The Skeptic: A Life of H.L. Mencken* (New York: HarperCollins, 2002), http://www.post-gazette.com/books/reviews/20021027mencken1027fnp5.asp.

[18] In *The Skeptic: A Life of H.L. Mencken* (New York: HarperCollins, 2002), Terry Teachout observes (p. 65): "Everything about Mencken—his politics, his religious beliefs, his personal relationships, his taste in literature—was conditioned by his certainty that life was a struggle for survival to which some men were ill-suited by the accident of birth. His philosophy would become more elaborate, especially after he began to read Nietzsche, but it never strayed far in spirit from the social Darwinism in shirtsleeves that he acquired as city editor of the *Herald*, listening to drunken reporters gripe about the unfairness of life."

[19] "People & Events: Henry Louis Mencken (1880–1956)," *Monkey Trial*, http://www.pbs.org/wgbh/amex/monkeytrial/peopleevents/p_mencken.html.

[20] Larson, p. 224.

[21] See the transcript of the show at http://www.pbs.org/wgbh/amex/monkeytrial/filmmore/pt.html.

[22] Edward J. Larson, *Summer for the Gods: The Scopes Trial and America's Continuing Debate over Science and Religion* (New York: Basic Books, 1997). *Summer*

won the Pulitzer Prize in 1998. It is indispensable for understanding the true context, as opposed to any fictional context, for the creation–evolution debate in the United States.

23 *Ibid.*, p. 240.

24 See *ibid.*, pp. 241–43. See also David N. Menton, "Inherently wind: a Hollywood history of the 1925 Scopes 'monkey' trial," www.gennet.org/facts/scopes.html. The site is sponsored by Missouri Association for Creation.

25 Gallup poll taken in November 1997, reported by ABC News, September 2, 1999. See p. 160–61 on possible weaknesses of these types of polls.

26 Letter, dated June 2, from Cynthia Anderson, Associate Superintendent for Educational Services to John Calvert, Celti Johnson's legal adviser.

Chapter 8: How Modern Evolutionists Have Evolved Away from Darwin (Pages 85–101)

1 See Roger Highfield, "DNA pioneers lash out at religion," *London Daily Telegraph* (March 24, 2003).

2 See "Do our genes reveal the hand of God," a *Daily Telegraph* "Science in the News" feature (March 20, 2003), http://www.science-writer.co.uk/news_and_pr/headline_mar_25_03_1.html.

3 Edward J. Larson, *Summer for the Gods: The Scopes Trial and America's Continuing Debate over Science and Religion* (New York: Basic Books, 1997), pp. 19–20. Paleontologist Niles Eldredge notes: "No doubt about it, the first two decades of the twentieth century were rough on Darwinians." *Reinventing Darwin* (New York: John Wiley, 1995), p. 16.

4 Niles Eldredge, *Reinventing Darwin* (New York: John Wiley, 1995), p. 14.

5 Michael Ruse, *The Evolution Wars: A Guide to the Debates* (Santa Barbara, CA: ABC-CLIO, 2000), pp. 53–57.

6 Stephen Jay Gould, "Evolution's erratic pace," *Natural History* (May 1977), 86, 5: 14.

7 See, for example, R.A. Kerr, "Evolution's Big Bang Gets Even More Explosive," *Science*, Vol. 261, 3 September 1993, pp. 1274–1275, and J.M. Nash, "When Life Exploded," *Time Magazine*, Vol. 146, No. 23, December 4, 1995, pp. 71–78, p. 72. Nash writes, "543 million years ago, in the early Cambrian, within the span of no more than 10 million years, creatures with teeth and tentacles and claws and jaws materialized with the suddenness of apparitions. In a burst of creativity like nothing before or since, nature appears to have sketched out the blueprints for virtually the whole of the animal kingdom. This explosion of biological diversity is described by scientists as biology's Big Bang."

[8] See, for example, "'Big bang' for tertiary birds?" A. Feduccia, *Trends in Ecology and Evolution* (April 2003), vol. 18, no. 4: 172–76.

[9] See, for example, "Early evolution of land plants: phylogeny, physiology, and ecology of the primary terrestrial radiation," *Annual Review Ecol. Syst.* (1998), 29: 263–92.

[10] For an interesting retrospective on the Piltdown fraud, including the fact that much of what happened remains a mystery, see "Too good to be true" by Tim Radford, *Guardian* (November 13, 2003), http://education.guardian.co.uk/print/0,3858,4795611-110865,00.html. "The cast of plausible potential pranksters in this anthropological whodunnit includes enthusiastic amateurs, passionate professionals and disinterested jokers." Fossil fraud is a lucrative business even today.

[11] Daniel Dennett, *Darwin's Dangerous Idea* (New York: Simon and Schuster, 1995), p. 21, quoted in Kenneth R. Miller, *Finding Darwin's God: A Scientist's Search for Common Ground Between God and Evolution* (New York: HarperCollins, 1999), pp. 12–13.

[12] Daniel Dennett, *Darwin's Dangerous Idea* (New York: Simon and Schuster, 1995), pp. 12–13.

[13] Douglas Futuyma, *Evolution* (Sunderland, MA: Sinauer Associates, 1986), p. 2, quoted in Kenneth R. Miller, *Finding Darwin's God: A Scientist's Search for Common Ground Between God and Evolution* (New York: HarperCollins, 1999), p. 168.

[14] Roger Highfield, "DNA pioneers lash out at religion," *London Daily Telegraph* (March 24, 2003).

[15] Colin Tudge, "Microscopes have no morals: science needs the ethical underpinning that religion can best provide," *Guardian* (September 13, 2003), http://www.guardian.co.uk/print/0,3858,4752915-103677,00.html.

[16] Michael Ruse, *The Evolution Wars: A Guide to the Debates* (Santa Barbara, CA: ABC-CLIO, 2000), p. 114. Ruse is a strong supporter of Darwinism.

[17] Collins was responding to Crick's and Watson's attacks on traditional religion, in "Do our genes reveal the hand of God," a *Daily Telegraph* "Science in the News" feature (March 20, 2003), http://www.science-writer.co.uk/news_and_pr/headline_mar_25_03_1.html.

[18] Ibid.

[19] See, for example, pp. 167, 187, and 219.

[20] Today, the students are actually taught "neo-Darwinian" evolution, which is a synthesis of Darwinism and Mendel's genetics. In this book, the distinction of terminology is not made except where the sense requires it.

[21] You can view the entire report at http://www.discovery.org/articleFiles/PDFs/ZogbyFinalReport.pdf.

[22] Lynn Margulis, "Gaia Is a Tough Bitch" in John Brockman, ed., *The Third*

Culture (New York: Simon and Schuster Touchstone, 1996), p. 133. You can read the chapter in which she makes this point online at http://www.edge.org/documents/ThirdCulture/n-Ch.7.html. The recent discovery that very simple (prokaryotic) organisms can have organelles has challenged Margulis's theory. See "Organelle's discovery challenges theory, could alter approach to disease treatment," *EurekAlert* (June 17, 2003), http://www.eurekalert.org/pub_releases/2003-06/uoia-odc061703.php.

23 Quoted in "Theory challenges Darwin doctrine of common descent" from *UniSci: Daily University Science News* (June 18, 2002), University of Illinois. See also http://unisci.com/stories/20022/0618021.htm.

24 Gordon Rattray Taylor, *The Great Evolution Mystery* (London: Secker & Warburg, 1982), pp. 14–15. If you want to know more about *microstomum*, search at http://www.teaching-biomed.man.ac.uk/bs1999/bs146/biodiversity/cnidaria.htm.

25 Gordon Rattray Taylor, *The Great Evolution Mystery* (London: Secker & Warburg, 1982), p. 15.

26 See Thomas Woodward, *Doubts About Darwin: A History of Intelligent Design* (Grand Rapids, MI: Baker, 2003), p. 37.

27 Michael J. Behe, *Darwin's Black Box: The Biochemical Challenge to Evolution* (New York: Free Press, 1996), p. 29. See also H. Yockey, *Information Theory and Molecular Biology* (Cambridge: Cambridge University Press, 1992), ch. 9; M. Kaplan, "Welcome to Participants" in *Mathematical Challenges to the Neo-Darwinian Interpretation of Evolution*, P.S. Moorhead and M.M. Kaplan, eds. (Philadelphia: Wistar Institute Press, 1967), p. vii; M.P. Schutzenberger, "Algorithms and Neo-Darwinian Theory of Evolution" in *Mathematical Challenges to the Neo-Darwinian Interpretation of Evolution*, P.S. Moorhead and M.M. Kaplan, eds. (Philadelphia: Wistar Institute Press, 1967), p. 75; S. Kauffman, *The Origins of Order* (Oxford: Oxford University Press, 1993), p. xiii. Phillip Johnson also provides some interesting reflections on the Wistar meetings in Phillip E. Johnson, *Darwin on Trial* (Downer's Grove. IL: InterVarsity Press, 1993), pp. 38–39.

28 Thomas Woodward, *Doubts About Darwin: A History of Intelligent Design* (Grand Rapids, MI: Baker, 2003), p. 37.

29 "DR. FRASER: It would seem to me that there have been endless statements made and the only thing I have clearly agreed with through the whole day has been the statement made by Carl [sic] Popper, namely, that the real inadequacy of evolution, esthetically and scientifically, is that you can explain anything you want by changing your variables around." A. Fraser, "Discussion: Paper by Dr. Wald," in P.S. Moorhead and M.M. Kaplan, eds., Mathematical challenges to the neo-Darwinian interpretation of evolution: a symposium held at the Wistar Institute of Anatomy and Biology, April 25 and 26, 1966, Wistar Institute Symposium Monograph no. 5 (Philadelphia: Wistar Institute Press, 1967), p. 67.

30 She was also the first wife of Carl Sagan, by whom she had a son, Dorion Sagan, with whom she co-authored *Microcosmos: Four Billion Years of Microbial Evolution* (University of California Press, 1997). At her home page, http://www.bio.umass.edu/faculty/biog/margulis.html, is a summary of some of her works.

31 Lynn Margulis, "Gaia Is a Tough Bitch" in John Brockman, ed., *The Third Culture* (New York: Simon and Schuster Touchstone, 1996), pp. 36–37, 129–51. Interestingly, she likens her discovery that she was not a supporter of neo-Darwinism to the recognition that one has ceased to believe in a religion (p. 133). Some still keep the faith. Her chapter in *The Third Culture* is available online at http://www.edge.org/documents/ThirdCulture/n-Ch.7.html.

32 David M. Raup, *Extinction: Bad Genes or Bad Luck?* (New York: W.W. Norton, 1991), p. 3. Taxonomists (people who catalogue species) tend to be either "lumpers" or "splitters," depending on whether they try to fit as many specimens as possible into one species or divide them up. Thus, estimates vary widely on the probable number of species. Either way, almost all life forms that have ever lived are now extinct.

33 David M. Raup, *Extinction: Bad Genes or Bad Luck?* (New York: W.W. Norton 1991), pp. 10–11.

34 Ibid., p. 6.

35 Ibid., p. 84.

36 Ibid., p. 118. The Big Five were the Ordovician, Devonian, Permian, Triassic, and Cretaceous (K–T) extinctions.

37 David M. Raup, *Extinction: Bad Genes or Bad Luck?* (New York: W.W. Norton,1991), p. 108.

38 "The disturbing reality is that for none of the thousands of well-documented extinctions in the geologic past do we have a solid explanation of why the extinction occurred. We have many proposals in specific cases, of course: . . . These are all plausible scenarios, but no matter how plausible, they cannot be shown to be true beyond reasonable doubt. Equally plausible alternative scenarios can be invented with ease, and none has predictive power in the sense that it can show *a priori* that a given species or anatomical type was destined to go extinct." David M. Raup, *Extinction: Bad Genes or Bad Luck?* (New York: W.W. Norton, 1991), p. 17. Interestingly, Raup encouraged Phillip Johnson to go ahead with his critique of Darwinism, though he never formally identified with the ID camp. See Thomas Woodward, *Doubts About Darwin: A History of Intelligent Design* (Grand Rapids, MI: Baker, 2003), pp. 82–83.

39 "This idea is appealing and has been learned by generations of biology students. But its verification from actual field data is negligible." David M. Raup, *Extinction: Bad Genes or Bad Luck?* (New York: W.W. Norton, 1991), pp. 184–85.

40 The whole passage reads: "I returned, and saw under the sun, that the race is not to the swift, nor the battle to the strong, neither yet bread to the wise, nor yet riches to

men of understanding, nor yet favour to men of skill; but time and chance happeneth to them all." Eccles. 9:11, KJV.

41 Darwin himself thought that there could have been more than one ancestor of life. For example, he wrote, "There is grandeur in this view of life, with its several powers, having been originally breathed by the Creator into a few forms or into one ...." Charles Darwin, *The Origin of Species by Means of Natural Selection*, [1872], Everyman's Library, 6th Edition, reprint, (London: J.M. Dent & Sons, 1928) p. 463. The main problem is that multiplying the number of times that a wildly improbable event is required compounds the improbability.

42 Quoted in "Theory challenges Darwin doctrine of common descent," *UniSci: Daily University Science News* (June 18, 2002), University of Illinois. See http://unisci.com/stories/20022/0618021.htm.

43 This was AAAS's 169th meeting, February 17, 2003. See http://www.stanford.edu/dept/news/pr/03/aaassocialselection219.html for more information on the dissenting researchers' views. Roughgarden is the author of *Evolution's Rainbow: Diversity, Gender and Sexuality in Nature and People* (University of California Press, 2003).

44 Ibid.

45 *Taylor*: Gordon Rattray Taylor, *The Great Evolution Mystery* (London: Secker & Warburg, 1983), pp. 87–88.

Hunter: "Darwinists claim that such adaptations are powerful evidence for their theory. Are new proteins and pesticide resistance not examples of evolution in progress? The problem is these adaptations are produced by a machine that appears to be set up to produce such changes. Rather than mutations aimlessly exploring new designs, we are apparently witnessing the actions of a complex and robust machine. . . . One study of the common fruit fly found that pesticide resistance arises from a gene that has been present all along. The gene serves to break down the pesticide. It used to be less active, but now it is more active in resistant flies. A special signal was inserted into the gene to lift production constraints. It appears that pesticide resistance is conferred by flipping a switch on the genetic production line rather than creating a new factory.

"These findings are awkward for evolution. Instead of single mutations leading to a new functionality one step at a time, we must believe that evolution produced this marvelous machine by which more complicated changes can occur." C.G. Hunter, *Darwin's Proof: The Triumph of Religion over Science* (Grand Rapids, MI: Brazos Press, 2003), pp. 24–25.

Gould: Stephen Jay Gould, *Wonderful Life: The Burgess Shale and the Nature of History* (New York: W.W. Norton, 1989.) See especially ch. 3, "Reconstruction of the Burgess Shale: Toward a New View of Life."

Woese: Quoted in "Theory challenges Darwin doctrine of common descent," *UniSci: Daily University Science News* (June 18, 2002), University of Illinois. See also http://unisci.com/stories/20022/0618021.htm.

Margulis: Lynn Margulis, "Gaia Is a Tough Bitch" in John Brockman, ed., *The*

Third Culture (New York: Simon and Schuster Touchstone, 1996), pp. 36–37,129–51.

Berlinski: See, for example, David Berlinski, "A scientific scandal," *Commentary* (April 2003). Incidentally, Berlinski is not the only person to complain about artificial life scenarios that supposedly demonstrate Darwinism that are too favorable or too simple compared to real life. See, for example, Nick Barton and Willem Zuidema, "Evolution: the erratic path towards complexity," *Current Biology* (August 19, 2003), vol. 13, R649–R651. They describe computer-generated Artificial Life models as "the study of life as it could be," noting that "real progress on this issue, however, requires Artificial Life researchers to take seriously the tools and insights from population genetics."

Wesson: "There are striking parallels of various Australian marsupials with placental mammals. The placental mole, flying and nonflying squirrels, jumping mice, ordinary mice, cats, and wolves all have marsupial counterparts. The resemblance of the (extinct) Tasmanian wolf to the northern wolf is especially close, down to the shape of teeth, claws, ears, and skull. That their convergences are beyond the needs of adaptation for their respective ways of life suggests that certain patterns are most compatible with the mammalian plan, that is the basic mammalian attractor. The way genes can be fitted together must be similar to marsupials and placentals, although their common ancestry lies at least 100 million years in the past. It is somehow inherent in the mammalian pattern that, in suitable environments, primitive mammals could radiate in similar directions, evolving similar burrowing insectivores, coursing carnivores, and so forth. . . . The idea that the direction of evolution is in any way predetermined is disliked because it seems to hint divine purpose." R.G. Wesson, *Beyond Natural Selection* [1991] (Cambridge, MA: MIT Press, 1994), repr., pp. 184, 186.)

Popper: Karl Popper, *The Logic of Scientific Discovery* (London: Hutchinson, 1959), p. 109. See http://plato.stanford.edu/entries/popper/ for more on Popper's thoughts.

Patterson: See p. 180, and Phillip E. Johnson, *Darwin on Trial* (Downer's Grove, IL: InterVarsity Press, 1993), pp. 23–24.

Eldredge: "Physics envy" means the desire for simple, comprehensive explanations that may not be suited to a discipline. For example, Eldredge writes: "Ultra-Darwinian desire has been great to deny the separateness of, the distinctions between, the economic and genealogical arenas. It is a desire to see evolution as an active process, like the sorts of dynamic processes studied by physicists, chemists, and ecologists. Evolutionists have consistently denied this separateness, have attributed economic properties to genealogic entities, and, most recently, as ultra-Darwinians, have insisted that competition for reproductive success drives economic systems. What is this but physics envy? Claiming that economic systems are really all about the transmission of genetic information is a fairly blatant distortion of natural systems." Niles Eldredge, *Reinventing Darwin* (New York: John Wiley, 1995), p. 197.

Grasse: "Panchronic species [living fossils], which like other species are subject to the assaults of mutations remain unchanged. . . . Cockroaches, which are one of the most venerable living relict groups, have remained more or less unchanged since the Permian, yet they have undergone as many mutations as Drosophila, a Tertiary insect.

It is important to note that relict species mutate as much as others do, but do not evolve, not even when they live in conditions favorable to change (diversity of environments, cosmopolitanism, large populations). How does the Darwinian mutational interpretation of evolution account for the fact that the species that have been the most stable—some of them for the last hundreds of millions of years have mutated as much as the others do?" (P.-P. Grasse, *Evolution of Living Organisms: Evidence for a New Theory of Transformation* [1973] (New York: Academic Press, 1977), pp. 87–88.

Denton: "Does Darwinian theory adequately explain the pervasive patterns of natural history? Well, the basic pattern it fails to explain is the apparent uniqueness and isolation of major types of organisms. My fundamental problem with the theory is that there are so many highly complicated organs, systems and structures, from the nature of the lung of a bird, to the eye of the rock lobster, for which I cannot conceive of how these things have come about in terms of a gradual accumulation of random changes. It strikes me as being a flagrant denial of common sense to swallow that all these things were built up by accumulative small random changes. This is simply a nonsensical claim, especially for the great majority of cases, where nobody can think of any credible explanation of how it came about. And this is a very profound question which everybody skirts, everybody brushes over, everybody tries to sweep under the carpet. The fact is that the majority of these complex adaptations in nature cannot be adequately explained by a series of intermediate forms. And this is a fundamental problem. Common sense tells me there must be something wrong." In "An interview with Michael Denton," Access Research Network, *Origins Research* (July 20, 1995), vol. 15, no. 2 www.arn.org/docs/orpages/or152/dent.htm

Kimura: "From the standpoint of population genetics, positive Darwinian selection represents a process whereby advantageous mutants spread through the species. Considering their great importance in evolution, it is perhaps surprising that well-established cases are so scarce; for example, industrial melanisms in moths and increases of DDT resistance in insects are constantly being cited. On the other hand, examples showing that negative selection is at work to eliminate variants produced by mutation abound." In "Population genetics and molecular evolution," *The Johns Hopkins Medical Journal* (June 1976), vol. 138, no. 6: 260.

Yockey: H. Yockey, *Information Theory and Molecular Biology* (Cambridge: Cambridge University Press, 1992), ch. 9.

Gould: Stephen Jay Gould, "Evolution's erratic pace," in *Natural History* (May 1977), vol. 136, no.5: p. 14.

Eldredge: "Dawkins's 'selfish genes' gambit posits, in effect, that genetic information, viewed as the instructions for constructing an organism, is more important than the system it builds—the organism itself. Evolution is strictly competition among genes for representation in the next generation. This is the ultimate reductionist scenario yet concocted in evolutionary biology." Niles Eldredge, *Reinventing Darwin* (New York: John Wiley, 1995), p. 169.

Roughgarden: See http://www.stanford.edu/dept/news/pr/03/aaassocialselec-

NOTES

tion219.html for more information on the dissenting researchers' views. Roughgarden is the author of *Evolution's Rainbow: Diversity, Gender and Sexuality in Nature and People* (University of California Press, 2003).

46 Walsh notes: "Even today it is virtually impossible for conscientious biologists to admit that the evidence for evolution is extraordinarily thin. We simply have little tangible proof that one species evolves into another," but he also notes that "by calling into question the Darwinian universe, we would at the same time be restoring the openness to the transcendent creator. It is in other words the fear of God that prevents the biological community from too openly discarding a theory they have long ceased to honor in practice." David Walsh, *The Third Millennium: Reflections on Faith and Reason* (Washington: Georgetown University Press, 1999), p. 86.

47 A.S. Wilkins, "Evolutionary processes: a special issue," *BioEssays* (2000), 22: 1051–52.

48 For example, R.G. Wesson writes: "Pointing out the need for a better explanation means attacking a theory that scientists find useful, if not always satisfying. They certainly do not want to surrender the accepted doctrine unless they have something better. A natural rejoinder to criticism is, What do you have better to put in its place? Natural selection is credited with seemingly miraculous feats because we want an answer and have no other. There probably cannot be another general answer—certainly no equally broad and basically simple answer. Biologists, it seems, must do without a comprehensive theory of evolution, just as social scientists have to make do without a comprehensive theory of society." R.G. Wesson, *Beyond Natural Selection* [1991] (Cambridge, MA: MIT Press, 1994), reprint, p. xiii. But one thing we can certainly expect is a lot of kicking and screaming while they adjust.

Chapter 9: Darwin's Quarreling Heirs: Dawkins vs. Gould (Pages 103–113)

1 From a review of *Blueprints: Solving the Mystery of Evolution* by Maitland A. Edey and Donald C. Johanson (Boston: Little, Brown, 1989), New York Times (April 9, 1989).

2 Gregg Easterbrook, "Bullied and brainwashed" on www.beliefnet.com (no date) http://www.beliefnet.com/frameset.asp?pageLoc=/story/86/story_8686_1.html&boardID=26156

3 See Note 56 for this chapter.

4 "The accidental creationist," *New Yorker* (December 13, 1999). The online version from which these quotations are taken is adapted from chs. 19 and 20 of *Nonzero: The Logic of Human Destiny* by Robert Wright, published by Pantheon Books in 2000 and by Vintage Books in 2001. Online at http://www.nonzero.org/newyorker.htm.

5 H. Allen Orr, "The descent of Gould," *New Yorker* (September 30, 2002), Web posted September 23, 2002. Online at http://www.newyorker.com/printable/?critics/020930crat_atlarge.

280

[6] Quoted in "Richard Dawkins's evolution: an irascible don becomes a surprising celebrity" by Ian Parker, *New Yorker* (September 9, 1996).

[7] "Ultra-Darwinist" should not be confused with "neo-Darwinist." The latter term refers to the 20th-century synthesis of Darwinism and modern genetics. Most Darwinists today are neo-Darwinists. The phrase "ultra-Darwinism" was probably popularized by Richard C. Lewontin, a Harvard-based collaborator of Stephen Jay Gould.

[8] From the Introduction to the 1976 edition of *The Selfish Gene* by Richard Dawkins (Oxford: Oxford University Press). You can read excerpts from this and other works by Dawkins at http://www.world-of-dawkins.com/Dawkins/Work/Books/.

[9] "Vision that is 5 per cent as good as yours or mine is very much worth having in comparison with no vision at all. So is 1 per cent vision better than total blindness. And 6 per cent is better than 5, 7 per cent better than 6, and so on up the gradual, continuous series." Richard Dawkins, *The Blind Watchmaker*, reprint [1986] (London: Penguin: 1991), p. 81. Quoted in Phillip E. Johnson, *Darwin on Trial* (Downer's Grove, IL: InterVarsity Press, 1993), p. 34.

[10] An article in which he explores this theme is "Viruses of the mind," *Free Inquiry* (summer 1993): 34–41, available online at http://www.world-of-dawkins.com/Dawkins/Work/Articles/1993-summervirusesofmind.htm.

[11] He is the Simonyi Professor of the Public Understanding of Science.

[12] Quoted in *Free Inquiry* (summer 1993): 34–41. http://www.world-of-dawkins.com/Dawkins/Work/Articles/1993-summervirusesofmind.htm.

[13] See "Richard Dawkins's evolution: an irascible don becomes a surprising celebrity" by Ian Parker, *New Yorker* (September 9, 1996).

[14] Quoted in Kim A. McDonald, "Oxford U. professor preaches Darwinian evolution to skeptics," *Chronicle of Higher Education* (November 29, 1996).

[15] Richard Dawkins, *The Devil's Chaplain* (London: Weidenfeld & Nicolson, 2003).

[16] See Michael Ruse, "Through a glass, darkly," a review of *A Devil's Chaplain: Reflections on Hope, Lies, Science, and Love* (New York: Houghton Mifflin, 2003), *American Scientist* (November–December, 2003), http://www.americanscientist.org/template/BookReviewTypeDetail/assetid/28365. Ruse notes: "I worry about the political consequences of Dawkins's message. If Darwinism is a major contributor to nonbelief, then should Darwinism be taught in publicly funded U.S. schools?"

[17] Ben Wattenberg, *Think Tank*, November 8, 1996. (Wattenberg seems to have been quoting things that Dawkins said in *The Selfish Gene*.)

[18] The Wattenberg–Dawkins interview transcript can be read at "Talking about Evolution with Richard Dawkins," http://www.pbs.org/thinktank/show_410.html.

[19] See "Richard Dawkins's evolution: an irascible don becomes a surprising celebrity"

by Ian Parker, *New Yorker* (September 9, 1996).

[20] Ibid.

[21] "Ignorance is no crime" by Richard Dawkins, *Free Inquiry* (Summer, 2001), vol.21, no.3, online at www.secularhumanism.org/library/fi/dawkins_21_3.html.

[22] See, for example, "Keeping an eye on evolution: Richard Dawkins, a relentless Darwinian spear carrier, trips over Mount Improbable," review of *Climbing Mount Improbable* by Richard Dawkins (New York: W.H. Norton,1996) by David Berlinski in *Globe and Mail* (November 2, 1996), which can be read online at http://www.discovery.org/viewDB/index.php3?program=CRSC&command=view&id=132.

[23] See "Richard Dawkins's evolution: an irascible don becomes a surprising celebrity" by Ian Parker, *New Yorker* (September 9, 1996).

[24] Sarah Harris, "Christians plan to set up six schools that doubt Darwin," *Daily Mail* (April 29, 2003).

[25] See pp. 90–91.

[26]i Michael Ruse, in *The Evolution Wars: A Guide to the Debates* (Santa Barbara, CA: ABC-CLIO, 2000), pp. 274–77, makes Dawkins's religious agenda quite clear, comparing his conversion to Darwinism with the conversion of St. Paul to Christianity.

[27] Teaching objections to Darwinism does not necessarily mean teaching creationism. We have encountered a number of non-creationist objections to Darwinism. That said, creationists would be anxious to teach objections to Darwinism.

[28] See "Anti-Dawkins" by Gabriel Dover, pp. 47–66, in Hilary Rose and Steven Rose, eds., *Alas, Poor Darwin: Arguments Against Evolutionary Psychology* (London: Vintage Random House, 2000).

[29] Michael J. Behe, *Darwin's Black Box: The Biochemical Challenge to Evolution* (New York: Free Press, 1996), pp. 18–22.

[30] "The fallacy in that argument is that '5 per cent of an eye' is not the same thing as '5 per cent of normal vision.' For an animal to have any useful vision at all, many complex parts must be working together. Even a complete eye is useless unless it belongs to a creature with the mental and neural capacity to make use of the information by doing something that furthers survival or reproduction. What we have to imagine is a chance mutation that provides this complex capacity all at once, at a level of utility sufficient to give the creature an advantage in producing offspring." (P.E. Johnson, *Darwin on Trial*, [1991], InterVarsity Press: Downers Grove IL, Second Edition, 1993, pp. 34–35). See also N. Broom, "What is Natural Selection? A Plea for Clarification," International Society for Complexity, Information, and Design, 2003, pp.4-5, http://www.iscid.org/papers/Broom_WhatIs_031202.pdf.

[31] David Berlinski, "A scientific scandal," *Commentary* (April 2003). Berlinski has certainly earned his place as possibly the "wicked" one in Dawkins's worldview. See p. 107.

32 See also "Why Memes?" by philosopher Mary Midgeley, pp. 67–84, in Hilary Rose and Steven Rose, eds., *Alas, Poor Darwin: Arguments Against Evolutionary Psychology* (London: Vintage Random House, 2000).

33 Richard Dawkins, *The Blind Watchmaker* [1986] (London: Penguin, 1991), reprint, p. 233.

34 See "Richard Dawkins's evolution: an irascible don becomes a surprising celebrity" by Ian Parker, *New Yorker* (September 9, 1996).

35 Quoted from a review of *Wonderful Life* by Stephen J. Gould, in *Sunday Telegraph* (February 25, 1990). The review is available at http://www.world-of-dawkins.com/Dawkins/Work/Reviews/1990-02-25wonderful.htm.

36 Kim Sterelny, *Dawkins vs. Gould: Survival of the Fittest* (Maryland: Totem Books, 2001). Incidentally, "Kim" is a man, not a woman, despite the mistaken implication of references to him in various works.

37 Stephen Jay Gould, From Brainy Quote, www.brainyquote.com/quotes/authors/s/stephen_jay_gould.html, accessed February 7, 2004.

38 Ibid.

39 Quoted in "Richard Dawkins's evolution: an irascible don becomes a surprising celebrity," by Ian Parker, *New Yorker*, September 9, 1996. Online at http://www.world-of-dawkins.com/Media/dawkny.htm. Similarly, intelligent design theorist Michael Behe comments (in "Dogmatic Darwinism," *Crisis*, June 1998): "It's lucky that Gould teaches at Harvard and Dawkins at Oxford. One continent wouldn't be big enough for the two of them." Behe's take on the conflict, available at www.catholiceducation.org/articles/science/sc0018.html, is an interesting read.

40 "The accidental creationist," *New Yorker*, December 13, 1999. Online at http://www.nonzero.org/newyorker.htm.

41 For details, plus an analysis of the episode from the perspective of an intelligent design advocate, see http://www.arn.org/docs/dembski1129.htm.

42 "Times obituary: Stephen Jay Gould," *The Times* (May 21, 2002).

43 Gould used this term in 1977. "The extreme rarity of transitional forms in the fossil record persists as the trade secret of paleontology. The evolutionary trees that adorn our textbooks have data only at the tips and nodes of their branches; the rest is inference, however reasonable, not the evidence of fossils." S.J. Gould, "Evolution's Erratic Pace," *Natural History*, The American Museum of Natural History, Vol. 86, No. 5, May 1977, pp. 12–16, p. 14.

44 Charles Darwin, *On the Origin of Species* (New York: Penguin, 1968), p. 296. You can read Darwin online at http://www.literature.org/authors/darwin-charles/the-origin-of-species.

45 Stephen Jay Gould, *Wonderful Life: The Burgess Shale and the Nature of History*

(New York: W.W. Norton, 1989).

[46] Kim Sterelny, an Australian philosopher, wrote a book that handily summarizes the differences between Gould's views and Dawkins's views, *Dawkins vs. Gould: Survival of the Fittest* (Maryland: Totem Books, 2001). He points out that, whereas Dawkins sees the unit of selection as the gene, Gould sees it as the organism. Dawkins believes that the patterns in the development of life are a succession of tiny selecting events, where Gould believes that key patterns are not best explained by selection. Sterelny supports Dawkins more than Gould, but provides a fair assessment of both.

[47] See, for example, Tom Bethell, "Against sociobiology" in *First Things* (January 2001): 18–24, www.arn.org/docs2/news/againstsociobiology0101.htm.

[48] That, for example, is the theme of *Alas, Poor Darwin*, to which Gould contributed. See Hilary Rose and Steven Rose, eds., *Alas, Poor Darwin: Arguments Against Evolutionary Psychology* (London: Vintage Random House, 2000).

[49] Paul R. Gross, "The apotheosis of Stephen Jay Gould" in *New Criterion* (October 2002), vol. 21, no. 2, available online at http://www.newcriterion.com/archive/21/oct02/gould.htm

[50] "Times obituary: Stephen Jay Gould", *The Times* (May 21, 2002).

[51] From a letter to the editor of *New York Review of Books* by John Tooby and Leda Cosmides of the Center for Evolutionary Psychology, UCSB, July 7, 1997, available online at http://cogweb.ucla.edu/Debate/CEP_Gould.html.

[52] Ibid.

[53] David P. Barash, "Grappling with the ghost of Gould: a review of *The Structure of Evolutionary Theory*," in *Human Nature Review* (July 9, 2002), vol. 2: 283–292, online at http://human-nature.com/nibbs/02/gould.html. On the other hand, leading evolutionary biologist Ernst Mayr defended Gould in 2001, saying: "One must not forget that chance always plays a considerable role even at the second step of evolution, that of survival and reproduction. And not all aspects of adaptedness are tested in every generation. Or let us look at the 35 or so living phyla of animals. They are the survivors of the 60 or more body plans that existed in the early Cambrian. When one studies their differences, one does not get the impression that they are necessities. Many or even most of their unique characteristics may have had their origin in a developmental accident that was tolerated by selection, while the seeming failure of those that became extinct may have been the result of a chance event (like the Alvarez asteroid extinction event). S.J. Gould (1989) made such contingencies a major theme in *Wonderful Life*, and I have come to the conclusion that here he may be largely right." E. Mayr, *What Evolution Is* (New York: Basic Books, 2001), p. 229. This must have been gratifying to Gould, who was to die the following year.

[54] For a socialist analysis of Gould's life and work see the obituary by Pete Mason in *Socialism Today* (July–August, 2002). Online at http://www.socialismtoday.org/67/gould.html. The analysis includes the Simpsons

episode. See also Simon Conway Morris's comments in Richard Monastersky, "Revising the book of life," *The Chronicle of Higher Education* (March 15, 2002), online at http://chronicle.com/free/v48/i27/27a01401.htm.

55 Stephen Jay Gould, "More Things in Heaven and Earth," in Hilary Rose and Steven Rose, eds., *Alas, Poor Darwin: Arguments Against Evolutionary Psychology* (London: Vintage Random House, 2000), p. 87.

56 This becomes clear from the long, angry letter to the editor of *New York Review of Books* by John Tooby and Leda Cosmides of the Center for Evolutionary Psychology, UCSB, July 7, 1997, available online at http://cogweb.ucla.edu/Debate/CEP_Gould.html. They're mad and they're not going to take it any more. They list, among Gould's many sins, the fact that he has "showered Dawkins with abuse." The ill-used Dawkins is, in their view, "the brilliant and authentic native voice of modern evolutionary biology." However, to judge from his own comments on Gould while the latter was alive (see p. 108), Dawkins seems quite able to defend himself, and return the fire.

57 "Darwinian Fundamentalism," *New York Review of Books* (June 12, 1997), vol.44, no. 10. Online at http://www.nybooks.com/articles/1151.

58 For example, *Alas, Poor Darwin*, a mainly British collection of essays against evolutionary psychology, features many examples of writers anxious to show that their Darwinism is orthodox even though they have no use for Dawkins or EP. See Hilary Rose and Steven Rose, eds., *Alas, Poor Darwin: Arguments Against Evolutionary Psychology* (London: Vintage Random House, 2000).

59 "The accidental creationist," *New Yorker* (December 13, 1999). The online version from which these quotations are taken is adapted from chs. 19 and 20 of *Nonzero: The Logic of Human Destiny*, by Robert Wright, published by Pantheon Books in 2000 and by Vintage Books in 2001. Online at http://www.nonzero.org/newyorker.htm.

60 Charles Jencks, "EP, Phone Home," in Hilary Rose and Steven Rose, eds., *Alas, Poor Darwin: Arguments Against Evolutionary Psychology* (London: Vintage Random House, 2000), p. 43.

61 Harvey Blume, in his summation of Stephen Jay Gould in "The origin of specious: and why reductionists are winning the Darwin wars," *American Prospect* (September 23, 2002), comments: "Gould's science and literary style owed more to art and artists than to algorithms. His opponents' approach to art, on the other hand, is, as a rule, so doggedly reductionist as to sow doubts about their whole enterprise. It is painful, for example, to read Wilson, so often a superb writer himself, as he attempts to squeeze every artistic motif known to man into a few universals consistent with a genetic approach to human culture."

62 From Introduction by Stephen Jay Gould to Carl Zimmer, *Evolution: The Triumph of an Idea* (New York: HarperCollins, 2002). Available online at www.harpercollins.com/hc/features/evolution/introduction.asp.

NOTES

63 Ibid.

64 Ibid.

65 Stephen Jay Gould, "Nonoverlapping magisteria" in *Natural History* (March 1997), 106: 16–22. Gould also says: "I do not see how science and religion could be unified, or even synthesized, under any common scheme of explanation or analysis; but I also do not understand why the two enterprises should experience any conflict. Science tries to document the factual character of the natural world, and to develop theories that coordinate and explain these facts. Religion, on the other hand, operates in the equally important, but utterly different, realm of human purposes, meanings, and values-subjects that the factual domain of science might illuminate, but can never resolve. . . . I propose that we encapsulate this central principle of respectful noninterference—accompanied by intense dialogue between the two distinct subjects, each covering a central facet of human existence—by enunciating the Principle of NOMA, or Non-Overlapping Magisteria. . . . To summarize, with a tad of repetition, the net, or magisterium, of science covers the empirical realm: what is the universe made of (fact) and why does it work this way (theory). The magisterium of religion extends over questions of ultimate meaning and moral value. These two magisteria do not overlap, nor do they encompass all inquiry (consider, for example, the magisterium of art and the meaning of beauty). To cite the old cliches, science gets the age of rocks, and religion the rock of ages; science studies how the heavens go, religion how to go to heaven." S.J. Gould, "Rocks of Ages: Science and Religion in the Fullness of Life," *The Library of Contemporary Thought* (New York: Ballantine, 1999), pp. 4–6.

66 If anyone doubts what this means in practice, consider the typical reaction of Darwinist-inspired researchers to religious objections to the use of abandoned human embryos in their research projects. They can hardly contain their contempt, even though this is a subject where the question of the importance of a human being (in other words, "values") would obviously be critical.

67 Dawkins's views on debating creationists: "The question of who would 'win' such a debate is not at issue. Winning is not what these people realistically aspire to. The coup they seek is simply the recognition of being allowed to share a platform with a real scientist in the first place. This will suggest to innocent bystanders that there must be material here that is genuinely worth debating, on something like equal terms." Richard Dawkins, "Creating such a fuss about nothing," *Times 2* (January 28, 2003). Gould may also have feared encountering Johnson again. See www.arn.org/arnproducts/books/b076.html. Interestingly, Gould ended up with a creationist grad student at one point. See Chapter 11.

68 Larry A. Witham, *Where Darwin Meets the Bible: Creationists and Evolutionists in America* (New York: Oxford University Press, 2002), p. 225.

69 See their FAQ at
http://www.ncseweb.org/resources/articles/5945_the_faqs_2_16_2003.asp.

Chapter 10: Creationism: Morphing into a Modern Movement (Pages 117–131)

[1] In his sermon "Hideous Discovery," preached on July 25, 1886.

[2] From *The Outline of History—Being a Plain History of Life and Mankind*, 4th ed. (London: Cassell & Company, 1925), p. 616. This is the fourth revision.

[3] John William Draper, *History of the Conflict Between Religion and Science* (New York: Appleton, 1874); Andrewe Dickson White, *A History of the Warfare of Science with Theology in Christendom* (London: King's, 1876).

[4] Edward J. Larson, *Summer for the Gods: The Scopes Trial and America's Continuing Debate over Science and Religion* (New York: Basic Books, 1997), p. 21. Colin Russell, Professor of History of Science and Technology at the Open University in England, describes Draper's and White's works as "pseudo-history," remarking: "My first encounter as a young scientist with White's book led to deep suspicion; the book did not describe any scientific attitude I had ever met and its thesis seemed inherently improbable." *Perspectives on Science and Christian Faith* (March 1993), 45: 219–21. Russell is Vice President of Christians in Science. The thesis could easily have been refuted by a careful historian or journalist, so the fact that it was a reigning orthodoxy for many years, during which refutations did not become popular knowledge, says something about the temper of the times in which Darwinists reigned.

[5] A.H. Strong, *Systematic Theology* [1907] (Valley Forge, PA: Judson Press, 1967, reprint), pp. 392–93.

[6] In the early 20th century, fundamentalism had nothing to do with violent political extremism, as in "Islamic fundamentalism." It was a religious movement that countered 19th-century religious liberalism by teaching orthodox Protestant Christian doctrine.

[7] Ronald L. Numbers, "Creationism" in Microsoft® Encarta® Reference Library 2003. © 1993–2002 Microsoft Corporation.

[8] Del Ratzsch, *Battle of the Beginnings: Why Neither Side Is Winning the Creation–Evolution Debate* (Downers Grove, IL: InterVarsity Press, 1996), p. 61.

[9] "Fighting Darwin's battles: symposium marks evolutionist victory, anti-evolution growth," by Eugene Russo in *The Scientist* (March 19, 2001), vol. 15, no. 6: 1.

[10] See Chapter 12.

[11] D.M.S. Watson, "Adaptation," *Nature* (August 10, 1929), vol. 124, no. 3119: 231–34.

[12] Ashley Montagu, *Science and Creationism* (Oxford: Oxford University Press, 1984). Incidentally, Montagu was famous in his time as a promoter of prepared childbirth, and a foe of racism. He was also part of a minor industry of anticreationist books, as the science establishment began to discover that creationism was growing. He is thought by some to have popularized the name Ashley for girls. See http://www.montagu.org/Ashley.htm.

[13] John MacArthur, *The Battle for the Beginning: The Bible on Creation and the Fall of Adam* (Nashville: W Publishing Group, 2001), p. 12.

[14] Forty-four percent of Americans said that they believed that God created humans in the last 10,000 years, 39% believed in evolution so long as it was understood as being guided by God, and 10% believed that evolution occurred without God's help. Seven percent had no opinion. Gallup poll taken in November 1997, reported by ABC News, September 2, 1999.

[15] Contrary to some popular accounts, creationists generally accept small instances of evolution (microevolution). They do not believe that evolution produces large changes in life forms (macroevolution).

[16] Kauffman is called an "evolutionist" here because he himself has some serious problems with Darwinism. See, for example, his comments quoted on p. 47.

[17] Stuart Kauffman, *At Home in the Universe: The Search for the Laws of Self-Organization and Complexity* (New York: Oxford University Press, 1995), p. 6.

[18] Kauffman is the point man for complexity theory and proposes that there is an inherent self-organization principle in nature—design without the intelligence. See p. 47, his book at Note 17 above, or his Web site at the Bios group, http://www.santafe.edu/sfi/People/kauffman/.

[19] This was largely true in Victorian England as well, and continued to be true until after the mid-twentieth century. A. Hayward writes, "It is only within the past couple of decades that the age of the earth has become a subject for debate in English religious circles. When I was a young Bible-believing Christian around nineteen-fifty, the matter was regarded as settled. There was only one creationist society in Britain in those days, the Evolution Protest Movement, and its leading members all accepted without question that the earth is very old. I must have rubbed shoulders with hundreds of ancient-creationists, but I only remember ever meeting one recent-creationist before 1960." A. Hayward, *Creation and Evolution: Rethinking the Evidence from Science and the Bible* [1985] (Minneapolis, MN: Bethany House, 1995), reprint, p. 69. He attributes the change to Whitcomb and Morris's *Genesis Flood*.

[20] P.A. Zimmerman, "The Age of the Earth," in P.A. Zimmerman, ed., *Darwin, Evolution, and Creation* [1959] (St. Louis, MO: Concordia,1966), 5th printing, p. 161.

[21] Line 199. You can read it in context at http://eir.library.utoronto.ca/rpo/display/poem2162.html. Tennyson was an old man when he wrote the poem (1886), and had had many years to think about the theory of evolution, and to misunderstand what Darwin meant to say.

[22] This information is the fifth stanza of a long poem, *The British Birds* (1872), alleged to have been communicated to Collins (1827–1876) by the Ghost of Aristophanes, the ancient Greek comic writer— surely as impeccable a source of information on human character as one could hope for. You can read other examples of Victoriana on the subject of Darwinian evolution, some of it still quite funny, at http://www.giga-

usa.com/gigaweb1/quotes2/qutopevolutionx001.htm. Incidentally, a Positivist was an atheist, probably after a philosophical movement called Logical Positivism.

23 Charles Hodge in M.A. Noll and D.N. Livingstone, eds., *What Is Darwinism?* [1874], (Grand Rapids MI: Baker, 1994) reprint, p.156.

24 See Larson, *Summer for the Gods: The Scopes Trial and America's Continuing Debate over Science and Religion* (New York: Basic Books, 1997), p. 20.

25 These terms are sometimes disputed. Terms other than "old earth creationism" and "progressive creationism" are sometimes used to describe a variety of day–age theories. Terms chosen here are for convenience.

26 Gaines Johnson maintains a Web site that defends Gap theory, on behalf of his one-man Christian Geology Ministry, http://www.kjvbible.org. He told me in an e-mail communication, "The 'Gap Theory' is the only interpretation that addresses both the literal wording of the Bible and the geological evidence. Consequently, it is despised by Young Earth Creationists because it proves an old Earth."

27 You can find out more about the life and teachings of Ellen G. White at her estate's official site, http://www.whiteestate.org/about/egwbio.asp#who.

28 Genesis does not say how old earth is. The 6000 years is the result of calculation. Anyway, definitions are perilous. Some young earth creationists allow an older age for earth. Some may allow that the universe is billions of years old, but earth is not. The primary way in which young earth creationism can be distinguished from other points of view is the literal reading of Genesis 1 and 2 where earth, life, and human beings are concerned. Those YECs who belong to non-Christian traditions would take scriptures (for example, the Koran) or an aboriginal oral creation tradition as the fact base with which they begin.

29 Henry M. Morris, *History of Modern Creationism* (San Diego: Master Book Publishers, 1984), p. 96.

30 One often encounters the claim that young earth creationists believe in a God who deceives, because the earth looks much older than it is. The underlying assumption is that one should look for a source other than the Bible. The YEC replies that the information was there all along but was rejected because the Bible was rejected.

31 This was the definition employed in a 1981 law in the state of Arkansas, quoted from Ronald L. Numbers, *The Creationists: The Evolution of Scientific Creationism* (New York: Random House, 1992), p. x.

32 Stephen Jay Gould provides an interesting essay on Ussher's chronology in "Fall in the House of Ussher," in *Natural History* (1991), 12 (11): 12–19.

33 They explain: "If the strict-chronology interpretation of Genesis 11 is correct, all the postdiluvian patriarchs, including Noah, would still have been living when Abram was fifty years old; three of those who were born before the earth was divided (Shem, Shelah, and Eber) would have actually outlived Abram; and Eber, the father of Peleg,

not only would have outlived Abram, but would have lived for two years after Jacob arrived in Mesopotamia to work for Laban! On the face of it, such a situation would seem astonishing, if not almost incredible." J.C. Whitcomb and Henry M. Morris, *The Genesis Flood: The Biblical Record and Its Scientific Implications* (Grand Rapids, MI: Baker, 1993), pp. 477–78.

[34] See "Teaching about evolution and the nature of science: a review by Dr. William B. Provine," at http://fp.bio.utk.edu/darwin/NAS_guidebook/provine_1.html.

[35] This book does not systematically distinguish between conservative, evangelical, and fundamentalist Christians. An illuminating article that tackles the subject is "Defining evangelicalism," available from the Institute for the Study of American Evangelicals, http://www.wheaton.edu/isae/defining_evangelicalism.html.

[36] To judge from some of their comments, the pundits probably consider this a worse outcome. See, for example, John Wilson, "Thou shalt not take cheap shots," in *Books & Culture* (September–October 1999), http://www.christianitytoday.com/bc/9b5/9b5003.html. Speaking of the high levels of education possessed by both key creationists and intelligent design theorists, Pennock creates the impression that they are engaged in a conspiracy. See Robert T. Pennock, *Tower of Babel: The Evidence Against the New Creationism* (Cambridge, MA: MIT Press, 1999). The idea that non-Darwinists might value education for its own sake seems not to have occurred to him.

[37] This episode is recounted in detail in Ronald L. Numbers's book, *The Creationists: The Evolution of Scientific Creationism* (New York: Random House, 1992).

[38] The idea of evolution was well known and accepted long before Darwin published his book (1859). Darwin's key contribution was to suggest a mechanism (natural selection working on random variations) that ruled out divine intervention, a move that suited the science of his day.

[39] See pp. 148–49 for the fate of Walter Hearn and the ASA members who tried to mediate the controversy over Darwinian evolution in the schools.

Chapter 11: Can a Scientist Be a Creationist? (Pages 133–150)

[1] Interview, June 2003.

[2] Interview, June 2003.

[3] Quoted from Henry M. Morris, *History of Modern Creationism* (San Diego: Master Book Publishers, 1984), pp. 71–72. Today, Huxley's speculations about the "divinized father," based on the theories of Freud, sound profoundly Eurocentric. Christianity is the only major world religion that assigns to God an explicit, primary role as Father. The concept is offensive to Muslims, for example. The persistent obsession on the part of some Darwinists to "explain" religion through various forms of Social

Darwinism is probably best seen in terms of the need to subvert existing religions in favor of their new one.

4 Ibid.

5 For an informative account of the role of museums in the spread of evolution as a religion, see Michael Ruse, *The Evolution Wars: A Guide to the Debates* (Santa Barbara, CA: ABC-CLIO, 2000), pp. 103–05. For his own ambivalent view, see pp. 113–14.

6 Interview, May 2003.

7 In an interview with the author.

8 Sebastian Kitchen, "Professor rigid on evolution," *Lubbock Online* (October 6, 2002). That was apparently the requirement posted at Dini's Web site at the time. It has since been changed.

9 Ibid.

10 Ibid.

11 Michael Duff, "Duff: evolution, religion conflicting theories," *Universitydaily.net* (October 31, 2002).

12 Michael Castellon, "Controversy arises from professor's policy," *Universitydaily.net* (September 18, 2003).

13 Sebastian Kitchen, "Tech professor's evolution policy prompts federal inquiry," *Lubbock Online* (January 30, 2003).

14 The site is at http://www2.tltc.ttu.edu/dini/Personal/letters.htm. It reads like a lecture in favor of Darwinism rather than a list of criteria for recommendation letters. But he does say at the end: "The designated criteria for a letter of recommendation should not be misconstrued as discriminatory against anyone's personal beliefs. Rather, the goals of these requirements are to help insure that a student who wishes my recommendation uses scientific thinking to answer scientific questions."

15 Sebastian Kitchen, "Feds drop case after professor changes evolution policy," Lubbock *Avalanche-Journal* (April 23, 2003).

16 See p. 60.

17 Ronald L. Numbers, *The Creationists: The Evolution of Scientific Creationism* (New York: Random House, 1992), p. xiv.

18 Ibid., pp. xiv–v.

19 Larry A. Witham, *Where Darwin Meets the Bible: Creationists and Evolutionists in America* (New York: Oxford University Press, 2002), p. 52.

20 E-mail to the author, July 5, 2003.

21 The idea is that God created "kinds," which may diversify, change, or become extinct, as laws of nature permit. Kinds are roughly equivalent to "families" of animals in the conventional classification. For more information on creationist classifications of animals, see "An evaluation of lineages and trajectories as baraminological membership

criteria" by Todd Wood and David Cavanaugh, www.bryancore.org/bsg/opbsg/002.pdf, and "A refined baramin concept" by Todd Wood, Kurt Wise, Roger Sanders, and Neal Doran at www.bryancore.org/bsg/opbsg/003.pdf. See also Todd Wood and Megan Murray, *Understanding the Pattern of Life: Origins and Organization of the Species* (Nashville, TN: Broadman & Holman, 2003). Interestingly, interbreeding between wolves, dogs, and coyotes is known to occur in North America.

[22] Kurt P. Wise in J.F. Ashton, ed., *In Six Days: Why 50 Scientists Choose to Believe in Creation* (Sydney NSW, Australia: New Holland, 1999), p. 329.

[23] Witham, *Where Darwin Meets the Bible: Creationists and Evolutionists in America* (New York: Oxford University Press, 2002), p. 103.

[24] See p. 105. The point here is not that young earth creationists are not motivated by a need to defend a philosophical position, but that they are hardly unique in that regard.

[25] Ibid., p. 107. In the context, it is interesting to read Richard Dawkins's take on Wise, whose testimony he regards as "quite moving, in a pathetic kind of way." See Richard Dawkins, "Sadly, an honest creationist," in *Free Inquiry*, vol. 21, no.4, http://www.secularhumanism.org/library/fi/dawkins_21_4.html.

[26] You can read more on Baumgardner's views at www.globalflood.org. See, for example, "Catastrophic plate tectonics: the physics behind the Genesis flood," http://www.globalflood.org/papers/2003ICCcpt.html.

[27] "Scientists who believe: an interview with Dr. John Baumgardner," *The Lookout* (February 8, 1998).

[28] You can read the paper, "Helium diffusion rates support accelerated nuclear decay," at http://www.icr.org/research/icc03/pdf/Helium_ICC_7-22-03.pdf. See also www.talkorigins.org/indexcc/CD/CD015.html for a rebuttal.

[29] Geocentrists interpret verses such as Joshua 10:12 (where the Israelite warrior commanded the sun to stand still) and Psalms 93:1 ("the world also is stablished, that it cannot be moved") literally, according to Numbers (pp. 237–38). There are geocentrists today, for example, Marshall Hall, who maintains a large and active geocentricity page at http://www.fixedearth.com/, and Gerardus D. Bouw, a professor at Baldwin-Wallace College in Berea, Ohio, in the Department of Math and Computer Science. You can also learn more about geocentricity at the Official Geocentricity Web site, http://www.geocentricity.com/aboutdrbouw.htm. (*Note*: Doubt that alien civilizations exist on other planets is not geocentrism. Science has no way at present of knowing whether earth is the *philosophical* center of the universe, in the sense that it is the only place where there are thinking life forms. A lonely prospect, but possible.)

[30] See, for example, Answers in Genesis's page on arguments that creationists should not use, http://www.answersingenesis.org/home/area/faq/dont_use.asp.

[31] *Teaching About Evolution and the Nature of Science* (National Academy of Sciences), a review by Dr. William B. Provine, Cornell University, May 8, 1998,

http://fp.bio.utk.edu/darwin/NAS_guidebook/provine_l.html. Provine was complaining about a National Academy of Sciences evolution handbook for teachers that, in his view, did more harm than good.

[32] There has been a tendency in recent years for young earth creationists to denounce the Big Bang theory, because it is seen as "watering down" the idea of instant creation. See Ken Ham, "What's wrong with 'progressive creation?'" http://www.answersingenesis.org/docs/4077.asp. However, despite creationist beefing, the psychological fit between Genesis and the Big Bang is much better than that between Genesis and any kind of Steady State theory.

[33] Some verses in the Bible that are relevant to the belief that death came into the world only on account of human sin are Genesis 3:19, Romans 5:12–14, and 1 Corinthians 15:22. Romans 5:14 is especially relevant: "Nevertheless, death reigned from the time of Adam to the time of Moses, even over those who did not sin by breaking a command, as did Adam, who was a pattern of the one to come" (NIV). You can read the Bible or search any Bible verse online at http://www.biblegateway.com. Old earth creationists and Christian evolutionists also generally accept the doctrines that flow from these verses, but they do not encourage literalism in their interpretation.

[34] There are many varieties of creationism, including Muslim creationism and Native American creationism. A case can likely be made that these forms of creationism also simplify a belief system. In the case of non-Christian Native Americans, for example, creationism underscores a complete rejection of European culture.

[35] Paul Davies, "A brief history of the multiverse," *New York Times* (April 12, 2003).

[36] Ibid. Davies himself is skeptical of these far-flung speculations. See p. 36.

[37] One difference is that ridicule of creationists tends to be tinged with contempt. Ridicule of the multiverse tends to be ironic, along the lines of: "In another universe, I might be an opponent of the many universes theory."

[38] See, for example, Henry M. Morris, *History of Modern Creationism* (San Diego: Master Book Publishers, 1984), pp. 71–72, 122, 285.

[39] John Morris, *Tracking Those Incredible Dinosaurs and the Men Who Knew Them* (San Diego: Creation-Life Publishers, 1980),

[40] Ballard's oceanographic institute, located in Connecticut, is at http://www.ife.org. For more on Pitman and Ryan's research, see Hannah Fairfield, "Finding Noah's flood: evidence of ancient disaster is linked to biblical legend," *Columbia University News* (November 19, 1999), http://www.columbia.edu/cu/pr/99/11/flood.html. Meanwhile, biblical scholar I. Wilson notes: "That such an event actually happened is now absolutely certain, accredited by scientists of international repute to the same degree of confidence with which, only a few years ago, the Noah story was being dismissed as nonsense." See I. Wilson, *Before the Flood: Understanding the Biblical Flood Story as Recalling a Real-Life Event* [2001], (London: Orion, 2002), pp. xiv–xv. It appears that the search for Noah's Ark is ridiculous if creationists are doing the searching, but not otherwise. This double

standard is a classic example of the social construction of facts.

41 See http://www.canoe.ca/CNEWSElection2000News/1115_religion-cp.html (November 15, 2000).

42 Ronnie J. Hastings, "The rise and fall of the Paluxy Mantracks" PSCF 40 (September 1988), pp. 144–54, http://www.asa3.org/ASA/PSCF/1988/PSCF9-88Hastings.html. More information is available from David J. Tyler, "Dinosaur and human trackways at Paluxy" at http://www.biblicalcreation.org.uk/scientific_issues/bcs106.html. A picture of one of the original carvings can be found at The "Burdick Print" (C) 1989-1996, Glen J. Kuban and Gregg Wilkerson, http://members.aol.com/Paluxy2/wilker5.htm.

43 Darwinists often write as though it is a given that birds evolved from dinosaurs. This idea is so wonderful that, surely, we all want it to be true. It means that the dinosaurs are not really extinct, and the monstrous Canada goose that threatens us at the picnic table is a living remnant of a great family of life forms. Still, can we really be sure it's true? See, for example, "Longisquama insignis," *Science* (June 23, 2000).

44 It was recently revealed that top Japanese archeologist Shinichi Fujimura had systematically faked finds of prehistoric human artifacts from 30,000 to 100,000 years ago at 159 of 178 sites on which he had worked. "Young archaeologists do not challenge revered senior scholars," anthropologist Hisao Baba of the National Science Museum, told *The Scotsman*. "It is extremely difficult to directly deny others' work because it is taken as a grave personal and professional insult." In other words, if a scientist is mainstream and famous, the *discovery* of dishonesty may be easier to prevent than the practice.

45 *Nature* (August 21, 2003): 868.

46 Michael LaBossière, "Provocations number six: fraud, science and ethics," The Philosophers' Magazine on the Internet, http://www.philosophers.co.uk/cafe/provocations6.htm.

47 In the article, LaBossière provides several examples of cheating. Note also the saga of academic shiftiness detailed in Robin McKiethe, "Fur flies as dinosaur experts feud" in the *Observer* (September 8, 2003), which raises a very real question about the quality of the evidence for the extinction of the dinosaurs by an asteroid. A prominent scientist is accused by colleagues of withholding evidence that questions the Big Blast (extinction by asteroid) theory. "This affair has become an object lesson on how partisan and unethical the whole dinosaur controversy has become," according to Norman MacLeod, keeper of paleontology at London's Natural History Museum. Online at http://www.taipeitimes.com/News/world/archives/2003/09/08/2003067003.

48 Richard Dawkins, *The Blind Watchmaker* (London: W.W. Norton, 1986), p. 159.

49 Michael J. Behe, *Darwin's Black Box: The Biochemical Challenge to Evolution* (New York: Free Press, 1996), pp. 249–50.

50 See Edward J. Larson and Larry Witham, "Leading scientists still reject God,"

Nature (1998), vol. 394: 313. See also Henry F. "Fritz" Schaefer, III, "Stephen Hawking, the Big Bang, and God," a public lecture available at http://www.origins.org/articles/schaefer_bigbangandgod.html.

[51] Edward J. Larson and Larry Witham, "Leading scientists still reject God," *Nature* (1998), vol. 394: 313.

[52] These findings are reviewed by Richard Morin, *Washington Post* Polling Director, in "Do Americans believe in God?" Monday, April 24, 2000. They were accessed at http://www.washingtonpost.com/wp-srv/politics/polls/wat/archive/wat042400.htm.

[53] Edward J. Larson and Larry Witham, "Leading scientists still reject God," Nature (1998), vol. 394: 313.

[54] Quoted in Henry F. "Fritz" Schaefer, III, "Stephen Hawking, the Big Bang, and God," a public lecture available at http://www.origins.org/articles/schaefer_bigbangandgod.html.

[55] For more on Christian evolutionism, see pp. 72–75.

[56] See Ronald Numbers, *The Creationists* (New York: Random House, 1992), p. 322. Historian of science Ted Davis of Messiah College in Grantham, Pennsylvania, comments that William "Vendetta" Bennetta, as he calls him, organized a polarized response to the booklet, and attributes the bad reception largely to his efforts. Fair enough, but that raises the question, why were so many prominent Darwinists willing to go along with it?

[57] Ibid.

[58] Phillip E. Johnson, *Darwin on Trial* (Downer's Grove, IL: InterVarsity Press, 1993), p. 130.

[59] Jonathan Wells, *Icons of Evolution* (Washington: Regnery, 2000), p. 58. The context was that a visiting Chinese paleontologist pointed out that the Cambrian explosion of life forms contradicts Darwin's theory of evolution. He was puzzled that during the question period, this topic was persistently avoided. Wells told him that criticizing Darwinism was unpopular in the United States. Elsewhere, at pp. 192–93, Wells quotes another example of self-suppression among scientists. One discussion participant suggested that criticizing Darwinism would "reduce their chances of getting money."

[60] The attack is presented in an undated document accessed at http://www.answersingenesis.org/docs/4077.asp in July 2003.

[61] Hugh Ross, *The Genesis Question* (Colorado Springs: NavPress, 1998), p. 66. See also *The Creator and the Cosmos* (Colorado Springs: NavPress, 1993), pp. 81–82. Interestingly, Ross's organization adheres to the doctrinal statements of the International Council on Biblical Inerrancy. The belief that the Bible does not err does not apparently require a belief in young earth creationism as a necessary outcome.

[62] Answers in Genesis also makes available a book, *Creation and Time: A Report on the Progressive Creationist Book by Hugh Ross* by Mark Van Bebber and Paul Taylor, about

which it advises: "This exhaustively researched book on the theological ramifications of Hugh Ross's 'progressive creationist' teaching is a wake-up call to all Christians concerned about Biblical inerrancy and the terrible divisiveness that erroneous theological beliefs can cause!" (Advertised at the AiG site January 2004.)

[63] "Hugh Ross proposes a debate with Russell Humphreys: response to Dr. Russell Humphreys' open letter of June 26, 2003," http://www.reasons.org/resources/apologetics/humphreys_debate_statement.shtml?main (August 2002, rev. July 2, 2003).

[64] In an e-mail to Denyse O'Leary, August 11, 2003.

[65] Ibid. Of course, the ID theorists probably want to avoid Ross's fate, that is, getting sucked into an unproductive conflict with Answers in Genesis at the expense of their research into design.

Chapter 12: Why Has Creationism Been Growing? (Pages 151–163)

[1] Stephen Jay Gould, "Evolution as Fact and Theory" in *Hen's Teeth and Horse's Toes* (New York: W.W. Norton, 1994), pp. 253–62.

[2] Neil Postman, *The End of Education* (New York: Alfred Knopf, 1995), p 107.

[3] The origin of life (abiogenesis) can be considered as separate from the study of evolution. Evolution is the study of the *alteration* of life forms over time. The origin of life is mysterious from any perspective because the chemical reactions that power life forms are not the ones that non-living matter usually undergoes. This problem is discussed lucidly in Michael J. Behe's *Darwin's Black Box: The Biochemical Challenge to Evolution* (New York: Free Press, 1996), pp. 166ff.

[4] According to a study by Steve Deckard et al., http://www.vision.edu/iws/, "attending a creation course seminar or presentation is a better predictor of a creationist worldview than having completed a college science class" at a Christian university that teaches YEC views. The Darwinists who ridicule the church basement have underestimated its impact.

[5] This is *not* an original insight. W.R. Fix, in *The Bone Peddlers: Selling Evolution* (New York: Macmillan, 1984), notes, "Scientists almost invariably overstate the case for evolution, and creationists have as much access to the critical literature as any one else.", p. 233.

[6] Michael Ruse, *The Evolution Wars* (Santa Barbara, CA: ABC-CLIO, 2000), p. 114.

[7] Quoted in Edward J. Larson, *Summer for the Gods: The Scopes Trial and America's Continuing Debate over Science and Religion* (New York: Basic Books, 1997), p. 261.

[8] For example, Ronald Numbers cites figures of 11% belief in "creationist sentiment" in liberal Protestant churches compared to 91% in the Assemblies of God. (*The Creationists*, p. 300.)

[9] See the timeline on p. 156–57 for key books in this area.

[10] An early effort along these lines was *The Inevitability of Patriarchy* by Steven Goldberg (New York: William Morrow, 1973), whose assertions of male power through evolution enraged feminists.

[11] Some Darwinists have pointed out to the author during interviews that establishment science does not accept intelligent design theory, with the implication that ID theory must be wrong. It is worth noting that the social science establishment overwhelmingly rejects Social Darwinism, but Darwinists rarely or never draw the same conclusion from the rejection.

[12] See Ronald Numbers, *The Creationists*, pp. 332–39, for historical details. The most recent European Creationism Conference was held in August 2003 near Malmo, Sweden. It featured speakers Ann-Sofie Albrekt, Lund University research engineer at the department of immunotechnology and bioinformatics, and Tom Zoutewelle, a sedimentologist from the Netherlands. See http://www.creaton.nl/. As in the United States, young earth creationism attracts some academics as well as lay people.

[13] Arimasa Kubo, *Science Comes Closer to the Bible: On the History of the Earth* (Phoenix: ACW Press, 2001), www.acwpress.com.

[14] Canadian, French Russian, Spanish, German, Portuguese, Australia, Swedish, Japanese, Chinese, Nederlands, Korean, Italiano, Hungarian, Turkish, Indonesian, United Kingdom, Other Countries, and Multi-National were all given as links in 2003 from http://www.nwcreation.net, a Christian public service megasite sponsored by creationist Web host, Creation Science Resource.

[15] You can read more about Islamic creationism online in an article by Taner Edis, originally published in *Creation/Evolution* (1994), 34:1, "Islamic creationism in Turkey," at http://www2.truman.edu/~edis/writings/articles/islamic.html.

[16] George Johnson, "Indian tribes' creationists thwart archeologists," *New York Times* (October 22, 1996), highlights recent controversies. Available online at http://www.santafe.edu/~johnson/articles.creation.html, as of July 2003. See also "Burying the evidence," at the *Spiked* site, http://www.spiked-online.com/articles/00000006DFDE.htm. Tiffany Jenkins makes some good points about the way in which the "cultural left" seeks to control science by exploiting the situation. That said, she obviously lacks sympathy with the idea that human remains should be respected, thus marginalizing her own views. In a conflict between naturalism and culturalism, culturalism will recruit many more supporters.

[17] Note, however, that many Native North Americans belong to evangelical Christian denominations; in that case, if they subscribe to creationism, it is more likely to be the Christian kind.

[18] New York: Scribner, 1995. You can read an excerpt from *Red Earth, White Lies* at the site of Fulcrum, the publisher of the paperback edition, http://www.fulcrum-books.com/html/red_earth_white_lies.html.

[19] See, for example, Donald MacLeod, "Dawkins criticises 'spread' of creationism,"

The Guardian online, June 19, 2002,
http://education.guardian.co.uk/aslevels/story/0,10495,740377,00.html.

20 Ibid.

21 For a history of the Internet, see the Internet Society's site,
http://www.isoc.org/internet/history/brief.shtml#Origins. Its origin and development provide many insights into changes in our society.

22 The peer principle was developed to enable the Internet to cope with war or sabotage. No single, central computer controls every other computer. Messages are routed along available servers, and usually find their destination somehow.

23 Quoted from the jacket copy of *democracy.com? Governance in a Networked World*, edited by Elaine Ciulla Kamarck and Joseph S. Nye, Jr. (New York: Puritan Press, 1999).

24 The 2002 PBS special *Monkey Trial*'s Web site,
http://www.pbs.org/wgbh/amex/monkeytrial/, is highly recommended as an example of the difference that the Internet makes.

25 This book has a Web site, www.designorchance.com, where you can read updated information on many of the issues covered.

26 The site was accessed in June 2003 at www.nwcreation.net/aboutCSR.html.

27 Gallup poll taken in November 1997, reported by ABC News, September 2, 1999. Seven percent had no opinion.

28 If you do not identify the furry hominids shrieking in the treetops as human, you might have no problem agreeing that "God created humans pretty much in their present form in the last 10,000 years," but that would certainly not make you a young earth creationist.

29 This approach might miss young earth creationists who are not from a Western culture, but it would prevent a huge number of "false positives."

30 See, for example, Timothy Noah, "George W. Bush, the last relativist," *Slate*, October 31, 2000, http://slate.msn.com/id/1006378/.

31 Ronald L. Numbers, *The Creationists*, p. 300. Larry Witham notes in *Where Darwin Meets the Bible: Creationists and Evolutionists in America* (New York: Oxford University Press, 2002), p. 137, that Reagan's views were sometimes hard to fathom, but he recognized the Transnational Association of Christian Colleges and Schools, organized in 1979. The Association accredited only colleges that taught a literal six-day creation. Carter and Gore, by contrast, are convinced evolutionists.

32 D. Young, "The Evolution of Creationism," *Australasian Science* (April 2002), vol. 23, no. 3:.20–21.

33 Michael Ruse, *Darwinism Defended: A Guide to the Evolution Controversies* [1982] (Reading, MA: Addison-Wesley, 1983), 3rd printing, pp. 322–23. Emphasis in original.

Chapter 13: Intelligent Design: Why So Controversial? (Pages 167–186)

[1] Charles Thaxton, "A New Design Argument," *Cosmic Pursuit* (March 1, 1998).

[2] From the Preface to *The Design Revolution: Answering the Toughest Questions About Intelligent Design*, by William A. Dembski (Downers Grove, IL: InterVarsity Press, 2004).

[3] Debbie Cafazzo, "Some teachers talk of alternatives to evolution theory," *Tacoma News Tribune* (May 7, 2001).

[4] Both teachers identified themselves as Christians but denied talking about religion or God, and tried to avoid letting students know their own views. DeHart assured the *Los Angeles Times* that he did not discuss God. See Teresa Watanabe, "Enlisting science to find the fingerprints of a creator," *Los Angeles Times* (March 25, 2001), www.arn.org/docs/news/fingerprints032501.htm. (Note: The article can also be accessed at the *Times* site, for a fee.) Cowan told the *Tacoma News* the same thing. See Debbie Cafazzo, "Some teachers talk of alternatives to evolution theory," *Tacoma News Tribune* (May 7, 2001). See also Nancy R. Pearcey, "Creation mythology: defenders of Darwinism resort to suppressing data and teaching outright falsehoods," *World Magazine* (June 24, 2000), vol. 15, no. 25, www.arn.org/docs/pearcey/np_world-creationmythology62400.htm.

[5] The full page attack ad ran against him on November 24, 1999. See Debbie Cafazzo, "Some teachers talk of alternatives to evolution theory," *Tacoma News Tribune* (May 7, 2001).

[6] According to DeHart, "One of the most dishonest pieces of journalism occurred when Channel 5 came to Burlington and interviewed several of my students. None of the students interviewed felt that I was doing anything inappropriate. It was then out of desperation to present a controversy that the reporter cornered a special education student and asked him if religion should be taught in a biology classroom. Of course, he answered that it was inappropriate to do so. The interview when aired gave the impression that the student was in my class and that he felt I was teaching religion." (DeHart's personal account, provided to author.)

[7] This letter was reproduced at www.idurc.org/itsm/itsm-061501.htm, a student intelligent design Web site, in the summer of 2003.

[8] The things he was not permitted to correct included the Miller-Urey experiment being treated as conclusive, the "peppered myth," and even, astonishingly, Haeckel's embryos, which have been known to be fraudulent drawings for many decades. Nancy R. Pearcey, "Creation mythology: defenders of Darwinism resort to suppressing data and teaching outright falsehoods," *World Magazine* (June 24, 2000), vol. 15, no. 25, www.arn.org/docs/pearcey/np_world-creationmythology62400.htm.

[9] Personal communication to author.

[10] Administratively, that move makes sense. A completely unqualified teacher would be most unwise to teach anything other than the text, right or wrong.

[11] There is not space to go into DeHart's story in detail in this book. It is as noteworthy for what it shows about what is wrong with public education as for what it shows about the intelligent design controversy, but the problems with public education deserve books to themselves.

[12] Debbie Cafazzo, "Some teachers talk of alternatives to evolution theory," *Tacoma News Tribune* (May 7, 2001).

[13] Creationists are essentially concerned with the defense of Scripture. They want to demonstrate that the creation account in Genesis 1–3 can and should be interpreted literally. Whatever the merits of their exegesis, attention increasingly focuses on the intelligent design hypothesis.

[14] "Follow the evidence wherever it leads" has become a slogan of ID advocates. See, for example, Jay Richards, a senior fellow at the Discovery Institute, which finances many ID projects, expressing the view at http://speakout.com/activism/opinions/3116-1.html that "many guardians of current scientific orthodoxy are casting aspersions to prevent these new insights from gaining a hearing, and even threatening the freedom of scientists to follow the evidence wherever it leads."

[15] Phillip E. Johnson, "The wedge: breaking the modernist monopoly on science," *Touchstone* (July/August 1999), vol. 12, no. 4: 22–23.

[16] Quoted by Charles Thaxton writing in *Cosmic Pursuit* (March 1, 1998). See http://www.arn.org/docs/thaxton/ct_newdesign3198.htm.

[17] See Faithnet, www.faithnet.org, maintained by religious education teacher Stephen Richards for a readable historical backgrounder on Paley, with a link to a backgrounder on Hume available through the site map.

[18] Ibid.

[19] A very similar point of view was expressed by Lucretius in the ancient world. See p. 11.

[20] Ibid.

[21] Ernst Mayr, Foreword to M. Ruse, *Darwinism Defended* (Reading, MA: Addison-Wesley, 1982), pp. xi–xii, quoted in Paul Nelson, "Unfit for Survival: The Fatal Flaws of Natural Selection" from Phillip E. Johnson and Denis O. Lamoureux, *Darwinism Defeated? The Johnson-Lamoureux Debate on Biological Origins* (Vancouver: Regent College Publishing, 1999), p. 138.

[22] Quoted in Robert F. DeHaan and John L. Weister, "The Cambrian Explosion," in William A. Dembski and James M. Kushiner, eds., *Signs of Intelligence: Understanding Intelligent Design* (Grand Rapids, MI: Baker House–Brazos Press, 2001), p. 146. Originally from J.H. Campbell and J.W. Schopf, eds., *Creative Evolution!?* (Sudberg, MA: Jones and Bartlett, 1994), pp. 4–5.

23 Richard Dawkins, *Climbing Mount Improbable* (New York: W.W. Norton, 1996) pp. 6–7.

24 For a fuller account, see Larry A. Witham, *Where Darwin Meets the Bible: Creationists and Evolutionists in America* (New York: Oxford University Press, 2002), pp. 219–23.

25 Media can be slow to pick up on the significance of a movement in science, but some journalists have been surprisingly quick to understand what the ID folk have undertaken. For example, L. Kern, writing in the *Dallas Observer*, noted: "But Dembski contends that if he can codify the process by which we recognize intelligence in other fields, he can justifiably apply that process to biology. If he can codify that process, he says, intelligent design is not a matter of religious belief but a matter of following the evidence wherever it leads. Such a codification is Dembski's contribution to the intelligent design movement, and his claim to fame. It is an explanatory process that can be used for judging objects, events, and information. It begins by ruling out chance and natural law as explanations, and then infers design." Lauren Kern, "Monkey Business," *Dallas Observer* (January 11, 2001), http://www.dallasobserver.com/issues/2001-01-11/feature2.html/page1.html.

26 Charles Thaxton, "A new design argument," *Cosmic Pursuit* (March 1, 1998), http://www.arn.org/docs/thaxton/ct_newdesign3198.htm.

27 This outline is based on ibid.

28 A good example of this sort of low information pattern in ordinary life is the stitch patterns in plain knitting and crochet work. These patterns, once learned, can be repeated by rote as desired.

29 The embryo as a whole is not a pattern or blueprint. The embryo *is* the kitten, as far as it has got in its development. The DNA of the embryo tells you what to expect as the embryo unfolds.

30 In "A new design argument," *Cosmic Pursuit* (March 1, 1998), http://www.arn.org/docs/thaxton/ct_newdesign3198.htm.

31 Stephen C. Meyer, "DNA and Other Designs," *First Things* (April 1, 2000).

32 Phillip Johnson in Phillip E. Johnson and Denis O. Lamoureux, eds., *Darwinism Defeated? The Johnson-Lamoureux Debate on Biological Origins* (Vancouver: Regent College Publishing, 1999), p. 51. Michael Behe indicated in an e-mail to the author (August 11, 2003) that he invented the term "irreducible complexity." Mathematician M.J. Katz used the term "irreducibly complex" in a 1986 book (*Templets and the Explanation of Complex Patterns*, Cambridge University Press, 1986, pp. 26–27). But he does not appear to have meant the same thing.

33 Interestingly, the old qwertyuiop keyboard was retained, even though its original purpose is said to have been to slow down typing, lest it damage the original typewriting machines. After that, it continued to be the keyboard of choice simply because the human

time cost of changeover is too high. There may be some lessons in this for design theory.

³⁴ William Dembski explains it like this: "Logically, intelligent design is compatible with everything from utterly discontinuous creation (e.g., God intervening at every conceivable point to create new species) to the most far-ranging evolution (e.g., God seamlessly melding all organisms together into one great tree of life). For intelligent design the primary question is not how organisms came to be . . . but whether organisms demonstrate clear, empirically detectable marks of being intelligently caused. In principle an evolutionary process can exhibit such 'marks of intelligence' as much as any act of special creation." William A. Dembski, *Intelligent Design: The Bridge Between Science and Theology* (Downers Grove, IL: InterVarsity Press, 1999), pp. 109–10. In other words, design is real and detectable by the methods of science. It does not need to be a miracle. On the other hand, design does not rule out miracles.

³⁵ See p. 38 for this concept.

³⁶ Michael J. Behe, *Darwin's Black Box: The Biochemical Challenge to Evolution* (New York: Free Press, 1996), p.46.

³⁷ For example, he argues, in a précis of his chapter, "Order for Free," in John Brockman, ed., *The Third Culture* (New York: Simon and Schuster Touchstone, 1996), that "the overall answer may be that complex systems constructed so that they're on the boundary between order and chaos are those best able to adapt by mutation and selection." See also p. 47.

³⁸ Thaxton is also the editor of an intelligent design textbook, *Of Pandas and People*, used as a supplementary text (Dallas: Haughton, 1990–2004).

³⁹ Richard Jenkyns, "Victorian selection," a review of Janet Browne, *Charles Darwin: The Power of Place* (New York: Knopf, 2003), in The New Republic Online, post date 02.13.03; issue date 02.24.03.
http://www.tnr.com/docprint.mhtml?i=20030224&s=jenkyns022403.

⁴⁰ See Chapter 3.

⁴¹ Cynthia Russett, *Darwin in America* (San Francisco: W.H. Freeman, 1976), p. 210. Quoted in Thomas Woodward, *Doubts About Darwin: A History of Intelligent Design* (Grand Rapids, MI: Baker, 2003), p. 65.

⁴² For more information, see John Myers, "The real issue: a Scopes trial in reverse," *Leadership U*, www.leaderu.com/real/ri9401/scopes.html.

⁴³ Denton was also a key influence on Michael Behe. See Thomas Woodward, *Doubts About Darwin: A History of Intelligent Design* (Grand Rapids, MI: Baker, 2003), p. 63.

⁴⁴ Michael Denton, *Evolution: A Theory in Crisis* (London: Burnett Books, 1985), p.16.

⁴⁵ Michael Denton, *Evolution: A Theory in Crisis* (Bethesda: Adler & Adler, 1986), p. 146.

46 Thomas Woodward, *Doubts About Darwin: A History of Intelligent Design* (Grand Rapids, MI: Baker, 2003), p. 72.

47 Ibid., pp. 43–44. Patterson spelled out his doubts to fellow scientists, not to the public. For example, addressing a gathering at the American Museum of Natural History, he said: "In general, I'm trying to suggest two themes. The first is that evolutionism and creationism seem to have become very hard to distinguish, particularly lately. I've just been showing how Gillespie's bitterest characterization of creationism seems to be, as I think, applicable to evolutionism—a sign that the two are very similar. . . . Well, here's Gillespie again on creationism in the 1850s. He says: 'Frequently, those holding creationist ideas could plead ignorance of the means and affirm only the facts.' That seems to summarize the feeling I get in talking, to evolutionists today. They plead ignorance of the means of transformation but affirm only the facts, knowing that it's taken place. Again the two points do seem hard to distinguish." Patterson, "Evolutionism and Creationism," transcript of address at the American Museum of Natural History, New York City, November 5, 1981, pp. 2–3. According to Phillip Johnson, someone circulated Patterson's views, and he was eventually forced by peer pressure to stop questioning Darwinism in public. Phillip E. Johnson, *Darwin on Trial* (Downer's Grove, IL: InterVarsity Press, 1993), p. 10. The transcript of Patterson's address is available at http://members.iinet.net.au/~sejones/pattamnh.html.

48 Thomas E. Woodward, "Doubts about Darwin: in the face of mounting evidence, more scientists are abandoning evolution," Apologetics.org, www.apologetics.org/articles/doubts.html.

49 Phillip E. Johnson, *Darwin on Trial* (Downer's Grove, IL: InterVarsity Press, 1993), p. 12.

50 Ibid., p. 16.

51 Stephen Jay Gould, "Impeaching a self-appointed judge," *Scientific American* (July 1992), 267 (1):118–21; reprinted in Liz R. Hughes, ed., *Reviews of Creationist Books* (Berkely, CA: The National Center for Science Education, 1992), pp. 79–84. Specifically, Gould says, "In a 'classic' of antievolutionary literature from the generation just past, lawyer Norman Macbeth (1971) wrote a much better book from the same standpoint, entitled *Darwin Retried* (titles are not subject to copyright). Macbeth ultimately failed (though he raised some disturbing points along the way) because he used an inappropriate legal criterion: the defendant (an opponent of evolution) is accused by the scientific establishment and must be acquitted if the faintest shadow of doubt can be raised against Darwinism. (As science is not a discipline that claims to establish certainty, all its conclusions would fall by this inappropriate procedure.)" Johnson wrote a detailed response to Gould, available at http://www.arn.org/docs/orpages/or151/151john-gould.htm. Apparently, when Johnson was invited to give at talk at the Campion Center in 1989, Gould, who was also invited, informed Johnson: "You're a creationist, and I've got to stop you." Then, amazingly, he went on to claim that the fossil record provided much evidence for Darwinism, contradicting his public stance. See Thomas Woodward,

Doubts About Darwin: A History of Intelligent Design (Grands Rapids, MI: Baker, 2003), pp. 82–83.

[52] For a fuller treatment of Johnson, see Larry A. Witham, *Where Darwin Meets the Bible: Creationists and Evolutionists in America* (New York: Oxford University Press, 2002), pp. 65–72, and Thomas Woodward, *Doubts About Darwin: A History of Intelligent Design* (Grand Rapids, MI: Baker, 2003), in which Johnson is a central figure.

[53] Thomas Woodward, *Doubts About Darwin: A History of Intelligent Design* (Grand Rapids, MI: Baker, 2003), p. 74.

[54] Phillip E. Johnson, *Darwin on Trial* (Downer's Grove, IL: InterVarsity Press, 1993), p. 169.

[55] Phillip E. Johnson, "Reflection 2," in J.P. Moreland and J.M. Reynolds, eds., *Three Views on Creation and Evolution* (Grand Rapids, MI: Zondervan,1999), pp. 273–74.

[56] Ibid.

[57] Steven Weinberg, *Dreams of a Final Theory* (New York: Pantheon, 1992), pp. 257–58. Weinberg is a Nobel Laureate who favors the multiple universes theory. Most intelligent design advocates who are Christians would be on the orthodox rather than the liberal side.

[58] Larry A. Witham, *Where Darwin Meets the Bible: Creationists and Evolutionists in America* (New York: Oxford University Press, 2002), p. 68.

[59] In this context, Phillip Johnson's refusal to spell out a point of view on evolution is probably also responsible, at least in part, for the uncertainty about intelligent design vs. creationism. For example, Niles Eldredge comments, in a book mainly dedicated to attacking ultra-Darwinism: "Yet I must mention one cultural phenomenon that has had a most salutary unifying effect—the one issue on which all at the High Table can agree. Just as neo-Darwinians united against the (rather slender) forces of saltationism, so we disputants around the High Table in the 1980s have been united in common opposition to a movement outside the confines of biology: creationism. Indeed, the cannier creationists (and others of unmistakable creationist bent who profess simple disagreement with evolution, such as the lawyer Philip Johnson) have long accused evolutionary biologists of hiding our very real disagreements under a cloak of unanimity—so united are we against the pseudoscience of creationism." Niles Eldredge, *Reinventing Darwin* (New York: John Wiley,1995), pp. 103–04.

[60] Kenneth Korey, "Selections and Commentary by Kenneth Korey," *The Essential Darwin*, in Masters of Modern Science Series, Robert Jastrow, general editor (Boston: Little, Brown, 1984), p. 140.

[61] Thomas Kuhn, *The Structure of Scientific Revolutions*, 2nd ed., enlarged (Chicago: University of Chicago Press, 1970), p. 171.

[62] Dembski is actually one of four younger scholars who are known as the "four

horsemen" of intelligent design. The other three are Steven Meyer, Paul Nelson, and Jonathan Wells.

63 Phillip Johnson in Phillip E. Johnson and Denis O. Lamoureux, eds., *Darwinism Defeated? The Johnson-Lamoureux Debate on Biological Origins* (Vancouver: Regent College Publishing, 1999), p. 51.

64 Stuart Kauffman, spokesman for complexity theory, has an interesting comment on the Cambrian explosion: "One of the wonderful and puzzling features of the Cambrian explosion is that the chart was filled in from the top down. Nature suddenly sprang forth with many wildly different body plans—the phyla—elaborating on these basic designs to form the classes, orders, families, and genera. . . . In the Permian extinction, 245 million years ago, 96 percent of all species disappeared. But in the rebound, during which many new species evolved, diversity filled in from the bottom up, with many new families, a few new orders, one new class, and no new phyla." Stuart Kauffman, *At Home in the Universe: The Search for the Laws of Self-Organization and Complexity* (New York: Oxford University Press, 1995), p. 13.

65 Behe neither invented the term "black box" nor was the first to apply it to ideas about evolution and biochemistry. He quotes University of California geneticist John Endler: "Although much is known about mutation, it is still largely a 'black box' relative to evolution. Novel biochemical functions seem to be rare in evolution, and the basis for their origin is virtually unknown." J.A. Endler, and T. McLellan, "The process of evolution: toward a newer synthesis," *Annual Review of Ecology and Systematics* (1988), 19, 397, quoted in Michael J. Behe, *Darwin's Black Box: The Biochemical Challenge to Evolution* (New York: Free Press, 1996), p. 29.

66 Of course, miracles may well occur. But whether they occur is a matter for evidence, and miracles—direct interventions by a deity—are a separate question from design. The question really depends on whether a universe that has an intelligent designer would also permit miracles. It could go either way.

67 The book went through 15 printings in the first year, and still sells about 20,000 copies per year. There are 15 foreign translations. Thomas Woodward, *Doubts About Darwin: A History of Intelligent Design* (Grands Rapids, MI: Baker, 2003), p. 155. In late 2003, it had sold 120,000 copies, according to Behe (conversation with author).

68 Tamler Sommers and Alex Rosenberg explain in "Darwin's nihilistic idea: evolution and the meaninglessless of life," *Biology and Philosophy* 18: 653–668, 2003 http://www.kluweronline.com/issn/0169-3867 that "Stalin or Osama bin Laden, or Michael Behe, or your favorite villain, is also "an utterly idiosyncratic structure ..." The message of the article is that Darwinism requires nihilism. It's not clear just how these folks understand the nihilism but the grouping of names is unsettling.

Chapter 14: Is ID Good Science? Is It Science at All? (Pages 187–206)

1 Victor J. Stenger, in a paper based on talks given in Kansas, September 2000, at the invitation of the Kansas Citizens for Science (revised May 5, 2001). http://www.infidels.org/library/modern/vic_stenger/stealth.pdf. Stenger is a Visiting Fellow in Philosophy, University of Colorado.

2 E-mail interview with the author, June 17, 2003.

3 Thomas Kuhn, *The Structure of Scientific Revolutions*, 2nd ed., enlarged (Chicago: University of Chicago Press, 1970), p. 77.

4 You can find out more about the Altair at the University of California (Davis) Computer Science Museum, www.virtualaltair.com.

5 Kiley Armstrong, "Creationist fired by *Scientific American*," Associated Press (1990), http://www.primepropertyofga.com/aog/ec/ec121.htm.

6 Mims told me: "I taped Piel with great reluctance, only after a well-known attorney friend, Ted Lee, urged me to do so, explaining it is legal under Texas law if I am a party to the conversation. He said that Piel would deny everything if I did not do so. That's exactly what happened. When questioned by the *Wall Street Journal*, Piel denied discrimination. They said they were printing that without my claim to the contrary unless I had evidence. Lee said to play the tape for me. I did, and they ran a quote from the tape that contradicted Piel's assertion." In fairness, Piel, as a convinced Darwinist, may not have known that he was discriminating, at least by the usual standards applied in media. He may have simply assumed that it was his duty to purge from his magazine any taint of non-Darwinism.

7 F.M. Mims, III, "Satellite monitoring error," *Nature* (1993), 361: 505.

8 See p. 184.

9 For example, philosopher Victor J. Stenger uses this term in "Intelligent Design: the new stealth creationism" at
http://www.infidels.org/library/modern/vic_stenger/stealth.pdf.

10 Michael J. Behe, *Darwin's Black Box: The Biochemical Challenge to Evolution* (New York: Free Press, 1996), p. 5.

11 William Dembski, *No Free Lunch* (Lanham: Rowman and Littlefield, 2002), p. 314.

12 Interview with the author, June 2003.

13 This is not an exhaustive list. These figures are chosen because their views on both religion and Darwinism are known. Some would argue that atheistic/agnostic views constitute a sort of religion. Fair enough, but these people are hardly supporters of any type of American fundamentalism. You can get further information about these thinkers as follows:

Berlinski:http://www.anova.org/bio/berlinski.

Denton: http://www.iscid.org/michael-denton.html.

Hoyle: http://www.panspermia.org/hoylintv.htm.

Interestingly, despite Hoyle's skepticism about Darwinism, many atheist, infidel, and skeptic Web sites see a major part of their mission as defending Darwinism. Their skepticism is selective; his wasn't.

[14] Sir Arthur Stanley Eddington, *The Philosophy of Physical Science* [Tarner Lectures, 1938] (Cambridge, 1939), quoted at a page of Eddington quotations, http://www-gap.dcs.st-and.ac.uk/~history/Quotations/Eddington.html, maintained by the School of Mathematics and Statistics at St. Andrew's University in Scotland, as part of a large collection of science biographies and memorabilia.

[15] Following this view, Robert Pennock refers to ID theorists as creationists in *Tower of Babel: The Evidence Against the New Creationism* (Cambridge, MA: MIT Press, 1999). You can read the first chapter online at MIT Press at http://mitpress.mit.edu/books/PENOH/ch01.pdf (accessed July 2003).

[16] There are, of course, other varieties of creationism than the young earth type. See p. 131.

[17] Geoscientist Marcus R. Ross addressed the issue of how to classify non-Darwinist positions at the 2003 meeting of the Geological Society of America. He argues that young earth creationism can be viewed as a specialized type of intelligent design argument but notes that an intelligent design argument need not entail any form of creationism, saying: "ID is classified as a philosophically minimalistic position, asserting that real design exists in nature and is empirically detectable by the methods of science." A summary of his approach can be read at Paper No. 249–4, "Intelligent design and young-earth creationism—investigating nested hierarchies of philosophy and belief," http://gsa.confex.com/gsa/2003AM/finalprogram/abstract_58668.htm.

[18] See Chapter 15, pp. 208–9. Note that some YECs actively support the intelligent design hypothesis. One example is philosopher Paul Nelson.

[19] Keith B. Miller, "Design and purpose within an evolving creation," in Phillip E. Johnson and Denis O. Lamoureux, *Darwinism Defeated? The Johnson–Lamoureux Debate on Biological Origins* (Vancouver: Regent College Publishing, 1999), p. 113.

[20] Nina Shapiro, "The new creationists: Seattle's Discovery Institute leads a national movement challenging Darwinism," *Seattle Weekly* (April 19–25, 2001). See also the National Center for Science Education's Web site www.ncse.org.

[21] See the quote from Newton on p. 170.

[22] You can learn more about these and other units of measurement at http://www.ex.ac.uk/cimt/dictunit/dictunit.htm.

[24] See "Newton voted greatest Briton," *BBC News* (August 14, 2003). Charles Darwin was fifth on the list. To put matters in perspective, Diana, Princess of Wales,

was third. You can read more at
http://news.bbc.co.uk/2/hi/entertainment/3151333.stm.

[25] It is a separate question whether those historical scientists would support the ID movement today. The point here is that assumption of design did not impede their practice of science.

[25] You can read more about Michael Polanyi (1891–1976) at Gospel & Culture, http://www.deepsight.org/articles/polanyi.htm, which gives an account of his life and a brief outline of his philosophy.

[26] I encountered a bit of this sentiment, though at the time I did not interpret it clearly. When I was working on a booklet for the DARE series published at Wycliffe College in Toronto, "Intelligent Design: Beyond Creation and Evolution?" (2001), an e-mail from a professor was forwarded to me by my editor, strictly for my information. The professor claimed to know Dembski, abused him in a very unprofessional manner, and demanded that our booklet project be slanted so as to attack ID. It wasn't.

[27] Personal communication to the author, July 2003.

[28] Tony Carnes, "Design interference: William Dembski fired from Baylor's Intelligent Design Center," *Christianity Today* (December 4, 2000), www.christianityto-day.com/ct/2000/014/18.20.html, as well as John Wilson, "Books and Culture Corner: Unintelligent designs," *Christianity Today* (week of October 23), www.christianityto-day.com/ct/2000/143/11.0.html. A search on the CT site will turn up a number of other articles about this controversy. See also Thomas Woodward, *Doubts About Darwin: A History of Intelligent Design* (Grand Rapids, MI: Baker, 2003), pp. 179–81, and Lauren Kern's "Monkey Business" in the *Dallas Observer* (January 11, 2001), http://www.dallasobserver.com/issues/2001-01-11/feature2.html.

[29] The accusation that one basketball player killed another triggered questions about Sloan's program. You can read about this at http://www.christianitytoday.com/ct/2003/130/21.0.html.

[30] Steve Benen, "Insidious design: disguising dogma as science, religious right activists have created a new scheme to wedge religion into public schools," *Church & State* (May 2002). This is the publication of Washington-based Americans United for Separation of Church and State. See http://www.au.org/churchstate/cs5022.htm.

[31] This and much more at http://www.txscience.org/files/icons-revealed/index.htm.

[32] From Phillip E. Johnson, "The Gorbachev of Darwinism," *First Things* (January 1998): 14–16, http://www.firstthings.com/ftissues/ft9801/johnson.html.

[33] Daniel Dennett, *Darwin's Dangerous Idea: Evolution and the Meanings of Life* (London: Penguin, 1995), pp. 250–51. Sterelny's review of Dawkins's *The Blind Watchmaker* was in the *Australasian Journal of Philosophy* (1988), vol. 66: 421–66.

[34] Franklin Harold, *The Way of the Cell* (New York: Oxford University Press, 2001), p. 205.

35 Sir Arthur Conan Doyle (1859–1930), *The Adventure of the Beryl Coronet* (1892). There are a number of variations on this quotation throughout Doyle's work. Ruling out the impossible in favor of the improbable seems to have been Holmes's primary detection method. It was characteristic of 19th-century science because it ignores the problem of how we decide what is possible and what is probable. A list of the quotes is available at http://www.bcpl.net/~lmoskowi/HolmesQuotes/q.detection.html. The text of the Holmes stories is also widely available online, for example at http://www.cit-soft.com/holmes3.html, so you can read these quotes in context. Doyle, who was born in the year that *On the Origin of Species* was published, wrote a story called *The Lost World* that deals with Darwinism (*The Lost World*, Oxford University Press, 1998.)

36 See p. 113.

37 Interview with Denyse O'Leary, June 2003. At this point in the interview, Ruse appeared to conflate creationists and ID advocates, though at other points he distinguished the two.

38 That is, in fact, how Michael Denton is sometimes described. For example, a press release from the Institute for Accelerating Change, dated August 18, 2003, announces a debate between futurist Ray Kurzweil and Michael Denton, as follows: "After his presentation, Kurzweil will debate Michael Denton, noted post-Darwinian biologist and Platonist ("Protein Folds as Platonic Forms," *J. Theoretical Bio*, 2002), who proposes that our living proteins have unique emergent properties that will not easily, or perhaps ever, be modeled by technological systems." Lynn Margulis has also been described as a post-Darwinian. See K. Kelly, *Out of Control: The New Biology of Machines* [1994] (London: Fourth Estate, 1995), reprint, pp. 470–471, "A number of microbiologists, geneticists, theoretical biologists, mathematicians, and computer scientists are saying there is more to life than Darwinism. They do not reject Darwin's contribution; they simply want to move beyond it. I call them the 'postdarwinians.'"

39 Quoted in Steve Benen, "Insidious design: disguising dogma as science, religious right activists have created a new scheme to wedge religion into public schools" *Church & State* (May 2002), the publication of Washington-based Americans United for Separation of Church and State. See http://www.au.org/churchstate/cs5024.htm.

40 See pp. 70–71, 86, 180–81 for more on these issues.

41 See also p. 228.

42 The concept of "proof" is not used here because proofs are difficult to obtain outside mathematics. Sciences operate on the balance of evidence rather than proof.

43 From his introduction to *Uncommon Dissent*, to be published by Intercollegiate Studies Institute in 2004.

44 *The Skeptic's Dictionary*'s entry on intelligent design, http://skepdic.com/intelligentdesign.html.

45 Interview, July 2003.

[46] Phillip Johnson quotes Darwin as saying: "If it could be proved that any part of the structure of any one species had been formed for the exclusive good of another species, it would annihilate my theory, for such could not have been produced through natural selection," but points that that "this was the same Darwin who insisted that he had never claimed that natural selection was the exclusive mechanism of evolution." Phillip E. Johnson, *Darwin on Trial* (Downer's Grove, IL: InterVarsity Press, 1993), p. 30. Darwin, like most scientists, often altered or kibitzed around with his theory, to protect it from falsification.

[47] See Chapter 8.

[48] A number of examples are given in this book. See, for example, pages 167, 187, and 219.

[49] Phillip E. Johnson, *Darwin on Trial* (Downer's Grove, IL: InterVarsity Press, 1993), p. 30. A classic along these lines may be Eldredge and Tattersall's statement: "The basic notion that life has evolved is as certain as the existence of gravity or the idea that the earth is spheroidal. We call such highly verified notions 'facts' when they consistently escape all attempts to prove them false. Evolution is no myth. But how life has evolved is another matter entirely." N. Eldredge and I. Tattersall, *The Myths of Human Evolution* (New York: Columbia University Press, 1982), p. 2. Note the last line. How life evolved is *precisely* the point at issue for everyone other than young earth creationists! What it means to describe evolution as a fact depends on what we think it is a fact *about*.

[50] Thomas Kuhn, *The Structure of Scientific Revolutions*, 2nd ed., enlarged (Chicago: University of Chicago Press, 1970), pp. 109–10.

[51] You can read more about Popper at *Stanford Encyclopedia of Philosophy*, http://plato.stanford.edu/entries/popper/.

[52] I have heard this advice given privately on several occasions.

[53] The magazine is *Faith Today*, the national Canadian evangelical Christian magazine. The interview with Durston can be read at http://www.canadianchristianity.com/cgi-bin/na.cgi?nationalupdates/031023evolution.

[54] Interview with the author.

[55] In this context, see also "Bad for the career" at www.alternativescience.com/censorship.htm, where the case of British biologist Warwick Collins is discussed. Collins was apparently driven out of the profession because he had expressed doubt in some of his papers about Darwinian theory. Incidentally, the AAAS, far from being a neutral arbiter of the controversy, has thrown itself into opposition to the intelligent design hypothesis. We are informed, for example, that as of November 29, 2002, "the AAAS Board of Directors has passed a resolution urging policy-makers, scientists, and other members of the public to oppose teaching 'intelligent design theory' (ID theory) in the nation's science classrooms, noting that the concept has so far not been supported by credible scientific evidence." (*Science*, no. 5599, vol., 298: 1804.) The problems with Darwinism do not seem to trouble AAAS at all.

[56] See Frank J. Tipler, "Refereed journals: do they insure quality or enforce orthodoxy?" in *Progress in Complexity, Information, and Design: The Journal of ISCID*, vols. 2.1 and 2.2 (double issue), January–June 2003. http://www.iscid.org/pcid/2003/2/1-2/tipler_refereed_journals.php. Note: This is an online journal only.

[57] Niles Eldredge, *Reinventing Darwin* (New York: John Wiley, 1995), p. xi.

[58] Ibid.

[59] See Frank J. Tipler, "Refereed journals: do they insure quality or enforce orthodoxy?" in *Progress in Complexity, Information, and Design: The Journal of ISCID*, vols 2.1 and 2.2 (double issue), January–June 2003. http://www.iscid.org/pcid/2003/2/1-2/tipler_refereed_journals.php. Note: This is an online journal only.

[60] "Scientific research put under spotlight," *BBC News* (August 10, 2003), http://news.bbc.co.uk/go/pr/fr/-/2/hi/science/nature/3140261.stm. The Royal Society is acting, in part, in response to false claims surrounding human cloning.

[61] All this creativity in relativity physics happened, Tipler notes, at a time when the government of Germany did not provide much funding for science!

[62] Stephen Hawking, in *The Illustrated A Brief History of Time* (New York: Bantam, 1996), p. 108, recounts that a journalist informed Sir Arthur Eddington that only three people in the world were thought to understand general relativity. Eddington's reply was: "I am trying to think who the third person is." Eddington and the journalist may have been exaggerating, but not by much.

[63] Frank J. Tipler, "Refereed journals: do they insure quality or enforce orthodoxy?" in *Progress in Complexity, Information, and Design: The Journal of ISCID*, vols. 2.1 and 2.2 (double issue), January–June 2003. http://www.iscid.org/pcid/2003/2/1-2/tipler_refereed_journals.php. Note: This is an online journal only.

[64] Phillip E. Johnson, "The Gorbachev of Darwinism," *First Things* (January 1998): 14–16, http://www.firstthings.com/ftissues/ft9801/opinion/johnson.html.

[65] R. Monastersky writes, "His new book sailed through the publishing process unreviewed and virtually unedited, because Harvard and all other publishers that have dealt with Mr. Gould know that he rarely allows changes to his manuscripts." See R. Monastersky, "Revising the Book of Life." Review of Stephen Jay Gould, *The Structure of Evolutionary Theory*, (Cambridge, MA: Harvard University Presss, 2002). *The Chronicle of Higher Education*, March 15, 2002, p. A14, http://chronicle.com/free/v48/i27/27a01401.htm.

[66] *Progress in Complexity, Information, and Design: The Journal of ISCID* is available at www.iscid.org.

[67] William Dembski told the author that he is responsible for this change.

[68] Personal communication to author, September 17, 2003.

[69] Ibid.

[70] See, for example, Thomas Woodward, *Doubts About Darwin: A History of Intelligent Design* (Grand Rapids, MI: Baker, 2003), p. 68.

Chapter 15: Is ID Good Theology? Is It Theology at All? (Pages 207–217)

[1] Howard Van Till, "Intelligent Design: The Celebration of Gifts Withheld?" in Phillip E. Johnson and Denis O. Lamoureux, eds., *Darwinism Defeated? The Johnson–Lamoureux Debate on Biological Origins* (Vancouver: Regent College Publishing, 1999), p. 84.

[2] William A. Dembski, "Intelligent design is not optimal design," *Metaviews* (February 2, 2000).

[3] There is some evidence of a trend to interdisciplinary discussions. For example, a landmark paper, "Science and God: a warming trend?" was published in *Science*, the journal of the American Academy for the Advancement of Science (August 15, 1997, 277: 890). The National Academy of Sciences and the American Association for the Advancement of Science have both launched projects to promote a dialogue between science and religion. Also, according to Denis Lamoureux, new institutions such as the Chicago Center for Religion and Science and the Center for Theology and Natural Sciences in Berkeley, California, as well as professorships and lectureships at Cambridge and Princeton aim at furthering mutual understanding. Lamoureux, a Christian evolutionist, joins a colleague in hoping that, "rather than being driven even farther apart, tomorrow's scientist and theologian may seek each other's solace." See Phillip E. Johnson and Denis O. Lamoureux, *Darwinism Defeated? The Johnson–Lamoureux Debate on Biological Origins* (Vancouver: Regent College Publishing), 1999, p. 17.

[4] See p. 47.

[5] E-mail interview with the author, June 2003.

[6] The post date for these statements is August 30, 2002, http://www.answeringenesis.org/docs2002/0830_IDM.asp.

[7] E-mail interview with the author, June 2003.

[8] Darwinists sometimes loosely label anyone who is not committed to metaphysical naturalism, whose prophet is Darwin, a "creationist." On that showing, as we have seen, nearly 90% of North Americans are creationists. This is *not* young earth creationism. See pp. 131 and 161.

[9] Julian Huxley is quoted from Encarta® Book of Quotations (1999). See p. 133–34 for Huxley's attempt to start a religion of science. The title of his book, *Religion Without Revelation* (New York: Harper & Brothers, 1957), pretty much gives the idea.

[10] The Cheshire Cat appears in Chapter 6, "Pig and Pepper," of *Alice in Wonderland*. You can read the whole passage online at http://the-office.com/bedtimestory/classics-alice-6.htm, sponsored by The Office.com, an office furniture sales firm.

Many classic illustrations are also reproduced.

[11] Denis Lamoureux, "Evangelicals Inheriting the Wind: The Phillip E. Johnson Phenomenon," in Phillip E. Johnson and Denis O. Lamoureux, eds., *Darwinism Defeated? The Johnson–Lamoureux Debate on Biological Origins* (Vancouver: Regent College Publishing, 1999), p. 19.

[12] Stephen C. Meyer, "Teleological Evolution: The Difference It Doesn't Make" in Phillip E. Johnson and Denis O. Lamoureux, eds., *Darwinism Defeated? The Johnson–Lamoureux Debate on Biological Origins* (Vancouver: Regent College Publishing), 1999, p. 92.

[13] Ernst Haeckel (1834–1919), the embryologist who popularized Darwin in Germany, claimed that a cell was a "simple lump of albuminous combination of carbon." M.J. Behe, *Darwin's Black Box: The Biochemical Challenge to Evolution* (New York: The Free Press, 1996), p. 24. Darwin and Huxley evidently agreed with him; in fact, Huxley named what he thought was a "half alive" life form after Haeckel (*Bathybius haeckelii*). See pp. 41–42. For an interactive look at how complex cells really are, see http://www.intelligentdesign.org/menu/cell/cell_life.htm.

[14] See p. 200 for William Dembski on how ID might be falsified.

[15] ASA is at www.asa3.org, and provides resources on Christianity and evolution at http://www.asa3.org/ASA/topics/Evolution/index.html.While the organization does not take an official position on the subject, its members seem generally to be Christian Darwinists, and the ASA's archived listserv, based at Calvin College, has been a major venue for anti-intelligent design argument, certainly in 2003, when the author monitored and sometimes participated in discussions. Canadian Christian and Scientific Affiliation is at http://www.csca.ca/.

[16] The term "Christian evolution" is used in this section rather than "theistic evolution," because the persons quoted apparently profess a traditional form of Christianity. Organizations like ASA and CSCA were founded by and for scientists of that persuasion. "Theistic evolution" involves the same questions, of course, but the range of beliefs may be much wider, and the options more complex.

[17] Other examples of prominent Christian or theistic evolutionist philosophers are Ian Barbour, John Haught, Philip Hefner, Robert John Russell, Nancey Murphy, and Arthur Peacocke. The John M. Templeton Foundation (www.templeton.org) supports much research and writing in this area.

[18] Howard Van Till, "What good is stardust," *Christianity Today* (August 6, 2001). In a similar spirit, geologist Keith B. Miller even *resists* scientific verification: "My objection to the arguments of the proponents of intelligent design is not that they posit design, but that they restrict its meaning to only certain structures or processes and make it subject to scientific verification." Quoted from Keith B. Miller, "Design and Purpose Within an Evolving Creation," in Phillip E. Johnson and Denis O. Lamoureux, eds., *Darwinism Defeated? The Johnson–Lamoureux Debate on Biological Origins*

(Vancouver: Regent College Publishing, 1999), pp. 110–11. Actually, the ID advocates make their theory subject to scientific falsification as well as verification.

[19] Dawkins makes clear in his published writings that he became an atheist at a young age. In an interview with Mark Sappenfield of the *Independent* (February 20, 2003) entitled "Richard Dawkins: you ask the questions," he said: "I toyed with atheism from the age of about nine . . ." Then, after a flirtation with pantheism, "around the age of 16, I first understood that Darwinism provides an explanation big enough and elegant enough to replace gods. I have been an atheist ever since."

[20] Rikki E. Watts, "Of Apples and Star Treks, Guidance and Gaps," in Phillip E. Johnson and Denis O. Lamoureux, eds., *Darwinism Defeated? The Johnson–Lamoureux Debate on Biological Origins* (Vancouver: Regent College Publishing, 1999), p. 159.

[21] Phillip E. Johnson, *The Wedge of Truth* (Downer's Grove, IL: InterVarsity Press, 2000), p. 90.

[22] Ibid.

[23] Interview June 2003. Ruse indicated during the interview that he was pretty much an atheist.

[24] Michael J. Behe in Phillip E. Johnson and Denis O. Lamoureux, eds., *Darwinism Defeated? The Johnson–Lamoureux Debate on Biological Origins* (Vancouver: Regent College Publishing), 1999, p. 106.

[25] Michael J. Denton in ibid., p. 153.

[26] Ibid.

[27] From the Preface to William A. Dembski, *The Design Revolution: Answering the Toughest Questions About Intelligent Design* (Downer's Grove, IL: InterVarsity Press, 2004.

[28] Crick's idea could be criticized as a science stopper on this account. If he is right, how will we know?

[29] Thomas Woodward, Doubts *About Darwin: A History of Intelligent Design* (Grand Rapids, MI: Baker, 2003), p. 45.

[30] From The *Catholic Encyclopedia Online*: "According to Greek philosophy the world maker is not necessarily identical with God, as first and supreme source of all things; he may be distinct from and inferior to the supreme spirit, though he may also be the practical expression of the reason of God, the Logos as operative in the harmony of the universe . . . a world-maker distinct from the Supreme God." The demiurge, whatever else may be said about him, was intelligent but free to make mistakes.

[31] For example, according to L.P. Gerson in *The Oxford Companion to Philosophy*, "Plato, in the *Timaeus*, uses the word for the maker of the universe. Plato says of this maker that he is unreservedly good and so desired that the world should be as good as possible. The reason why the world is not better than it is that the demiurge had to work on pre-existing chaotic matter. Thus, the demiurge is not an omnipotent creator."

32 The *Catholic Encyclopedia Online*'s article is at
http://www.newadvent.org/cathen/04707b.htm. Note that early Christians quickly
identified the Logos with Jesus Christ, which meant that, in the Christian view, the
Logos was God, as the Gospel of St. John (1:1) makes clear.

33 Traditional Christian doctrine teaches that the universe would be perfect except
for the entrance of sin, which is freely chosen evil. For an excellent discussion of this
subject from a traditional philosophical point of view,

http://www.newadvent.org/cathen/05649a.htm.

34 "'Intelligent design' and public schools: covert evangelism?" *Church & State*
(May 2002), http://www.au.org/churchstate/cs5024.htm.

35 Edward J. Larson, *Summer for the Gods: The Scopes Trial and America's Continuing
Debate over Science and Religion* (New York: Basic Books, 1997), p. 17. Darwin's loss of faith
probably had far more to do with the slow death of his beloved 10-year-old daughter Annie
in 1851 than with the misfortunes of his garden's pests. See Randal Keynes, *Annie's Box:
Charles Darwin, His Daughter and Human Evolution* (Fourth Estate, 2002). Keynes, a great-
great-grandson of Darwin, happened to discover the box where Emma Wedgewood
Darwin kept her deceased daughter's mementos. You can read an excerpt online at
http://www.amazon.com/exec/obidos/tg/detail/-/1573229555/ref=pm_dp_ln_b_3/103-
3516224-3850264?v=glance&s=books&n=507846&vi=excerpt.
Jon Turney, a teacher of science communication at University College London, reviewed
the book for the *Guardian* (June 8, 2002), noting that Darwin "found it impossible to
see this death as part of any divine plan. It might have an explanation, even a cause, but
no reason. Keynes's Darwin, in other words, is a thinker facing up to the realities of the
secular world most of us now live in." Incidentally, the Ichneumon wasp lays its eggs in
the bodies of caterpillars, which the wasp offspring then use as a food source. Organic
gardening mavens promote the use of the wasp because it is more environmentally
friendly than pesticides, which kill small life forms indiscriminately.

36 If there is an intrinsic principle of "self-organization" in the universe, as Stuart
Kauffman believes, surely it is a form of design. It does not require God, but it does
require actual rather than apparent design.

37 From a traditional Christian perspective, imperfection in a design does not
establish that it cannot be authored by God. When God works with finite, limited, and
transient material, he does not, as a necessary consequence, make the material infinite,
perfect, or immortal. For example, we are told in the Gospel of St. John that Jesus raised
Lazarus from the dead (see John 11: 1–44), but Lazarus must certainly have died again
in the course of nature. Direct divine intervention did not bring about a permanent
change in Lazarus's body, only a reprieve.

38 William Dembski, Introduction, *No Free Lunch* (Lanham: Rowman and
Littlefield, 2002), p. 16. You can read the Introduction online at
http://www.arn.org/docs/dembski/wd_nfl_intro.htm. Dembski also fleshes out his

views on the issue of design and evil in considerable detail at "Intelligent design is not optimal design," *Metaviews* (February 2, 2000), http://www.leaderu.com/offices/dembski/docs/bd-optimal.html.

[39] William A. Dembski, "Intelligent design is not optimal design," *Metaviews* (February 2, 2000).

[40] Science can be objective where no great issues are at stake. The same is true of many endeavors in life, such as law, medicine, or firefighting. The difficulty is that great issues often *are* at stake. Controversialists seize the mantle of objectivity, without even knowing, in many cases, that they have no claim to it.

[41] The Christian view is emphasized here for economy of space. Devout Jews and Muslims, and perhaps believers of other major religions, would have the same problem. See, for example, an online essay by Dave Hernandez, a student at Michigan State University, LBS 492, "Response to 'evolution is only believed by dogmatic atheists,'" http://www.msu.edu/~hernan94/, for a discussion of the diversity of Jewish, Muslim, and Hindu views of evolution, including links.

Chapter 16: The Future of Design (Pages 219–235)

[1] David Papineau; "Natural Selections," *New York Times* (May 14, 1995), a review of Niles Eldredge, *Reinventing Darwin: The Great Debate at the High Table of Evolutionary Theory* (New York: John Wiley, (1995); Richard Dawkins, *River out of Eden: a Darwinian View of Life* (New York: Basic Books. (1996); and Daniel C. Dennett, *Darwin's Dangerous Idea: Evolution and the Meanings of Life* (New York: Simon & Schuster, (1996). Papineau thinks that questioning Darwinism is a bad thing.

[2] From Laurence J. Peter, *Peter's Quotations: Ideas for Our Time* (New York: William Morrow & Company, 1977).

[3] From his RAPID address, 2002. The whole of the address can be read online at http://www.arn.org/docs/dembski/wd_disciplinedscience.htm

[4] Jonathan H. Esensten, "Death to intelligent design," *The Crimson* (March 31, 2003). Http://www.thecrimson.com/article.aspx?ref=347206.

[5] Ibid.

[6] Ibid.

[7] Ibid.

[8] See pp. 167 and 187.

[9] Columnist Halvorson had tried to get his piece, "Confessions of a skeptic," published in mid-March, but two editors told him that they were rejecting it because they disagreed with the opinion. The official reason given later was a technicality: Halvorson had failed to note that Darwinists are constantly changing their theory. Two weeks later, the editors ran the piece by Esensten, explicitly advocating censorship. Halvorson slightly revised and resubmitted his column, and it ran. The editors should be Crimson

with embarrassment; otherwise, their publication hardly deserves to be read.

[10] Richard T. Halvorson, "Confessions of a skeptic," *The Crimson* (April 7, 2003), http://www.thecrimson.com/article.aspx?ref=347399.

[11] Ibid. (*Note*: Thankfully for physics, Max Planck and Albert Wiens were Einstein's editors in 1906, so enforced orthodoxy was not a likely misfortune for the young patent clerk.)

[12] Ibid.

[13] Chapman had a long career in both the federal and Washington State civil service. This included stints as a former Director of the United States Census Bureau (1981–1983), Deputy Assistant to President Ronald Reagan (1983–1985), and United States Ambassador to the United Nations Organizations in Vienna (1985–1988). See http://www.discovery.org/fellows.

[14] Richard Lewontin, "Billions and billions of demons," *New York Review of Books* Z9 January 9, 1997), p. 31. Lewontin was reviewing *The Demon-Haunted World: Science as a Candle in the Dark* by Carl Sagan (1934–1996). You can read the whole review at www.csus.edu/indiv/m/mayesgr/Lewontin1.htm. It is well worth the read, not for what it tells you about Sagan's demons, which are minimally described, but for what it tells you about the context of metaphysical naturalism.

[15] Phillip E. Johnson, *Defeating Darwinism by Opening Minds* (Downers Grove, IL: InterVarsity Press, 1997), p. 80. Some would go further than Johnson and deny the very existence of a distinction between methodological and metaphysical naturalism. For example, philosopher of science A.G. Padgett writes: "Some authors on both sides of the religion–science debate argue that natural science must include a 'methodological naturalism.' I should like to propose a bold hypothesis: there is no such thing as methodological naturalism in natural science. Rather, the term 'methodological naturalism' is always and everywhere a front for full-blown philosophical naturalism. Those who defend this 'mere' methodology always end up resorting to naturalism pure and simple. And those who attack it, like William Dembski or Phillip Johnson, are in fact attacking philosophical naturalism. There just is no such thing, then, as a merely 'methodological' naturalism that is limited to the actual practice of modern natural science." (A.G. Padgett, "Creation by design: is the intelligent-design movement asking natural scientists to work outside their proper focus?", *Books & Culture* (July/August 2000), http://www.christianitytoday.com/bc/2000/004/13.30.html.

[16] For example, physicist Lawrence Krauss argued that the ID is "not science" at an Ohio school board meeting. Quoted by Steve Benen, "Insidious design: disguising dogma as science, religious right activists have created a new scheme to wedge religion into public schools," *Church & State* (May 2002), http://www.au.org/churchstate/cs5022.htm. This is the publication of Washington-based Americans United for Separation of Church and State.

[17] ID can be consistent with methodological naturalism if the latter includes design

as a possibility, where the evidence warrants. However, current definitions of method-ological naturalism do not allow for design.

[18] Originally, it was called Center for Science & Cultural Renewal, but the name was later changed to Center for Science & Culture.

[19] See Steve Benen, "Insidious design: disguising dogma as science, religious right activists have created a new scheme to wedge religion into public schools," *Church & State* (May 2002), http://www.au.org/churchstate/cs5022.htm.

[20] One rarely hears about Christian Reconstructionism in the Christian media today, though it created a minor, mostly negative, flurry in the early 1990s.

[21] This has come up in a number of discussions with the author.

[22] See p. 208.

[23] Dembski has been urged to renounce the friendship of Phillip Johnson as well, for the sake of respectability. See the note immediately following.

[24] He expresses this view in an article called "Cards on the table" at http://www.meta-library.net/id-wd/index-body.html, accessed August 13, 2003.

[25] Computer savvy sources have suggested that the hacker tried a number of guesses about the names of documents put up for discussion in a non-public area of the site, and then downloaded the one that worked. However, Jay Richards, spokesman for Discovery Institute, says: "Actually, we're not quite sure how the document came into 'enemy hands.' It was a summary of a talk given to the board of one of our foundation supporters in September 1998, and there were only about 10 hard copies of it made. It never was on a Web site (although we long had similar language on our Web site). So the short answer is either that someone got hold of one of those 10 copies, or came into our office in down-town Seattle and found it, or printed it off of a computer in our office. We do know that it was originally uploaded from an Internet café in Seattle." (E-mail, December 3, 2003.) Discovery's official response is at www.discovery.org/csc/TopQuestions/wedgeresp.pdf.

[26] Larry A. Witham, *Where Darwin Meets the Bible: Creationists and Evolutionists in America* (New York: Oxford University Press, 2002), p. 68.

[27] Portions of the "Wedge document" can be found floating around the Internet at official "unbelief" sites to this day.

[28] This quotation has appeared on several sites. Jay Richards says: "The quote you cite is, I believe, accurate. Although we now describe our project a bit differently, there's nothing in the Wedge document posted on the Internet that we disagree with, or even con-sider particularly controversial, no matter how shrill the cries of the self-named 'Internet Infidels' may become." The Internet Infidels' cries can be viewed at http://www.infidels.org/secular_web/feature/1999/wedge.html. These people's skepticism is remarkably selective.

[29] Note that this differs from the creationist's desire to disprove or eliminate Darwinism.

30 He said as much in "Becoming a Disciplined Science," an address to an intelligent design conference in 2002. The whole of the address can be read online at http://www.arn.org/docs/dembski/wd_disciplinedscience.htm.

31 Phillip Johnson, *The Wedge of Truth* (Downer's Grove, IL: InterVarsity Press, 2000), p. 168.

32 Phillip E. Johnson and Nancy Pearcey, *The Right Questions: Truth, Meaning and Public Debate* (Downer's Grove, IL: InterVarsity Press, 2002), appears to be a transitional book. See http://www.arn.org/arnproducts/books/b070.htm for more information.

33 "Insidious design: disguising dogma as science, religious right activists have created a new scheme to wedge religion into public schools" and "The Discovery Institute: genesis of 'intelligent design,'" *Church & State* (May 2002), http://www.au.org/church-state/cs5024.htm and /cs5023.htm.

34 The outraged letters from Darwinists (July–August 2003) are free, but the article, "A scientific scandal" (April 2003), must be purchased, both at www.commentary.org. The article is worth the price, to provide a context for the free uproar in the Letters pages.

35 The phrase is Michael Behe's, from "Fatuous filmmaking," *World Net Daily* (September 28, 2001). He argues: "While ostensibly about science, it's plain that the overriding purpose of the series—financed in its entirety by Microsoft billionaire Paul Allen—is to change people's religious beliefs. The series wallows in religion—from the fictional opening scene, where Robert FitzRoy, captain of the H.M.S. Beagle, banters with Charles Darwin about Noah's Ark, through the choice of Handel's Messiah as a supposed example of human creativity driven by sexual selection, to the closing program 'What About God?' Through many, many unsubtle clues, we learn there is good religion—incarnated in a down-the-line Darwinist professor shown receiving communion—and bad religion—represented by fundamentalist Ken Ham, whose supporters are shot in choir robes and sing their objections to evolution. Good religion cheerfully accommodates Darwinism. Bad religion doesn't."

36 While we are on the subject of good and bad religion, as per Behe's comments in the note above, the American Darwin lobby, National Center for Science Education, put out a publication, *Voices for Evolution*, calling attention to the fact that "mainstream Judaism and the major Christian denominations, both Protestant and Catholic, have no difficulty accommodating evolution to their religious perspectives." The publication was financed by the Deer Creek Foundation, the Carnegie Foundation of New York, the Richard Lounsbery Foundation, and "a foundation that wishes to remain anonymous." One wonders what the reaction would be if a foundation offering support to ID elected to remain anonymous. For the record, the Esther and Joseph Klingenstein Foundation helped fund the second edition of NCSE's publication.

37 It is worth remembering that Darwin himself was a wealthy man. With money as with the habit of publishing books, he established a pattern for the controversy.

38 Of course, a Darwinist might reply that Ken Miller, author of *Finding Darwin's*

God, is also a Roman Catholic biochemist—one who argues for Darwinism. That is true, and it is a good argument for leaving religion out of the discussion of intelligent design, and focusing on the science issues instead.

[39] The whole of the address can be read online at http://www.arn.org/docs/dembski/wd_disciplinedscience.htm.

[40] The main problem is that the experiments were staged. In nature, the moths generally do not rest on tree trunks during the day, providing a target for predators. They in fact hide from their predators, so the differences between dark and light moths would not normally be evident, and would not be a source of selection. See Jonathan Wells, *Icons of Evolution* (Washington: Regnery Press, 2000), pp. 137–59. See also Judith Hooper, *Of Moths and Men: Intrigue, Tragedy and the Peppered Moth* (London: Fourth Estate, 2002). "Darwinism in a flutter," a review of Hooper's work by Peter D Smith appeared in the *Guardian* (May 11, 2002), http://books.guardian.co.uk/reviews/scienceandnature/0,6121,713294,00.html. It gives a good sense of the valuable details that Hooper provides about what went wrong.

[41] See Jonathan Wells, *Icons of Evolution* (Washington: Regnery Press, 2000), pp. 9–28.

[42] See also, Denton, *Evolution: A Theory in Crisis*, pp. 145–49.

[43] The biologist was Michael Behe, who is not a creationist. Behe accepts common descent.

[44] Personal communication to the author, June 17, 2003.

[45] Ibid.

[46] See, for example, "Backgrounder and summary of publisher's proposed revision to biology textbooks," October 30, 2003, http://www.discovery.org/scripts/viewDB/index.php?program=News-CSC&command=view&id=1619, which gives an overview of errors publishers have offered to correct. However, the publishers are always under pressure to retain convenient errors, so they may back off.

[47] Ibid.

[48] Karl W. Giberson and Donald A. Yerxa, *Species of Origins: America's Search for a Creation Story* (Lanham: Rowman and Littlefield, 2002), p. 210.

[49] Interview with the author, June 2003.

[50] Good comparative photos are available at www.uwgb.edu/biodiversity/news/photo_ofthe–week/pow20020920main.htm, a page maintained by the Cofrin Center for Biodiversity, University of Wisconsin-Green Bay.

[51] There are many good examples in nature of Batesian mimicry. For example, certain beetles that live in anthills resemble ants in appearance, presumably for their own protection. However, Darwinism resulted in a tendency to identify as Batesian mimicry some situations that are much more complex and questionable, and may not even be

mimicry at all, such as the Monarch–Viceroy situation.

[52] J. Vz. Brower, "Experimental studies of mimicry in some North American butterflies," *Evolution* (1958). 35: 32–47.

[53] United States Geological Survey,

http://www.npsc.nbs.gov/resource/distr/lepid/bflyusa/wa/92.htm. Accessed August 14, 2003. The information is under "Comments."

[54] The site is http://www.uky.edu/Ag/Entomology/ythfacts/mystery/mystry50.htm, accessed August 14, 2003.

[55] David Ritland and Lincoln Brouwer, "The viceroy butterfly is not a batesian mimic," *Nature* (1991), 350: 497–98.

[56] Both *Danaus* and *Archippus* belong to the Nymphalidae family, and but *Danaus* is a member of the Danainae subfamily and *Archippus* is a member of the Limenitidinae subfamily.

[57] Kim A. Pike, "Antipredator adaptations by monarch butterflies," http://www.colostate.edu/Depts/Entomology/courses/en507/papers_1999/pike.htm.

[58] David B. Ritland, Erskine College, Department of Biology, "More about viceroy mimicry" http://www.erskine.edu/academics/biology/biology.mimicry.html.

[59] Akira Sato, "Mimicry in butterflies: microscopic structure" *Forma* (2002), 17: 133–39. The complex studied was *Hypolimnas anomala* and *Euploea mulciber*. The female of the former species imitates the male of the latter.

[60] "Family nymphalidae," Canadian Biodiversity Information Facility, www.cbif.gc.ca/spp_pages/butterflies/families/nymphalidae_e.php.

[61] Personal comment to Dembski, noted in RAPID address, 2002. The whole of the address can be read online at http://www.arn.org/docs/dembski/wd_disciplined-science.htm.

[62] See Lauren Kern, "Monkey business," *Dallas Observer* (January 11, 2001). http://www.dallasobserver.com/issues/2001-01-11/feature2.html/page1.html.

[63] William Dembski, "Positive research program," reprinted from *Cosmic Pursuit* (spring 1998) http://www.arn.org/docs/dembski/wd_idmovement.htm.

[64] Scientists who believe in God start with theology as a foundation for their vocation and life, but the purpose of a research project is not to examine God.

[65] G.C. Williams, "A Package of Information" in J Brockman, ed., *The Third Culture: Beyond the Scientific Revolution* (New York: Simon & Schuster, 1995), p. 43. http://www.edge.org/documents/ThirdCulture/h-Ch.1.html).

[66] Jacob D. Bekenstein, "Information in the holographic universe," *Scientific American* (July 14, 2003), http://www.sciam.com/print_version.cfm?articleID=000AF072-4891-1F0A-97AE80A84189EEDF.

[67] Ibid.

^{68} Ibid.

^{69} See, for example, information about a paper published in *Nature Genetics* (May 13, 2002), at http://www.eurekalert.org/pub_releases/2002-05/uomh-pop051002.php.

^{70} Wojciech Makalowski, "Not junk after all," *Science* (May 23, 2003). (*Note*: A *clochard* is a hobo or tramp, in French.)

^{71} University of Michigan Health System, May 13, 2002; Louisiana State University, May 14, 2002. Much of the material in this sidebar first appeared as a news item in Science Teachers' Association of Ontario's magazine, *Crucible* (September 2002).

Afterword (Pages 237–244)

^{1} A relevant verse from the Bible is Romans 1:20 (NIV): "For since the creation of the world God's invisible qualities—his eternal power and divine nature—have been clearly seen, being understood from what has been made, so that men are without excuse." Biblical writers assume that God's handiwork in nature is self-evident, and that radical disbelief is perverse. But they also recognize that, by its very nature, belief cannot be compelled.

^{2} "I have no metaphysical necessity driving me to propose the miraculous action of the evident finger of God as a scientific hypothesis. In my world view, all natural forces and events are fully contingent on the free choice of the sovereign God. Thus, neither an adequate nor an inadequate 'neo-Darwinism' (as mechanism) holds any terrors. But that is not what the data [look] like. And I feel no metaphysical necessity to exclude the evident finger of God." This statement by D.L. Wilcox in "Tamed Tornadoes," in J. Buell and V. Hearn, eds., *Darwinism: Science or Philosophy?* (Richardson, TX: Foundation for Thought and Ethics, 1994), www.leaderu.com/orgs/fte/darwinsim/chapter136.html, sums up my own view.

3 Notice that Dawkins protects himself by referring to "evolution," not to "Darwinism," which is his motive force. Suppose he had said: "If you meet somebody who claims not to believe in *Darwinism*, that person is ignorant, stupid or insane (or wicked, but I'd rather not consider that)." Darwinists often retreat to general talk of "evolution" when confronted about Darwinism.

^{4} Phillip E. Johnson, *Darwin on Trial* (Downer's Grove, IL: InterVarsity Press, 1993), p. 91.

^{5} See, for example, Mary Wakefield, "The mystery of the missing links" in the *Spectator* (October 25, 2003). Wakefield was dismayed by the fact that a well-educated friend questioned Darwinism, but when she went home to discuss the subject with her three flatmates, she discovered that they all questioned it, too. See http://www.arn.org/docs2/news/missinglinkmystery102803.htm. Wakefield believes that the Discovery Institute (see pp. 221–25) is to blame for this situation, but that is implausible. One little institute could not do that much damage to a major worldview all by itself. This book has attempted to provide a detailed roadmap to the changes in public perception that have resulted in her flatmates' surprising views.

6 C.S. Lewis has written: "Ever since I became a Christian I have thought that the best, perhaps the only, service I could do for my unbelieving neighbours was to explain and defend the belief that has been common to nearly all Christians at all times. . . . what Baxter calls 'mere' Christianity." (C.S. Lewis, *Mere Christianity* [1952], London: Fount, 1997, reprint, p. vi.) Evangelical Anglicanism stands in the tradition Lewis is referring to, of the great Anglican scholars of mainstream *orthodoxy*.

7 Kenneth R. Miller, *Finding Darwin's God: A Scientist's Search for Common Ground Between God and Evolution* (New York: HarperCollins, 1999), p. 246.

8 See pp. 133–34. Michael Ruse also makes this point. See p. 91.

9 "There are many things we can never know about those long ago experiments in Dorset and Birmingham, since Kettlewell's field notes have never been found (a circumstance that Bruce Grant calls 'very peculiar'). E.B. Ford, for his part, destroyed all his papers, as well as his breeding material in certain pivotal experiments. Another celebrated experiment of Ford's was possibly fraudulent, certainly irregular. The best that can be said of Kettlewell's studies of dominance and of background choice is that they have not been replicated by a great number of scientists. 'It doesn't happen,' says Bruce Grant, of Kettlewell's dominance breakdown/buildup studies. 'David West tried it. Cyril Clarke tried it. I tried it. Everybody tried it. No one gets it.' As for the background matching experiments, Mikkola, Grant and Sargent, among others, repeated what Kettlewell did and got results contrary to his. 'I am careful not to call Kettlewell a fraud,' says Bruce Grant after a discreet pause. 'He was just a very careless scientist.'" From J. Hooper, *Of Moths and Men: An Evolutionary Tale* (New York: W.W Norton, 2002), p. 295. The remarkable thing about the experiment is not that it turned out to be of questionable value but that it has been regarded, for so long, as a demonstration of Darwinian evolution in action and is still defended as such, for example by the National Center for Science Education. (See, for example, "Icons of evolution? Why much of what Jonathan Wells writes about evolution is wrong" by Alan D. Gishlick, Peppered Moths, http://www.ncseweb.org/icons/icon6moths.html). One wonders what other problems with demonstrations of Darwinism lurk out there, waiting for another enterprising researcher.

10 T.H. Huxley, "The Coming of Age of the 'Origin of Species,'" in *Darwiniana: Essays by Thomas H. Huxley* [1896], (New York: AMS Press, 1970), p. 229.

Index